GLOBAL PLATFORM GOVERNANCE

GLOBAL PLATFORM GOVERNANCE

Regulating Big Tech Beyond the Trans-Atlantic

Edited by

NANJALA NYABOLA

TAYLOR OWEN

HEIDI TWOREK

BLOOMSBURY ACADEMIC

LONDON • NEW YORK • OXFORD • NEW DELHI • SYDNEY

BLOOMSBURY ACADEMIC
Bloomsbury Publishing Plc, 50 Bedford Square, London, WC1B 3DP, UK
Bloomsbury Publishing Inc, 1359 Broadway, New York, NY 10018, USA
Bloomsbury Publishing Ireland, 29 Earlsfort Terrace, Dublin 2, D02 AY28, Ireland

Published in Great Britain 2026

Cover design by Aneeka Makwana
Cover Image: Avenue © Wonman Kim via Getty Images

A catalogue record for this book is available from the British Library.

Library of Congress Cataloging-in-Publication Data available

ISBN: HB: 978-1-3505-8011-4
PB: 978-1-3505-8010-7
ePDF: 978-1-3505-8014-5
eBook: 978-1-3505-8013-8

Typeset by Amnet
Printed and bound in Great Britain

CONTENTS

ACKNOWLEDGMENTS

This project is funded with the generous support of Reset, the Centre for International Governance Innovation, the Canada Research Chairs Program, and the Centre for Media, Technology and Democracy at McGill University. We are tremendously grateful to all our authors for continuing with the project despite the many challenges presented by the COVID-19 pandemic.

CONTRIBUTORS

Pınar Akman is a leading expert in competition law at the University of Leeds and is a senior advisor at White & Case LLP. Previously, she served as a judge at the UK Competition Appeal Tribunal and also as a member of the UK Financial Conduct Authority's Innovation Advisory Group. Her research, notably on abuse of dominance and digital markets, includes the acclaimed monograph *The Concept of Abuse in EU Competition Law*. A recipient of the Philip Leverhulme Prize, she has advised international institutions such as the IMF and the UN. Akman is a nongovernmental advisor to the International Competition Network and has received multiple global recognitions for her work.

Elettra Bietti is an assistant professor of law and computer science at Northeastern University. She is a faculty associate at the Berkman Klein Center for Internet and Society at Harvard University and an affiliated fellow at Yale Law School's Information Society Project (ISP). Elettra completed her doctorate on the regulation of digital platform companies and data at Harvard Law School in 2022 and holds an LLM from Harvard Law School and an LLB from University College London.

Siddharth Peter de Souza is an assistant professor in AI and Society at the Centre for Interdisciplinary Methodologies (CIM), University of Warwick. He studies developments in law and technology from a legal pluralist, data justice, and decolonial perspective. His work explores how data is governed globally in contested and plural settings, and he is interested in the role that civil society and social movements play in shaping data governance and data law frameworks. Siddharth is the founder of Justice Adda, a law and design social venture that works on access to justice in the Indian context.

Iginio Gagliardone is the inaugural SA-UK Chair in the Digital Humanities at Wits University, professor of media studies at Wits University in Johannesburg, South Africa, and an inaugural fellow of Wits Machine Intelligence and Neural Discovery (MIND) Institute. He is the author of *The Politics of Technology in Africa* (2016) and *China, Africa, and the Future of the Internet* (2019). His most recent work examines the international politics of artificial intelligence and the emergence of new imageries of technological evolution in Africa.

Ivar A. Hartmann is an associate professor of law at Insper in São Paulo, Brazil. He is a founding member of the Platform Governance Research Network and an affiliate of the International Panel on the Information Environment. His research focuses on online content moderation and technology applied to quantitative legal research.

Jazmia Henry is an AI professional with a 15-year career spanning quantitative methods, reinforcement learning, machine learning, and natural language processing. She is currently an early employee at Collide AI, where she is building domain-specific foundational models for the oil and gas industry. She has held technical and leadership roles at Microsoft, Morgan Stanley, and The Motley Fool. Jazmia was previously a PhD candidate at St. Hilda's College at the University of Oxford. She also completed a technical fellowship at Stanford University, holds a master's degree from Columbia University, and earned her undergraduate degree from Tulane University.

Lilly Irani is an associate professor of communication & science studies at the University of California, San Diego, where she is the faculty director of the UC San Diego Labor Center. She holds an affiliation in the Department of Computer Science. She is the author of *Chasing Innovation: Making Entrepreneurial Citizens in Modern India* (2019) and *Redacted* (with Jesse Marx) (2021), as well as numerous articles on the cultural politics of high-tech work and the counterpractices they generate. She was a cofounder of the digital worker advocacy organization Turkopticon.

David Kaye is a law professor at the University of California, Irvine School of Law. He served as United Nations Special Rapporteur on the right to freedom of opinion and expression from 2014 to 2020 and, since 2024, has been the US member of the Venice Commission. His publications include landmark reports on human rights and technology for the United Nations and the 2019 book *Speech Police: The Global Struggle to Govern the Internet*.

Jose Mari Hall Lanuza is an assistant professor of political science at the University of the Philippines Manila and a communication PhD candidate at the University of Massachusetts Amherst. He is also currently the Head of Research for Sigla Research Center, studying hyperlocal influence operations for the 2025 Philippine midterm elections. He holds a Dissertation Innovation Fellowship from the Mellon Foundation and the American Council for Learned Societies. He also serves as an assessor for the International Fact-Checking Network.

Grace Mutung'u is a digital policy researcher and a research student at the University of Nairobi, Kenya. She has been involved in ICT policy development over the past fifteen years. Her current interests include digital ID, digital rights, data governance, and development.

Nanjala Nyabola is a researcher and writer. Her research focuses on the politics of and decolonial approaches to digital technology. She has a PhD in Digital Humanities from King's College London and has held several academic and professional positions. She is the author of several titles, including *Digital Democracy, Analogue Politics: How the Internet Era Is Transforming Politics in Kenya* (2018) and *Travelling While Black: Essays Inspired by a Life on the Move* (2020).

Jonathan Corpus Ong is a professor of Global Digital Media and director of the Global Technology for Social Justice Lab (GloTech) at the University of Massachusetts, Amherst. He is also the founder of the nonprofit Sigla Research Center, which supports community-engaged research in the Global South. He is the coauthor of "Architects of Networked Disinformation," an ethnographic study of disinformation-for-hire workers in the Philippines. He is a coeditor-in-chief of the *International Journal of Cultural Studies*.

Taylor Owen is the Beaverbrook Chair in Media, Ethics, and Communications, the founding Director of The Centre for Media, Technology and Democracy, the Principal Investigator of The Media Ecosystem Observatory, and an associate professor at the Max Bell School of Public Policy at McGill University. He is the host of *The Globe and Mail*'s *Machines Like Us* podcast and is a senior fellow at the Center for International Governance Innovation and the Public Policy Forum.

Amin Parsa is an associate professor of sociology of law at Halmstad University in Sweden. His primary research interest concerns the use of advanced digital technologies in the context of armed conflicts and border control practices.

Hong Shen is an assistant professor in the Human-Computer Interaction Institute at Carnegie Mellon University (CMU). She received her PhD from the University of Illinois Urbana-Champaign (UIUC). Her research focuses on the social, ethical, and policy dimensions of digital platforms and algorithmic systems.

Berhan Taye is an independent researcher, analyst, and facilitator who investigates the relationship between technology, society, and social justice. She is currently a part-time PhD student at the University of Amsterdam. Berhan was previously a practitioner fellow at Stanford University, a research fellow at the University of Toronto, and has affiliations with the Center for Intellectual

Property and IT at Strathmore University. Previously, Berhan was the Africa Policy Manager at Access Now and led the #KeepItOn campaign, a global campaign that fights against internet shutdown with a coalition of more than 220 member organizations worldwide.

Heidi Tworek is a Canada Research Chair (Tier II) and professor of history and public policy at the University of British Columbia, Vancouver, where she directs the Centre for the Study of Democratic Institutions. She is the author of the multiaward-winning *News from Germany: The Competition to Control World Communications, 1900–1945* (2019) and has published extensively on the history and policy of new communications technologies. She is a coeditor of the *Journal of Global History* and senior fellow at the Centre for International Governance Innovation.

Angela Huyue Zhang is a professor of law at the University of Southern California. Her scholarship explores the intersection of law, technology, and geopolitics, with a focus on the US–China tech rivalry and the global regulation of artificial intelligence. She is the author of two widely acclaimed books: *Chinese Antitrust Exceptionalism: How the Rise of China Challenges Global Regulation* (2021) and *High Wire: How China Regulates Big Tech and Governs Its Economy* (2024). Before joining the University of Southern California, Zhang taught at the University of Hong Kong, New York University School of Law, and King's College London.

INTRODUCTION

Nanjala Nyabola, Taylor Owen, and Heidi Tworek

The emergence of digital platforms and their integration into so many aspects of modern life has not only brought tremendous social, political, and economic benefits but also created significant costs. What was once a far more decentralized infrastructure is now dominated by a small number of global companies that hold and process much of the world's digital content and data. In the two decades since the first commercially available social networking platforms were launched, the online world has been largely privatized, allowing companies' interests to determine the quality of civic discourse, the character of the digital economy, and the integrity of democracies. Data collection at unprecedented scales has become routine and unchallenged, even while it is increasingly unclear who is collecting this data, what they are collecting it for, how they intend to use it, and how long they are empowered to keep it. Today, the harms attributed to platforms include election interference, the amplification of mis- and disinformation, harmful and hate speech, siloed epistemic communities, and economic inequalities.

Governments have taken notice. Several new large-scale governance regimes, such as the European Union Digital Services Act and the Digital Markets Act, the Australian Online Safety Commission, and the Online Safety Bill in the UK, have been introduced. The Association of African Election Authorities, under the auspices of the African Union, has adopted the Principles and Guidelines for Social and Digital Media in elections, targeting platform use during election periods. Even in the United States, where platform regulation has long seemed unlikely, substantive antitrust and data privacy regimes have been debated and proposed in Congress, although adoption remains subject to political transformations.

Some regions are also adopting a market-oriented approach, where competition authorities are taking a far more assertive approach to extending their power into digital markets. Under former US President Joe Biden, the Federal Trade Commission sued Meta for their purchase of Within, the UK blocked Meta's purchase of GIPHY, and the European Commission fined Google €2.42 billion for breaching EU antitrust rules.

Similarly, the Indonesian government blocked PayPal and many large gaming platforms for not complying with its new regulations. Brazilian officials asked WhatsApp to postpone launching a new feature until several months after the Brazilian election in 2022 because they were worried that this feature might undermine information integrity during the election. And in China, President Xi Jinping announced at the World Internet Conference in 2022 that China plans to morph the gathering into an international organization that will implicitly compete with the International Telecommunication Union and other organizations that determine internet protocols.

Academic discourse about platform governance around the world has evolved alongside these developments. A once small community of loosely connected interdisciplinary scholars is maturing and today includes research from around the world, asking local questions of platforms as global entities. However, literature on Western Europe and North America is preponderant, and even scholarship that seeks to engage directly with public policy remains disconnected from those in government. There has been little systematic treatment of what platform governance looks like outside those regions, even while other jurisdictions around the world tighten regulation in this space. With both research and policy moving quickly, how do people interested in this space make sense of all of this rapid transformation?

This volume is premised on an expansive understanding of what platforms are and how to regulate them. When we think of platforms, we often first think about social media because this is the most public-facing incarnation. But platformization is about more than social media. It is about the increasing use of digital tools to collect, sort, and manage data related to a variety of goods and service provisions. All social networking sites are platforms, but not all platforms are social networking sites. Governments use platforms to manage borders or identity systems. Businesses use platforms to manage employees or inventory. Platforms show up in both the private and the public sector as solutions to the datafication of our contemporary lives, and their proliferation makes the question of governing them urgent.

The volume is designed as a guide for people looking for a global approach to addressing the challenge of platform governance. Bringing together writers and practitioners from various national and regional contexts, the text teases out the social, political, and economic upheavals caused by platformization alongside the potential consequences of leaving them unaddressed. We suggest that the complex ecosystem of platforms might be broken down into four main domains: content, data, competition, and infrastructure. Each author writes from a different global and disciplinary perspective on one of these four domains. The book therefore speaks to multiple audiences: academics, policymakers, and a broader public invested in these issues. It is a guide for anyone who is curious about what it means to manage the power that platformization creates and to make sure that it is wielded in ways that do not create new or compound existing harms.

Overall, the book reflects the growing consensus that the problems exist and that there is significant ambiguity and uncertainty about the nature and scale of an appropriate response. Governments around the world have made tentative attempts at a strategy to govern the digital world, converging on what might be called a platform governance agenda. But the prioritization within this agenda varies considerably.

Meanwhile, scholars have leaned toward an interdisciplinary approach to better understand the roles platforms play in societies, interrogating whether existing governance regimes will suffice or if it is necessary to develop new legal and regulatory frameworks. This tendency toward interdisciplinarity is reflected in the backgrounds of those who have contributed to this book, bringing together scholars in communications, media studies, science and technology studies (STS), history, law, geography, computer science, psychology, political science, sociology, and anthropology. After all, a global challenge requires global thinking to lead to global solutions.

We have also gathered a group to try to address the current transatlantic bias of extant scholarship, in part reflecting the geographies within which these platforms emerge but also the disparate resources available to researchers. This limitation is particularly problematic given the speed at which platforms—even those that are not public-facing—globalized. Consider, for example, the discourse on free speech, which privileges US or European definitions of free speech because these are the geographies from which many platforms emerge or are their biggest markets. That approach becomes problematic in countries where public speech is more strictly curtailed for political reasons, and a technical challenge where companies have not made necessary investments to monitor speech because they do not prioritize certain markets. Countries with histories of genocide, for instance, are stricter on permissible public speech, yet many platforms do not even have the basic language and translation capacities to monitor said speech.

No single state can address the challenges emerging from the platform economy alone. The challenge demands a global response, even if this need for global governance is complicated by a parallel need for subsidiarity and complementarity in policy responses. On some issues, such as speech regulation, policy might best be nationally implemented; on others, such as advertisement transparency and a new data rights agenda, global coordination is required; and for even more, such as artificial intelligence (AI) standards, global collaboration is needed to ensure uniform application and enforcement. And in each of these levels of governance, there are radically different policies and economic and historical contexts in which platforms must be governed.

This book defines a new global approach to the academic and policy discourse on platform governance, imagining a new global agenda for digital governance.

It began with a series of deliberations within which we brought together fifteen globally recognized scholars who are based around the world to develop a global approach to understanding the regulatory challenges that platforms present and what an international response to these challenges could look like. We invited this group of scholars to work within four distinct domains of the platform governance discourse: content policy, data policy, competition policy, and infrastructure. Each of these domains is defined in greater detail as follows:

1 **Content:** The highest priority problems concerning the negative impact of technology, including hate speech, harassment, and violent extremism. Platform companies have struggled for strategies to moderate this content, settling for deleting it rapidly or down-ranking its visibility in the automated curation of social media feeds. Other forms of problematic or illegal activity—including state-sponsored disinformation campaigns, hacking, commercial fraud, and other forms of abusive deception—also fall into this policy bucket, implicating new security and transparency measures. Policies often discussed in this domain include content moderation, ad transparency, bot and agent identification, civic journalism, digital literacy, and liability.

2 **Data:** Data policies will be more important in the medium term because they have the power to change how the market is structured and how technology products are built. Consequently, restrictions on data collection and use could reduce these effects in a content-neutral manner, steering business models in directions that are healthier for public welfare. Some of these policy agendas can be implemented under existing data protection laws. Other elements will require new regulations. Policies often discussed in this domain include algorithmic accountability, a wide range of AI governance, increased data privacy protection, new IP standards and global regimes, and data localization.

3 **Competition:** The vast scale of the digital platform economy affords near-unassailable competitive advantages to the largest players; it also invites abuses of power in ways that raise barriers to market entry. Moreover, the ubiquity of the platform companies in the consumer marketplace creates special vulnerabilities because of the amount of control they wield over data, advertising, and the curation of information. Several governments—including the European Union, the United Kingdom, and China—are exploring and implementing ways to curb the power of digital giants. Focused efforts to promote and grow competition in the digital platform sector create an environment where disruptive innovation can occur, which, in turn, provides greater opportunities to improve consumer welfare, rather than an environment

in which dominant platforms create products that are conducive to maintaining the current market structure. Policies often discussed in this domain include modernized antitrust, mergers and acquisitions restrictions, and data portability and interoperability.

4 **Infrastructure:** Underlying the platform ecosystem is the communications, computational, and human infrastructure on which it is built. Understanding the political economy, geopolitics, and culture of these infrastructures is therefore critical to contextualizing the platform discourse and policy agenda. This section will engage with the design, incentives, politics, and labor underlying our global infrastructure. Policies and topics include 5G and physical infrastructure, the cloud, labor rights, the geopolitics of infrastructure, and the internet of things (IoT).

Academic Context

This text is presented as an introduction to global platform governance while also cementing it as a field. We see platform governance as the latest stage in a longer debate on tech governance. International governance has always lain at the heart of new media technologies, and governing communications technologies arguably stretches back to the postal system. For example, the first international organization, the International Telegraph Union, was created in 1865 to govern the new electric medium of telegraphy.[1] The history of governance is also intertwined with the history of information: who controls it, who creates it, and who owns it.[2] The nineteenth-century imperial history of information and communications created path dependency for where the world has arrived in the twenty-first century, whether it is where major platforms are based, where fiber-optic cables are laid, or how states organized international governance.[3]

The history of platform governance is rooted in various developments. The more immediate precursors of platform governance are computing and internet regulation. Scholars have connected the broader history to Silicon Valley and its libertarian beliefs to the free market sensibilities that underlie many of the most successful global platforms.[4] Others have shown how computing increasingly excluded women, erased space for nonbinary people, and even required people to adapt their aching bodies to the computer, rather than the other way around.[5] Some texts trace the "prehistory of social media" in bulletin boards and other networks.[6]

By 2011, a few scholars had started to point out the "dark side" of platforms or the potential problems of platforms' overweening power.[7] In the last five to ten years, an increasing number of scholars have shown the discrimination baked into platforms, particularly through the intersectional lens of race and gender.[8]

Much of the work that has so far been done on platform governance has focused on social networking and its implications. For instance, sociologist Zeynep Tufekci examined the implications of social media on the arc of protest and democracy in the Middle East, foreshadowing the growing interest in the space.[9] Political analyst Nanjala Nyabola considered the implications of social networking sites on democracy and politics in Kenya, exploring the regulatory space that exists and the challenges that lie ahead.[10] Nathaniel Persily and Joshua Tucker produced a volume on social media and democracy that brought together scholars from the United States to consider how the structures of social media enable specific harms.[11] Many more volumes exist that consider the specific regional implications of social networking sites, but many of these volumes are either national in focus or specifically restricted to social networking sites and not platforms more broadly, as the current volume does.

A transatlantic or Global North geographical focus characterizes most of the major programmatic texts in the field.[12] Some work has explored the question of data governance through the lens of sovereignty, for instance, in an edited volume on digital sovereignty in BRICS countries.[13] More scholars have started to focus on China, particularly in the realms of data and infrastructure.[14] But the challenges extend far beyond contemporary centers of power and must be understood as such. A growing number of scholars outside these large nations are producing important scholarship reflecting this, including many of our authors in this volume.[15] Sarah Ganter and Hanan Badr's edited volume takes a similar approach to ours for media governance, as it seeks "to enhance media governance literature beyond the West and regional foci."[16] What remains is an opportunity like that provided by this book to put these varied perspectives into conversation with each other in a truly global discourse.

It's worth noting as well that the lack of visibility of key texts in platform regulation in other parts of the world doesn't imply an absence of regulation or action in this space. Rather, it indicates more systemic challenges of institutional power and visibility. In many parts of the world, key intellectual work is done in spaces of advocacy and litigation, for instance, where lawyers in Kenya are litigating urgent questions of content moderation and outsourcing. The first successful litigation against a mobile telecommunications company for participating in an internet shutdown was decided through the Economic Community of West African States (ECOWAS) court in Togo against the leading African mobile network corporation, MTN.[17] Governments such as Kenya, Uganda, and Nigeria have—for better or worse—made significant inroads into defining their regulatory space. The work exists, but it is not visible to institutional academia: a limitation our volume tries to resolve by working with practitioners, as well as academics.

Many previous volumes have explored particular aspects of the platform governance agenda and provide critical contributions to our understanding of, for example, the social, economic, and political contexts of AI,[18] the collective action potential of social media,[19] the discriminatory attributes of data,[20] the legal underpinnings of our digital infrastructure,[21] the labor dimensions of the platform economy,[22] and how infrastructures could operate as public goods.[23] With this volume, however, we bring these diverse disciplinary and epistemological approaches to understanding our platform infrastructure into conversation with each other. In all of these fields, the United States tends to attract the greatest amount of scholarship, even if its citizens only comprise 4 percent of the world's population.[24] If the platform governance discourse has a chance of growing beyond its initial decade, it will need to radically broaden its regional representation and relevance. Some work has attempted to take global approaches to individual themes. For example, David Kaye, one of our authors, examined content regulation as a global phenomenon, and there are others who have examined speech in global contexts.[25] Others have used a multiauthored volume to reflect on data, COVID-19, and global justice[26] or to coalesce global Indigenous perspectives on data and sovereignty.[27]

We do not know of any volume, though, that brings together all the strands of platform governance into one accessible book.

Chapter Summaries

This book, therefore, presents an overview of the state of the discipline and conversation on platform governance around the world, providing policymakers and the curious with a global understanding of the challenges they must respond to.

Former UN Special Rapporteur on freedom of expression, David Kaye, reminds policymakers that private platforms have become so potent that their content decisions may start to influence public speech norms offline. Kaye reminds us that the challenge has evolved: Rather than platforms incorporating extant speech law into their terms of service, building an increasingly elaborate structure, policymakers should begin by returning to the first principles of governance. Specifically looking at content moderation, Kaye suggests that transparency, as well as principles of democracy and human rights, could guide a more malleable and portable approach to managing content.

Similarly, Berhan Taye uses the example of Ethiopia to emphasize that the challenge of content is multinational and transnational, compounded by the failures of existing platforms to understand this fundamental principle. Ethiopia is the second-largest country in Africa by population, but while platforms have demonstrated great interest in expanding into the Ethiopian market, there has been no similar investment in safety for users of these platforms, particularly in languages other than English. Yet, following the onset of conflict in the country in 2019, these platforms are increasingly used to disseminate inflammatory messages with minimal response from the platforms. Taye reminds readers that these platforms are even more important in contexts where freedom of expression is otherwise circumscribed. This lack of investment is not just bad business—it puts lives at risk.

Ivar Hartmann contemplates Latin America as a single market and examines the state of platform governance discourse across the region. Hartmann focuses on the three most common approaches to regulation in the region—automation, paid moderation, and judicial review—and evaluates the relative successes or failures of each approach. Content moderation is often offered as a solution to the many challenges that platforms have created in the region, but Hartmann sees in Latin America a greater interest from the judiciary in intervening in the space—perhaps more than any other region. What are the consequences of these three strategies as currently applied, and do they offer a way forward for other parts of the world? Hartmann also pursues a parallel ambition of emphasizing that a significant body of work has developed in the region around these challenges, inviting those who are operating in the space to engage with it to build a truly international response to platform governance.

Jonathan Corpus Ong and Jose Mari Hall Lanuza describe how anti-disinformation work from civil society groups in the Global South are pushing back against platform deterministic discourses that depict platform and tech-centric causes and solutions to problems of civic participation. These explanations miss the local context for political change and minimize the agency of those working for progressive policy change. Instead, they argue for a "whole-of-society" approach to addressing misinformation that situates the specific country context of the platform experience. Doing so highlights both the challenges faced by those leading anti-disinformation efforts, as well as the opportunity for meaningful policy alternatives to top-down platform governance models. While dominant platform governance frames risk propagating policy solutions that could further entrench illiberal governance, Ong and Lanuza argue for an alternative whole-of-society platform governance agenda grounded in local context and politics.

The challenge of managing data occurs at the intersection of human and technical challenges. To date, most responses to the data dimension of platform governance have focused on the technical challenges, ignoring the fact that all data is subject to interpretation, and the human dimension is not just supplementary context. Our chapters on data invite policymakers to think about data at the human and technical interface and to consider the real-world implications of how humans interpret data generated and used by platforms.

Siddharth Peter de Souza focuses on ratings systems used by food delivery systems and what they reveal about power relations between those who build platforms and those who use them as consumers and as service providers. Ratings promise to transform interactions into quantifiable data, and that this data will, in turn, motivate users while creating a sense of objectivity that protects both service providers and users. De Souza argues that instead, ratings have become weapons of control wielded harshly against service providers by tilting power heavily toward consumers, particularly in the absence of comprehensive labor rights. De Souza coins the term "data theater" to refer to this use of data to inflict violence, engender silences, and deny justice to these service providers, reminding us that the externalities of reducing labor and justice protections in the name of efficiency must be absorbed somewhere, in this case by vendors.

Amin Parsa shifts the reader's attention toward the border to remind us that not all platforms are public-facing, and, indeed, many are built and deployed by governments to serve specific governance functions. Borders are highly contested sites, and this intensifies the social impact of platformizing the management of migration. Parsa's analysis focuses on Europe, where border management is a data-intensive process focused on the collection of personal identity data and the sharing of it between the various border management institutions. Parsa argues that platformization in this context inadvertently or intentionally intensifies cultures of exclusion and that the false promise of efficiency incubates the developers and users of these technologies from much-needed scrutiny. Data used and generated to manage highly contested contexts remains as susceptible to racism and structural violence, but with less scrutiny, as assessments of who is a threat and who borders must defend against are often uninterrogated, leading to compounded harms against specific groups.

Jazmia Henry's chapter invites policymakers into a technical conversation on what platform governance, particularly in relation to AI, involves while proposing a potential solution to one of the recurring challenges of bias in AI. Henry, a Machine Learning Operations (MLOps) expert, proposes an approach to addressing bias embedded in MLOps to avoid compounding the harms of racism highlighted by other writers. This chapter is crucial for policymakers as it offers insight into the decision-making processes that go into building the technology that runs the platforms that we use. Henry focuses our attention sharply on the interpretive aspects of data and what steps can minimize the impact of bias in the configuration of data. Henry allows policymakers to peer behind the veil and contemplate what is possible beyond the rhetoric shared with platforms, empowering readers to ask some of the difficult questions that might be shrouded in arguments about industrial secrecy or academic specialization.

Elettra Bietti's chapter also focuses on antitrust law, specifically the importance of reducing the exceptions and exemptions that currently insulate platforms from the social and political implications of their participation in markets. She argues that the dominance of neoliberal paradigms in both the EU and the United States places undue expectation on individual action to govern experiences on platforms, leaving crucial factors such as democracy or distributive justice by the wayside. Bietti argues that it is important to engage the "antimonopoly" momentum that characterizes current efforts at platform regulation to deliver a more socially aware and politically grounded paradigm. Self-regulation can no longer be the primary strategy employed to regulate platforms as their efficiency as markets so evidently fails. Bietti proposes a strategy to reintroduce normative and distributive justice into the regulation of digital platform markets.

Most platforms that are in use in the world right now operate as private corporations, even in nominally communist countries such as China. Yet regulators seem reluctant to apply many of the principles of commercial governance to these entities, resulting in a chaotic competition environment that these writers aim to reorganize. Pınar Akman focuses on the potential utility of antitrust regulation as a policy response to the incredible sway and influence of the largest platforms in the world. Akman notes that there is a perceived enforcement gap in tech that has led to a frenzy of policymaking, particularly in the United States and Europe. But in contrast to other uses of competition law, most of these policies are being developed after the proverbial horse has left the stable and based on what regulators think might happen (*ex ante*) rather than on what has actually happened (*ex post*). Akman invites policymakers to look beyond the hype and view platforms primarily as what they are—companies—and thus, they could be effectively regulated by addressing the policy gaps that preexisted in competition law. Such an approach allows policymakers to maintain complexity and avoid unforced errors and politicization of crucial issues.

Grace Bomu Mutung'u invites the reader to contemplate the importance of transmutable principles of platform governance by considering the impact of a large domestic platform in Kenya, looking to expand into Ethiopia. The vast majority of internet users in the world still use their mobile phones to connect to the internet, and, in much of the world, the first platform that users will interact with will be built and operated by a telco. Mutung'u considers the significant influence of platforms, both on the telecommunications and the platform markets, not merely operating in a regulatory space but shaping the market around their commercial interests. Yet many of the debates on platform governance do not examine the position that these companies hold within their specific countries as large corporations that are usually dominant in their market of operation and often exempted from key regulatory frameworks because of their perceived strategic value to the government of the day. Mutung'u's contribution challenges many of the presumptions embedded in how we propose rules on platform governance—that other regulatory guardrails not only exist but are also inconsistently applied. This is the reality of platform governance for the majority of the world and must be contended with in order to build any international response.

Angela Huyue Zhang adds another dimension to the antitrust discourse, this time from the perspective of China. Zhang argues that outsiders have misunderstood some of the efforts to bring order into China's hitherto unruly tech space and uses her chapter to bring deeper context. The dominance of two companies, each prohibiting interoperability and the sharing of information across their various platforms, entrenches their dominant position while preventing new players from entering the space. Risks that occur on the platforms are compounded by the sheer size of these companies, with significant knock-on factors for the economy and society in general. Zhang argues that much of the crackdown and wave of regulations that have emerged since 2020 are efforts to address the regulatory lag within China's tech space, albeit in a distinctly Chinese approach shaped by the government's approach to policy and governance.

In the final section, the authors delve into three aspects of infrastructure. Hong Shen delves into the complexity of China's global push to construct digital infrastructure. Beyond simplistic characterizations of Chinese infrastructure building since the early 2000s, Shen uses a political economy approach to move the debate past a simplistic dichotomy of either state owned or private owned. Rather, Shen highlights conflicts between the state and businesses, as well as internal rifts within China, to reveal a more nuanced classification. Huawei and ZTE, for instance, started Chinese companies' push abroad, partly because of their intense domestic competition. Shen also disaggregates internet infrastructure into hardware, networking, and web applications before tracing how Chinese companies have tried to expand their reach. The chapter offers three broad insights for policymakers: that China's infrastructural expansion dates back at least to the late 1990s; that foreign capital played a crucial role in supporting "Chinese" companies such as Alibaba; and that internal and domestic power struggles complicate any notions of a monolithic plan to expand Chinese-built internet infrastructure.

Iginio Gagliardone similarly offers a more nuanced approach to understanding the expansion of internet infrastructure, centering his analysis on Africa, where much of the competition to build new infrastructure is taking place. Gagliardone emphasizes the agency of African nations when choosing which digital infrastructure they acquire, pointing out that African nations have combined technologies and infrastructures from the United States and China. The debate on China's role on the continent is still best understood through debates on neocolonialism. While some Africans view Chinese actors and companies as "replacing" colonial and development actors, others see it as fundamentally upending those power dynamics. Gagliardone cautions against the hype of Chinese surveillance technologies, which have yet to deliver promised results, even while Chinese ideas of internet sovereignty hold appeal for some more authoritarian African leaders, who increasingly use tools like internet shutdowns.

Finally, Lilly Irani's chapter investigates the people who power platform work and how algorithms written by white-collar engineers render suspicious workers who do not behave as assumed or predicted. Gig workers are the labor by-product of platformization, yet, too often, they are not considered in regulatory discussions. Using methods such as community-based participatory research and design justice, Irani takes a deep dive into the problems that workers encounter on Amazon Mechanical Turk, such as account suspensions for supposedly inauthentic behavior, sharing wifi, or even moving across borders. Humans, Irani shows, do not behave like algorithms project they will. By paying close attention to workers' frontline experiences, Irani shows the opacity of platform practices in dealing with workers and resolving disputes. Algorithms create part of the black box; corporate secrecy creates the rest, including patents for fraud detection. Irani invites policymakers to better respond to such disputes and protect workers from discriminatory and AI-driven rules.

Conclusion

Overall, this volume invites policymakers working on platform governance issues to look beyond technical solutions to problems that mostly arise at the interface of human and technical questions. For too long, platforms have escaped in-depth regulatory and legislative scrutiny by shrouding their data and infrastructure in secrecy and jargon. Even where concerns are raised, they have focused on the management of content and, therefore, on technical solutions to managing content. This volume demonstrates that both the challenge and the solution must look beyond this level.

By keeping their responses to many of the challenges that have been leveled against them hidden under the guise of proprietary or technical information, those who build and deploy these platforms have often managed to keep policymakers at bay. This volume addresses this gap by demystifying many of the challenges that arise from platformization, by clearly demonstrating that they are not merely technical issues, and by reminding policymakers that they do indeed have significant scope for action.

At the same time, the volume demonstrates that effective responses to the challenges of platform governance cannot be developed in silos. As much as platforms might be legally domiciled in specific jurisdictions, their impacts are routinely global. The dominance of Western, and specifically the United States, platforms in the broad understanding of what a platform is has resulted in policy responses that do not capture the nuances of how platforms behave elsewhere in the world. This volume demonstrates that platforms are not a monolith, nor are the politics of which platform is deployed in a particular context and by whom. Platforms are not simply shaped by preexisting norms; they create new norms that intersect with these preexisting norms to define new social and political possibilities. Therefore, a meaningful response to the challenges of platform governance must have a solid grasp of how national and regional histories intersect with the challenges that emerge from platforms so as to propose solutions that have import beyond the social and political context in which these platforms are developed.

Most importantly, this book emphasizes that platform governance is a human project and not merely a technical one. As such, policy responses must take into account all the people who use platforms, not just those who build them or experience them as consumers. Refugees and migrants can be victims of poor platformization policy, even where the customer is the state purchasing the platform technology. Vendors are as much affected by harsh ratings systems as the customers around whose experiences these ratings are optimized.

The nascent academic and public policy discipline of platform governance has proven prescient for a range of growing challenges faced by governments around the world. But while much of this work has found purchase in Western capitals, which have been the first to develop new digital policies, the discourse has suffered from a lack of global representation and context. We hope that this volume contributes to a range of efforts to broaden the platform governance discourse and to ensure that it represents the challenges and opportunities of this policy agenda around the world.

Notes

1 Gabriele Balbi and Andreas Fickers, eds., *History of the International Telecommunication Union (ITU): Transnational Techno-Diplomacy from the Telegraph to the Internet* (De Gruyter, 2020).

2 Ann Blair et al., eds., *Information: A Historical Companion* (Princeton University Press, 2021).

3 Heidi Tworek, "Policy Lessons from Five Historical Patterns in Information Manipulation," in *The Disinformation Age: Politics, Technology, and Disruptive Communication in the United States*, ed. W. Lance Bennett and Steven Livingston (Cambridge University Press, 2020).

4 Margaret O'Mara, *The Code: Silicon Valley and the Remaking of America* (Penguin, 2020). On contemporary Silicon Valley, see Jillian York, *Silicon Values: The Future of Free Speech Under Surveillance Capitalism* (Verso, 2022).

5 Thomas S. Mullaney et al., *Your Computer Is on Fire* (MIT Press, 2021).

6 Kevin Driscoll, *The Modem World: A Prehistory of Social Media* (Yale University Press, 2022).

7 Evgeny Morozov, *The Net Delusion: The Dark Side of Internet Freedom* (PublicAffairs, 2012); Siva Vaidhyanathan, *The Googlization of Everything (And Why We Should Worry)* (University of California Press, 2012).

8 For some crucial texts, see Safiya Umoja Noble, *Algorithms of Oppression* (New York University Press, 2018); Ruha Benjamin, *Race After Technology: Abolitionist Tools for the New Jim Code* (Polity, 2019); Abeba Birhane, "Algorithmic Injustice: A Relational Ethics Approach," *Patterns* 2, no. 2 (2021): 100205.

9 Zeynep Tufekci, *Twitter and Tear Gas: The Power and Fragility of Networked Protest* (Yale University Press, 2017).

10 Nanjala Nyabola, *Digital Democracy, Analogue Politics: How the Internet Era Is Transforming Politics in Kenya* (Zed Books, 2018).

11 Nathaniel Persily and Joshua Tucker, eds., *Social Media and Democracy: The State of the Field, Prospects for Reform* (Cambridge University Press, 2020).

12 Annabelle Gawer, ed., *Platforms, Markets and Innovation* (Edward Elgar, 2011); Dal Yong Jin, *Digital Platforms, Imperialism and Political Culture* (Routledge, 2015); Geoffrey G. Parker et al., *Platform Revolution: How Networked Markets Are Transforming the Economy and How to Make Them Work for You* (W. W. Norton, 2016); José van Dijck, Thomas Poell, and Martijn de Waal, *The Platform Society: Public Values in a Connective World* (Oxford University Press, 2018); Nick Srnicek, *Platform Capitalism* (Wiley, 2017); Shoshana Zuboff, *The Age of Surveillance Capitalism: The Fight for a Human Future at the New Frontier of Power* (PublicAffairs, 2019); Jathan Sadowski, *Too Smart: How Digital Capitalism Is Extracting Data, Controlling Our Lives, and Taking over the World* (MIT Press, 2020).

13 Min Jiang and Luca Belli, eds., *Digital Sovereignty in the BRICS Countries: How the Global South and Emerging Power Alliances Are Reshaping Digital Governance* (Cambridge University Press, 2025).

14 Yun Wen, *The Huawei Model: The Rise of China's Technology Giant* (University of Illinois Press, 2020); Yu Hong and Eric Harwit, "China's Globalizing Internet: History, Power, and Governance," *Chinese Journal of Communication* 13, no. 1 (2020): 1–7; Aynne Kokas, *Trafficking Data: How China Is Winning the Battle for Digital Sovereignty* (Oxford University Press, 2022).

15 Herman Wasserman and Dani Madrid-Morales, *Disinformation in the Global South* (Wiley, 2022).

16 Sarah Anne Ganter and Hanan Badr, "Introduction: Re-Examining Media Governance Through Cosmopolitan Critique," in *Media Governance*, ed. Sarah Anne Ganter and Hanan Badr (Palgrave Macmillan, 2022), 1–12.

17 Natalia Krapiva, "ECOWAS Togo Court Decision: Internet Access Is a Right That Requires Protection of the Law," *Access Now*, July 14, 2020, available online: https://www.accessnow.org/ecowas-togo-court-decision/.

18 Kate Crawford, *The Atlas of AI: Power, Politics, and the Planetary Costs of Artificial Intelligence* (Yale University Press, 2021).

19 Tufekci, *Twitter and Tear Gas*.

20 Wendy Chun, *Discriminating Data: Correlation, Neighborhoods, and the New Politics of Recognition* (MIT Press, 2021).

21 Julie E. Cohen, *Between Truth and Power: The Legal Constructions of Informational Capitalism* (Oxford University Press, 2019).

22 Rafael Grohmann and Jack Qiu, "*Contextualizing Platform Labor," Contracampo: Brazilian Journal of Communication* 39, no. 1 (2020), https://doi.org/10.22409/contracampo.v39i1.42260.

23 Ethan Zuckerman, "The Case for Digital Public Infrastructure," Knight First Amendment Institute, January 17, 2020, available online: https://knightcolumbia.org/content/the-case-for-digital-public-infrastructure.

24 See, for example, the wide range of work on privacy and data in the United States, such as Woodrow Hartzog, *Privacy's Blueprint: The Battle to Control the Design of*

New Technologies (Harvard University Press, 2018); Helen Nissenbaum, *Privacy in Context: Technology, Policy, and the Integrity of Social Life* (Stanford Law Books, 2009); Frank Pasquale, *The Black Box Society: The Secret Algorithms That Control Money and Information* (Harvard University Press, 2015); Ari Ezra Waldman, *Industry Unbound: The Inside Story of Privacy, Data, and Corporate Power* (Cambridge University Press, 2021); Danielle Citron, *The Fight for Privacy: Protecting Dignity, Identity, and Love in the Digital Age* (W. W. Norton, 2022).

25 David Kaye, *Speech Police: The Global Struggle to Govern the Internet* (Columbia Global Reports, 2019); Sahana Udupa, Iginio Gagliardone, and Peter Hervik, *Digital Hate: The Global Conjuncture of Extreme Speech* (Indiana University Press, 2021); Monroe Price and Nicole Stremlau, eds., *Speech and Society in Turbulent Times: Freedom of Expression in Comparative Perspective* (Cambridge University Press, 2018).

26 Linnet Taylor et al., eds., *Data Justice and Covid-19: Global Perspectives* (Meatspace Press, 2020).

27 Tahu Kukutai and John Taylor, eds., *Indigenous Data Sovereignty: Toward an Agenda* (ANU Press, 2016); Maggie Walter et al., *Indigenous Data Sovereignty and Policy* (Taylor & Francis, 2021).

Bibliography

Balbi, Gabriele, and Andreas Fickers, eds. *History of the International Telecommunication Union (ITU): Transnational Techno-Diplomacy from the Telegraph to the Internet*. De Gruyter, 2020.

Benjamin, Ruha. *Race After Technology: Abolitionist Tools for the New Jim Code*. Polity, 2019.

Birhane, Abeba. "Algorithmic Injustice: A Relational Ethics Approach." *Patterns* 2, no. 2 (2021): 100205.

Blair, Ann, Paul Duguid, Anja-Silvia Goeing, and Anthony Grafton, eds. *Information: A Historical Companion*. Princeton University Press, 2021.

Chun, Wendy Hui Kyong. *Discriminating Data: Correlation, Neighborhoods, and the New Politics of Recognition*. MIT Press, 2021.

Citron, Danielle. *The Fight for Privacy: Protecting Dignity, Identity, and Love in the Digital Age*. W. W. Norton, 2022.

Cohen, Julie E. *Between Truth and Power: The Legal Constructions of Informational Capitalism*. Oxford University Press, 2019.

Crawford, Kate. *The Atlas of AI: Power, Politics, and the Planetary Costs of Artificial Intelligence*. Yale University Press, 2021.

Driscoll, Kevin. *The Modem World: A Prehistory of Social Media*. Yale University Press, 2022.

Ganter, Sarah Anne, and Hanan Badr. "Introduction: Re-examining Media Governance Through Cosmopolitan Critique." In *Media Governance*, edited by Sarah Anne Ganter and Hanan Badr. Palgrave Macmillan, 2022.

Gawer, Annabelle, ed. *Platforms, Markets and Innovation*. Edward Elgar, 2011.

Grohmann, Rafael, and Jack Qiu. "Contextualizing Platform Labor." *Contracampo: Brazilian Journal of Communication* 39, no. 1 (2020). https://doi.org/10.22409/contracampo.v39i1.42260.

Hartzog, Woodrow. *Privacy's Blueprint: The Battle to Control the Design of New Technologies*. Harvard University Press, 2018.

Hong, Yu, and Eric Harwit. "China's Globalizing Internet: History, Power, and Governance." *Chinese Journal of Communication* 13, no. 1 (2020): 1–7.

Jiang, Min, and Luca Belli, eds. *Digital Sovereignty in the BRICS Countries: How the Global South and Emerging Power Alliances Are Reshaping Digital Governance*. Cambridge University Press, 2025.

Jin, Dal Yong. *Digital Platforms, Imperialism and Political Culture*. Routledge, 2015.

Kaye, David A. *Speech Police: The Global Struggle to Govern the Internet*. Columbia Global Reports, 2019.

Kokas, Aynne. *Trafficking Data: How China Is Winning the Battle for Digital Sovereignty*. Oxford University Press, 2022.

Krapiva, Natalia. "ECOWAS Togo Court Decision: Internet Access Is a Right that Requires Protection of the Law." *Access Now*, July 14, 2020. Available online: https://www.accessnow.org/ecowas-togo-court-decision/.

Kukutai, Tahu, and John Taylor, eds. *Indigenous Data Sovereignty: Toward an Agenda*. ANU Press, 2016.

Morozov, Evgeny. *The Net Delusion: The Dark Side of Internet Freedom*. PublicAffairs, 2012.

Mullaney, Thomas S., Benjamin Peters, Mar Hicks, and Kavita Philip, eds. *Your Computer Is on Fire*. MIT Press, 2021.

Nissenbaum, Helen. *Privacy in Context: Technology, Policy, and the Integrity of Social Life*. Stanford Law Books, 2009.

Noble, Safiya Umoja. *Algorithms of Oppression*. New York University Press, 2018.

Nyabola, Nanjala. *Digital Democracy, Analogue Politics: How the Internet Era Is Transforming Politics in Kenya*. Zed Books, 2018.

O'Mara, Margaret. *The Code: Silicon Valley and the Remaking of America*. Penguin, 2020.

Parker, Geoffrey G., Marshall W. Van Alstyne, and Sangeet Paul Choudary. *Platform Revolution: How Networked Markets Are Transforming the Economy and How to Make Them Work for You*. W. W. Norton, 2016.

Pasquale, Frank. *The Black Box Society: The Secret Algorithms That Control Money and Information*. Harvard University Press, 2015.

Persily, Nathaniel, and Joshua A. Tucker, eds. *Social Media and Democracy: The State of the Field, Prospects for Reform*. Cambridge University Press, 2020.

Price, Monroe, and Nicole Stremlau, eds. *Speech and Society in Turbulent Times*. Cambridge University Press, 2018.

Sadowski, Jathan. *Too Smart: How Digital Capitalism Is Extracting Data, Controlling Our Lives, and Taking over the World*. MIT Press, 2020.

Srnicek, Nick. *Platform Capitalism*. Wiley, 2017.

Taylor, Linnet, G. Sharma, A. Martin, and Shazade Jameson, eds. *Data Justice and COVID-19: Global Perspectives*. Meatspace Press, 2020.

Tufekci, Zeynep. *Twitter and Tear Gas: The Power and Fragility of Networked Protest*. Yale University Press, 2017.

Tworek, Heidi. "Policy Lessons from Five Historical Patterns in Information Manipulation." In *The Disinformation Age: Politics, Technology, and Disruptive Communication in the United States*, edited by W. Lance Bennett and Steven Livingston. Cambridge University Press, 2020.

Udupa, Sahana, Iginio Gagliardone, and Peter Hervik. *Digital Hate*. Indiana University Press, 2021.

Vaidhyanathan, Siva. *The Googlization of Everything (And Why We Should Worry)*. University of California Press, 2012.

van Dijck, José, Thomas Poell, and Martijn De Waal. *The Platform Society: Public Values in a Connective World*. Oxford University Press, 2018.

Waldman, Ari Ezra. *Industry Unbound: The Inside Story of Privacy, Data, and Corporate Power*. Cambridge University Press, 2021.

Walter, Maggie, Tahu Kukutai, Stephanie Russo Carroll, and Desi Rodriguez-Lonebear, eds. *Indigenous Data Sovereignty and Policy*. Taylor & Francis, 2021.

Wasserman, Herman, and Dani Madrid-Morales, eds. *Disinformation in the Global South*. Wiley, 2022.

Wen, Yun. *The Huawei Model: The Rise of China's Technology Giant*. University of Illinois Press, 2020.

York, Jillian C. *Silicon Values: The Future of Free Speech Under Surveillance Capitalism*. Verso, 2022.

Zuboff, Shoshana. *The Age of Surveillance Capitalism: The Fight for a Human Future at the New Frontier of Power*. PublicAffairs, 2019.

Zuckerman, Ethan. "The Case for Digital Public Infrastructure." Knight First Amendment Institute, January 17, 2020. Available online: https://knightcolumbia.org/content/the-case-for-digital-public-infrastructure.

PART ONE
CONTENT

1 PLATFORM RULES AND PUBLIC NORMS

David Kaye*

Introduction

During their nascence, American social media companies adopted modest sets of rules to govern user-generated content on their platforms.[1] As they grew in popularity, their seeming openness to free exchange of information and ideas transformed into a liability as they became known less as places of social connection than as lawless environments of harassment and hatred. Instances of public harm proliferated: Infamously, Facebook failed to act when its platform was used to incite violence and genocide in Myanmar against the Rohingya community; Twitter, the platform now known as X, became a place where American white supremacists felt comfortable; and YouTube deleted video evidence of war crimes in Syria.[2] Human rights defenders, journalists, governments, advertisers, and the United Nations began to pay attention to how the companies dealt with content widely seen as harmful to individuals and public discourse, such as racism, misogyny, terrorist content, glorification of violence and self-harm, disinformation, and physical threats. In response, the companies developed increasingly detailed rules and bureaucracies for content moderation, along with armies of content moderators.[3] Yet they generally operated in the shadows, rarely disclosing decisions to the public.

Outsiders have found it difficult to determine whether these companies exercise their power responsibly. Thus, calls for transparency have proliferated in tandem with demands that the companies pay attention to the public interest (e.g., the harms caused by harassment, disinformation, and hate speech). In turn, when they do go public, their explanations often involve a rhetoric of public law. This is new. Once upon a time, the companies would have defended their

* U.C. Irvine School of Law. Thanks to Julia Kim for outstanding research assistance.

rights to run their companies according to their brand, perhaps subject to legal requests from governments. They argued that they enjoy the right to determine their own speech rules according to their contractual terms of service. They may still make those arguments. But it became common for social media companies to justify their decisions according to domestic legal norms and human rights frameworks that govern freedom of expression and the limitations the right to free speech imposes on the state. In some cases, they began to do this under the requirements of local law, such as in Germany, whose Network Enforcement Act requires platforms to assess certain kinds of content on the basis of its criminal code and to disclose their actions regularly through transparency reporting. At other times, they do it in the shadow of government or public pressure, even if not required. Facebook established an oversight mechanism to address some instances of content controversies, which, in turn, draws explicitly from human rights law in making its decisions. Twitter's former CEO, Jack Dorsey, tweeted about the need for the company to root its decisions in human rights norms. TikTok, Spotify, and many other online platforms face the same pressure and exhibit similar responses.

Transparency is a tool to ensure that company decisions are understood and assessed by the public. But it is more than a one-way ratchet to promote good content moderation practices. Increasing disclosure of the reasoning behind content moderation will almost certainly also influence public policy and law. Industry standards around online speech could converge, and in turn, companies and experts will explain and defend them, courts will defer to them, and legislators will accept them.[4] Publicly reasoned content moderation decisions will exist as part of a global argument about the appropriate standards for online speech regulation. As governments move to regulate social media and promote transparency, should they promote industry-wide development of normative standards? Or should they seek to channel company decisions regarding public norms into democratically legitimate forums?

The likelihood of private influence over public norms should be explored and considered by policymakers and legislators.[5] This chapter first provides an overview of how company content moderation standards evolved toward a kind of publicly understandable set of rationales for their decisions. It then highlights some legislative trends that may mandate public reasoning and other sorts of disclosures, opening up pathways for platforms to influence public policy. It then borrows from some of the theorizing others have done pertaining to corporate influence over public policy—apart from the common examples of adversarial argument and legislative or regulatory lobbying—to consider ways in which this reciprocal impact could play out. It concludes with an assessment of how transparency may be harnessed for democratic and human rights principles.

Governing Through Content Moderation

Commercial content moderation is a major function—perhaps the key platform function—according to which social media companies adopt and enforce rules concerning unacceptable content.[6] Increasingly bureaucratized, "governing" aptly characterizes the work the companies do.[7] The term has a decidedly *internal* character, referring to how the companies develop and enforce their own private terms of service, articulated through variously named guidelines, rules, or standards, with respect to content that users upload to their privately owned platforms. It suggests that the relationship between the companies and their users is one between the governors and the governed. Platform rules may take into account the off-platform consequences of user-generated content, but they essentially look inward in an effort to create an internally coherent kind of platform law.[8] As long as they are inward-looking, contained within a supposed bubble of company governance, one might imagine their influence is cabined within the particular private realm they rule.

Over time, however, broadly worded and generic standards evolved into "an intricate system of rules."[9] At first, the American companies rested their approach on a US-centric view of speech norms under the First Amendment of the US Constitution, but as they globalized, they struggled to locate the source of their values to determine what speech would be inappropriate. Simply saying that they had terms of service to which users must adhere was not satisfying to those subjected to harassment or hatred, for instance, certainly not in environments where off-platform harms—such as political and public health disinformation, hate speech and misogyny, and incitement to discrimination or violence—seemed to be on the rise. In the United States and Europe, among other jurisdictions, the companies were under no *legal* pressure to infuse their rules with some public value, as Section 230 of the Communications Decency Act in the United States and the e-Commerce Directive in the European Union, did not impose upon them any foundational free speech or antiharm norms to carry out their content moderation. This author, as a special rapporteur for the United Nations, encouraged the companies to adopt the UN Guiding Principles on Business and Human Rights to ensure that their activities would prevent or mitigate human rights harms.[10]

Companies' development of rules appeared from the outside to be so opaque, and their enforcement so capricious and responsive to powerful political actors, that the pressure increased to justify rules and their application according to publicly understandable reasoning and norms. In 2018, former Twitter CEO Jack Dorsey noted, "Our early values informed our rules. We likely overrotated on one value, & then let the rules react to rapidly changing circumstances (some we helped create). We need to root these values in human rights law."[11] Meta

CEO Mark Zuckerberg mused with an interviewer, "How can you set up a more democratic or community-oriented process that reflects the values of people around the world?"[12]

These kinds of references to public values did not emerge from some internal and independent assessment of their roles as would-be custodians of a new digital public square. They came because of public advocacy, media reporting, and political pressure. This was not exactly new. As far back as the establishment of the Global Network Initiative (GNI) in 2008 and the adoption of its Principles on Freedom of Expression and Privacy, several companies, along with civil society organizations, academics, and investors, committed to observing fundamental human rights in the way they assess government restrictions on speech or demands for private data.[13] In doing so, the companies committed to independent assessment, a process that involves interactions with academic and civil society experts, if not full public disclosure of the assessment itself. It nonetheless reflects a corporate familiarity with the standards of human rights law and the call of the UN Human Rights Council that companies respect human rights and remedy violations where they occur.[14] Around 2008, the US public had focused on company complicity with government repression of online speech and privacy; this focus helped generate the GNI's establishment. Only later—and certainly by social media's influence during the United Kingdom's 2016 vote to leave the European Union, the US election of Donald Trump as president that same year, and the genocidal attack on the Rohingya community in Myanmar in 2017—did global attention turn to internal company content moderation rules and their enforcement.

The technology titans started out not wanting any particular rules or responsibilities for their internal content governance. They saw themselves as mere hosts for others' expression, not their police. As that seemingly free speech-friendly argument fell apart in the face of the reality that companies' hunger for content served an advertising-centered business model, scholars, activists, and governments increasingly pushed the companies to adopt public interest norms to moderate content. This pressure came from governments as early as 2015, when Germany's minister of justice wrote to Facebook of his dismay that application of the company's community standards did not result in the deletion of content considered illegal under German law.[15] A cascade of efforts followed. Germany developed a code of conduct with several of the companies, urging them to take down content illegal under domestic law.[16] The European Union followed with a similar code in 2016.[17] In 2018, as German politicians became frustrated with the companies' failure to modify their behavior concerning far-right and discriminatory content (and incitement to hatred and violence), Germany enacted its Network Enforcement Act (NetzDG), requiring the platforms to adopt systemic approaches to ensure that illegal content under German law would be deleted. Across Europe, the same demands followed, from the United Kingdom to France and elsewhere.

The legislative pressure tracked widespread disgruntlement; in turn, the biggest of the platforms began to explain their decisions around high-profile cases. The trend was haphazard, a dip into the waters of content moderation transparency. Even so, the research and advocacy organization, Ranking Digital Rights, in evaluating twenty-six of the leading actors in technology and communications, noted in 2020 that "the global internet is facing a systemic crisis of transparency and accountability."[18] In the context of some of the platforms' decisions and rulemaking, the companies began deploying a public-facing rhetoric that drew upon the vocabulary of public law. It may be that public disclosures and reasoning were merely a public relations tool to help the companies argue that they were acting to protect the public interest. It may be that the language of content moderation decision-making and rulemaking necessarily and incidentally borrowed from public law terminology and frameworks, given the kinds of issues at stake. Approaching content moderation explanations from this perspective may reflect no more than an effort to create or borrow from a shared language so that company decisions, standards, and processes would be understandable to a public that increasingly saw the companies as powerful state-like forces within society. It may also have reflected a desire to avoid legislation that would push them beyond mere public disclosures of rules and processes, and the occasional high-profile case, in ways that are inconsistent with their perceived business interests. In any event, the motivation is less salient than their impact on public norm development.

For an example of that trend, who is better to demonstrate the changed attitudes than Donald Trump, the US president, who infamously used (and continues to use) social media to promote his brand and conduct public business? The three major American platforms signaled their actions concerning Donald Trump with varying degrees of detail. Throughout his first presidential term, they responded to him with limited, if any, moderation. In 2017, Trump tweeted, "Just heard Foreign Minister of North Korea speak at U.N. If he echoes thoughts of Little Rocket Man, they won't be around much longer!"[19] Twitter responded to calls for the tweet to be treated as a violent threat. It noted that the tweet alluded to "a number of factors" Twitter considered when evaluating a tweet's consistency with its rules, and then it added, "Among the considerations is 'newsworthiness' and whether a Tweet is of public interest."[20] That was the extent of the reasoning. It served as a contrast to Twitter's decision in 2021 to permanently remove Trump from the platform (though "permanent" proved an overstatement). On January 8, 2021, Twitter released a statement indicating that it had "permanently suspended" the Trump account, providing a "comprehensive analysis" of the reasons.[21] The company pointed to the overall context of the tweets and found that they constituted incitement to violence. While the post may be less comprehensive than advertised, it clearly aligns the decision with a public-oriented approach to understanding when speech may constitute incitement subject to restriction. YouTube, by contrast, explained its decision to suspend Trump's channel with something much less comprehensive, curiously posting its decision on Twitter.[22]

Facebook, now under the umbrella of Meta, went further. As with Twitter, Facebook suspended Trump, doing so with indefinite application on January 7, 2021, just after the Trump-inspired attack on the US Capitol.[23] It then referred its decision to the Facebook (now Meta) Oversight Board, which it had created the year before to address content moderation decisions.[24] Together, the two statements established a public-oriented argument as to why the company believed that it was right to suspend Trump. In the referral, Nick Clegg, the company's vice president of Global Affairs at the time, noted, "It would be better if these decisions were made according to frameworks agreed by democratically accountable lawmakers. But in the absence of such laws, there are decisions that we cannot duck."[25] Four months later, in language with remarkably juridical tones, the Oversight Board "upheld" the Facebook decision, providing a rationale drawn not only from Facebook's Community Standards but also from international human rights law.[26]

There is, of course, significant variation among these public-facing rationales for action against Trump's accounts. They nonetheless move toward public reasoning, both in the context of the content decisions and the process for grievance and appeal. This has been repeated following Russia's invasion of Ukraine. For instance, Twitter explained its approach to content moderation by emphasizing that "we have a responsibility to the public," *inter alia*, to "elevate credible and reliable information," a policy it described in detailed public-minded terms.[27] With less explanation, YouTube announced (on Twitter) that it would address "deceptive practices and misinformation" in part by blocking Russian state media in Europe.[28] Meta, then the rebranded Facebook, similarly announced that it would restrict access to state media from Russia given the "exceptional circumstances."[29] Whether express or implied, the companies took a position about propaganda and the public interest.

The most far-reaching instance of public reasoning is the Facebook/Meta Oversight Board. Whether one sees it as a net-positive or net-negative for the impact of Meta platforms (Facebook, Instagram, WhatsApp) on public life, the board has initiated a practice in which it, a private entity established by and for a private entity, assesses content moderation standards at least in part according to the public norms of human rights law. It may be that the practice will not gain traction among other companies or across the industry, but given the pressures that will be evident in the context of government transparency proposals, the Facebook approach is likely not to be the last of its kind.

Transparency demands are not only pushing the companies toward public reasoning of their content moderation decisions but also pushing them toward a kind of procedural fairness in which individuals gain increasing access to notice, grievance mechanisms, and appeals processes. At the time, Twitter presented some basic information around user notifications and appeals processes following account action (or inaction).[30] YouTube developed an appeals process for "strikes" under its community guidelines.[31] Facebook has gone further than others in developing an internal mechanism for notice and appeal, enabling not only on-platform appeal but also the potential for recourse through its Oversight Board.[32] The Oversight Board may be generating outsize interest in North America and Europe, with global submissions modest in numbers.[33] Yet the trend toward decisions and processes that at least echo public law norms had generally taken root at the time of the deplatforming of Trump.

It may also be the case that companies prefer, and will advocate, transparency obligations (to a point) over specific obligations to remove content absent an official legal order to that effect. Responding to public demands and anticipating the regulatory moment, Google, Twitter/X and Facebook/Meta have developed transparency reports that disclose (mostly in the aggregate) a range of their activities, from the demands they field from governments to the steps they take to moderate content even beyond the shadow of such legal requests. They have also taken cues from members of the public and legislators, who see in the platforms a significant degree of opacity that interferes with their ability to know exactly how company terms of service (and content rules or standards) are applied.[34] Transparency in their decisions, at a more granular level than they do now, may be a trade-off they are willing to embrace to avoid content-specific rules. Such obligations would not have the force of a specific rule demanding the companies respond in particular ways to certain kinds of content. From the perspective of human rights, and especially the rights to freedom of expression and privacy, the specter of governments making content decisions or making demands of companies regarding categories of content or user data easily lead to concerns of official abuse, overremoval by companies, interference with the companies' rights to shape their platforms and brands in a competitive market, and the security of individuals. There are examples enough of governments legislating against broad, poorly defined categories of harm and then using that legal tool to target journalists, human rights defenders, opposition political figures, historically oppressed communities, and the global media for censorship, punishment, or worse.

Transparency, by contrast, seems to satisfy several public priorities.[35] If performed by companies in good faith and with appropriate disclosure, transparency can provide governments with the information to identify risks and public harms and then take appropriate (i.e., lawful) action. It can disclose to users and potential users the nature of the platform's activities, risks, and actions taken against those risks, giving users a measure of autonomy in deciding whether to engage on the platform and how to do so. Transparency mandates, if done right, may also help incentivize internal company cultures of rights-sensitive practices, with the companies knowing that their decisions will see the sunlight of public critique. They can, moreover, productively feed into a debate that is often strong on rhetoric and weak on evidence.[36]

The Regulatory Move Toward Transparency Requirements

In the debate over the regulation of online platforms, the shape and resilience of global norms governing online speech are at stake. The European Union's Digital Services Act (DSA), adopted in 2022, could incentivize companies to articulate why they take action on accounts, though that remains to be seen. A German federal court determined that the failure of Facebook to provide adequate notice about its rules and actions interfered with the rights of users in Germany.[37] Transparency mandates have been considered in the United States, Canada, France, and the United Kingdom (in the last of which they were adopted). Australia has already adopted regulations to incentivize the development of industry codes.

These regulatory moves involve an often-unstated question at their core: To what extent should private platforms be adjudicating claims essentially arising from public law norms? Its corollary: To what extent should the state direct the platforms in how they adjudicate content claims? Put another way, content claims—that is, demands that companies either leave up or take down or otherwise take actions for or against specific posts or tweets—are typically framed as public rights. *The platform is interfering with my legal right to express my opinion.* Or: *The platform is enabling others to interfere with my right to be free from discrimination, hostility, or violence.* As legal rights that must arise from some domestic or international source, these are claims seeking the legitimacy of public standards even though the platforms, as private actors, are not subject to the same obligations or limitations (or authorities) that law imposes on (or grants) the state. A state that adopts a content-regulation model, requiring action against certain categories of content, is signaling that it wishes to limit the discretion of the platform to make content decisions, imposing at least some set of rules pertaining to certain harms on the companies' freedom to shape their rules and enforcement of them. A state that adopts a rule-transparency model is signaling a view that the sunlight of public knowledge will enable policymakers to make better decisions about their governance of the platforms and subject them to implicit public oversight.

Transparency provisions typically involve one of two categories, or both: (1) transparency *to users* regarding content moderation decisions and (2) transparency to governments (and thus the public) through scheduled "transparency reports." Two examples may be helpful in considering the future of transparency mandates.

The European Union's Digital Services Act: Article 17 of the DSA requires internet service providers that restrict or remove content to inform the affected user of their decision as well as provide a "clear and specific statement of reasons" for that decision, regardless of whether the reason is based on the content's lawfulness or its consistency with company terms of service.[38] Providers are also required to ensure that notice is given to users "at the latest at the time of the removal or disabling of access."[39] Such notices are to include the result and territorial scope of the decision; the facts and circumstances relied on in making the decision; whether automated technology was involved; if deemed illegal, a reference to and explanation of the legal ground relied on; and if deemed inconsistent with terms of service, an explanation and information on the user's redress possibilities.[40] Platforms would also be required to publish content moderation decisions and the "statement of reasons" for those decisions in a publicly accessible database managed by the European Commission.[41]

In addition to an obligation to publish content moderation decisions and statements of reasons, providers must also publish an annual transparency report on the content moderation they engaged in during the relevant period.[42] The reports, as specified in Article 15, are to include aggregate data on such matters as orders received from member states, the number of reports through user flagging, and, most pertinent here, the content moderation engaged in at the provider's own initiative, including the number and type of measures, categorized by the type of reason and basis for taking those measures.[43]

Germany's NetzDG: The 2017 Network Enforcement Act obligates social media and video sharing platform providers with two million or more users to remove content that is "manifestly illegal" within twenty-four hours after notification of a user complaint.[44] If the illegality of the content is not obvious on its face, the provider has up to seven days to investigate and decide on the case.[45] Providers must refer to the German Criminal Code (StGB) when determining which content requires removal as NetzDG defines illegal online content in relation to twenty-two provisions in the Criminal Code.[46] A social media network may be fined up to fifty million euros for noncompliance by the Federal Office of Justice,[47] which oversees provider compliance with the law. On June 28, 2021, the Act to Amend the Network Enforcement Act[48] entered into force.[49] The recent amendments to the law grant supervisory and injunctive powers to the Federal Office of Justice while seeking to improve the user-friendliness of reporting channels for complaints and efforts to mitigate "over-blocking" of content through a user-initiated review of content moderation decisions.[50] Under NetzDG, providers are required to immediately notify the complainant and the user about any decision regarding reported content, as well as the reasons for the provider's decision.[51] NetzDG does not outline specific requirements for the contents of the disclosure notices, leaving it up to the individual providers to determine how much information to provide to affected users with respect to their content moderation decisions.

Under the 2021 amendment, complainants and affected users may request reviews of the provider's decision to remove or retain reported content through an appeals process, where the reported content is reviewed by a reviewer who was not involved in the original decision-making process.[52] The network provider is obligated to notify the user and complainant when an appeal is filed, and give the complainant an opportunity to comment within a reasonable period of time when a user requests a review of the original decision.[53] The result of the review, as well as justifications for the result, must also be immediately communicated to the user or complainant appealing the decision. If it is determined through the appeals process that the removed content was, in fact, legal content, users can request that the content be restored.[54] However, an affected user or complainant must file an appeal within two weeks of being informed of the original decision.[55] Furthermore, the amendment authorizes the Federal Office of Justice to approve arbitration bodies for voluntary out-of-court settlements of disputes between complainants/users and social media providers.[56]

Under NetzDG, providers that receive more than a hundred complaints about illegal content in a calendar year are required to publish biannual reports in German on how they deal with these complaints.[57] Large social media platforms complying with the reporting requirements have published their biannual reports online on their own websites and in the Federal Gazette.[58] The 2021 amendment requires the inclusion of additional information in the reports, including information on procedures for automated detection of illegal content, as well as general information on training data and internal procedures for quality assurance or evaluation.[59] In addition, reports must subdivide the numbers of complaints received according to the amount of time it took to remove the flagged content (within twenty-four hours, within forty-eight hours, within a week, or longer).[60] Complaints must also be broken down according to the reason for the complaint.[61] The reports must also include information on the new appeals process, including the number of appeals filed and the number of cases in which the original decision was revised.[62]

Pathways to Influence

The preceding legislative efforts rest on an assumption that transparency mandates feed a public need for and right to information about the nature and enforcement of platform rules, processes, impacts on the public, and so forth. Two trends appear to have emerged and intersected—on the one hand, increasing company publicity over their rules and enforcement, at least in the highest profile cases, and, on the other, regulatory initiatives to expand that publicity and legally mandate certain kinds of disclosures. As such, the argument for transparency has been focused on its value as a tool to change company behavior and as a benefit to public policy and decision-making. The argument may uncover only one side of the potential dynamism that public access to company reasoning may trigger and how transparent company practice may itself influence social and public norms themselves. The platforms have already begun to internalize and implement a version of public norms (e.g., freedom of expression and limitations on it) and develop new ones ("trust and safety") that themselves create "a private legal order in its own right."[63]

A rich literature explores how public law and policy may develop in reaction to, or be influenced by, the activities of private business. While there is variation among company practices, their practices and public reasoning tend, as Edelman and Suchman noted in general application, to "mimic[] and absorb[]" the vocabulary and practices of public law.[64] The episodes concerning Trump's use of online platforms during his presidency and the run-up to and aftermath of the November 2020 presidential election in the United States further pushed the companies in the direction of *sounding like* public authorities. The same can be said for the platforms' decisions to limit or remove Russian state media following Russia's invasion of Ukraine. They expressly evaluated questions that sit at the heart of public lawmaking, examining the rights at issue for speakers and audiences (the right to express oneself, the right to seek and receive that expression) as against the public values of safety and democratic legitimacy. Their previous (and recurrent) failure to articulate their rules and enforcement practices and reasoning in a consistent way has fed a public debate over the roles that the platforms should play in a democratic society. Lately, recognizing that their failures are incentivizing legislative and regulatory proposals that ultimately may harm their business models or, more seriously, the freedom of expression of their users, they have begun to borrow heavily from the structure and content of public rights reasoning, most evident in the Meta Oversight Board.

In short, the companies generally seek to "construct their own legitimacy,"[65] becoming more than mere actors in a legal system that are subject to the rules of particular domestic jurisdictions where they operate and litigate (particularly attenuated in an environment where their content decisions are largely immune from liability). As transparency forces them to be increasingly public in their rulemaking and enforcement, the companies may create implicit or explicit industry-wide standards, something the DSA, in fact, encourages, and thereby "gain control over the construction, implementation and impact of law, not only within their own boundaries, but also throughout their organizational field."[66] Put another way, their standards—which are conceived, articulated, and enforced to take into account their private shareholder interests far more than public lawmaking would—may, over time, structure the public debate and scope of what seems amenable to public regulation. They may begin to "manage, transform, and even supplant external societal rules."[67] Over time, as the rules and enforcement gain a certain legitimacy within society and its institutions (legislatures, courts, social discourse), it becomes more difficult to push back and articulate "plausible alternatives" to company practice.[68]

Gregory Shaffer has noted how "public law and business internal policies are interpenetrated, reciprocally and dynamically affecting each other."[69] On the one hand, Shaffer notes, "public law can catalyze more transparent and principled decision-making within decentralized, private 'new governance' processes that fall outside of traditional conceptions of law."[70] This is a principal intention of most transparency legislation concerning social media. But the impact of business decisions on law may work reciprocally as well, as legislators codify and courts enforce emerging company practices and industry standards.[71] Perhaps most importantly in the dynamic public space in which companies, civil society, and policymakers/legislators debate the limits of expression in democratic society, platform rules may, to borrow from Shaffer, "reciprocally shape the understanding of existing law within public institutions, including courts."[72] In short, "organizational behavior. . . affects public law."[73] Moreover, the process of interpenetration between public and private rulemaking and enforcement may happen globally as well, as bureaucratic companies and nongovernmental organizations "have all become not only subjects and objects of international law, but also creators and shapers of law."[74]

As (or if) the companies become transparent about their policies toward content and enforcement of their rules, and as (or if) they develop increasingly dense avenues to enable grievance mechanisms to be applied for their users and the public, outside observers will respond. Internal process standards and rule enforcement outcomes will increasingly interact with legal and cultural norms concerning expression in democratic, rights-respecting societies. They may do more than interact. Under international human rights law, for instance, the state must show that a given restriction on the right to freedom of expression (a law or a restriction under law) is provided by law and necessary to protect a particular public interest (the rights or reputations of others, national security or public order, or public health or morals).[75] A rich jurisprudence has developed around these standards.[76] Private rulemaking—the social media platforms themselves and their private oversight mechanisms—may put pressure on those standards. The companies may articulate rules and enforcement patterns that make sense for them as business entities, even if they take seriously and seek to mitigate their impact on human rights, and yet they may be out of step with the public norms or, more specifically, human rights law obligations of the state. It is also plausible that their articulation of human rights law principles (or other public norms) could reinforce or influence the development of international standards.

Recognizing Transparency's Impact

If the supporters of transparency mandates are correct, increased disclosure and information about platform rules, enforcement, impact, and other issues will inure to the benefit of public policy. Transparency should enable debate based on evidence, to the extent such mandates are carried out in good faith and enforced fairly by public authorities. Particularly as the disclosures are translated into publicly digestible conclusions, users will also gain more insights into the platforms, enabling them a firmer basis for deciding whether and how to participate on them. This could facilitate more individual autonomy, peeling away the opacity that fuels so much of the politicized debate over platform speech.

Yet as transparency mandates begin to materialize, policymakers may want to consider the likelihood of reciprocal impact. What might that impact look like? What kinds of tools may be available to harness the democratic potential of transparency to democratically legitimate outcomes? What kinds of constraints may governments wish to consider to ensure that platform rulemaking does not come to supplant public norms? The DSA already includes some potential avenues of prophylaxis, such as the requirement that very large online platforms (VLOPs) conduct systemic risk assessment and be subject to independent auditing.[77] That said, it may not be enough to require generic forms of risk assessment that involve any negative effects for the exercise of fundamental rights.[78] Rather, regular public evaluation of the normative approaches adopted by the platforms in their rulemaking and enforcement may profitably accompany transparency mandates. This is not to say that such an evaluation should involve legal enforcement of domestic standards pertaining to freedom of expression or other human rights norms. It may be sufficient, for purposes of constraining the reciprocal impact of platform decisions on public law, for an independent auditor or regulator to conduct regular evaluations of platform decision-making and identify in clear terms how they diverge from the norms to which states are obligated under, for instance, human rights law.

The reciprocal impact of company rulemaking and enforcement counsels in favor of treating it seriously. It may be easy to disregard company rules as merely the activities of private actors, nongovernmental businesses unbound by the rules applicable to the state, or corporations that have the freedom to adopt and enforce whatever rules they deem appropriate. Analysts may be tempted to consider company self-regulatory efforts such as the Meta Oversight Board as minor tools that hardly address the extraordinary impact the platforms have on democratic institutions, individual mental health, public debate, and countless other areas of concern. They may be correct. But as transparency mandates increasingly push for company disclosures and rationales for platform actions, it would be a mistake to put those rationales in an impenetrable box labeled "private actor." In the multistakeholder environment of internet governance, company rationales will likely have an impact. It will be up to scholars, activists, intergovernmental organizations, human rights monitors, and, yes, governments, to ensure that their impact advances the public interest.

Notes

1. See Kate Klonick, "The New Governors: The People, Rules and Processes Governing Online Speech," *Harvard Law Review* 131, no. 6 (2018): 1598, 1619–21.
2. See, for example, Business for Social Responsibility, "Human Rights Impact Assessment: Facebook in Myanmar," 2018, available online: https://about.fb.com/wp-content/uploads/2018/11/bsr-facebook-myanmar-hria_final.pdf; J. M. Berger, "Nazis vs. ISIS on Twitter: A Comparative Study of White Nationalist and ISIS Online Social Media Networks," September 2016, available online: https://extremism.gwu.edu/sites/g/files/zaxdzs2191/f/downloads/Nazis%20v.%20ISIS.pdf; David Kaye, *Speech Police: The Global Struggle to Govern the Internet* (Columbia Global Reports, 2019), 22–8.
3. See Kaye, *Speech Police*, 45.
4. That convergence is encouraged by such organizations as the Digital Trust and Safety Partnership, a US-based cross-industry entity "committed to developing industry best practices." See https://dtspartnership.org/.
5. To be clear, I am not here concerned with the private influence driven by lobbying, the revolving door from government to platform, and various other forms of corporate capture. Those are also key influences, but here I am concerned with the normative influence driven by public articulation of content moderation decisions.
6. See Sarah Roberts, "Commercial Content Moderation: Digital Laborers' Dirty Work," in *The Intersectional Internet: Race, Sex, Class and Culture Online*, ed. Safiya U. Noble and Brendesha Tynes (Peter Lang, 2016).
7. See generally Klonick, "The New Governors."
8. Report of the Special Rapporteur on the promotion and protection of the right to freedom of opinion and expression, Online Content Moderation, A/HRC/38/35 (2018) ("UN Report").
9. Klonick, "The New Governors," 1631–5. See also Kaye, *Speech Police*, 45–8.
10. See UN Report.
11. See Jack Dorsey, Tweet, available online: https://twitter.com/jack/status/1027962500438843397?lang=en.
12. Quoted in Kaye, *Speech Police*, 19.
13. In disclosure, the author served as Independent Chair of the Board of the Global Network Initiative from 2020 to 2024.
14. See UN Report.

15 See Kaye, *Speech Police*, 66–7.

16 Government of Germany Task Force, "Together against Hate Speech: Ways to Tackle Online Hateful Content Proposed by the Task Force Against Illegal Online Hate Speech," December 15, 2015, available online: https://edri.org/files/12152015_TaskForceErgebnispapier_eng.pdf.

17 European Commission, "Code of Conduct on Countering Illegal Hate Speech Online," 2016, available online: https://ec.europa.eu/info/policies/justice-and-fundamental-rights/combatting-discrimination/racism-and-xenophobia/eu-code-conduct-countering-illegal-hate-speech-online_en#theeucodeofconduct.

18 See Ranking Digital Rights, "2020 Corporate Accountability Index," available online: https://rankingdigitalrights.org/index2020/executive-summary.

19 Bill Chappel, "'Declaration of War' Means North Korea Can Shoot Down U.S. Bomber, Minister Says," NPR, September 25, 2017, available online: https://www.npr.org/sections/thetwo-way/2017/09/25/553475174/declaration-of-war-means-north-korea-can-shoot-down-u-s-bombers-minister-says.

20 See Twitter Global Governmental Affairs (tweet), available online: https://twitter.com/Policy/status/912438046515220480.

21 Twitter, Inc., "Permanent Suspension of @realDonaldTrump," January 8, 2021, available online: https://blog.twitter.com/en_us/topics/company/2020/suspension.

22 See @UpdatesfromYT, Twitter, January 13, 2021, available online: https://twitter.com/YouTubeInsider/status/1349205688694812672?ref_src=twsrc%5Etfw%7Ctwcamp%5Etweetembed%7Ctwterm%5E1349205688694812672%7Ctwgr%5E%7Ctwcon%5Es1_&ref_url=https%3A%2F%2Fwww.washingtonpost.com%2Ftechnology%2F2021%2F01%2F12%2Ftrump-youtube-ban%2F.

23 Guy Rosen, "Our Response to the Violence in Washington," January 7, 2021, available online: https://about.fb.com/news/2021/01/responding-to-the-violence-in-washington-dc/.

24 Nick Clegg, "Referring Former President Trump's Suspension from Facebook to the Oversight Board," January 21, 2021, available online: https://about.fb.com/news/2021/01/referring-trump-suspension-to-oversight-board/.

25 Ibid.

26 See Facebook Oversight Board, "Oversight Board Upholds Former President Trump's Suspension, Finds Facebook Failed to Impose Proper Penalty," May 2021, available online: https://oversightboard.com/news/226612455899839-oversight-board-upholds-former-president-trump-s-suspension-finds-facebook-failed-to-impose-proper-penalty/.

27 Sinead McSweeney, Twitter Vice-President of Global Public Policy, "Our Ongoing Approach to the War in Ukraine," Twitter Blog, March 16, 2022, available online: https://blog.twitter.com/en_us/topics/company/2022/our-ongoing-approach-to-the-war-in-ukraine.

28 See updates from YouTube (tweet), available online: https://twitter.com/YouTubeInsider/status/1498772480034365440.

29 See Meta, "Meta's Ongoing Efforts Regarding Russia's Invasion of Ukraine," February 26, 2022, available online: https://about.fb.com/news/2022/02/metas-ongoing-efforts-regarding-russias-invasion-of-ukraine/.

30 Twitter, "Our Range of Enforcement Options," available online: https://help.twitter.com/en/rules-and-policies/enforcement-options. Those options are not clearly available under X, as owned and managed by Elon Musk.

31 YouTube, "Appeal Community Guideline Actions," available online: https://support.google.com/youtube/answer/185111?hl=en.

32 Facebook, "How to Appeal to the Oversight Board," available online: https://transparency.fb.com/oversight/appealing-to-oversight-board/.

33 See Heidi Tworek, "Could E-courts Help Fix Facebook's Inadequate Oversight Board?," Centre for International Governance Innovation, available online: https://www.cigionline.org/articles/could-e-courts-help-fix-facebooks-inadequate-oversight-board/.

34 For an example of a constructive response to that concern, see "The Santa Clara Principles on Transparency and Accountability in Content Moderation," May 7, 2018, available online: https://newamericadotorg.s3.amazonaws.com/documents/Santa_Clara_Principles.pdf.

35 For an instructive catalog of some of the purposes supporting transparency in the context of intermediaries in the business sector, see, for example, European Union, Regulation (EU) 2019/1150 of the European Parliament and of the Council of June 20, 2019, on Promoting Fairness and Transparency for Business Users of Online Intermediation Services, available online: https://eur-lex.europa.eu/legal-content/EN/TXT/PDF/?uri=CELEX:32019R1150&from=EN. The recitals in particular articulate a view that transparency can foster consumer trust, business understanding, and the prevention of unfair practices.

36 See especially Annenberg Public Policy Center of the University of Pennsylvania, Transatlantic Working Group on Content Moderation Online and Freedom of Expression, "Freedom and Accountability: A Transatlantic Framework for Moderating Speech Online," 2020, available online: https://www.annenbergpublicpolicycenter.org/feature/transatlantic-working-group-freedom-and-accountability/. In a clear statement of how transparency advocates see such tools, the report noted, "Transparency is not an end in itself, but a prerequisite to establish accountability, oversight, and a healthy working relationship between tech companies, government, and the public." Id. at 7.

37 Bundesgerichtshof, "Bundesgerichtshof zu Ansprüchen gegen die Anbieterin eines sozialen Netzwerks, die unter dem Vorwurf der 'Hassrede' Beiträge gelöscht und Konten gesperrt hat," July 29, 2021, available online: https://www.bundesgerichtshof.de/SharedDocs/Pressemitteilungen/DE/2021/2021149.html.

38 Digital Services Act (DSA), art. 17.

39 Ibid.

40 Ibid., para. 2.

41 Ibid., para. 4.

42 Digital Services Act, art. 13.

43 Ibid., para 1(c).

44 Gesetz zur Verbesserung der Rechtsdurchsetzung in sozialen Netzwerken [Netzwerkdurchsetzungsgesetz—NetzDG] [Network Enforcement Act], January 9, 2017, BGBl I at 3352, § 3, para. 2, last amended by Gesetz [G], June 3, 2021, BGBl. I at 1436, art 1 (Ger.), available online: http://www.gesetze-im-internet.de/netzdg/NetzDG.pdf.

45 Ibid.

46 "Unlawful content shall be content within the meaning of subsection (1) which fulfils the requirements of the offences described in sections 86, 86a, 89a, 91, 100a, 111, 126,129 to 129b, 130, 131,140, 166,184b in connection with 184d, 185 to 187, 241 or 269 of the Criminal Code and which is not justified." NetzDG, § 1, para. 3.

47 Federal Ministry of Justice and Consumer Protection (Bundesministerium der Justiz und für Verbraucherschutz, BMJV), "Network Enforcement Act Regulatory Fining Guidelines," 2018, available online: https://www.bmjv.de/SharedDocs/Downloads/DE/Themen/Fokusthemen/NetzDG_Bußgeldleitlinien_engl.pdf;jsessionid=D683AE485A9BD7DD2F4A7EF10D8BFEBA.1_cid289?__blob=publicationFile&v=2.

48 Gesetzes zur Änderung des Netzwerkdurchsetzungsgesetz [Act to Amend the Network Enforcement Act], June 3, 2021, BGBl. I at 1436, art 1 (Ger.), available online: https://www.bgbl.de/xaver/bgbl/start.xav?startbk=Bundesanzeiger_BGBl&jumpTo=bgbl121s1436.pdf#__bgbl__%2F%2F*%5B%40attr_id%3D%27bgbl121s1436.pdf%27%5D__1639175827769.

49 Library of Congress, "Germany: Network Enforcement Act Amended to Better Fight Online Hate Speech," July 6, 2021, available online: https://www.loc.gov/item/global-legal-monitor/2021-07-06/germany-network-enforcement-act-amended-to-better-fight-online-hate-speech//.

50 Ibid.

51 NetzDG, § 3, para. 5.

52 Ibid., § 3b.

53 Ibid.

54 Ibid., § 3b, para. 2.

55 Ibid., § 3b, para. 1.

56 Ibid., § 3c.

57 Ibid., § 2, para. 1.

58 Network Enforcement Act ("NetzDG"), Facebook, available online: https://www.facebook.com/help/285230728652028; "*Where Can I See Instagram's NetzDG Transparency Reports?*," Instagram, available online: https://help.instagram.com/704881976636188/?helpref=related; "Removals under the Network Enforcement Law—YouTube," Google, available online: https://transparencyreport.google.com/netzdg/youtube?hl=en; "Removals under the Network Enforcement Law—Google+," Google, available online: https://transparencyreport.google.com/netzdg/googleplus?hl=en; "Transparency—Germany," Twitter, available online: https://transparency.twitter.com/en/reports/countries/de.html;

59 NetzDG, § 2, para. 2.

60 Ibid.

61 Ibid.

62 Ibid.

63 Lauren Edelman and Mark Suchman, "When the 'Haves' Hold Court: Speculations on the Organizational Internalization of Law," *Law & Society Review* 33, no. 4 (1999): 941, 943.

64 Ibid., 943.

65 Ibid.

66 Ibid., 976.

67 Ibid.

68 Ibid.

69 Gregory C. Shaffer, "How Business Shapes Law: A Socio-Legal Framework," *Connecticut Law Review* 42 no. 1 (2009): 147, 169.

70 Ibid.

71 Ibid.

72 Ibid., 170.

73 Ibid.

74 Ralf Michaels and Nils Jansen, "Private Law Beyond the State? Europeanization, Globalization, Privatization," *American Journal of Comparative Law* 54, no. 4 (2006): 843, 868.

75 International Covenant on Civil and Political Rights, Article 19(3).

76 See Human Rights Committee, General Comment 34, UN Doc. CCPR/C/GC/34 (2011), available online: https://www2.ohchr.org/english/bodies/hrc/docs/gc34.pdf.

77 See DSA, articles 34–5.

78 DSA Article 34(1)(b).

Bibliography

Berger, J. M. "Nazis vs. ISIS on Twitter: A Comparative Study of White Nationalist and ISIS Online Social Media Networks." September 2016. Available online: https://web.archive.org/web/20180522195803/https://extremism.gwu.edu/sites/g/files/zaxdzs2191/f/downloads/Nazis%20v.%20ISIS.pdf.

Business for Social Responsibility. "Human Rights Impact Assessment: Facebook in Myanmar." 2018. Available online: https://about.fb.com/wp-content/uploads/2018/11/bsr-facebook-myanmar-hria_final.pdf.

Chappel, Bill. "'Declaration of War' Means North Korea Can Shoot Down U.S. Bomber, Minister Says." National Public Radio, September 25, 2017. Available online: https://www.npr.org/sections/thetwo-way/2017/09/25/553475174/declaration-of-war-means-north-korea-can-shoot-down-u-s-bombers-minister-says.

Clegg, Nick. "Referring Former President Trump's Suspension from Facebook to the Oversight Board." January 21, 2021. Available online: https://about.fb.com/news/2021/01/referring-trump-suspension-to-oversight-board/.

Dorsey, Jack. Tweet. Available online: https://twitter.com/jack/status/1027962500438843397?lang=en.

Edelman, Lauren, and Mark Suchman. "When the 'Haves' Hold Court: Speculations on the Organizational Internalization of Law." *Law & Society Review* 33, no. 4 (1999): 941–91.

European Commission. "Code of Conduct on Countering Illegal Hate Speech Online." 2016. Available online: https://ec.europa.eu/info/policies/justice-and-fundamental-rights/combatting-discrimination/racism-and-xenophobia/eu-code-conduct-countering-illegal-hate-speech-online_en#theeucodeofconduct.

European Union. "Regulation (EU) 2019/1150 of the European Parliament and of the Council of 20 June 2019 on Promoting Fairness and Transparency for Business Users of Online Intermediation Services." Available online: https://eur-lex.europa.eu/legal-content/EN/TXT/PDF/?uri=CELEX:32019R1150&from=EN.

Facebook Oversight Board. "Oversight Board Upholds Former President Trump's Suspension, Finds Facebook Failed to Impose Proper Penalty." May 2021. Available online: https://oversightboard.com/news/226612455899839-oversight-board-upholds-former-president-trump-s-suspension-finds-facebook-failed-to-impose-proper-penalty/.

Federal Ministry of Justice and Consumer Protection (Bundesministerium der Justiz und für Verbraucherschutz, BMJV). "Network Enforcement Act Regulatory Fining Guidelines." 2018. Available online: https://www.bmjv.de/SharedDocs/Downloads/DE/Themen/Fokusthemen/NetzDG_Bußgeldleitlinien_engl.pdf;jsessionid=D683AE485A9BD7DD2F4A7EF10D8BFEBA.1_cid289?__blob=publicationFile&v=2.

Gesetz zur Änderung des Netzwerkdurchsetzungsgesetz [Act to Amend the Network Enforcement Act], June 3, 2021, BGBl. I at 1436, art 1 (Ger.). Available online: https://www.bgbl.de/xaver/bgbl/start.xav?startbk=Bundesanzeiger_BGBl&jumpTo=bgbl121s1436.pdf#__bgbl__%2F%2F*%5B%40attr_id%3D%27bgbl121s1436.pdf%27%5D__1639175827769.

Gesetz zur Verbesserung der Rechtsdurchsetzung in sozialen Netzwerken [Netzwerkdurchsetzungsgesetz—NetzDG] [Network Enforcement Act], Jan. 9, 2017, BGBl I at 3352, § 3, para. 2, last amended by Gesetz [G], June 3, 2021, BGBl. I at 1436, art 1 (Ger.). Available online: http://www.gesetze-im-internet.de/netzdg/NetzDG.pdf.

Government of Germany Task Force. "Together Against Hate Speech: Ways to Tackle Online Hateful Content Proposed by the Task Force against Illegal Online Hate Speech." December 15, 2015. Available online: https://edri.org/files/12152015_TaskForceErgebnispapier_eng.pdf.

Human Rights Committee. General Comment 34: Article 19. UN Doc. CCPR/C/GC/34 (2011). Available online: https://www2.ohchr.org/english/bodies/hrc/docs/gc34.pdf.

International Covenant on Civil and Political Rights, Article 19(3). Available online: https://www.ohchr.org/en/instruments-mechanisms/instruments/international-covenant-civil-and-political-rights.

Kaye, David. "Report of the Special Rapporteur on the Promotion and Protection of the Right to Freedom of Opinion and Expression: Online Content Moderation." UN Doc. A/HRC/38/35 (2018). Available online: https://ap.ohchr.org/documents/dpage_e.aspx?si=A/HRC/38/35.

Kaye, David. *Speech Police: The Global Struggle to Govern the Internet*. Columbia Global Reports, 2019.

Klonick, Kate. "The New Governors: The People, Rules and Processes Governing Online Speech." *Harvard Law Review* 131, no. 6 (2018): 1598–670.

Library of Congress. "Germany: Network Enforcement Act Amended to Better Fight Online Hate Speech." July 6, 2021. Available online: https://www.loc.gov/item/global-legal-monitor/2021-07-06/germany-network-enforcement-act-amended-to-better-fight-online-hate-speech//.

McSweeney, Sinead. "Our Ongoing Approach to the War in Ukraine." Twitter Blog, March 16, 2022. Available online: https://blog.twitter.com/en_us/topics/company/2022/our-ongoing-approach-to-the-war-in-ukraine.

Meta. "How to Appeal to the Oversight Board." Available online: https://transparency.meta.com/oversight/appealing-to-oversight-board/.

Meta. "Meta's Ongoing Efforts Regarding Russia's Invasion of Ukraine." February 26, 2022. Available online: https://about.fb.com/news/2022/02/metas-ongoing-efforts-regarding-russias-invasion-of-ukraine/.

Michaels, Ralf, and Nils Jansen. "Private Law Beyond the State? Europeanization, Globalization, Privatization." *American Journal of Comparative Law* 54, no. 4 (2006): 843–90.

Ranking Digital Rights. "2020 Corporate Accountability Index." Available online: https://rankingdigitalrights.org/index2020/executive-summary.

Roberts, Sarah. "Commercial Content Moderation: Digital Laborers' Dirty Work." In *The Intersectional Internet: Race, Sex, Class and Culture Online*, edited by Safiya U. Noble and Brendesha Tynes. Peter Lang, 2016.

Rosen, Guy. "Our Response to the Violence in Washington." Meta, January 7, 2021. Available online: https://about.fb.com/news/2021/01/responding-to-the-violence-in-washington-dc/.

"The Santa Clara Principles on Transparency and Accountability in Content Moderation." May 7, 2018. Available online: https://newamericadotorg.s3.amazonaws.com/documents/Santa_Clara_Principles.pdf.

Shaffer, Gregory C. "How Business Shapes Law: A Socio-Legal Framework." *Connecticut Law Review* 42, no. 1 (2009): 147–83.

Transatlantic Working Group on Content Moderation Online and Freedom of Expression. "Freedom and Accountability: A Transatlantic Framework for Moderating Speech Online." 2020. Available online: https://www.annenbergpublicpolicycenter.org/feature/transatlantic-working-group-freedom-and-accountability/.

Twitter Global Governmental Affairs (tweet). Available online: https://twitter.com/Policy/status/912438046515220480.

Twitter Global Governmental Affairs (tweet). "Our Range of Enforcement Options." Available online: https://help.twitter.com/en/rules-and-policies/enforcement-options.

Twitter Global Governmental Affairs (tweet). "Permanent Suspension of @realDonald Trump." January 8, 2021. Available online: https://blog.twitter.com/en_us/topics/company/2020/suspension.

Tworek, Heidi. "Could E-Courts Help Fix Facebook's Inadequate Oversight Board?" Centre for International Governance Innovation, October 29, 2021. Available online: https://www.cigionline.org/articles/could-e-courts-help-fix-facebooks-inadequate-oversight-board/.

Updates from YouTube (tweet). Available online: https://twitter.com/YouTubeInsider/status/1498772480034365440.

YouTube. "Appeal Community Guideline Actions." Available online: https://support.google.com/youtube/answer/185111?hl=en.

2

FACEBOOK'S CONTENT MODERATION ECO SYSTEM IN ETHIOPIA

"Until the Machine Learns Your Language, You Stay Put"

Berhan Taye

As the war between the Tigray People's Liberation Front (TPLF) and the Ethiopian federal government raged on and as TPLF controlled more towns in the Amhara region in October and November 2021,[1] Mesay Mekonnen, a famous TV journalist,[2] called on the Ethiopian government to put all Tigrayans outside of Tigray in "concentration camps."[3] Mesay, posting a lengthy message on Facebook, justified his call for the mass detention of the fourth-largest ethnic group because, according to him, Tigrayans who lived outside of Tigray were "helping TPLF win the war against the Federal government."[4] Although Mesay's post violated Facebook's Community Standards, this content was only taken down after twenty-four hours. Users who used Facebook's in-app reporting tool to report Mesay's post received a reply that Facebook would not be able to take down this content because it did not violate its Community Standards. Instead, Facebook advised users offended or bothered by this content to block the person if they found the content offensive.[5]

Mesay's post on Facebook was shared over six hundred times, screenshots created, and reposted. This post, because of the profile of the speaker, normalized and justified the assault, detention, and disappearance of Tigrayans in the public sphere and potentially helped escalate the assault against Tigrayans.[6] Tigrayans in different parts of the country continued to be rounded up and sent to unknown locations,[7] vigilante groups, particularly in Addis Abeba, were formed to "protect" the city from Tigrayans,[8] and many were harassed, profiled, and targeted because they were Tigrayans.[9] By the time Facebook took down this post, the damage had already been done.[10]

This is not just a Tigray or an Ethiopian story. In India, Facebook's largest market, minority groups have faced similar, if not worse, problems due to Facebook's lack of due diligence and care.[11] During Delhi's Assembly elections in February 2020, Bharatiya Janata Party (BJP) affiliates and far-right Hindutva leaders live streamed content with calls to violence against Muslims and Dalits.[12] Facebook, as it failed in Ethiopia, also failed to act in India, and "when it did [act] much later, it was already too late."[13] Muslims and Dalits, the targets of this content, were killed, and their mangled bodies were left on the streets of Delhi and dumped in drains.[14] The perpetrators of the violence used Facebook's other platform, WhatsApp, to spread disinformation and misleading narratives about the cause of the violence.[15] This is not an isolated event in India. Muslims, Dalit communities, and other minority groups have been calling on the platform to act against hate speech and violence-inciting content for years before the Delhi pogrom.[16]

In Myanmar, similar to India and Ethiopia, Facebook chose not to act. The Rohingya, a predominantly Muslim ethnic minority in Myanmar, have been subjected to state-sanctioned persecution, oppression, and discrimination for generations.[17] According to the latest Facebook whistleblower, Sarah Wynn-Williams, media reports, and a collective of researchers, practitioners, and advocates from Myanmar, Facebook facilitated the rise of the mass Buddhist nationalist movement in Myanmar.[18] As this movement rose on the platform, so did anti-Rohingya sentiment, followed by the military's clearance operation against the Rohingya community in Rakhine State.[19] Facebook, even though it was aware of the situation on the platform, failed to take action.[20] Later, the head of the United Nations Independent Fact-Finding Mission on Myanmar blamed Facebook for "substantively contribut[ing] to the level of acrimony and dissension and conflict [. . .] within the public" and effectively against the Rohingya in Myanmar.[21]

Minorities in Ethiopia, Muslims and Dalit communities in India, and the Rohingya are not the first nor the only groups that have been targeted because of viral content on social media. Thus, if this is not just a single-country problem, why does Facebook fail to take down hate speech and violence-inciting content year after year? After claiming to invest in languages, machines, code, and humans,[22] why does the platform fail to take down the most obvious content like Mesay's? This chapter, by taking Ethiopia as a case study, will provide an analysis of Facebook's content moderation ecosystem. After providing a brief overview of Ethiopia's internet landscape, it examines Facebook's automated and human moderation systems. It further explores how the Oversight Board and the Trusted Partner program, which are institutional mechanisms designed to fill the gap created by automated and human moderation, result in systemic failure.

Internet in Ethiopia—101

Ethiopia was estimated to have a population of 125 million people in 2025, comprising more than eighty ethnic groups. Oromos, Amhara, Somalis, and Tigrayans are the four largest ethnic groups and languages spoken in the country, respectively. These ethnic groups, while they make up their own regions, also use their respective languages in schools and for government services. In February 2020, Afan Oromo, Tigrinya, Somali, and Afar were introduced as working federal languages in addition to Amharic. By 2024, approximately 20 percent of Ethiopians were online, and less than 10 percent of those online, or around seven million, used social media platforms such as Facebook.[23] Although Ethiopia has a relatively low level of internet access compared to other African countries, the internet and communication infrastructure have had a significant impact on its people. The most predominant platforms frequented by Ethiopians are Facebook and Telegram.[24] Ethiopians, like others around the world, use social media for various reasons: to connect with their friends, share and source information, earn money, organize for war and peace, and document atrocities.

Social media, in the past ten years, have significantly influenced how the public and the private sphere discourse is in contention with subsequent Ethiopian governments. Often, this tension arises out of the government's attempt to be the only source of "truth" and social media's ability to entertain and allow numerous narratives to flourish. Between 2005 and 2016, the then-ruling party introduced numerous laws and regulations that closed independent media and ultimately made state-affiliated media the only source of information in the country.[25] This made social media, for better or worse, the only avenue where people could seek alternative sources of information, debate issues, and organize for change. The autonomy presented on social media did not go unchallenged—on numerous occasions, the government blocked social media, filtered content, shut down the internet, and arrested those who used social media to challenge the government's narratives.[26]

The rise of Prime Minister Abiy Ahmed (2018–) changed how social media is used in the country. Unlike his predecessor, Abiy, his cabinet and extended government use social media. For instance, the conflict between the TPLF and the federal forces was announced on the prime minister's Facebook page and state media almost simultaneously. State media now quotes the government from its social media pages. Still, old habits die hard. Abiy's reformer government also uses social media for its public relations and propaganda, continues to spy on citizens and dissidents, has been accused of spreading hate speech and violence-inciting content online,[27] and has shut down social media and the internet numerous times.[28]

By the time of writing, the monopoly of violence in Ethiopia is shared between the federal government and numerous regional armed groups. Ethnic violence is rampant in the country, and the government is at war with itself. The ruling party, which used to be a federation of four major ethnic-based political parties, coalesced to form a unitary party, and this move fractured the fragile federation within the ruling elites. The TPLF, the former minority ruling elites, bruised by the changes brought forward by the new government, attacked the federal government's biggest military base in the North, leading to one of the most devastating civil wars in Africa. Human suffering and the egregious crimes committed by all the warring parties, including Eritrean forces and Amhara paramilitary groups, have been declared crimes against humanity and war crimes by the United Nations, Amnesty International, Human Rights Watch, and the Ethiopian Human Rights Commission.[29] This war has forced millions to leave their homes; women and men have been raped, and many are living in displacement camps under dire circumstances, without access to basic necessities and telecommunications services.

After two years of war, in November 2022, TPLF and the federal government declared a truce and signed a cessation of hostilities agreement in Pretoria, South Africa.[30] Soon after this agreement was signed, alliances shifted, and old friends became new enemies. Amhara nationalists and paramilitary groups, armed by the federal government to fight in Tigray, turned their muzzles to Addis Abeba and fought against the federal government. The rest is history, and history is on a loop. The same atrocities documented in Tigray are now taking place in the Amhara region.[31]

As this war claims its victims offline, it also targets and kills its victims online. The self-proclaimed defenders of an ethnic group use social media platforms to live stream, write, and perform their call of the mass extensions of ethnic groups, deny claims of violence and rape of the most vulnerable, organize for war, and fundraise for weapons. Facebook, YouTube, X (previously Twitter), TikTok, Telegram, and Instagram are instruments of war and, at times, peace in Ethiopia. The codes, design, algorithms, and business models of social media platforms have helped hate speech and violence-inciting content go viral. The platforms have turned a blind eye as groups fundraise for weapons, organize militias, recruit fighters, facilitate mob justice, and as content on the platforms sow and fan animosity in the country. Facebook, due to its popularity and reach in the country,[32] causes the lion's share of this problem, and at the core of this problem is Facebook's content moderation system.

Automated Moderation: Death by Default

Facebook, on numerous occasions, has confirmed that it applies proactive and reactive moderation in Ethiopia.[33] A report from Facebook during Ethiopia's 2021 election confirmed: "We've [. . .] invested in proactive detection technology that helps us catch violating content before people report it to us. We're now using this technology to proactively identify hate speech in Amharic and Oromo, alongside over 40 other languages globally."[34] Facebook asserts that, between March 2020 and March 2021, it removed 87,000 pieces of hate speech in Ethiopia, and almost 90 percent of this content was proactively detected.[35] The black box nature of these systems and numbers makes it difficult to fully discern how these systems work and which methods were used to classify and take down 87,000 pieces of content. The key question is, then, if Facebook's systems are effective at proactively and reactively taking down content, then why is Facebook unable to take down content that is facilitating and amplifying grave atrocities against minority groups in Ethiopia? When users report hateful, dangerous, and insightful content, why does the company fail to take down the content, and why do users get a reply that the content reported does not violate the company's Community Standards? To fully understand the company's failure in Ethiopia and other places, it is essential to look into the content moderation system, both the technical and political.

According to Facebook, it employs two approaches to content moderation: proactive measures that utilize machine learning and human content moderators.[36] The proactive measures and detection systems are Facebook's flagship program, utilizing machine learning to proactively examine content and enforce measures in line with the Community Standards and Facebook's rules of engagement. This system simply attempts to "identify, match, predict, or classify some pieces of content (e.g. [words], text, images, or video) on the basis of its exact properties or general features."[37] Content that is moderated through these systems is either flagged for human moderators or deleted.[38] Depending on the format and features of the content, this system can either use keyword matching, *hash, or classify* content to either automatically delete, remove, or flag for human review.[39] Platforms like Facebook, through keyword matching, can flag specific words, phrases, or terms against previously identified terms compiled against a specific database. In addition to keyword matching, platforms, through hashing, create unique identifiers for content, often flagging images or videos that violate the platform's standards.

Whenever text containing pre-identified words, phrases, terms, or images is uploaded to the platform, it is checked against this database of content. If a positive match is found, this content is either deleted, barred from being uploaded, or flagged for human moderation.[40] Facebook has been forthcoming about this process and even indicates that it has removed more than 1.9 million pieces of content related to Islamic State of Iraq and Syria (ISIS) and Al-Qaeda using this system.[41] According to thousands of documents leaked by whistleblower Frances Haugen in 2021, Facebook also employs a fairly new, untested, and experimental content moderation method called *network-based modeling*.[42] Network-based modeling, rather than depending on previously identified content like images or videos and keyword matching such as slur lists, bases its content moderation "on identifying patterns of behavior that are consistent with malicious activity."[43] A Facebook spokesperson has publicly denied using network-based modeling.[44] However, contrary to this claim, the Facebook papers leaked by Frances Haugen show that Facebook is keen to use this method of moderation in Ethiopia and Myanmar, where, according to these internal documents, the company has poor language or context capacity.[45]

For this proactive technology to accurately detect hateful, violence-inciting, and dangerous speech in Ethiopian languages, it requires an extensive amount of data relevant to the Ethiopian context. Not just any data, "the more examples of correctly labeled data there are, the better the algorithm will be at producing accurate predictions, [matches, and decisions]."[46] In addition to contextualized and accurate data, the proactive technology, if it is to perform well, needs "rigorous evaluation, audit, curation and management [. . .]."[47]

However, the reality is that online content and labeled data in Ethiopian languages such as Afaan Oromo, Tigrinya, Amharic, or Somali are limited. For languages like Amharic and Tigrinya, which use their own script, this might not be that easy. For any of these languages, according to scholars working on machine learning in Ethiopian languages, such as Professor Wondwossen Mulugeta, there are no machine-readable dictionaries or WordNet available, and if they are available, they are often limited and experimental.[48] Amharic, as widely used and a hundred years old, still does not have an automated spelling or grammar checker. For instance, it was only in 2021 that Apple added the Geez alphabet to its list of keyboards on the iPhone. Therefore, until the recent iOS update, those communicating in Geez languages on iOS, such as Amharic and Tigrinya, had to depend on third-party apps that provided this specific service, at times at a cost.

For a language like Amharic that's not yet fully present online, when present, it is mostly social media data.[49] Datasets trained using social media and content in the internet-sourced data are riddled with mistakes.[50] In this case, the machine learning's ability to learn, understand the nuances, and respond correctly is very limited and prone to failure. For instance, while Google Translate has been enabled for Amharic for a few years now, it was only in 2022 that it rolled out its Tigrinya and Afaan Oromo services.[51] This service is prone to mistranslations and errors.[52] Moreover, Google Search autocompletes for Amharic "are influenced by the search behaviors of other Amharic speakers"[53] and return sexualized, with "profane" search results for the words *"women" and "girls*."[54] On Google, scholars have identified that since Amharic uses its own script and has a small number of users compared to other languages, the algorithm seems to work differently.[55]

Amharic's lack of an expanded WordNet, its non-Latin script, limited online presence, and other factors make it challenging to automate content moderation in Amharic. Therefore, in such circumstances, Facebook's "proactive technology" or automated content moderation might heavily depend on limited slur and hate speech terms developed in Ethiopian languages and limited content available on social media platforms. To keep up with the changing dynamics on the ground, slur and hate speech lists must be updated frequently. Facebook, in response to a request from the Oversight Board, confirmed that its automated systems are "audited and refreshed every six months."[56] A Securities and Exchange (SEC) filing by the anonymous Whistleblower Aid, a nonprofit organization, indicated that hate speech classifiers for Myanmar/Burmese are currently not in use or being maintained.[57] The rich and intricate history and reality of these languages are not readily available online. This is not just an Ethiopian problem—this is a problem for all languages that are not English, Spanish, and Mandarin.[58]

Determined social media users understand these limitations. Users learn and adapt as the platform struggles to keep up with new slurs and hateful terms. As hateful, derogatory, and violent terms are added as key terms to filter and automatically take down or flag for human moderation, users have learned to adapt together with the slur lists. For instance, while Facebook was considering adding words such as በሎም ("*belom*" translated as "hit them") to its incitement list, social media users flipped the spelling of the word and changed it to ምሎብ (*moleb*). When the term ፎጣ ለባሽ ("*fota Lebash*," which means "someone wearing a towel") was being flagged as a hateful term against Amharas, those determined to bypass the platform's detection system started to use the term ፎጤ (*fote*), which has the same meaning but a different spelling.

To bypass the "proactive technology" and game Facebook's automated moderation, savvy users tweak the hateful and derogatory terms or mix English and Amharic alphabets. For instance, rather than writing the word "Amhara," which automatically tells the "proactive technology" that the content is in reference to a protected group, users use Aማራ. For Amharic or Tigrinya speakers, it means Amhara; for Facebook's "proactive technology," it is meaningless. While users learn to circumvent the fragile guards put up by the platform quickly, according to the Oversight Board, Facebook only reviews and audits its automated systems every six months. The platform is unable to move at the pace of its most determined users and consequential users. A quick curation of these terms using Facebook's public insight tools, CrowdTangle,[59] shows that there are still thousands of hateful and violence-inciting content using the above terms.

Moreover, since hateful words are not enough, the "proactive" technology often cross-references terms from other languages, such as English.[60] Facebook claims that learning hate speech terms from languages such as English "enables [it] to better understand concepts like hate speech across languages and, most crucially, it means that training done in one language, such as English, can improve the quality of classifiers across other languages."[61] Facebook AI researchers further assert that this is essential for low-resourced languages.[62] There are numerous problems with this approach. First, cross-referencing from high-resource languages to low-resource languages is heavily dependent on machine translations, and machine translations are prone to mistakes.[63] Such attempts to use English as the reference language for all others often are nominal and fail to rectify the underlying gaps of content moderation in low-resourced languages such as Amharic.[64] Second, they do not account for context or cultural differences.[65] For instance, the term "the color of your eyes" in English might usually be flagged on the platform because, in Western cultures, there is a history of discrimination based on eye color.[66] However, in Amharic, Tigrigna, or Afaan Oromo, this term does not mean much because, in these societies, people rarely discriminate based on eye color. Once an automated content moderation system starts cross-referencing terms from other languages, it imposes values and realities that are foreign to low-resource languages; it soon loses context and nuance. It likely implements a top-down censorship system prone to taking down content that does not violate Community Standards.

Third, cross-language reference is dependent on linguistic typology databases such as the World Atlas of Language Structures (WALS).[67] This database classifies and compares languages based on their structural and semantic properties and "provide[s] . . . guidance for multilingual Natural Language Processing (NLP), particularly for languages that suffer from the lack of human labeled resources."[68] This database, however, ignores at least nine important typological features for Amharic.[69] As a result, researchers have found that the translations of English to Amharic using this model have an error rate of 60.71.[70] While Amharic and Arabic are Semitic languages, the WALS database documents all typological features of Arabic. Therefore, the model's error rate for English to Arabic is only 7.8.[71] Last, when cross-referencing languages fail, it is difficult to understand the underlying cause and fix it.[72] Cross-referencing from other languages, such as English, to inform hate speech in radically different places like Ethiopia and more sophisticated languages like Amharic or Tigrinya will, at best, result in errors and will, at worst, lead to significant human tragedy.

However, the reality is that the need for African or other languages to be fully present online is a double-edged sword. The availability of languages online could help facilitate moderation, but at the same time, "standardized script use, standardized spelling, and NLP systems in particular increase a language community's legibility for digital surveillance."[73]

When the Default Is Human, It Results in PTSD

Where proactive technology fails and its accuracy is questionable, the only alternative is human moderation. Human beings would need to sit in front of a computer and review content.[74] In most contexts, especially for high-resource languages, human moderators teach the automated system by "manually identifying content that breaks the rules"[75] so that it updates and learns these new rules. In languages like Amharic and others, where automated content moderation fails repeatedly, these human moderators not only teach the automated system about its often costly mistakes but are also the only source of recourse.

However, internal documents leaked by Frances Haugen indicate that Facebook proactively and consciously divested human moderators in favor of automated moderation, even though it knew its automated moderation was ineffective.[76] The *Wall Street Journal*, in an expose of the company's practices, quotes a Facebook manager saying, "Within our total budget, hate speech is clearly the most expensive problem."[77] Human moderators were costing the company $104 million a year, and, in 2019, Facebook took measures to decrease this cost by 15 percent.[78] Rather than hiring human moderators to take action against hate speech and other inflammatory content, it shifted about 75 percent of the human content moderation budget to hire more people to train the algorithm.[79]

In addition to decreasing the number of human content moderators, Facebook also planned to reduce user-reported content by 5 percent.[80] It intentionally made it difficult for users to find and report content using their in-platform reporting system.[81] This new change enforced a mechanism that allowed the remaining human content moderators to ignore vast amounts of user reports. Vulnerable communities in India, Ethiopia, and Myanmar were left to depend on an algorithm and a machine that did not understand their language. To make matters worse, Facebook also interfered and limited vulnerable communities' interactions with human content moderators.

While working in the background to reduce user reporting and actively divest from human moderation, Facebook has, on numerous occasions, advised minority and civil society groups to use the in-app reporting mechanism to report hate speech and inflammatory content.[82] Puzzled by the dissonance, the Next Billion Network, a collective of frontline civil society groups, researchers, and activists from the global majority, audited Facebook's in-app reporting system in six countries, including India and Myanmar. This audit, which happened during the platform's attempt to cut down on the number of user reports that reached human moderators, found that the user reporting systems in these countries "was broken, inadequately staffed, [lacked] localization, and [was] rigged with critical technical and UI issues."[83]

The human content moderators who survived the cut were normally outsourced, overworked, underpaid, and exploited. In 2019, Facebook outsourced its African language moderation to Samasource. Samasource, rebranded as Sama, is a US-based company with a content moderation and data annotation center in Nairobi, Kenya. Sama hired about two hundred African content moderators to review content in more than eleven African languages. Facebook and Sama have been unwilling to publicly declare how many content moderators they have assigned for Ethiopian languages. However, court documents filed by two Ethiopians challenging Facebook's content moderation practices allege that the company only has twenty-five human content moderators serving all Ethiopian languages.[84] Compared to Facebook's impact on the country and its role in the conflict, the number of human moderators is not enough to deal with the hateful, dangerous, and violent content on the platform.

Content moderators working out of Sama are unable to effectively moderate content due to deplorable labor conditions, and reports indicate that their working conditions directly contribute to Facebook's failure in Ethiopia. The workers describe "a workplace culture characterized by mental trauma, intimidation, and alleged suppression of the right to unionize."[85] Moderators have fifty seconds to review traumatic content that contains deadly violence, child abuse, and other disturbing content and make policy-informed decisions.[86] This seems to be an industry-wide practice. Others moderating dating apps and online platforms also normally have seconds to decide.[87]

Unable to unionize and negotiate better pay, moderators were making about $2.20 per hour.[88] More than 140 Sama moderators were later diagnosed with post-traumatic stress disorder (PTSD).[89] Mental health issues were not just limited to the experience of Facebook content moderators. Most recently, Sama workers were tasked with training and moderating the outputs of OpenAI's ChatGPT. These workers describe the same work conditions and challenges with PTSD.[90] These and many other reasons have also led many content moderators to quit Sama; however, many, who depended on the $2.20 per hour pay and do not have other feasible alternatives, continued to work for inadequate pay.

Both Facebook and Sama have been taken to court by content moderators in Nairobi for allegedly barring unionization and engaging in forced labor. In the lawsuit against Facebook and Sama, the content moderators allege that they did not know they would be working on Facebook content moderation and expected to review traumatizing content. Most, when they applied for the job, were responding to "misleading" job ads that made it seem as though they would be working on administrative tasks rather than reviewing content that would impact their mental health and general well-being.[91] Deceptive hiring appears to be an industry-wide practice: OpenAI's ChatGPT moderators only discovered they were working for ChatGPT when ChatGPT was officially launched.[92] Similarly, dating app content moderators in the Philippines described applying for call center jobs but being offered a content moderation position instead. Others in Silicon Valley described the job as "you don't really know what [this job] means until you are actually doing the job."[93]

The lawsuit further alleges that "these misleading ads were targeted deliberately at Kenyans and Africans from disadvantaged backgrounds who, after being tricked into a job they had not realized they had applied for, were trapped in a dangerous job without a safety net."[94] The lawsuit against Facebook and Sama does not stop there—it alleges that both companies violated their workers' rights to association, freedom of expression, privacy, and fair wages.[95]

African content moderators are not the first to sue Facebook. In May 2020, Facebook agreed to pay $52 million to content moderators who developed PTSD while moderating content on the platform.[96] This settlement aimed to support more than 11,250 content moderators in the United States in receiving at least $1,000 in compensation and further entitling them to additional compensation if they develop mental health issues as a result of their work with Facebook.[97]

A group of researchers, focused on tackling harmful content while meaningfully supporting moderators, ran experiments to identify what an ideal content moderation system would look like in contexts such as Tigray.[98] Their findings reveal a significant disconnect between the skills needed for meaningful moderation and the skills social media platforms value. While social media platforms set the threshold for content moderation skills at superficial levels of basic language skills and cultural awareness, researchers show that what is needed more is deep cultural understanding, detailed and up-to-date knowledge of local issues and dialects, open dialogue and deliberation, and proactive mental health support, among others.[99] Human content moderators, if adequately trained, compensated, and supported, are potentially the only piece in Facebook's content moderation ecosystem that would be able to correctly discern content, context, and languages to minimize their impact on the most vulnerable. However, the everyday realities of these workers and the dire working conditions, lack of due care, infringement of the fundamental rights of workers, and, most importantly, the difficulty in processing and labeling traumatic content play a significant part in Facebook's failure to protect the most vulnerable in Ethiopia.

The tech industry's decision to outsource content moderation to third-party companies such as Sama, Accenture, and others is deliberate and "done to achieve desired ends."[100] Facebook outsources its moderation to third-party companies, allowing the demand for better pay and decent working conditions to occur within these companies rather than within Facebook itself. It creates distance between the platform and the moderators. While the languages being underdeveloped online might not be within Facebook's control, Facebook, with its vast resources, can hire trained content moderators with decent pay and dignity. The working conditions of content moderators are within Facebook's control.

Facebook argues that the working conditions of its third-party contractors are not its responsibility, and workers employed in business processing units, such as Sama, are not Facebook employees.[101] What Facebook fails to see is that, at least in Ethiopia, its inability to take down violence-inciting content and hate speech is affected by the working conditions of its content moderators. The high turnover of content moderators and the deplorable working conditions affect the accuracy and effectiveness of content moderation. Without improving the working conditions of human content moderators, Facebook will be unable to bridge the gap created by proactive technologies and their limitations in accurately removing content and preventing online incitement that leads to offline violence and harm.

The Oversight Board Without Any Oversight

In 2020, Facebook established the Oversight Board so that Facebook would not decide "what to take down, what to leave up and why" on its own.[102] The Oversight Board, comprising twenty-one panels of experts from various parts of the world and funded by Facebook, makes binding decisions on how content should be moderated on Facebook and Instagram. Among the many contents reviewed by the board, the board has, until mid-2025, reviewed three cases related to Ethiopia, all of which pertain to the armed conflict in the country.

All three cases reveal the challenges with Facebook's content moderation ecosystem in Ethiopia, and the board, similar to Facebook, fails to see the impacts of its decisions. In the most recent case reviewed by the board, a user appealed Facebook's decision to leave content on its platform. According to the details from the board, a user in April 2023, during the height of protests in the Amahara region, posted a picture of a hotel, claiming it was owned by a military official and calling for it to be burned down. The content had a picture of the hotel, the address, and the name of the military official.[103] When users reported the content to Facebook, even though the post violated Facebook's Community Standards, Facebook refused to take it down. It was only after the user appealed to the Oversight Board and the board flagged it that Facebook reversed its original and flawed decision and took down the post.

Although Facebook complied with the board and reversed its original decision, the board failed to ask an important question: Why does Facebook, after claiming to have made significant investments in proactive technology and human content moderators, fail to take down content that clearly violates its Community Standards? This seemingly simple but magnanimous error has such deadly consequences far away from the people who make this decision, and the board, similar to its funder, fails to adequately understand this chasm and is unable to address this critical issue.

The second case reviewed by the board relates to content taken down by Facebook, and a user appeals to the board, imploring it to reinstate the content.

A user, again at the height of the war in Tigray, posted content claiming that the TPLF killed civilians, raped women and children, and, among other crimes, looted properties in Raya Kobo and other towns in Ethiopia's Amhara region.[104] The Raya man, who lived in Ethiopia but was currently not in Raya, further claimed that Tigrayan civilians assisted the TPLF in carrying out these crimes.[105] According to the board, this content was viewed 5,000 times, shared 30 times, received fewer than 35 comments, and garnered 140 reactions.[106]

This content, when it was first posted by the user, was automatically taken down by Facebook but later restored. During the period the content was taken down, the user appealed Facebook's decision to remove his content and insisted that his post was not hate speech, but rather, the truth. The man from Raya, in his appeal to the board, stated that "the TPLF targeted his community of one million people and left them without food, water, and other basic necessities."[107] The board, applying Facebook's Violence and Incitement Community Standard, rendered its decision in December 2021. It upheld Facebook's original decision to remove the content and argued that the post contained an "unverifiable rumor" and further asserted that "rumors alleging that an ethnic group is complicit in mass atrocities, as found in this post, are dangerous and significantly increase the risk of imminent violence."[108] The board acknowledged that civilians were involved in atrocities committed in other parts of the country and admitted that it did not have information about civilian involvement in Raya Kobo and that Facebook was unable to verify allegations made by the man from Raya at the time he posted the content. It also admitted that "true reports can save lives in conflict zones, while unsubstantiated claims regarding civilian perpetrators are likely to heighten risks of near-term violence."[109]

In contexts such as Ethiopia, the Oversight Board's actions are far from just deciding "what to take down, what to leave up, and why." In a country like Ethiopia, where the conflict in different parts of the country is happening under a communication blackout and where local and international journalists, human rights organizations, and observers do not have access to sites where atrocities are being committed, people who are looking for information about their loved ones retreat to social media platforms like Facebook to follow how the war is unfolding. Almost everything that is going to be posted on social media, in a context like Ethiopia's war, is an unverified rumor until the war is over or survivors reach IDP (internally displaced people) camps and give their testimonies. Numerous independent reports that were published after the board made its decision indicate that there were indeed mass atrocities, rapes, and lootings committed in Raya Kobo and its surrounding areas during the time and after this post went online.[110] As to the involvement of Tigrayan civilians, many of the investigations are not clear on whether civilians were involved or not. However, one of the testimonies of a fourteen-year-old-girl collected by Amnesty International notes at least one incident of rape where a man in civilian clothes was involved.[111] Many testimonies revealed that the forces committing the atrocities wanted revenge.[112] Where atrocities and mass killings of civilians have no witnesses, taking down content that claims mass atrocities because it is an unverified rumor can also mean deleting the few pieces of evidence that might exist and rendering hundreds, if not thousands, of victims who are in mass graves forever silent and invisible. The Oversight Board's decisions have significant consequences.

The Oversight Board, similar to Facebook, is not a subject matter expert on Ethiopia. By the time of writing, the board's decisions in Amharic were still prone to grammatical and other errors that indicated that native speakers did not review the translation for context, semantics, or edit for policy and consistency. For instance, in the Amharic version, "the board" is translated as "monitoring board" rather than an oversight board. It sometimes writes "Facebook" and "Meta" in English, and at times in Amharic and Tigrinya, dates are not translated into the Ethiopian calendar.[113] No glossary of terms is provided so that those mentioned in this report can understand it better. If those affected by this content, whether people from Raya Kobo or Tigray, read this report, it would leave them as bystanders and onlookers to the issue that displaced them and left them without a home.

Facebook's Trusted Partner Program: "It's Like Being Taken Hostage"

Facebook, through its trusted partner system, collaborates with nongovernmental organizations around the world. The Trusted Partner program introduces "local context" into its global standards and approaches.[114] The program currently brings together four hundred organizations that work on numerous issues, including hate speech and peacebuilding.[115] It helps Facebook get insight into trends, address "problematic content," prevent harm, enable online safety and security, and support the development of effective and transparent policies.[116]

Organizations in Ethiopia that are part of the Trusted Partner program have nicknamed this the "local context" program, where Facebook's policy and human rights team not only reach out to ask about trends and patterns in the country but also ask endless questions about the local context around events that happen in the country. Often, even though these partners in Ethiopia and other places are underfunded, underrepresented, and overworked and take the heavy burden of content moderation in Ethiopia, they cannot afford to miss the calls from Facebook. Without these trusted partners, there's no one who could provide essential context that could potentially impede Facebook's dangerous global and Western approach to all things non-Western.

Trusted partners are given special access to report content using Facebook's in-app reporting tool and are provided an email to reach out to, with the assumption that contents reported by these trusted partners skip the queue and are given extra attention by content moderators. Yet again, Facebook outsources its content filtering and moderation work to underfunded civil society organizations that do this work for free; however, Facebook keeps the profit for itself.[117] One member of the Trusted Partner program described this program as being held hostage by the platform.[118] They describe spending hours and hours collecting content, categorizing, and reporting it to the platform, not because they enjoy doing this work but because they have seen the impact of the lack of content moderation and the deaths and destruction it had in the country. They describe the mental toll, the time it takes to report this content, and the vicious cycle of needing to do this over and over again.

Just like Facebook's proactive technology, the Trusted Partner program does not work. Once a trusted partner reports content to the platform, it takes, at times, more than two months for the platform to act.[119] While some trusted partners document hundreds of posts that incite violence, Facebook can only process their request if they send twenty at a time.[120] Facebook employees, while aware of the limitations of the program and its ineffectiveness in moderating content in fragile situations like Ethiopia, continued to recruit local civil society organizations as trusted partners and continued to give them false hope.

Conclusion

Since June 2019, almost every week, there has been news of violence in Ethiopia. In the past few years, millions have been displaced, many children have become orphans, many more have crossed to Sudan and Kenya, and women, girls, boys, and men have been brutally raped. What the country shares in common is the collective trauma and violence it continues to experience and the role social media plays in automating this violence.

Professor Meareg Amare Abrha was a professor of chemistry at Bahir Dar University, Amhara Regional State's capital's university. A Tigrayan by birth, the professor had lived and worked in Bahir Dar for all his adult life. In October 2021, a Facebook page with over 50,000 followers posted a picture of the professor, claiming he was a spy for the TPLF.[121] A few weeks later, the professor was gunned down by armed groups in front of his house. When Abraham, the late professor's son, reported the content, Facebook refused to take down the post. Facebook's trusted partners and other users also reported the content.[122] However, even after unknown gunmen killed Professor Meareg, Facebook refused to take down the content and insisted the content did not violate its Community Standards. In 2022, Abraham sued Facebook for aiding and abetting the murder of his father.[123]

Facebook, despite its claims of investing in technology and human content moderators, is making deadly mistakes. Abraham's tragic loss is not an isolated incident. Freweyni Hetsay also lost her father and brother due to a post on Facebook that falsely linked her family to armed groups in the Oromia region.[124] Both families had desperately pleaded with Facebook to remove the content before their loved ones were killed.[125] However, all they received was an automated message advising them to block the page or the person if they were "offended" by the content.

Proactive technology makes deadly mistakes because it is not trained on correct data using relevant Ethiopian languages. The Facebook in-app reporting system rarely works, and when it does, it takes a long time to remove content. To exacerbate the situation, Facebook has intentionally diverted funding from the in-app reporting mechanism, making it less likely for users to report content. Human content moderators, who have the potential to correct the "proactive technology" deadly mistake, are underfunded and work in miserable conditions that make it difficult for them to shield millions who depend on them. The Oversight Board, just like the platform, does not engage earnestly with those most affected by its decisions. The Trusted Partner program, which is intended to fill all these gaps, is ineffective.

This is not just an Ethiopian problem, nor is it only an Amharic language problem or just a Facebook problem. Many languages, such as Afaan Oromo, Tigrinya, Somali, Afar, and others, are rarely moderated, and when they are, they face the same problems as Amharic. Platforms such as X, YouTube, and Telegram are equally problematic, if not worse. X and YouTube rarely accurately moderate user-reported content, and when they do, it sometimes takes more than two to three months.[126] Their policy teams, unlike Facebook's, are under-resourced and inaccessible. Telegram is in a different league of its own. Currently, Telegram does not have content moderation. The need for improvement in content moderation across all languages and platforms is urgent and cannot be ignored.

These systemic failures render the most vulnerable—those who speak beautiful and diverse languages and those living within the global majority—obsolete. In some places, such as Myanmar, Facebook was aware of what was happening on its platform but failed to act.[127] In India, Facebook has been accused of being too close to the ruling party, the BJP, and this connection is helping automate its oppression.[128] In places like Ethiopia, it claimed that it had done everything it could, even though the opposite is true. Unfortunately, even this inefficient and lackluster response from platforms such as Facebook might drastically change in the era of the European Union's (EU) Digital Services Act (DSA). The EU's DSA sets new requirements for platforms to establish transparency and accountability frameworks and measures, provides EU users with new rights, such as the right to complain to platforms, and seeks out-of-court settlements, among others. Moreover, it creates "privileged channels" for trusted flaggers who flag illegal content such as hate speech and terrorist or child abuse content.[129]

Looking at the current *modus operandi* of platforms such as Facebook, Africans and others who are not citizens of the EU will once again be relegated to the back of the queue. Unless those in the global majority are willing to collectively bargain for their right to have a decent existence online and unless global majority states, rather than cracking down on legitimate speech online, organize to hold platforms accountable and force them to see their citizens, there will be many more who will perish because the system is systematically broken. This is not by accident; this is by design.

Notes

1. Jamal Osman, "Ethiopia Civil War: Stories of War Crimes Uncovered in Amhara," *Channel 4 News*, January 25, 2022, available online: https://www.channel4.com/news/ethiopia-civil-war-stories-of-war-crimes-uncovered-in-amhara.
2. Mesay Mekonnen, "Mesay Mekonnen—Profile on Facebook," available online: https://www.facebook.com/mesay.mekonnen.7.
3. Mesay Mekonnen, "**አሁን ነገሮች ጥሩ መልክ ይዘዋል**," Facebook Page, Screenshot, October 2021, available online: https://drive.google.com/file/d/1TRbelt8SFuh6Aod5Hk96W7TX6_PNY3lB/view?usp=sharing&usp=embed_facebook.https://drive.google.com/file/d/1TRbelt8SFuh6Aod5Hk96W7TX6_PNY3lB/view?usp=sharing&usp=embed_facebook Mekonnen.
4. Mekonnen, "**አሁን ነገሮች ጥሩ**."
5. Berhan Taye [@btayeg], "Content Calling for All Tigrayans to Be Put in Concentration Camps Does Not Violate Facebook's CS. FB Is Divesting from Human Moderators, Content Moderation AI Does Not Work, & We Depend on Emailing FB's Human Rights Team on a Sunday-Knowing That They Will Only See It on Monday. Https://T.Co/NxerE9qJJS," Tweet, *Twitter*, October 31, 2021, available online: https://drive.google.com/file/d/1SKLbR_OCi0B-nDnmlfIlrO78j0TAQ7bp/view?usp=drive_link.
6. Human Rights Watch, "'We Will Erase You from This Land' Crimes Against Humanity and Ethnic Cleansing in Ethiopia's Western Tigray Zone" (Human Rights Watch, April 6, 2022), available online: https://www.hrw.org/report/2022/04/06/we-will-erase-you-land/crimes-against-humanity-and-ethnic-cleansing-ethiopias.
7. Lucy Kassa, "'They Just Vanished': Tigrayans Disappear for Months in Secret Ethiopian Detention Camps," *The Globe and Mail*, November 7, 2021, available online: https://www.theglobeandmail.com/world/article-they-just-vanished-tigrayans-disappear-for-months-in-secret-ethiopian/.
8. Jamal Osman, "UN Demands Answers from Ethiopia over Aid Blockade as Conflict Fuels Ethnic Divisions," *Channel 4 News*, November 10, 2021, available online: https://www.channel4.com/news/un-demands-answers-from-ethiopia-over-aid-blockade-as-conflict-fuels-ethnic-divisions.

9 Human Rights Watch, "Ethiopia: Ethnic Tigrayans Forcibly Disappeared: Discriminatory Arrests, Detentions, Business Closures in Addis Ababa," Ethnic Tigrayans Forcibly Disappeared, Human Rights Watch, August 18, 2021, available online: https://www.hrw.org/news/2021/08/18/ethiopia-ethnic-tigrayans-forcibly-disappeared.

10 Kassa, "They Just Vanished."

11 T. Soundararajan, *Facebook India: Towards the Tipping Point of Violence: Caste and Religious Hate Speech* (Equality Labs, 2019).

12 Shakuntala Banaji and Ramnath Bhat, *Social Media and Hate* (Routledge, 2021), https://doi.org/10.4324/9781003083078.

13 Ibid.

14 Ibid.

15 Ibid.

16 Soundararajan, *Facebook India*.

17 Amnesty International, "Myanmar: The Social Atrocity: Meta and the Right to Remedy for the Rohingya" (Amnesty International, September 29, 2022), available online: https://www.amnesty.org/en/documents/asa16/5933/2022/en/.

18 Myanmar Internet Project, "Rohingya Crisis" (Myanmar Internet Project, September 2022), available online: https://www.myanmarinternet.info/rohingya-crisis; Sarah Wynn-Williams, *Careless People: The Explosive Memoir That Meta Doesn't Want You to Read* (Macmillan, 2025); Robert Smith and Nucharee Smith, "Use and Abuse of Social Media in Myanmar Between 2010 and 2022," *Athens Journal of Law* 8, no. 3 (2022): 309–28, https://doi.org/10.30958/ajl.8-3-5.

19 Myanmar Internet Project, "Rohingya Crisis;" Wynn-Williams, *Careless People*.

20 Amnesty International, "The Social Atrocity;" Wynn-Williams, *Careless People*.

21 *Al Jazeera*, "Meta Owes Rohingya Reparations for Myanmar Violence, Says Amnesty," *Al Jazeera*, available online: https://www.aljazeera.com/news/2022/9/29/meta-owes-rohingya-reparations-for-myanmar-violence-says-amnesty.

22 Miranda Sissons, "Letter from Facebook to Berhan Taye and Peter Micek in Response to an Open Letter Penned by Berhan Taye and Javier Pallero," October 2020, available online: https://www.accessnow.org/wp-content/uploads/2020/12/Ethiopia-Response.pdf.

23 Mercy Ndegwa and Mark Smith, "An Update on Our Longstanding Work to Protect People in Ethiopia," Meta Newsroom (blog), November 9, 2021, available online: https://about.fb.com/news/2021/11/update-on-ethiopia/; DataReportal, "Digital 2024: Ethiopia," DataReportal—Global Digital Insights, February 23, 2024, available online: https://datareportal.com/reports/digital-2024-ethiopia.

24 Abdi Latif Dahir, "In a Continent Dominated by WhatsApp, Ethiopia Prefers Telegram," *Quartz*, available online: https://qz.com/gateway/faa-nominee-says-he-will-hold-boeing-accountable-in-senate-hearing.

25 Committee to Protect Journalists, "Ethiopia Archives," Committee to Protect Journalists (blog), December 29, 2014, available online: https://cpj.org/africa/ethiopia/; Tracy J. Ross, "A Test of Democracy: Ethiopia's Mass Media and Freedom of Information Proclamation," *Penn State Law Review* 114 (2010): 1047–73, available online: https://www.pennstatelawreview.org/print-issues

/comments/a-test-of-democracy-ethiopias-mass-media-and-freedom-of-information-proclamation/.

26 Felix Horne, "'Journalism Is Not a Crime' Violations of Media Freedoms in Ethiopia," Human Rights Watch, January 21, 2015, available online: https://www.hrw.org/report/2015/01/21/journalism-not-crime/violations-media-freedoms-ethiopia.

27 Nathaniel Gleicher, "Removing Coordinated Inauthentic Behavior from Ethiopia," Meta Newsroom (blog), June 16, 2021, available online: https://about.fb.com/news/2021/06/removing-coordinated-inauthentic-behavior-from-ethiopia/.

28 Berhan Taye, "Old Habits Die Hard: Ethiopia Blocks Internet in the Eastern Part of the Country Again," Access Now (blog), August 7, 2018, available online: https://www.accessnow.org/ethiopia-blocks-internet-in-eastern-part-of-country-again/.

29 Report of the Ethiopian Human Rights Commission (EHRC) and Office of the United Nations High Commissioner for Human Rights (OHCHR), "EHRC-OHCHR Joint Investigation Report on Tigray Conflict," Ethiopian Human Rights Commission (EHRC), available online: https://ehrc.org/download/ehrc-ohchr-joint-investigation-report-on-tigray-conflict/; Amnesty International, "Ethiopia: Summary Killings, Rape and Looting by Tigrayan Forces in Amhara" (Amnesty International, February 16, 2022), available online: https://www.amnesty.org/en/documents/afr25/5218/2022/en/; Human Rights Watch, "We Will Erase You from This Land."

30 "Ethiopia's Tigray Conflict: Truce Agreed," BBC News, November 2, 2022, sec. Africa, available online: https://www.bbc.com/news/world-africa-63490546.

31 Human Rights Watch, "Ethiopia: Events of 2024," in *World Report 2025*, 2024, available online: https://www.hrw.org/world-report/2025/country-chapters/ethiopia.

32 Ndegwa and Smith, "An Update on Our Longstanding Work to Protect People in Ethiopia."

33 The Oversight Board, "Alleged Crimes in Raya Kobo," Facebook Oversight Board, available online: https://www.oversightboard.com/decision/fb-mp4zc4cc/.

34 Mercy Ndegwa, "How Facebook Is Preparing for Ethiopia's 2021 General Election," Meta Newsroom (blog), June 10, 2021, available online: https://about.fb.com/news/2021/06/how-facebook-is-preparing-for-ethiopias-2021-general-election/.

35 Ibid.

36 Meta, "How Technology Detects Violations," available online: https://transparency.meta.com/en-gb/enforcement/detecting-violations/technology-detects-violations/.

37 Robert Gorwa, Reuben Binns, and Christian Katzenbach, "Algorithmic Content Moderation: Technical and Political Challenges in the Automation of Platform Governance," *Big Data & Society* 7, no. 1 (2020): 205395171989794, https://doi.org/10.1177/2053951719897945.

38 Gorwa, Binns, and Katzenbach, "Algorithmic Content Moderation."

39 Emma J. Llansó, "No Amount of 'AI' in Content Moderation Will Solve Filtering's Prior-Restraint Problem," *Big Data & Society* 7, no. 1 (2020): 205395172092068, https://doi.org/10.1177/2053951720920686.

40 Ibid.

41 Gorwa, Binns, and Katzenbach, "Algorithmic Content Moderation."

42 Zecharias Zelalem and Peter Guest, "Why Facebook Keeps Failing in Ethiopia," Rest of World, November 13, 2021, available online: https://restofworld.org/2021/why-facebook-keeps-failing-in-ethiopia/.

43 Ibid.

44 Ibid.

45 Ibid.

46 Kate Crawford, *Atlas of AI* (Yale University Press, 2021).

47 Abeba Birhane, "Algorithmic Injustice: A Relational Ethics Approach," *Patterns* 2, no. 2 (2021): 100205, https://doi.org/10.1016/j.patter.2021.100205.

48 በዶ/ር ወንደሰን ሙሉጌታ ናቹራል ላንጉዌጅ ፕሮሰሲንግን አስመልክቶ የቀረበ ገለጻ (ክፍል ሁለት), 2022, available online: https://www.youtube.com/watch?v=coOzxgB6JAY.

49 Ibid.

50 Abeba Birhane et al., "On Hate Scaling Laws for Data-Swamps," arXiv, 2023, https://doi.org/10.48550/ARXIV.2306.13141.

51 "Google Translate Adds 24 New Languages," BBC News, May 12, 2022, sec. Technology, available online: https://www.bbc.com/news/technology-61416757.

52 "Google Afaan Oromoo dabalatee afaanota Afrikaa kudhaniin tajaajila kennuu eegale," BBC News Afaan Oromoo, available online: https://www.bbc.com/afaanoromoo/oduu-61412485.

53 Peter Chonka, Stephanie Diepeveen, and Yidnekachew Haile, "Algorithmic Power and African Indigenous Languages: Search Engine Autocomplete and the Global Multilingual Internet," *Media, Culture & Society* 45, no. 2 (2023): 246–65, https://doi.org/10.1177/01634437221104705.

54 Ibid.

55 Ibid.

56 The Oversight Board, "Alleged Crimes in Raya Kobo."

57 CBS News, "Whistleblower's SEC Complaint: Facebook Knew Platform Was Used to 'Promote Human Trafficking and Domestic Servitude,'" CBS News, October 7, 2021, available online: https://www.cbsnews.com/news/facebook-whistleblower-sec-complaint-60-minutes-2021-10-04/.

58 Billy Perrigo, "Facebook Says It's Removing More Hate Speech Than Ever Before. But There's a Catch," *Time*, November 28, 2019, available online: https://time.com/5739688/facebook-hate-speech-languages/.

59 CrowdTangle, available online: https://help.crowdtangle.com/en/articles/4201940-about-us [Facebook has pulled the plug on the tool CrowdTangle and this is no longer available].

60 Meta, "Community Standards Report," Community Standards Report (blog), 2019, available online: https://drive.google.com/file/d/152XTOF_RxSisab6yPWo949L9niwLHnRx/view?usp=drive_link.

61 Ibid.

62 Meta, "Community Standards Report," Community Standards Report (blog), 2019, available online: https://ai.meta.com/blog/community-standards-report/.

63 Aliya Bhatia and Gabriel Nicholas, "Lost in Translation: Large Language Models in Non-English Content Analysis," Center for Democracy and Technology, June 20, 2023, available online: https://cdt.org/insights/mind-the-language-gap-nlp-researchers-advocates-weigh-in-on-automated-content-analysis-in-non-english-languages/.

64 Helm, Paula, Gábor Bella, Gertraud Koch, and Fausto Giunchiglia, "Diversity and Language Technology: How Language Modeling Bias Causes Epistemic Injustice," *Ethics and Information Technology* 26, no. 1 (2024): 8, https://doi.org/10.1007/s10676-023-09742-6.

65 Ibid.

66 United States Holocaust Memorial Museum, "Nazi Racism: In Depth," Nazi Racism: In Depth (blog), available online: https://encyclopedia.ushmm.org/content/en/article/racism-in-depth.

67 Edoardo Maria Ponti et al., "Modeling Language Variation and Universals: A Survey on Typological Linguistics for Natural Language Processing," *Computational Linguistics* 45, no. 3 (2019): 559–601, https://doi.org/10.1162/coli_a_00357.

68 Ibid.

69 Pratik Joshi et al., "The State and Fate of Linguistic Diversity and Inclusion in the NLP World," arXiv, 2020, https://doi.org/10.48550/ARXIV.2004.09095.

70 Ibid.

71 Ibid.

72 Bhatia and Nicholas, "Lost in Translation."

73 Isabelle Zaugg, "Digital Surveillance and Digitally-Disadvantaged Language Communities," *AfricArXiv*, December 4, 2019, https://doi.org/10.5281/ZENODO.5272640.

74 Sarah T. Roberts, *Behind the Screen: Content Moderation in the Shadows of Social Media* (Yale University Press, 2019), https://doi.org/10.2307/j.ctvhrcz0v.

75 Billy Perrigo, "WhatsApp Content Moderators Review the Worst Material on the Internet. Now They're Alleging Pay Discrimination," *Time*, July 15, 2021, available online: https://time.com/6080450/facebook-whatsapp-content-moderators/.

76 Deepa Seetharaman, Jeff Horwitz, and Justin Scheck, "Facebook Says AI Will Clean Up the Platform. Its Own Engineers Have Doubts," *Wall Street Journal*, October 17, 2021, sec. Tech, available online: https://www.wsj.com/tech/facebook-ai-enforce-rules-engineers-doubtful-artificial-intelligence-11634338184.

77 Ibid.

78 Ibid.

79 Ibid.

80 Ibid.

81 Ibid.

82 Author's private conversation with researchers from India, Ethiopia, and Myanmar.

83 Next Billion Network, "FACEBOOK AUDIT: Reporting System," Medium (blog), October 24, 2021, available online: https://nextbillion.network/facebook-audit-reporting-system-529863313343.

84 Abraham Meares, Fisseha Tele, and Katiba Institute v Meta, No. HCCHRPET E541/2022 (The High Court of Kenya 2022).

85 Billy Perrigo, "Inside Facebook's African Sweatshop," *Time*, February 14, 2022, available online: https://time.com/6147458/facebook-africa-content-moderation-employee-treatment/.

86 Ibid.

87 Roberts, *Behind the Screen*, 170–200.

88 Perrigo, "Inside Facebook's."

89 Robert Booth, "More Than 140 Kenya Facebook Moderators Diagnosed with Severe PTSD," *The Guardian*, December 18, 2024, sec. Media, available online: https://www.theguardian.com/media/2024/dec/18/kenya-facebook-moderators-sue-after-diagnoses-of-severe-ptsd.

90 Karen Hao, *Empire of AI: Dreams and Nightmares in Sam Altman's OpenAI* (Penguin, 2025).

91 Billy Perrigo, "Meta Accused of Human Trafficking and Union-Busting in Kenya," *Time*, May 10, 2022, available online: https://time.com/6175026/facebook-sama-kenya-lawsuit/.

92 Hao, *Empire of AI*.

93 Roberts, *Behind the Screen*.

94 Perrigo, "Meta Accused of Human Trafficking."

95 Ibid.

96 Casey Newton, "Facebook Will Pay $52 Million in Settlement with Moderators Who Developed PTSD on the Job," *The Verge*, May 12, 2020, available online: https://www.theverge.com/2020/5/12/21255870/facebook-content-moderator-settlement-scola-ptsd-mental-health.

97 Ibid.

98 Nuredin Ali Abdelkadir et al., "The Role of Expertise in Effectively Moderating Harmful Social Media Content," *Proceedings of the 2025 CHI Conference on Human Factors in Computing Systems*, April 26, 2025, 1–21, available online: https://doi.org/10.1145/3706598.3714010.

99 Ibid.

100 Roberts, *Behind the Screen*.

101 Perrigo, "Facebook Faces New Lawsuit."

102 "Oversight Board," April 28, 2024, available online: https://www.oversightboard.com/our-work/.

103 "Hotel in Ethiopia" | Oversight Board, 2023, available online: https://www.oversightboard.com/decision/fb-iulhg7jk/.

104 The Oversight Board, "Alleged Crimes in Raya Kobo."

105 Ibid.

106 Ibid.

107 Ibid.

108 Ibid.

109 Ibid.

110 Ethiopian Human Rights Commission (EHRC), "Investigation into Human Rights and Humanitarian Law Violations in Areas of Amhara Region Affected by the Conflict" (Ethiopian Human Rights Commission [EHRC], February 2, 2022), available online: https://ehrc.org/download/investigation-into-human-rights-and-humanitarian-law-violations-in-areas-of-amhara-region-affected-by-the-conflict/.

111 Amnesty International, "Summary Killings," 14.

112 Ibid.

113 The Oversight Board, "Alleged Crimes in Raya Kobo."

114 Meta, "Bringing Local Context to Our Global Standards," Transparency Centre (blog), available online: https://transparency.meta.com/en-gb/policies/improving/bringing-local-context/.

115 Ibid.

116 Ibid.

117 Facebook annually offers a lump sum funding to its trusted partners. However, this funding rarely covers the time and resources CSOs need to review and report content, and at times trusted partners decline this funding as it comes with strings attached and consequences.

118 Author's private conversation with one trusted partner in May 2022.

119 Tekendra Parmar, "A Professor Was Murdered After a Facebook Post Branded Him a Traitor. Was Facebook Complicit in His Death?," *Business Insider*, available online: https://www.businessinsider.com/facebooks-local-partners-say-hate-speech-stays-on-the-platform-2023-4.

120 The author saw an email from Facebook Trusted Partner personnel to the organization instructing them to only report 20 links and content at a time in an email.

121 Abraham Meares, Fisseha Tele & Katiba Institute v Meta.

122 Parmar, "A Professor Was Murdered After a Facebook Post Branded Him a Traitor."

123 Abraham Meares, Fisseha Tele & Katiba Institute v Meta.

124 "A Facebook Post 'Killed' My Father and Younger Brother," 2023, available online: https://www.youtube.com/watch?v=fjml9uySms4.

125 Abraham Meares, Fisseha Tele & Katiba Institute v Meta; "A Facebook Post 'Killed' My Father and Younger Brother.

126 Private conversation with those reporting content on YouTube and Twitter.

127 Wynn-Williams, *Careless People*.

128 Billy Perrigo, "Facebook's Ties to India's Ruling Party Complicate Its Fight Against Hate Speech," *Time*, August 28, 2020, available online: https://time.com/5883993/india-facebook-hate-speech-bjp/.

129 European Commission, "Questions and Answers on the Digital Services Act," Text, European Commission, available online: https://ec.europa.eu/commission/presscorner/detail/en/qanda_20_2348.

Bibliography

Abraham Meares, Fisseha Tele, and Katiba Institute v Meta, No. HCCHRPET E541/2022. The High Court of Kenya, 2022. Available online: https://new.kenyalaw.org/akn/ke/judgment/kehc/2025/4362/eng@2025-04-03.

Al Jazeera. "Meta Owes Rohingya Reparations for Myanmar Violence, Says Amnesty." *Al Jazeera*. Available online: https://www.aljazeera.com/news/2022/9/29/meta-owes-rohingya-reparations-for-myanmar-violence-says-amnesty.

Amnesty International. "Ethiopia: Summary Killings, Rape and Looting by Tigrayan Forces in Amhara." Amnesty International, February 16, 2022. Available online: https://www.amnesty.org/en/documents/afr25/5218/2022/en/.

Amnesty International. "Myanmar: The Social Atrocity: Meta and the Right to Remedy for the Rohingya." Amnesty International, September 29, 2022. Available online: https://www.amnesty.org/en/documents/asa16/5933/2022/en/.

Banaji, Shakuntala, and Ramnath Bhat. *Social Media and Hate*. Routledge, 2021. https://doi.org/10.4324/9781003083078.

BBC News. "Ethiopia's Tigray Conflict: Truce Agreed." November 2, 2022, sec. Africa. Available online: https://www.bbc.com/news/world-africa-63490546.

BBC News. "Google Translate Adds 24 New Languages." May 12, 2022, sec. Technology. Available online: https://www.bbc.com/news/technology-61416757.

BBC News Afaan Oromoo. "Google Afaan Oromoo dabalatee afaanota Afrikaa kudhaniin tajaajila kennuu eegale." Available online: https://www.bbc.com/afaanoromoo/oduu-61412485.

Bhatia, Aliya, and Gabriel Nicholas. "Lost in Translation: Large Language Models in Non-English Content Analysis." *Center for Democracy and Technology*, June 20, 2023. Available online: https://cdt.org/insights/mind-the-language-gap-nlp-researchers-advocates-weigh-in-on-automated-content-analysis-in-non-english-languages/.

Birhane, Abeba. "Algorithmic Injustice: A Relational Ethics Approach." *Patterns* 2, no. 2 (2021): 100205. https://doi.org/10.1016/j.patter.2021.100205.

Birhane, Abeba, Vinay Prabhu, Sang Han, and Vishnu Naresh Boddeti. "On Hate Scaling Laws for Data-Swamps." *arXiv*, 2023. https://doi.org/10.48550/ARXIV.2306.13141.

Booth, Robert. "More than 140 Kenya Facebook Moderators Diagnosed with Severe PTSD." *The Guardian*, December 18, 2024, sec. Media. Available online: https://www.theguardian.com/media/2024/dec/18/kenya-facebook-moderators-sue-after-diagnoses-of-severe-ptsd.

Chonka, Peter, Stephanie Diepeveen, and Yidnekachew Haile. "Algorithmic Power and African Indigenous Languages: Search Engine Autocomplete and the Global Multilingual Internet." *Media, Culture & Society* 45, no. 2 (2023): 246–65. https://doi.org/10.1177/01634437221104705.

Committee to Protect Journalists. "Ethiopia Archives." *Committee to Protect Journalists (blog)*, December 29, 2014. Available online: https://cpj.org/africa/ethiopia/.

Crawford, Kate. *Atlas of AI*. Yale University Press, 2021.

DataReportal. "Digital 2024: Ethiopia." DataReportal—Global Digital Insights, February 23, 2024. Available online: https://datareportal.com/reports/digital-2024-ethiopia.

Ethiopian Human Rights Commission (EHRC). "Investigation into Human Rights and Humanitarian Law Violations in Areas of Amhara Region Affected by the Conflict." Ethiopian Human Rights Commission (EHRC), February 2, 2022. Available online: https://ehrc.org/download/investigation-into-human-rights-and-humanitarian-law-violations-in-areas-of-amhara-region-affected-by-the-conflict/.

European Commission. "Questions and Answers on the Digital Services Act." Text. European Commission—European Commission. Available online: https://ec.europa.eu/commission/presscorner/detail/en/qanda_20_2348.

"A Facebook Post 'Killed' My Father and Younger Brother." 2023. Available online: https://www.youtube.com/watch?v=fjml9uySms42348.

Gleicher, Nathaniel. "Removing Coordinated Inauthentic Behavior from Ethiopia." Meta Newsroom (blog), June 16, 2021. Available online: https://about.fb.com/news/2021/06/removing-coordinated-inauthentic-behavior-from-ethiopia/.

Gorwa, Robert, Reuben Binns, and Christian Katzenbach. "Algorithmic Content Moderation: Technical and Political Challenges in the Automation of Platform Governance." *Big Data & Society* 7, no. 1 (2020): 205395171989794. https://doi.org/10.1177/2053951719897945.

Hao, Karen. *Empire of AI: Dreams and Nightmares in Sam Altman's OpenAI*. Penguin, 2025.

Horne, Felix. "'Journalism Is Not a Crime' Violations of Media Freedoms in Ethiopia." Human Rights Watch, January 21, 2015. Available online: https://www.hrw.org/report/2015/01/21/journalism-not-crime/violations-media-freedoms-ethiopia.

Human Rights Watch. "Ethiopia: Ethnic Tigrayans Forcibly Disappeared: Discriminatory Arrests, Detentions, Business Closures in Addis Ababa." Ethnic Tigrayans Forcibly Disappeared. Human Rights Watch, August 18, 2021. Available online: https://www.hrw.org/news/2021/08/18/ethiopia-ethnic-tigrayans-forcibly-disappeared.

Human Rights Watch. "Ethiopia: Events of 2024." In *World Report 2025*, 2024. Available online: https://www.hrw.org/world-report/2025/country-chapters/ethiopia.

Human Rights Watch. "'We Will Erase You from This Land' Crimes Against Humanity and Ethnic Cleansing in Ethiopia's Western Tigray Zone." Human Rights Watch, April 6, 2022. Available online: https://www.hrw.org/report/2022/04/06/we-will-erase-you-land/crimes-against-humanity-and-ethnic-cleansing-ethiopias.

Joshi, Pratik, Sebastin Santy, Amar Budhiraja, Kalika Bali, and Monojit Choudhury. "The State and Fate of Linguistic Diversity and Inclusion in the NLP World." *arXiv*, 2020. https://doi.org/10.48550/ARXIV.2004.09095.

Kassa, Lucy. "'They Just Vanished': Tigrayans Disappear for Months in Secret Ethiopian Detention Camps." *The Globe and Mail*, November 7, 2021. Available online: https://www.theglobeandmail.com/world/article-they-just-vanished-tigrayans-disappear-for-months-in-secret-ethiopian/.

Latif Dahir, Abdi. "In a Continent Dominated by WhatsApp, Ethiopia Prefers Telegram." *Quartz*. Available online: https://qz.com/gateway/faa-nominee-says-he-will-hold-boeing-accountable-in-senate-hearing.

Llansó, Emma J. "No Amount of 'AI' in Content Moderation Will Solve Filtering's Prior-Restraint Problem." *Big Data & Society* 7, no. 1 (2020): 205395172092068. https://doi.org/10.1177/2053951720920686.

Mekonnen, Mesay. "Mesay Mekonnen—Profile on Facebook." Available online: https://www.facebook.com/mesay.mekonnen.7.

Mekonnen, Mesay. "አሁን ነገሮች ጥሩ መልክ ይዘዋል (Now Things Are in Order)." Facebook Page. Screenshot, October 2021. Available online: https://drive.google.com/file/d/1TRbelt8SFuh6Aod5Hk96W7TX6_PNY3lB/view?usp=sharing&usp=embed_facebook.

Meta. "Bringing Local Context to Our Global Standards." Transparency Centre (blog). Available online: https://transparency.meta.com/en-gb/policies/improving/bringing-local-context/.

Meta. "Community Standards Report." Community Standards Report (blog), 2019. Available online: https://drive.google.com/file/d/152XTOF_RxSisab6yPWo949L9niwLHnRx/view?usp=drive_link.

Meta. "How Technology Detects Violations | Transparency Centre." Available online: https://transparency.meta.com/en-gb/enforcement/detecting-violations/technology-detects-violations/.

Myanmar Internet Project. "Rohingya Crisis." Myanmar Internet Project, September 2022. Available online: https://www.myanmarinternet.info/rohingya-crisis.

Ndegwa, Mercy. "How Facebook Is Preparing for Ethiopia's 2021 General Election." Meta Newsroom (blog), June 10, 2021. Available online: https://about.fb.com/news/2021/06/how-facebook-is-preparing-for-ethiopias-2021-general-election/.

Ndegwa, Mercy, and Mark Smith. "An Update on Our Longstanding Work to Protect People in Ethiopia." Meta Newsroom (blog), November 9, 2021. Available online: https://about.fb.com/news/2021/11/update-on-ethiopia/.

Newton, Casey. "Facebook Will Pay $52 Million in Settlement with Moderators Who Developed PTSD on the Job." *The Verge*, May 12, 2020. Available online: https://www.theverge.com/2020/5/12/21255870/facebook-content-moderator-settlement-scola-ptsd-mental-health.

Next Billion Network. "FACEBOOK AUDIT: Reporting System." Medium (blog), October 24, 2021. Available online: https://nextbillion.network/facebook-audit-reporting-system-529863313343.

Osman, Jamal. "Ethiopia Civil War: Stories of War Crimes Uncovered in Amhara." *Channel 4 News*, January 25, 2022. Available online: https://www.channel4.com/news/ethiopia-civil-war-stories-of-war-crimes-uncovered-in-amhara.

Osman, Jamal. "UN Demands Answers from Ethiopia over Aid Blockade as Conflict Fuels Ethnic Divisions." *Channel 4 News*, November 10, 2021. Available online: https://www.channel4.com/news/un-demands-answers-from-ethiopia-over-aid-blockade-as-conflict-fuels-ethnic-divisions.

The Oversight Board. "Alleged Crimes in Raya Kobo." The Oversight Board. Available online: https://www.oversightboard.com/decision/fb-mp4zc4cc/.

"Oversight Board," April 28, 2024. Available online: https://www.oversightboard.com/our-work/.

Parmar, Tekendra. "A Professor Was Murdered After a Facebook Post Branded Him a Traitor. Was Facebook Complicit in His Death?" *Business Insider*. Available online: https://www.businessinsider.com/facebooks-local-partners-say-hate-speech-stays-on-the-platform-2023-4.

Perrigo, Billy. "Facebook's Ties to India's Ruling Party Complicate Its Fight Against Hate Speech." *Time*, August 28, 2020. Available online: https://time.com/5883993/india-facebook-hate-speech-bjp/.

Perrigo, Billy. "Inside Facebook's African Sweatshop." *Time*, February 14, 2022. Available online: https://time.com/6147458/facebook-africa-content-moderation-employee-treatment/.

Perrigo, Billy. "Meta Accused Of Human Trafficking and Union-Busting in Kenya." *Time*, May 10, 2022. Available online: https://time.com/6175026/facebook-sama-kenya-lawsuit/.

Perrigo, Billy. "WhatsApp Content Moderators Review the Worst Material on the Internet. Now They're Alleging Pay Discrimination." *Time*, July 15, 2021. Available online: https://time.com/6080450/facebook-whatsapp-content-moderators/.

Ponti, Edoardo Maria, Helen O'Horan, Yevgeni Berzak, Ivan Vulić, Roi Reichart, Thierry Poibeau, Ekaterina Shutova, and Anna Korhonen. "Modeling Language Variation and

Universals: A Survey on Typological Linguistics for Natural Language Processing." *Computational Linguistics* 45, no. 3 (2019): 559–601. https://doi.org/10.1162/coli_a_00357.

Report of the Ethiopian Human Rights Commission (Ehrc), and Office of the United Nations High Commissioner for Human Rights (OHCHR). "EHRC-OHCHR Joint Investigation Report on Tigray Conflict." Ethiopian Human Rights Commission (Ehrc). Available online: https://ehrc.org/download/ehrc-ohchr-joint-investigation-report-on-tigray-conflict/.

Roberts, Sarah T. *Behind the Screen: Content Moderation in the Shadows of Social Media*. Yale University Press, 2019. https://doi.org/10.2307/j.ctvhrcz0v.

Ross, Tracy J. "A Test of Democracy: Ethiopia's Mass Media and Freedom of Information Proclamation." *Penn State Law Review* 114 (2010): 1047–73. Available online: https://www.pennstatelawreview.org/print-issues/comments/a-test-of-democracy-ethiopias-mass-media-and-freedom-of-information-proclamation/.

Seetharaman, Deepa, Jeff Horwitz, and Justin Scheck. "Facebook Says AI Will Clean Up the Platform. Its Own Engineers Have Doubts." *Wall Street Journal*, October 17, 2021, sec. Tech. Available online: https://www.wsj.com/tech/facebook-ai-enforce-rules-engineers-doubtful-artificial-intelligence-11634338184.

Sissons, Miranda. "Letter from Facebook to Berhan Taye and Peter Micek in Response to an Open Letter Penned by Berhan Taye and Javier Pallero." October 2020. Available online: https://www.accessnow.org/wp-content/uploads/2020/12/Ethiopia-Response.pdf.

Smith, Robert, and Nucharee Smith. "Use and Abuse of Social Media in Myanmar Between 2010 and 2022." *Athens Journal of Law* 8, no. 3 (2022): 309–28. https://doi.org/10.30958/ajl.8-3-5.

Soundararajan, T. *Facebook India: Towards the Tipping Point of Violence: Caste and Religious Hate Speech*. Equality Labs, 2019. Available online: https://southasiacommons.net/artifacts/5034988/facebook-india/5800485/.

Taye, Berhan [@btayeg]. "Content Calling for All Tigrayans to Be Put in Concentration Camps Does Not Violate Facebook's CS. FB Is Divesting from Human Moderators, Content Moderation AI Does Not Work, & We Depend on Emailing FB's Human Rights Team on a Sunday-Knowing That They Will Only See It on Monday. Https://T.Co/NxerE9qJJS." Tweet. *Twitter*, October 31, 2021. Available online: https://drive.google.com/file/d/1SKLbR_OCi0B-nDnmlfIlrO78j0TAQ7bp/view?usp=drive_link.

Taye, Berhan. "Old Habits Die Hard: Ethiopia Blocks Internet in the Eastern Part of the Country Again." *Access Now* (blog), August 7, 2018. Available online: https://www.accessnow.org/ethiopia-blocks-internet-in-eastern-part-of-country-again/.

United States Holocaust Memorial Museum. "Nazi Racism: In Depth." Nazi Racism: In Depth (blog). Available online: https://encyclopedia.ushmm.org/content/en/article/racism-in-depth.

Wynn-Williams, Sarah. *Careless People: The Explosive Memoir That Meta Doesn't Want You to Read*. Macmillan, 2025.

Zaugg, Isabelle. "Digital Surveillance and Digitally-Disadvantaged Language Communities." *AfricArXiv*, December 4, 2019. https://doi.org/10.5281/ZENODO.5272640.

Zelalem, Zecharias, and Peter Guest. "Why Facebook Keeps Failing in Ethiopia." Rest of World, November 13, 2021. Available online: https://restofworld.org/2021/why-facebook-keeps-failing-in-ethiopia/.

"በዶ/ር ወንደሰን ሙሉጌታ ናቹራል ላንጉዌጅ ፕሮሰሲንግን አስመልክቶ የቀረበ ገለጻ (ክፍል ሁለት) (Presentation by Dr. Wondonsen Mulugeta on Natural Language Processing (Part Two))." 2022. Available online: https://www.youtube.com/watch?v=coOzxgB6JAY.

3
ONLINE CONTENT MODERATION IN LATIN AMERICA

Ivar A. Hartmann

Introduction

Latin Americans, like people from any other region in the world, have a legitimate expectation that their online speech is moderated with respect to their local legal traditions, culture, realities, and needs. How close are we to that goal today? Private content moderation has failed to consider geopolitical context: The tragedy in Myanmar offers the most vivid of several examples.[1] Facebook itself conceded that it had underestimated the need for culturally mindful moderation.[2]

If context matters, why discuss content moderation in Latin America instead of diagnosing problems and drafting solutions for Mexico, Uruguay, or Nicaragua separately? Unlike some regions, Latin America appears to exhibit significantly common traits among its over thirty countries. Granted, it is anything but homogeneous from a cultural, political, or legal perspective. Upon closer examination, it becomes obvious that the challenges of platform governance in Venezuela are not the same as in Brazil. An overview of content moderation in Latin America will necessarily lack attention to national specificities that additional studies need to address.

This chapter aims to uncover characteristics, problems, and potential solutions for regulating online content that illustrate the multiple Latin American realities. The regulation of hate speech, defamation, fake news, and image-based sexual abuse are all current, substantial, and equally pressing issues in the region. However, my analysis here will focus less on black letter law and private terms of use taken at face value and more on how the local ensemble of public and private platform rules, cultural norms, and practice positively or negatively affects freedom of expression.

Four common themes connect most Latin American experiences of content moderation, enabling me to treat it as a singular region within a global context. First, the most important regional trait is poverty and concentration of wealth.[3] The colonial origin and development of almost every Latin American nation meant that for centuries, racism guided power relations, whereby European-descended whites harnessed "control of productive resources and capital."[4] Online content moderation in Latin America should be, at least partly, about ameliorating inequalities in how disenfranchised minorities access and use media.

Second, unlike Europe, Africa, and Asia, the number of major languages in Latin America is small. Although many local and Indigenous languages exist today, all the countries have either Spanish or Portuguese as their sole or main official language. The ubiquity of these two languages in schools and the press creates certain commonalities around instances of hate speech and how narratives are framed in different countries.

Third, several Latin American countries suffered under military dictatorships and authoritarian rule in recent history. This has impaired and, perhaps, in some cases, even prevented the development of a culture of free speech. The level of censorship that is socially and politically tolerated is much higher than in North America or Europe. State intervention into private content policy is not always feared upfront as many Latin Americans accept and sometimes even desire the influence of the executive branch of government on matters that elsewhere would be understood as akin to the private sphere. This peculiar view about authority and speech extends to the relationship between users and social media platforms. Platforms' exploitation of personal data might be swiftly denounced as unlawful, an abuse of consumer protection guarantees, whereas private censorship is usually perceived as an acceptable clause of a private contract.

A fourth common theme is the role and attitude of courts. The region's judicial activism is commonly explained away as necessary to consolidate young democracies. A strong judiciary and especially a powerful constitutional court have also been the vehicle for the justiciability of social rights. In many respects, including speech, however, judges are fairly conservative. Courts, therefore, represent a significant hurdle to novel arrangements designed to tackle the complex problems of content moderation, even when implemented by legislation but certainly when adopted by social media companies. For example, lower courts questioned the judicial notice-and-takedown model enshrined in Brazil's 2014 Internet Civil Rights Framework as an unconstitutionally insufficient protection of the right to honor from the very beginning.

The chapter will offer a sociologically mindful account of platform content regulation in Latin America, based on a close analysis of three commonly adopted alternatives for deciding the limits of online expression: automated moderation, paid moderation, and judicial review. Taken together, the inquiry on these three fronts will address the main question: Is current online content moderation practice compatible with the realities and necessities of Latin American speakers? This chapter evaluates these mechanisms in light of regional specificities and contributes to developing a critique of corporate social media moderation in developing countries, especially when platforms underestimate the necessary level of cultural adaptation. As such, this study could prove valuable to policymakers worldwide. The policy responses to corporate moderation's lack of attention to regional context could be replicable.

A parallel goal of this chapter is to increase the visibility of scholarship by Latin American authors and enhance the circulation of studies that have narrowed down their scope to the region. As someone born and educated in Latin America, I expect to have legitimacy to entertain the research question. Nevertheless, it would be paradoxical if this chapter were supported by sources exclusively from North America and Europe in its attempt to discuss how well online content moderation has suited the interests of Latin Americans so far. Despite my conscious efforts to seek out and interact with literature by Latin Americans and researchers from developing countries, the geographical origin distribution of my bibliography is still heavily tilted toward North America and Europe. This might reveal a failure in my mission while also confirming that "Latin American communication scholarship has never been purely Latin American. Rather, it is premised on a distance from, and a reference to, a central 'other.'"[5]

Automated Moderation

Social media platforms employ some variation of artificial intelligence (AI)[6] for automated moderation that is operated opaquely[7] and, above all, designed and executed centrally.[8] In less than a decade, AI moderation has risen from a cost-effective cog in the larger moderation engine to the very center of complex "decision factory" moderation systems.[9] Recommender systems also influence the public sphere in an affirmative role,[10] making decisions regarding speech placement, timing, and visibility.[11] Software makes nonrandom decisions to increase the frequency that specific messages—either user-generated content[12] or commercial speech[13]—are shown to carefully targeted users. This is precisely the democratically relevant task that has always been performed by the press, except recommender system decisions about information are individualized, invisible to anyone except the user herself, and rendered under constantly changing rules always unknown to the user.[14]

Academic research on automated moderation discloses tested accuracy and comments on the areas where models perform better or worse.[15] Not so with corporate content moderation.[16] Even minimally accurate content moderation AI needs to be incredibly sophisticated, with novel techniques such as generative adversarial networks[17] to enhance the fight against context-dependent and culturally grounded hate speech.[18] The high and increasing cost of sophisticated AI and, especially, of effective content moderation AI, maximizes inequality and concentration of power in the field. With few nonprofit exceptions,[19] machine moderation of the vast majority of user-generated content today is executed by social media platforms—mostly based in the United States. They are a natural monopoly with immense commercial and political strength that have remained largely unregulated so far and are seen by their own government as "national champions" with a "strategic role" in the country's economy.[20]

Social media AI in either an affirmative or negative role is decisive in shaping the public debate in Latin American countries as much as anywhere else and, lately, has caused increasing concern worldwide. However, Latin Americans have particular apprehensions that are not necessarily shared by users from developed countries.

First, the very notion of AI—its design goals, its role, its possibilities, its imperfections—derives from a concept of intelligence in Western thought and science rooted in colonial ideas and their justifications. Intelligence is not only a charged word but also an idea that has evolved within a "matrix of domination"[21] in the relationship between Europe and its colonies. Far from a neutral concept, AI stems from an idea of intelligence developed to concoct and emphasize the alleged substantive difference between the intellect of Europeans and that of native peoples in different regions, including Latin America.

A second concern is that public authorities in rich nations, especially in Europe, exercise pressure on private platforms, effectively steering AI moderation of Latin American speech. This is a reality of the international platform governance triangle, where states, nongovernmental organizations (NGOs), and private companies operate in an intertwined fashion to configure and influence private and public regulation.[22] In many platforms, opaque automated moderation arguably violates the basic free speech standard in Article 13 of the American Convention of Human Rights, which requires restrictions of speech to be proportional.[23] Under pressure from European Union (EU) governmental bodies, platforms obscurely carry out automated moderation of, for example, terrorist and extremist content with disregard to the law in other countries, resulting in over-censorship and lack of transparency.[24]

Public authorities exert nonlegislative pressure over companies to get them to privately censor their users, thus avoiding legal challenges of government censorship.[25] For example, platforms use highly unaccountable automated moderation to voluntarily censor far more than what copyright law requires.[26] Strong rules and pressure dictate the restrictions of Latin American online speech that states want private platforms to institutionalize, while soft law and principles[27] are the only things governments are willing to offer in defense of user expression against corporate power.

EU state power sways the architectural power of platforms[28] in such a way that, four centuries later, Europeans still hold considerable influence over the scope of protection of the fundamental rights of Latin Americans. One possible solution would be to enforce basic international human rights law standards on automated moderation, identifying the threats that such systems pose to freedom of expression, access to information, and diversity.[29] This would shift the locus of state power over AI decisions about speech from a handful of powerful players at the national and regional levels to the legitimate, inclusive, global level of human rights law.

A third concern is with the design and implementation of private automated moderation. The impact of the United States legal tradition of free speech[30] on community guidelines and human moderation decisions made at the main social media companies is well documented.[31] Automated moderation systems add another layer to this problem. More often than not, developers born and/or educated and/or located in North America and Europe, working for technology companies based in these countries, create and oversee the execution of AI that makes decisions impacting people in the Global South. This is evidence of "algorithmic coloniality" enhancing "data colonialism in the context of the interactions of algorithms across societies, which impact the allocation of resources, human socio-cultural and political behaviour and extant discriminatory systems."[32]

The demographic makeup of engineering teams in such companies does not reflect even that of their host countries. Before being let go from Google, Eritrean computer scientist Timnit Gebru understood that striving for diverse AI development teams would yield ethical,[33] social, as well as technical returns.[34] For the same reason that a female engineer is more likely than a male one to identify and diagnose a bias in the statistical model that negatively impacts women, a Latin American engineer is more likely to spot, comprehend, and solve a problem with regional hate speech detection AI than a North American engineer.[35] Even strictly from a quality of software perspective, less regionally and nationally diverse developer teams produce worse automated moderation solutions.[36] A Latin American engineer is the only one fully equipped to select and assess not only the best machine learning models for automated moderation but also—crucially—the best training sets of Latin American social media speech. After all, "taken out of context, Big Data loses its meaning."[37]

The social aspect and its impact are controlling variables in how intelligence has been defined and conceptualized and how AI has been created and operated on digital platforms.[38] AI applications are assembled in the Global North and purposefully trained in the Global South, where the human cost of the machines acquiring "real world experience" and slowly becoming more accurate is almost insignificant in the eyes of the constituents where the companies are based.[39] The need to decolonize AI stems from the current roles in the industry and market, where Latin Americans are subject to automated decisions about their expression but are not active or significant players in the production of such technology. They are allowed only one opportunity for meaningful contribution: low-cost labor reviewing machine decisions or coding social media speech datasets to allow for machine learning. Social media companies deprive Latin Americans of agency.[40]

So far, user moderation schemes merely enable unpaid moderation work that benefits the platform, without extending actual leverage to users over their own speech. User decisions to flag content do not bind the platform in any way and are usually not final.[41] Flagging influences moderation AI only indirectly, from the bottom and at the will and guidance of developer teams. Automated moderation of expression has fortified a preexisting divide within corporate social media moderation. On one side, a small group of engineers steers automated moderation systems with phenomenal impact over the public sphere. On the other side, along with general users, are disadvantaged groups whose speech platforms censor at scale, who "have borne the brunt of surveillance: often women, people who are Black, Indigenous, LGBT+, poor or disabled."[42]

Declarative ethical AI documents, as well as principled legislation,[43] have become a common first step to improve the situation. They signal points of consensus between governments, civil society, and the private sector—such as inclusion and diversity in automated moderation design. At this point, however, the discussion must move beyond principles into actual governance mechanisms for AI with practical effect.[44] Latin American governments should consider regulation pushing social media companies to increase the proportion and active participation of locals in the crews responsible for automated moderation design and improvement. In reality, part of the problem is that the actual composition of such groups is simply not known. Regarding the transparency of AI teams, prompt disclosure obligations constitute a lesser restriction on corporate autonomy and arguably stand next in line as regulatory measures. Before any other government intervention, social media platforms should inform civil society about the demographic and geographic configuration of automated content moderation departments.

Today, Latin Americans either feed or suffer the consequences of AI moderation systems. It is time to include engineers from the region—and other developing countries—as designers and implementers of automated decisions about freedom of expression worldwide.

Contracted Moderators

Social media platforms exploit at least three types of unpaid or low-paid work related to user-generated content. First, there is the production of text, pictures, and videos. The vast majority of immaterial goods posted by users are not compensated at all, even though they generate value for the platform. Second, there is a set of curation tasks performed by users, also for free, consisting of not only voluntary moderation but also "maintenance, selection and promotion" of other users' content.[45] This directly improves user experiences and, importantly, also further teaches curation algorithms, increasing the value of a company's software.[46] Third, there is paid content moderation work, often performed by workers in developing countries, which falls in the category of "clerical, low-end" labor, where Latin Americans often find themselves responsible for "cleaning the web."[47]

From the perspective of labor, concentration of wealth, and power, the platform economy is a digital architecture that repeats "political and historical patterns of domination," whereby, in Latin America and other developing countries that are targeted for cheap labor, gig work falls "outside regulatory frameworks," leading "to workers' loss of bargaining power, underbidding and risky race-to-the-bottom dynamics."[48] This replicates long-standing patterns of gig work worldwide.[49]

Platforms deploy contracted moderators in much larger numbers than before. In 2012, the first widely circulated report on their work shocked many, both because of the rules moderators were told to apply and because of the utter secrecy that had shrouded this process until then.[50] The troubling lack of transparency about the profile and work of contracted moderators and how it benefits social media companies continues to this day.

As outsourced workers, the usual compensation of moderators and employment benefits differ vastly from those of actual social network employees, with meager pay, limited health-care plans, and workplaces resembling low-ceiling and poorly lit telemarketing rooms.[51] They are told to apply extremely detailed sets of rules for speech, without overthinking the rules themselves, and prioritizing the value of consistency and coherency in repetitive tasks "designed around [corporate content moderation] systems."[52] Even though they perform essentially the same job as judges deciding about freedom of expression, private moderators receive nowhere near the same training.[53] Because only questionable content is directed to their attention, private moderators are consistently exposed to the most vile and terrifying expressions. The profound and long-lasting negative effects on their mental health have been documented by qualitative studies.[54]

From an ethical perspective, then, it is troubling to demand that more people be exploited in this type of job. This is fundamentally at odds with the proposal for companies to increase the number of paid moderators from Latin America.[55] Most, if not all, types of abusive speech suppressed by companies are directly tied to a particular language and set of mores. Addressing hate speech produced in a cultural and geographic setting with groups of moderators who are disconnected from it results in an unacceptable number of both false positives and false negatives[56]

Unfortunately, if platforms were to just hire more Latin American moderators, they would actually exacerbate the problem of colonial exploitation already described earlier—tech giants in developed countries profit from the anonymous, poorly compensated digital labor of fungible workers in communities and countries that see no collective social gain deriving from those companies' success.[57] It would seem digital platforms' current practices of paid moderation make a zero-sum game inevitable: Either Latin American expression struggles with culturally ignorant moderation or Latin American paid moderators suffer in a hellish job. But it does not have to be so.

First, paid moderation working conditions and compensation need to significantly improve, considering the particular challenges of each part of the world and, especially, the pitfalls of platform economy work in developing countries. The obvious starting point is direct compensation, which should be comparable to that of platform employees. Especially for the purposes of improving working conditions, state regulation of paid moderator work is long overdue. As far back as 2010, there were already legislative proposals for "government [to] consider incentives for service providers to create wellness programs for employees tasked with viewing disturbing imagery" in online environments.[58]

Outsourcing moderation work should receive special scrutiny from labor authorities, and the law should establish mandatory special physical and psychological health-care support for workers. Governments in developed countries do not shy away from opportunities to impose their freedom of expression standards in ways that directly affect users in developing countries, so they should not shirk their responsibility in regulating paid moderation. To be coherent, they should demand that platforms offer comprehensive health care to paid moderators regardless of the country where they are employed. There is no need to wait until each country in Latin America enacts protective legislation. The regulation of paid moderation work should follow the successful example of the United States Foreign Corrupt Practices Act framework,[59] making social media corporate misbehavior overseas also the responsibility of the developed country's government.

The root of the problem is the rationale of paid moderation work chosen by platforms. Workers are required to behave as much as possible to resemble machines, churning out repeated decisions within seconds in a logic that denies them any creative problem-solving input whatsoever. The role of paid moderators should revert to the "logic of care" that inspired online community moderation two decades ago. Instead of manual laborers, they have to be accepted as protagonists of a "self-aware conversational culture."[60] Platforms need to provide more information to moderators about, for example, the context of flagged posts or how exactly their decisions influence the training of statistical models. Platform workers feed machines, but they are kept in the dark regarding how exactly the data they produce is used.[61] The contracting company does not explain to a moderator why or how that specific set of tasks was designated to her.[62]

Moderators should also receive, as a start, a modicum of decision-making power, including more general moderation rules and community guidelines, similar to the actual employees in the legal departments of social media companies. As Facebook promises to give up some corporate power over expression, it is astounding to see the monumental contrast between the treatment, compensation, staff, and overall prerogatives it extends to members of its Oversight Board[63] and the second-grade status of its outsourced moderators. This is a blatant example of inequality in content moderation.

For any of this to even be discussed and properly considered, there needs to be substantially more publicly available information about the profile of moderators—including their nationality and native language, their employment contracts, and their working conditions. The law should force platforms to produce reports on the numbers, profiles, work conditions, and decision reversal rate of private moderators. In Brazil, a draft known as "the Fake News Bill" was quickly approved in the Senate in 2020 and is under consideration in the House of Deputies as of August 2022, titled "Brazilian Law for Internet Freedom, Responsibility and Transparency." Among a number of reforms to social media regulation, including problematic ones,[64] the current version of the bill requires platforms to include in periodic transparency reports information about human moderators, "including the number of people involved in the activity, the contract model, as well as statistics on their nationality, work language, qualification and indicators of diversity, such as declared gender and ethnicity."[65]

Courts

Considering how automated moderation and paid moderation negatively impact Latin Americans, could judicial review offer a more sensible alternative? In other words: Are Latin American courts the answer?

Courts have some advantages over private human and automated moderation. This avenue reduces the already unsustainable privatization of freedom of expression balancing and addresses the troubling legitimacy deficit in the prevailing system, where speech is controlled by a private police.[66] The model of private, centralized freedom of expression courts has not shown much promise so far. The Facebook Oversight Board, the more prominent example, does a poor job of adequately protecting Latin American speech as it inherently lacks representative elements and might reduce even further whatever legitimacy Facebook currently has if it proves to be "a body that would create and interpret privately legislated law alone."[67]

Judicial notice and takedown is a liability model adopted by countries with legal traditions that exert significant influence in the region, such as Brazil,[68] Colombia, Chile, and Argentina.[69] The traditional notice-and-takedown model, which bypasses court analysis of online free speech challenges, has failed miserably[70] as it risks curtailing free expression. On one hand, the law aligns all incentives for a private platform to remove content upon extrajudicial notice in order to avoid liability with difficult-to-predict outcomes, and on the other, it offers no pragmatic reason for upholding user-generated content.[71] Naturally, more court influence might lead to more, but arguably also less, speech protection, depending on the attitude of judges, the legal tradition, and national freedom of expression law.

There is a particularly strong case for local-context-oriented judicial review of online hate speech. In light of a long history of disenfranchisement of native populations, people of African descent, and women, protecting freedom of expression is equally about ensuring access to media and enabling communicative capacity as it is about warding off government censorship.[72] Inequality shapes hate speech content, use, and its social effects in the region. The reality of online hate speech in Latin America today reflects "the experiences of a region that has both endured historical censorship of voices of dissent, while racial minorities have been stigmatized and exposed to racial violence most typically at the hands of law enforcement officials."[73]

Recent legal measures to combat online hate speech in Latin America present three main characteristics. First, many come as legislative changes to create or amend penal law dispositions, increasing the hold of criminal law logic over online speech. Second, in some countries, the executive branch has maneuvered presidential decrees, administrative orders, and other tools against allegedly abusive online speech, an avenue that is constitutionally unfit for restricting online speech. Third, countries have enacted legislation that holds digital platforms liable for hate speech without offering clear substantive standards, inviting even more private control of expression.[74] Therefore, improvements in liability rules have not been enough in countries such as Ecuador to offer adequate protection either for expression or for the victims of abusive speech.[75]

Historically oppressed groups targeted by online hate speech are also the ones traditionally excluded from private media. The legislator is often slow to improve the law on online content moderation. The executive branch frequently wields censorship measures under the guise of curbing abusive speech. Many would therefore believe the perfect solution to be Latin American transformative constitutionalism. One of the main characteristics of this movement, celebrated by legal scholars, is the ascension of courts with stronger procedural and substantive powers that will help reverse historical inequality by protecting minorities and their fundamental rights.[76]

It is true that the Inter-American Court of Human Rights has made strides in its freedom of expression case law in the last few decades, with some impact on national legislation.[77] However, the track record of Latin American courts on this issue has been poor. Courts apparently lean too conservative, often accepting unreasonable restrictions of speech, which leads one to believe they would not strongly oppose excessive corporate moderation. In certain countries, they have failed as constitutionally "endogenous controls" against censorship, as they sided with governments for political reasons. In Argentina, for example, courts have adopted a hostile stance on social protests, assuming unimpeded streets have intrinsic value, and one that trumps freedom of expression.[78] Though scholarship and higher court rulings in the region prescribe the principle of proportionality and balancing as sophisticated tools to help judges decide cases where free speech collides with other fundamental rights such as equality, privacy, and the right to honor,[79] statistical evidence from the trial court level shows cases about internet expression are often decided arbitrarily.[80]

Courts have missed the opportunity to adequately help minorities in speech cases by favoring powerful plaintiffs, suppressing speech based on erratic legal reasoning, while at the same time refusing to enforce criminal sanctions that would protect historically oppressed groups. In Brazil, for instance, trial courts have historically rejected convicting online and offline racist speech by creating a theory that offenses meant as humor are not punishable, a doctrine that has been described by scholarship as "recreative racism."[81] Part of the reason why Latin American courts have been remiss at using such transformative constitutionalism tools to criminally prosecute racist speech is that "the criminal context with its threat of imprisonment can inhibit judicial willingness to make racist expressions legally actionable because they are a predominant feature of the culture."[82] Part of the reason is also that judges are not immune to their ideology when deciding about speech, which means a conservative judicial body will likely decide conservatively on hate speech cases.[83] And the composition of the judiciary in Latin America is far from diverse and inclusive, with the effects of sexism, for example, palpable even today.[84] A more conservative judiciary is also ill-equipped to review online misinformation.

It would appear that many have been fooled by the promised efforts of inclusive rights protection by courts in the battle against hate speech, assuming bold progressive statements in constitutional court rulings were a signal of change. There is no evidence, however, that courts in Latin America have contributed to systematic suppression of hate speech, despite constitutional and legal provisions spurring and empowering them to do so. This phenomenon has been described as the "mission accomplished syndrome."[85] Are there any hopes, then, for courts as agents of change against online hate speech? Getting judges to adopt a more progressive stance on freedom of expression would mean somehow exerting an external check on their autonomy.

Ironically, the main external check on judicial power in Latin America comes from concentrated political power, especially in the hands of the administration.

An alternative way forward, then, would be to gradually educate judges on the novel aspects of online hate and their relationship with social inequality: It is less about the content itself and more about the digital hate culture and the virtual spaces hate speech groups foster.[86] This might prove fruitful as when it comes to protecting freedom of expression, judge ideology is a factor that explains the readiness of Latin American courts to sometimes oppose executive branch arbitrariness.[87] This, arguably, has important effects way beyond hate speech in the battle against many other types of online abuse as fake news,[88] image-based sexual abuse,[89] and terrorist content.[90]

Ultimately, even at their best, courts in Latin America cannot be democratically legitimate anchors that would check the power of exclusively private content moderation by digital platforms from the Global North. They can only review a fraction of abusive content, lack technical knowledge, and, what is especially problematic regarding online speech that disproportionately impacts disenfranchised groups, courts could operate as barriers to minority plaintiffs due to unequal access to justice.[91] I would argue that courts are not the appropriate arena for a substantive review of decisions by platforms on the merits of speech. Judicial notice and takedown is a significantly better liability model than notice-and-takedown, but it will not address many of the challenges of online content moderation in Latin America. Alternatively, courts could play a leading role in enforcing *procedural* content moderation guarantees.[92]

Conclusion

Stakeholders in most countries understand that curbing abuse in social media without excessively restricting freedom of expression is an extremely complex task. There are culture-specific and region-specific challenges around abusive content *and* adequate solutions.

Whatever the cost–benefit analysis of moderation efforts and mechanisms is for a developed country, it is usually different from a developing country. The debate on online content moderation needs to be global, but not all research and studies should be region-agnostic. This chapter on Latin America shows why. Social media companies established and based in rich countries embrace moderation mechanisms that are first and foremost profitable, financially efficient, and thus disenfranchise the speech of the Global South. They also underestimate cultural diversity. Without any course correction, platforms will perpetuate the exclusion of people in Latin America from the processes that decide the worth and limits of their expression. Increasing the influence of courts in moderating online speech will have varied outcomes, depending on the country and legal culture. So far, providing more power to Latin American courts does not seem to offer a promising solution for guaranteeing online speech.

The goal is not to find one global mode of moderation. In any part of the world, the best possible solution will require an understanding of how automation, paid moderation, courts, and other means can complement each other. Given the history of colonial relationships of power, the more recent authoritarian regimes, and significant social inequality, one alternative for social media companies is decentralized moderation.[93]

The most promising mechanism for increasing the legitimacy of content moderation in Latin America is not judicial review, but rather increasing formal and informal participation of civil society in the decisions about abstract rules, as well as how to apply them to specific cases. Identity-based social movements have surged in the region in the last two decades, strengthened by online mobilization.[94] Civil society organizations in Latin America actively participate in content moderation, although "the timing and scope of the engagements provide little opportunity for meaningful input, and the obscure internal structure of companies leaves stakeholders in the shadows as to how that input is processed."[95] What we need is legislation to structure sophisticated, inclusive participation mechanisms for users themselves in content moderation[96] so that the people of Latin America do not have to depend on the generosity of private platforms to play a role in determining the limits of their own freedom of expression online.

Notes

1 Robyn Caplan, *Content or Context Moderation? Artisanal, Community-Reliant, and Industrial Approaches* (Data & Society Report, 2018), 25.

2 Mark Zuckerberg, "A Blueprint for Content Governance and Enforcement," 4, available online: https://m.facebook.com/nt/screen/?params=%7B%22note_id%22%3A751449002072082%7D&path=%2Fnotes%2Fnote%2F&refsrc=deprecated&_rdr.

3 Fernando Calderón and Manuel Castells, *A nova América Latina*, trans. Eliana Aguiar (Companhia das Letras, 2021).

4 Aníbal Quijano, "Coloniality of Power and Eurocentrism in Latin America," *International Sociology* 15, no. 2 (2000): 215–32, 218.

5 Florencia Enghel and Martín Becerra, "Here and There: (Re)Situating Latin America in International Communication Theory," *Communication Theory* 28 (2018): 122.

6 "'artificial intelligence' refers to machines that are capable of performing tasks that, if performed by a human, would be said to require intelligence." Matthew Scherer, "Regulating Artificial Intelligence Systems: Risks, Challenges, Competencies, and Strategies," *Harvard Journal of Law & Technology* 29 (2016): 362.

7 Frank Pasquale, *The Black Box Society: The Secret Algorithms that Control Money and Information* (Harvard University Press, 2016).

8 James Grimmelman, "The Virtues of Moderation," *Yale Journal of Law and Technology* 17, no. 1 (2015): 42–109, 63.

9 Caplan, *Content or Context Moderation?*, 24.

10 Tim Wu, "Will Artificial Intelligence Eat the Law? The Rise of Hybrid Social-Ordering Systems," *Columbia Law Review* 119 (2019): 1–29, 14.

11 Jennifer Cobbe and Jatinder Singh, "Regulating Recommending: Motivations, Considerations, and Principles," *European Journal of Law and Technology* 10, no. 3 (2019): 13.

12 User-generated content or UGC is "third-party content that Internet users send via [intermediaries]" such as social media platforms. Frank La Rue, *Report of the Special Rapporteur on the Promotion and Protection of the Right to Freedom of Opinion and Expression* (United Nations General Assembly, 2011), 11.

13 Joshua A. Braun and Jessica L. Eklund, "Fake News, Real Money: Ad Tech Platforms, Profit-Driven Hoaxes, and the Business of Journalism," *Digital Journalism* 7, no. 1 (2019): 1–21, 2.

14 Zeynep Tufekci, "Algorithmic Harms Beyond Facebook and Google: Emergent Challenges of Computational Agency," *Colorado Technology Law Journal* 13 (2015): 203–18, 208.

15 Thomas Davidson et al., "Automated Hate Speech Detection and the Problem of Offensive Language," *Proceedings of the 11th International AAAI Conference on Web and Social Media* (2017): 512–15.

16 Robert Gorwa, Reuben Binns, and Christian Katzenbach, "Algorithmic Content Moderation: Technical and Political Challenges in the Automation of Platform Governance," *Big Data & Society* 7, no. 1 (2020): 1–15, 11.

17 Generative Adversarial Networks (GANs) involve a zero-sum game where two models compete. A generative model artificially produces a fake new object from a preexisting dataset—e.g., of defamation posts—and a discriminator model tries to correctly guess whether that object was indeed artificially created by the generative model or actually drawn from the dataset. The theory and implementation were proposed by Ian Goodfellow et al., "Generative Adversarial Nets," *NIPS'14: Proceedings of the 27th International Conference on Neural Information Processing Systems* 2 (2014): 2672–80. A proposal for improved architecture was made by Tim Salimans et al., "Improved Techniques for Training GANs," *NIPS'16: Proceedings of the 30th International Conference on Neural Information Processing Systems* (2016): 1–9.

18 Social media companies likely already use GANs, as they can greatly improve automated moderation systems. OFCOM, *Use of AI in Online Content Moderation* (OFCOM, 2019).

19 Milena Tsvetkova et al., "Even Good Bots Fight: The Case of Wikipedia," *PLoS One* 12, no. 2 (2017): 1–13.

20 "In sum, Google and Facebook have the power of ExxonMobil, the New York Times, JPMorgan Chase, the NRA, and Boeing combined. Furthermore, all this combined power rests in the hands of just three people." Luigi Zingales and Filippo Maria Lancieri, *Committee on Digital Platforms: Policy Brief* (Stigler Center for the Study of the Economics and the State, 2019), 10.

21 Stephen Cave, "The Problem with Intelligence. Its Value-Laden History and the Future of AI," *AIES'20,* February 7–8, 2020, New York, NY, USA (2020): 29–35, 32.

22 Robert Gorwa, "The Platform Governance Triangle: Conceptualising the Informal Regulation of Online Content," *Internet Policy Review* 8, no. 2 (2019): 1–22.

23 Manuel Ernest Larrondo and Nicolás Mario Grandi, "Inteligencia Artificial, algoritmos y libertad de expresión," *Universitas* 34 (2021): 177–94, 191.

24 César Francisco Gallegos Pazmiño and Eddy Ismael Villacís Flores, "Discurso Extremista y la Expansión de la Censura," *Revista CAP Jurídica Central* 6 (2020): 147–205.

25 Yochai Benkler, "A Free Irresponsible Press: WikiLeaks and the Battle Over the Soul of the Networked Fourth Estate," *Harvard Civil Rights-Civil Liberties Law Review* 46 (2011): 311–97.

26 Maayan Perel and Niva Elkin-Koren, "Accountability in Algorithmic Copyright Enforcement," *Stanford Technology Law Review* 19 (2016): 473–533, 508.

27 The most useful OECD AI principles in the context of content moderation are "There should be transparency and responsible disclosure around AI systems to ensure that people understand AI-based outcomes and can challenge them" and "Organisations and individuals developing, deploying or operating AI systems should be held accountable for their proper functioning in line with the above principles," available online: https://oecd.ai/en/ai-principles.

28 Lawrence Lessig, "The New Chicago School," *The Journal of Legal Studies* 27, no. 2 (1998): 661–91.

29 Thiago Dias Oliva, "Content Moderation Technologies: Applying Human Rights Standards to Protect Freedom of Expression," *Human Rights Law Review* 20, no. 4 (2020): 607–40.

30 With its historical roots described by James Whitman, "Enforcing Civility and Respect: Three Societies," *Yale Law Journal* 109 (1999): 1279–398. The shortcomings of such tradition as applied to online speech are described by Marvin Ammori, "Another Worthy Tradition: How the Free Speech Curriculum Ignores Electronic Media and Distorts Free Speech Doctrine," *Missouri Law Review* 70 (2005): 59–123.

31 Kate Klonick, "The New Governors: The People, Rules, and Processes Governing Online Speech," *Harvard Law Review* 131 (2018): 1598–670.

32 Shakir Mohamed, Marie-Therese Png, and William Isaac, "Decolonial AI: Decolonial Theory as Sociotechnical Foresight in Artificial Intelligence," *Philosophy & Technology* 405 (2020): 659–84, 665.

33 A thorough study of 36 AI principles documents found that "the Fairness and Non-discrimination theme is the most highly represented theme in our dataset" Jessica Jeld et al., *Principled Artificial Intelligence: Mapping Consensus in Ethical and Rights-Based Approaches to Principles for AI* (Berkman Klein Center for Internet & Society, 2020), 47.

34 Tom Simonite, "What Really Happened When Google Ousted Timnit Gebru," *WIRED*, June 8, 2021, available online: https://www.wired.com/story/google-timnit-gebru-ai-what-really-happened/.

35 "Machine learning algorithms work by selecting salient features (variables) in the data that telegraph or correlate with various behaviors. Behaviors that are culturally mediated may lead to inequitable [machine] behavior." Osonde Osoba and William Welser IV, *An Intelligence in Our Image. The Risks of Bias and Errors in Artificial Intelligence* (RAND Corporation, 2017), 20.

36 Caitlin Kuhlman, Latifa Jackson, and Rumi Chunara, "No Computation Without Representation: Avoiding Data and Algorithm Biases through Diversity," *arXiv:2002.11836* (2020): 1–10.

37 danah boyd and Kate Crawford, "Critical Questions for Big Data," *Information Communication & Society* 15, no. 5 (2012): 662–79, 670.

38 Rachel Adams, "Can Artificial Intelligence be Decolonized?," *Interdisciplinary Science Reviews* 46, no. 1–2 (2021): 176–97, 191.

39 "Facewatch is fast becoming the standard for retail sector facial recognition in the UK and this has led to huge interest across Europe and the World. In 2016 we launched our first version of Facewatch facial recognition in Brazil and using our real world experience and early adoption of the GDPR privacy principles we have created an incredibly simple and effective system that is fully GDPR compliant." Facewatch, "Facewatch Launches in Spain with the Appointment of Retail Technology Business Leader SBT," available online: https://www.facewatch.co.uk/2020/01/06/facewatch-launches-in-spain-with-the-appointment-of-retail-technology-business-leader-sbt/.

40 Eugenia Siapera, "AI Content Moderation, Racism and (De)coloniality," *International Journal of Bullying Prevention* 4 (2022): 55–65, 56.

41 Given the current governance arrangement of social media platforms, perhaps user flagging indeed shouldn't be final. Kate Crawford and Tarleton Gillespie, "What Is a Flag for? Social Media Reporting Tools and the Vocabulary of Complaint," *New Media & Society* 18, no. 3 (2016): 410–28.

42 Pratyusha Kalluri, "Don't Ask If AI Is Good or Fair, Ask How It Shifts Power," *Nature* 583 (2020): 169.

43 Thomas Burri, "The New Regulation of the European Union on Artificial Intelligence: Fuzzy Ethics Diffuse into Domestic Law and Sideline International Law," *SSRN*, 14, available online: https://papers.ssrn.com/sol3/papers.cfm?abstract_id=3865149.

44 Julia Black and Andrew Murray, "Regulating AI and Machine Learning: Setting the Regulatory Agenda," *European Journal of Law and Technology* 10, no. 3 (2019): 1–21.

45 Antonio Casilli, "Digital Labor Studies Go Global: Toward a Digital Decolonial Turn," *International Journal of Communication* 11 (2017): 3934–54, 3937.

46 Kalluri, 'Don't Ask If AI Is Good or Fair," 169.

47 Uma Rani and Parminder Jeet Singh, "Digital Platforms, Data, and Development: Implications for Workers in Developing Economies," *Comparative Labor Law & Policy Journal* 41, no. 1 (Fall 2019): 263–88, 267.

48 Casilli, "Digital Labor Studies Go Global," 3943.

49 Mark Graham, Isis Hjorth, and Vili Lehdonvirta, "Digital Labour and Development: Impacts of Global Digital Labour Platforms and the Gig Economy on Worker Livelihoods," *Transfer* 23, no. 2 (2017): 135–62, 140.

50 Adrian Chen, "Inside Facebook's Outsourced Anti-Porn and Gore Brigade, Where 'Camel Toes' Are More Offensive Than 'Crushed Heads,'" *Gawker*, February 16, 2012, available online: https://www.gawkerarchives.com/5885714/inside-facebooks-outsourced-anti-porn-and-gore-brigade-where-camel-toes-are-more-offensive-than-crushed-heads.

51 Sarah Roberts, *Behind the Screen: Content Moderation in the Shadows of Social Media* (Yale University Press, 2019).

52 S. Waschull et al., "The Redesign of Blue- and White-Collar Work Triggered by Digitalization: Collar Matters," *Computers & Industrial Engineering* 165 (2022): 1–14, 3.

53 "Facebook says in a company statement that moderators receive 'extensive training' that includes 'on-boarding, hands-on practice, and ongoing support and training.' Gray describes his training as only eight days of 'pretty cursory' PowerPoint displays presented in rote fashion by a CPL staff member." Paul Barrett, *Who Moderates the Social Media Giants? A Call to End Outsourcing* (NYU Stern Report, 2020), 13.

54 Miriah Steiger et al., "The Psychological Well-Being of Content Moderators: The Emotional Labor of Commercial Moderation and Avenues for Improving Support," *CHI'21,* May 8–13, 2021, Yokohama, Japan (2021): 1–14, 3.

55 Barrett, for example, suggests social media companies should "Further expand moderation in at-risk countries in Asia, Africa, and elsewhere." Barrett, *Who Moderates the Social Media Giants?*, 25.

56 Timothy McLaughlin, "How Facebook's Rise Fueled Chaos and Confusion in Myanmar," *WIRED,* July 6, 2018, available online: https://www.wired.com/story/how-facebooks-rise-fueled-chaos-and-confusion-in-myanmar/.

57 Shoshana Zuboff, "Big Other: Surveillance Capitalism and the Prospects of an Information Civilization," *Journal of Information Technology* 30 (2015): 75–89, 80.

58 Anna Drootin, "'Community Guidelines': The Legal Implications of Workplace Conditions for Internet Content Moderators," *Fordham Law Review* 90, no. 3 (2021): 1197–244, 1227.

59 Anne H. Lippitt, "An Empirical Analysis of the Foreign Corrupt Practices Act," *Virginia Law Review* 99, no. 8 (2013): 1893–930, 1928.

60 Minna Ruckenstein and Linda Lisa Maria Turunen, "Re-Humanizing the Platform: Content Moderators and the Logic of Care," *New Media & Society* 22, no. 6 (2019): 1026–42, 1036, available online: https://doi.org/10.1177/146144481987599.

61 Graham, Hjorth and Lehdonvirta, "Digital Labour and Development," 152.

62 Rani and Singh, "Digital Platforms, Data, and Development," 271.

63 Kate Klonick, "Inside the Making of Facebook's Supreme Court," *The New Yorker*, February 12, 2021, available online: https://www.newyorker.com/tech/annals-of-technology/inside-the-making-of-facebooks-supreme-court.

64 Previous versions of the bill tried to produce a viewpoint-specific concept of fake news that would invite state censorship while also creating exacting requirements for people subscribing to social networks. See Raphael Tsavkko Garcia, "Brazil's 'Fake News' Bill Won't Solve Its Misinformation Problem," *MIT Technology Review*, September 10, 2020, available online: https://www.technologyreview.com/2020/09/10/1008254/brazil-fake-news-bill-misinformation-opinion/. The draft eventually approved by the Senate was "considerably dehydrated" but still contained a few controversial elements. Angelica Mari, "Brazilian Senate Passes Fake News Bill," *ZDNet*, July 1, 2020, available online: https://www.zdnet.com/article/brazilian-senate-passes-fake-news-bill/.

65 Draft Legislation 2630/20, Brazilian House of Deputies. Art. 9, paragraph 2, section VII.

66 David Kaye, *Speech Police: The Global Struggle to Govern the Internet* (Columbia Global Reports, 2019).

67 Centro de Estudios en Libertad de Expresión y Acceso a la Información, *Considering Facebook Oversight Board: Turning on Expectations* (CELE, 2019), 3.

68 Nicolo Zingales, "The Brazilian Approach to Internet Intermediary Liability: Blueprint for a Global Regime?," *Internet Policy Review* 4, no. 4 (2015): 1–14.

69 Rodrigo Vargas Acosta, *Sucesos regulatorios en materias de libertad de expresión e internet en Latinoamérica* (Derechos Digitales América Latina, 2020). In Argentina the rule is private notice and takedown, with harder cases subject to judicial notice.

70 Wendy Seltzer, "Free Speech Unmoored in Copyright's Safe Harbor: Chilling Effects of The DMCA on the First Amendment," *Harvard Journal of Law and Technology* 24, no. 1 (2010): 171–232.

71 Rebecca Tushnet, "Power without Responsibility: Intermediaries and the First Amendment," *The George Washington Law Review* 76, no. 4 (2008): 986–1016.

72 Catalina Botero, "Diversidad, pluralismo y libertad de expresión," in *Libertad de expresión: debates, alcances y nueva agenda*, ed. María Paz Ávila Ordoñez, Ramiro Ávila Santamaría, and Gustavo Gómez Germano (UNESCO, 2011), 181–92.

73 Tanya K. Hernandez, "Hate Speech and the Language of Racism in Latin America: A Lens for Reconsidering Global Hate Speech Restrictions and Legislation Models," *University of Pennsylvania Journal of International Law* 32, no. 3 (2010): 805–42, 840.

74 Marianne Díaz Hernández, *Discurso de Odio en América Latina. Tendencias de regulación, rol de los intermediarios y riesgos para la libertad de expresión* (Derechos Digitales América Latina, 2020).

75 Mercedes Coronel Gómez, "El Principio de Libertad de Expresión en Las Redes Sociales y su Regulación en el Ordenamiento Jurídico Ecuatoriano," *Revista Científica ECOCIENCIA* December (2019): 1–24, 17.

76 Rodrigo Uprimny, "Las transformaciones constitucionales recientes en América Latina: Tendencias y desafíos," in *El derecho en América Latina: un mapa para el pensamiento jurídico del siglo XXI*, ed. César Rodríguez Garavito (Siglo Veintiuno Editores, 2011), 109–38.

77 Eduardo A. Bertoni, "Jurisprudencia interamericana sobre libertad de expresión: Avances y desafíos," in *Libertad de expresión: debates, alcances y nueva agenda*, ed. María Paz Ávila Ordoñez, Ramiro Ávila Santamaría, and Gustavo Gómez Germano (UNESCO, 2011), 349–72, 353.

78 Roberto Gargarella, "Constitucionalismo y libertad de expresión," in *Libertad de expresión: Debates, alcances y nueva agenda*, ed. María Paz Ávila Ordoñez, Ramiro Ávila Santamaría, and Gustavo Gómez Germano (UNESCO, 2011), 30–62, 56.

79 For Colombia, see Rodrigo Vargas Acosta, *Sucesos regulatorios en materias de libertad de expresión e internet en Latinoamérica* (Derechos Digitales América Latina, 2020), 9. In Brazil, that is the claim of (now) Supreme Court Justice Luís Roberto Barroso, "Colisão entre liberdade de expressão e direitos da personalidade. Critérios de ponderação. Interpretação constitucionalmente adequada do Código Civil e da Lei de Imprensa," *Revista de Direito Administrativo* 235 (2004): 1–36.

80 Studies produced with data science and random sampling show that state trial courts in Rio de Janeiro, the second largest court in the country, when deciding about freedom of expression, apply balancing or cite any jurisprudence at all in only half of the rulings. Ivar A. Hartmann, "A Liberdade de Expressão na Primeira Instância do TJ-RJ," *Revista Opinião Jurídica* 18, no. 27 (2020): 13–44. Furthermore, when the Brazilian Supreme Court decided this type of case in the last two decades, 70% of its citations to precedent referred to rulings by the Court itself where no workable substantive standard on freedom of expression had been presented. Ivar A. Hartmann, "A Crise dos Precedentes no Supremo: O Caso dos Precedentes sobre Liberdade de Expressão," *Revista Estudos Institucionais* 6, no. 1 (2020): 109–28.

81 Adilson Moreira, *Racismo Recreativo* (Jandaíra, 2019).

82 Hernandez, "Hate Speech and the Language of Racism in Latin America," 834.

83 Lee Epstein, Christopher M. Parker, and Jeffrey A. Segal, "Do Justices Defend the Speech They Hate? In-Group Bias, Opportunism, and the First Amendment," *American Political Science Association Annual Meeting* (2013): 1–16.

84 Judiciary composition and interactions are still plagued by the long-term effects of the structural exclusion of women. See Maria Gloria Bonelli, "Profissionalismo, gênero e significados da diferença entre juízes e juízas estaduais e federais," *Contemporânea: Revista de Sociologia da UFSCar* 1 (2011): 103–23.

85 "[B]ecause we are satisfied that judges have changed the way they talk about a given issue in their decisions, we move to the next item on our list of transformative promises to be redeemed." Diego Werneck Arguelhes, "Transformative Constitutionalism: A View from Brazil," in *The Global South and Comparative Constitutional Law*, ed. Philipp Dann, Michael Riegner, and Maxim Bönnemann (Oxford University Press, 2020), 165–89, 168.

86 "Rather than focus on content moderation, governments, technology companies, and civil society should cooperate to focus on disrupting individuals, accounts, and movements that use emotive messaging and extreme worldviews." Bharath Ganesh, "The Ungovernability of Digital Hate Culture," *Journal of International Affairs* 71, no. 2 (2018): 30–49, 44.

87 Matthew C. Ingram, "Judicial Power in Latin America," *Latin American Research Review* 50, no. 1 (2015): 250–60.

88 Ideology plays a strong role in not only fake news dissemination but also detection and review. See David Lazer et al., "The Science of Fake News," *Science* 359, no. 6380 (2018): 1094–6, 1095.

89 Clare McGlynn, Erika Rackley, and Ruth Houghton, "Beyond 'Revenge Porn': The Continuum of Image-Based Sexual Abuse," *Feminist Legal Studies* 25 (2017): 25–46.

90 Namosha Veerasamy, "Cyberterrorism and the Spectre that Is the Convergence of the Physical and Virtual Worlds," in *Emerging Cyber Threats and Cognitive Vulnerabilities*, ed. Vladlena Benson and John McAlaney (Elsevier, 2020), 27–52, 32.

91 Clara Iglesias Keller, "Policy by Judicialisation: The Institutional Framework for Intermediary Liability in Brazil," *International Review of Law, Computers & Technology* 35, no. 3 (2021): 185–203.

92 Ivar A. Hartmann, "A New Framework for Online Content Moderation," *Computer Law & Security Review* 36 (2020): 1–10.

93 Ivar A. Hartmann, "Let the Users Be the Filter? Crowdsourced Filtering to Avoid Online Intermediary Liability," *Journal of the Oxford Centre for Socio-Legal Studies* 1 (2017): 21–47.

94 Calderón and Castells, *A nova América Latina*.

95 Brenda Dvoskin, *Social Media Platforms and Civil Society in Latin America: A View from the Nonprofit Organizations*. Documentos de trabajo CETyS #26 (Universidad de San Andrés, 2020).

96 In "digital juries" as discussed and empirically tested by Jenny Fan and Amy X. Zhang, "Digital Juries: A Civics-Oriented Approach to Platform Governance," *CHI'20,* April 25–30, 2020, Honolulu, HI, USA (2020): 1–14.

Bibliography

Acosta, Rodrigo Vargas. *Sucesos regulatorios en materias de libertad de expresión e internet en Latinoamérica*. Derechos Digitales América Latina, 2020.

Adams, Rachel. "Can Artificial Intelligence Be Decolonized?" *Interdisciplinary Science Reviews* 46, no. 1–2 (2021): 176–97.

Ammori, Marvin. "Another Worthy Tradition: How the Free Speech Curriculum Ignores Electronic Media and Distorts Free Speech Doctrine." *Missouri Law Review* 70 (2005): 59–123.

Arguelhes, Diego Werneck. "Transformative Constitutionalism: A View from Brazil." In *The Global South and Comparative Constitutional Law*, edited by Philipp Dann, Michael Riegner, and Maxim Bönnemann. Oxford University Press, 2020.

Barrett, Paul M. *Who Moderates the Social Media Giants? A Call to End Outsourcing*. NYU Stern Report, 2020.

Barroso, Luís Roberto. "Colisão entre liberdade de expressão e direitos da personalidade. Critérios de ponderação. Interpretação constitucionalmente adequada do Código Civil e da Lei de Imprensa." *Revista de Direito Administrativo* 235 (2004): 1–36.

Benkler, Yochai. "A Free Irresponsible Press: Wikileaks and the Battle over the Soul of the Networked Fourth Estate." *Harvard Civil Rights-Civil Liberties Law Review* 46 (2011): 311–97.

Bertoni, Eduardo A. "Jurisprudencia interamericana sobre libertad de expresión: Avances y desafíos." In *Libertad de expresión: debates, alcances y nueva agenda*, edited by María Paz Ávila Ordoñez, Ramiro Ávila Santamaría, and Gustavo Gómez Germano. UNESCO, 2011.

Black, Julia, and Andrew Murray. "Regulating AI and Machine Learning: Setting the Regulatory Agenda." *European Journal of Law and Technology* 10, no. 3 (2019): 1–21.

Bonelli, Maria Gloria. "Profissionalismo, gênero e significados da diferença entre juízes e juízas estaduais e federais." *Contemporânea: Revista de Sociologia da UFSCar* 1 (2011): 103–23.

Botero, Catalina. "Diversidad, pluralismo y libertad de expresión." In *Libertad de expresión: debates, alcances y nueva agenda*, edited by María Paz Ávila Ordoñez, Ramiro Ávila Santamaría, and Gustavo Gómez Germano. UNESCO, 2011.

boyd, danah, and Kate Crawford, "Critical Questions for Big Data." *Information Communication & Society* 15, no. 5 (2012): 662–79.

Braun, Joshua A., and Jessica L. Eklund. "Fake News, Real Money: Ad Tech Platforms, Profit-Driven Hoaxes, and the Business of Journalism." *Digital Journalism* 7, no. 1 (2019): 1–21.

Burri, Thomas. "The New Regulation of the European Union on Artificial Intelligence: Fuzzy Ethics Diffuse into Domestic Law and Sideline International Law." SSRN. Available online: https://papers.ssrn.com/sol3/papers.cfm?abstract_id=3865149.

Calderón, Fernando, and Manuel Castells. *A nova América Latina*. Translated by Eliana Aguiar. Companhia das Letras, 2021.

Caplan, Robyn. *Content or Context Moderation? Artisanal, Community-Reliant, and Industrial Approaches*. Data & Society Report, 2018.

Casilli, Antonio. "Digital Labor Studies Go Global: Toward a Digital Decolonial Turn." *International Journal of Communication* 11 (2017): 3934–54.

Castells, Manuel. "Informationalism, Networks, and the Network Society: A Theoretical Blueprint." In *The Network Society: A Cross-Cultural Perspective*, edited by Manuel Castells. Edward Elgar, 2004.

Cave, Stephen. "The Problem with Intelligence: Its Value-Laden History and the Future of AI." *AIES'20,* February 7–8, 2020, New York, NY, USA (2020): 29–35.

Centro de Estudios en Libertad de Expresión y Acceso a la Información. *Considering Facebook Oversight Board: Turning on Expectations*. CELE, 2019.

Chen, Adrian. "Inside Facebook's Outsourced Anti-Porn and Gore Brigade, Where 'Camel Toes' Are More Offensive than 'Crushed Heads'." *Gawker*, February 16, 2012. Available online: https://www.gawkerarchives.com/5885714/inside-facebooks-outsourced-anti-porn-and-gore-brigade-where-camel-toes-are-more-offensive-than-crushed-heads.

Cobbe, Jennifer, and Jatinder Singh. "Regulating Recommending: Motivations, Considerations, and Principles." *European Journal of Law and Technology* 10, no. 3 (2019): 1–37.

Crawford, Kate, and Tarleton Gillespie. "What Is a Flag for? Social Media Reporting Tools and the Vocabulary of Complaint." *New Media & Society* 18, no. 3 (2016): 410–28.

Davidson, Thomas, Dana Warmsley, Michael Macy, and Ingmar Weber. "Automated Hate Speech Detection and the Problem of Offensive Language." *Proceedings of the 11th International AAAI Conference on Web and Social Media* (2017): 512–15.

Drootin, Anna. "'Community Guidelines': The Legal Implications of Workplace Conditions for Internet Content Moderators." *Fordham Law Review* 90, no. 3 (2021): 1197–244.

Dvoskin, Brenda. *Social Media Platforms and Civil Society in Latin America: A View from the Nonprofit Organizations*. Documentos de trabajo CETyS #26. Universidad de San Andrés, 2020.

Enghel, Florencia, and Martín Becerra. "Here and There: (Re)Situating Latin America in International Communication Theory." *Communication Theory* 28 (2018): 111–30.

Epstein, Lee, Christopher M. Parker, and Jeffrey A. Segal. "Do Justices Defend the Speech They Hate? In-Group Bias, Opportunism, and the First Amendment." *American Political Science Association Annual Meeting* (2013): 1–15.

Facewatch. "Facewatch Launches in Spain with the Appointment of Retail Technology Business Leader SBT." Available online: https://www.facewatch.co.uk/2020/01/06/facewatch-launches-in-spain-with-the-appointment-of-retail-technology-business-leader-sbt/.

Fan, Jenny, and Amy X. Zhang. "Digital Juries: A Civics-Oriented Approach to Platform Governance." *CHI'20, April 25–30, 2020, Honolulu, HI, USA* (2020): 1–14.

Ganesh, Bharath. "The Ungovernability of Digital Hate Culture." *Journal of International Affairs* 71, no. 2 (2018): 30–49.

Garcia, Raphael Tsavkko. "Brazil's 'Fake News' Bill Won't Solve Its Misinformation Problem." *MIT Technology Review*, September 10, 2020. Available online: https://www.technologyreview.com/2020/09/10/1008254/brazil-fake-news-bill-misinformation-opinion/.

Gargarella, Roberto. "Constitucionalismo y libertad de expresión." In *Libertad de expresión: debates, alcances y nueva agenda*, edited by María Paz Ávila Ordoñez, Ramiro Ávila Santamaría, and Gustavo Gómez Germano. UNESCO, 2011.

Gómez, Mercedes Coronel. "El Principio de Libertad de Expresión en las redes sociales y su Regulación en el Ordenamiento Jurídico Ecuatoriano." *Revista Científica ECOCIENCIA* December (2019): 1–24.

Goodfellow, Ian, Jean Pouget-Abadie, Mehdi Mirza, Bing Xu, David Warde-Farley, Sherjil Ozair, Aaron Courville, and Yoshua Bengio. "Generative Adversarial Nets." *NIPS'14: Proceedings of the 27th International Conference on Neural Information Processing Systems* 2 (2014): 2672–80.

Gorwa, Robert. "The Platform Governance Triangle: Conceptualising the Informal Regulation of Online Content." *Internet Policy Review* 8, no. 2 (2019): 1–22.

Gorwa, Robert, Reuben Binns, and Christian Katzenbach. "Algorithmic Content Moderation: Technical and Political Challenges in the Automation of Platform Governance." *Big Data & Society* 7, no. 1 (2020): 1–15.

Graham, Mark, Isis Hjorth, and Vili Lehdonvirta. "Digital Labour and Development: Impacts of Global Digital Labour Platforms and the Gig Economy on Worker Livelihoods." *Transfer* 23, no. 2 (2017): 135–62.

Grimmelmann, James. "The Virtues of Moderation." *Yale Journal of Law and Technology* 17, no. 1 (2015): 42–109.

Hartmann, Ivar A. "A Crise dos Precedentes no Supremo: O Caso dos Precedentes sobre Liberdade de Expressão." *Revista Estudos Institucionais* 6, no. 1 (2020): 109–28.

Hartmann, Ivar A. "Let the Users Be the Filter? Crowdsourced Filtering to Avoid Online Intermediary Liability." *Journal of the Oxford Centre for Socio-Legal Studies* 1 (2017): 21–47.

Hartmann, Ivar A. "A Liberdade de Expressão na Primeira Instância do TJ-RJ." *Revista Opinião Jurídica* 18, no. 27 (2020): 13–44.

Hartmann, Ivar A. "A New Framework for Online Content Moderation." *Computer Law & Security Review* 36 (2020): 1–10.

Hernández, Marianne Díaz. *Discurso de Odio en América Latina: tendencias de regulación, rol de los intermediarios y riesgos para la libertad de expresión*. Derechos Digitales América Latina, 2020.

Hernandez, Tanya K. "Hate Speech and the Language of Racism in Latin America: A Lens for Reconsidering Global Hate Speech Restrictions and Legislation Models." *University of Pennsylvania Journal of International Law* 32, no. 3 (2010): 805–42.

Ingram, Matthew C. "Judicial Power in Latin America." *Latin American Research Review* 50, no. 1 (2015): 250–60.

Jeld, Jessica, Nele Achten, Hannah Hilligoss, Adam Nagy, and Madhulika Srikumar. *Principled Artificial Intelligence: Mapping Consensus in Ethical and Rights-Based Approaches to Principles for AI*. Berkman Klein Center for Internet & Society, 2020.

Kalluri, Pratyusha. "Don't Ask If AI Is Good or Fair, Ask How It Shifts Power." *Nature* 583 (2020): 169.

Kaye, David. *Speech Police: The Global Struggle to Govern the Internet*. Columbia Global Reports, 2019.

Keller, Clara Iglesias. "Policy by Judicialisation: The Institutional Framework for Intermediary Liability in Brazil." *International Review of Law, Computers & Technology* 35, no. 3 (2021): 185–203.

Klonick, Kate. "Inside the Making of Facebook's Supreme Court." *The New Yorker*, February 12, 2021. Available online: https://www.newyorker.com/tech/annals-of-technology/inside-the-making-of-facebooks-supreme-court.

Klonick, Kate. "The New Governors: The People, Rules, and Processes Governing Online Speech." *Harvard Law Review* 131 (2018): 1598–670.

Kuhlman, Caitlin, Latifa Jackson, and Rumi Chunara. "No Computation Without Representation: Avoiding Data and Algorithm Biases Through Diversity." *arXiv:2002.11836* (2020): 1–10.

La Rue, Frank. *Report of the Special Rapporteur on the Promotion and Protection of the Right to Freedom of Opinion and Expression*. United Nations General Assembly, 2011.

Larrondo, Manuel Ernesto, and Nicolás Mario Grandi. "Inteligencia Artificial, algoritmos y libertad de expresión." *Universitas* 34 (2021): 177–94.

Lazer, David M. J., Matthew A. Baum, Yochai Benkler, Adam J. Berinsky, Kelly M. Greenhill, Filippo Menczer, Miriam J. Metzger, Brendan Nyhan, Gordon Pennycook, David Rothschild, Michael Schudson, Steven A. Sloman, Cass R. Sunstein, Emily A. Thorson, Duncan J. Watts, and Jonathan L. Zittrain. "The Science of Fake News." *Science* 359, no. 6380 (2018): 1094–6.

Lessig, Lawrence. "The New Chicago School." *The Journal of Legal Studies* 27, no. 2 (1998): 661–91.

Lippitt, Anne H. "An Empirical Analysis of the Foreign Corrupt Practices Act." *Virginia Law Review* 99, no. 8 (2013): 1893–930.

Mari, Angelica Mari. "Brazilian Senate Passes Fake News Bill." *ZDNet*, July 1, 2020. Available online: https://www.zdnet.com/article/brazilian-senate-passes-fake-news-bill/.

McGlynn, Clare, Erika Rackley, and Ruth Houghton, "Beyond 'Revenge Porn': The Continuum of Image-Based Sexual Abuse." *Feminist Legal Studies* 25 (2017): 25–46.

McLaughlin, Timothy. "How Facebook's Rise Fueled Chaos and Confusion in Myanmar." *WIRED*, July 6, 2018. Available online: https://www.wired.com/story/how-facebooks-rise-fueled-chaos-and-confusion-in-myanmar/.

Mohamed, Shakir, Marie-Therese Png, and William Isaac. "Decolonial AI: Decolonial Theory as Sociotechnical Foresight in Artificial Intelligence." *Philosophy & Technology* 33 (2020): 659–84.

Moreira, Adilson. *Racismo Recreativo*. Jandaíra, 2019.

OECD. "OECD AI Principles." Available online: https://oecd.ai/en/ai-principles.

OFCOM. *Use of AI in Online Content Moderation*. OFCOM, 2019.

Oliva, Thiago Dias. "Content Moderation Technologies: Applying Human Rights Standards to Protect Freedom of Expression." *Human Rights Law Review* 20, no. 4 (2020): 607–40.

Osoba, Osonde, and William Welser IV. *An Intelligence in Our Image: The Risks of Bias and Errors in Artificial Intelligence*. RAND Corporation, 2017.

Pasquale, Frank. *The Black Box Society: The Secret Algorithms that Control Money and Information*. Harvard University Press, 2016.

Pazmiño, César Francisco Gallegos, and Eddy Ismael Villacís Flores. "Discurso Extremista y la Expansión de la Censura." *Revista CAP Jurídica Central* 6 (2020): 147–205.

Perel, Maayan, and Niva Elkin-Koren. "Accountability in Algorithmic Copyright Enforcement." *Stanford Technology Law Review* 19 (2016): 473–533.

Quijano, Aníbal. "Coloniality of Power and Eurocentrism in Latin America." *International Sociology* 15, no. 2 (2000): 215–32.

Rani, Uma, and Parminder Jeet Singh. "Digital Platforms, Data, and Development: Implications for Workers in Developing Economies." *Comparative Labor Law & Policy Journal* 41, no. 1 (Fall 2019): 263–88.

Roberts, Sarah T. *Behind the Screen: Content Moderation in the Shadows of Social Media*. Yale University Press, 2019.

Rodríguez, Oscar Luis Figueroa. "Indigenous Policy and Indigenous Data in Mexico. Context, Challenges and Perspectives." In *Indigenous Data Sovereignty and Policy*, edited by Maggie Walter, Tahu Kukutai, Stephanie Russo Carroll, and Desi Rodriguez-Lonebear. Routledge, 2021.

Ruckenstein, Minna, and Linda Lisa Maria Turunen, "Re-Humanizing the Platform: Content Moderators and the Logic of Care." *New Media & Society* 22, no. 6 (2019): 1026–42, 1036. https://doi.org/10.1177/146144481987599.

Salimans, Tim, Ian Goodfellow, Wojciech Zaremba, Vicki Cheung, Alec Radford, and Xi Chen. "Improved Techniques for Training GANs." *NIPS'16: Proceedings of the 30th International Conference on Neural Information Processing Systems* (2016): 1–9.

Scherer, Matthew. "Regulating Artificial Intelligence Systems: Risks, Challenges, Competencies, and Strategies." *Harvard Journal of Law & Technology* 29 (2016): 353–400.

Seltzer, Wendy. "Free Speech Unmoored in Copyright's Safe Harbor: Chilling Effects of the DMCA on the First Amendment." *Harvard Journal of Law and Technology* 24, no. 1 (2010): 171–232.

Siapera, Eugenia. "AI Content Moderation, Racism and (De)coloniality." *International Journal of Bullying Prevention* 4 (2022): 55–65.

Simonite, Tom. "What Really Happened When Google Ousted Timnit Gebru." *WIRED*, June 8, 2021. Available online: https://www.wired.com/story/google-timnit-gebru-ai-what-really-happened/.

Steiger, Miriah, Timir J. Bharucha, Sukrit Venkatagiri, Martin J. Riedl, and Matthew Lease. "The Psychological Well-Being of Content Moderators: The Emotional Labor of Commercial Moderation and Avenues for Improving Support." *CHI'21, May 8–13, 2021, Yokohama, Japan* (2021): 1–14.

Tsvetkova, Milena, Ruth García-Gavilanes, Luciano Floridi, and Taha Yasseri. "Even Good Bots Fight: The Case of Wikipedia." *PLoS One* 12, no. 2 (2017): 1–13.

Tufekci, Zeynep. "Algorithmic Harms Beyond Facebook and Google: Emergent Challenges of Computational Agency." *Colorado Technology Law Journal* 13 (2015): 203–18.

Tushnet, Rebecca. "Power Without Responsibility: Intermediaries and the First Amendment." *The George Washington Law Review* 76, no. 4 (2008): 986–1016.

Uprimny, Rodrigo. "Las transformaciones constitucionales recientes en América Latina: tendencias y desafíos." In *El derecho en América Latina: un mapa para el pensamiento jurídico del siglo XXI*, edited by César Rodríguez Garavito. Siglo Veintiuno Editores, 2011.

Veerasamy, Namosha. "Cyberterrorism and the Spectre that Is the Convergence of the Physical and Virtual Worlds." In *Emerging Cyber Threats and Cognitive Vulnerabilities*, edited by Vladlena Benson and John McAlaney. Elsevier, 2020.

Waschull, Sabine, Jos A. C. Bokhorst, Johan C. Wortmann, and Eric Molleman. "The Redesign of Blue- and White-Collar Work Triggered by Digitalization: Collar Matters." *Computers & Industrial Engineering* 165 (2022): 1–14.

Whitman, James. "Enforcing Civility and Respect: Three Societies." *Yale Law Journal* 109 (1999): 1279–398.

Wu, Tim. "Will Artificial Intelligence Eat the Law? The Rise of Hybrid Social-Ordering Systems." *Columbia Law Review* 119 (2019): 1–29.

Zingales, Luigi, and Filippo Maria Lancieri. *Committee on Digital Platforms: Policy Brief*. Stigler Center for the Study of the Economics and the State, 2019.

Zingales, Nicolo. "The Brazilian Approach to Internet Intermediary Liability: Blueprint for a Global Regime?" *Internet Policy Review* 4, no. 4 (2015): 1–14.

Zuboff, Shoshana. "Big Other: Surveillance Capitalism and the Prospects of an Information Civilization." *Journal of Information Technology* 30 (2015): 75–89.

Zuckerberg, Mark. "A Blueprint for Content Governance and Enforcement." Available online: https://m.facebook.com/nt/screen/?params=%7B%22note_id%22%3A751449002072082%7D&path=%2Fnotes%2Fnote%2F&refsrc=deprecated&_rdr.

4

THE PERILS OF PLATFORM DETERMINISM

Reimagining Global South Disinformation Interventions

Jonathan Corpus Ong and Jose Mari Hall Lanuza

In much of the Global South, platform determinist discourses are convenient and persuasive yet deeply problematic organizing frames for many civil society actors seeking to justify their counterdisinformation efforts. Critical disinformation researchers Robyn Caplan, Meredith Clark, and Will Partin have observed that in the Global North, "technological determinism, the idea that technology is a dominant factor in social change, has seeped into how we talk about platforms."[1] Similarly, discourses about omniscient platforms holding sway on local markets, politics, and social life prevail in the Global South—with pernicious consequences for political organizing and coalition-building.

For countries that have been part of a global populist swing, platform determinism has functioned as a quick and seductive cross-national explanatory frame for liberals seeking answers to perplexing questions of how social media shaped "surprising" electoral outcomes or why voters have grown disenchanted with their traditional leaders and institutions. For leading advocates in the Global South counterdisinformation space, platform determinism has also served as an umbrella narrative, connecting various attempts to demand platform accountability for the wide range of hateful online speech that has occasionally escalated to direct physical harm in places with long histories of ethno-religious conflict.[2]

As engaged researchers highly involved in both policy debate and community interventions addressing disinformation in the Philippines, we both acknowledge the importance of platform accountability as a central component of creating healthy information ecosystems. Indeed, we excitedly welcome new opportunities for Global South–focused researchers like us to ride global momentum around platform accountability. We join other colleagues in advocating for more independent researchers to have a say in platform governance, access, and audit of social media data and algorithms, and to comparatively review platforms' investments in addressing digital harms, especially those affecting marginalized communities in the Global South. While platforms' attempts at engaging academic and legal experts have been fairly criticized as seeming like public relations exercises, we agree that platforms are not monoliths and have "many faces."[3] For example, we do not discount that Meta's own Oversight Board could shape content policy in international contexts in meaningful ways,[4] even while perhaps lacking teeth to address broader structural features of their platforms like Instagram or Facebook.

This chapter offers a critical reflection on how platform determinist discourse, and the platform- and tech-centric solutionism that follows from it, present real obstacles to antidisinformation work as well as to progressive coalition-building in the Global South. With a specific analysis of the internal politics within antidisinformation networks in the Philippine context, we argue that platform determinism helpfully draws global attention to various digital harms that are accelerated and left unaddressed by social media platforms.

However, we highlight that this discourse can perpetuate social divisiveness and moral displacement in specific expressions that blame Facebook or—more recently—TikTok for the digital practices and voting behaviors of so-called uneducated and manipulable poor on social media. Crucially, platform determinism silences imperatives for community dialogue and listening as urgent components of prodemocratic groups' rebuilding and reorganizing strategy. The assumption that social media have brainwashed poor voters directs investments in antidisinformation interventions in the country lopsidedly toward content takedowns, user bans, bot and troll detections, and legal penalties that could be filed against lower-class "fake news peddlers." These top-down approaches, overtly or inadvertently, exclude ordinary people from participating in community-level solutions and from innovating bespoke antidisinformation interventions that could potentially address the political economy of disinformation and also do bridge-building work with communities whose socioeconomic grievances have been stoked by recent populist leaders.

The aim of this chapter, then, is to invite and manifest a truly "whole-of-society" approach to addressing misinformation[5]—one that situates it within a specific country context. By focusing our discussion on the gaps and failures of antidisinformation coalition work, this chapter does not intend to name and shame any of our colleagues or allies, but rather to shed light on what we could all be doing better in representing and advocating for society's most marginalized groups. Our sociological approach recognizes that the internal politics of antidisinformation work in the Global South is part of, and mirrors, the larger context of Left infighting that is exacerbated in contexts of intense political repression.[6]

This chapter begins by reviewing local popular expressions of platform determinism that have circulated in key moments of Left electoral and political defeat in the past six years. Then, we discuss the mainstream antidisinformation interventions advanced by leading advocates who subscribe to platform- and tech-centric frameworks. We argue that the real danger posed by platform determinism as the umbrella frame of antidisinformation work in the country is that it fails to address key features of the local disinformation economy and political system that require localized approaches, thoughtful strategic organizing, and inclusive messaging that neither alienate diverse local communities nor play directly into the hands of chief disinformation architects.

When Platform Determinism Connects with "The Brainwashed Voter" Trope

In May 2022, Ferdinand "Bongbong" Marcos Jr., son of the late dictator Ferdinand Marcos Sr., won the presidential race with over 31 million votes, almost twice the number of votes as the liberal candidate and runner-up, Leni Robredo. While a few academics offered critical analysis of his electoral victory that astutely focused on his strategic political alliance with powerful elite families, including the incumbent President Rodrigo Duterte,[7] many were quick to embrace a readily available explanatory frame that social media had brainwashed voters into supporting Marcos Jr.

Some of the most vocal proponents of this theory are antidisinformation advocates in journalism and civil society. There is a version of this narrative that insinuates that Marcos' campaign team had enlisted the disreputable consultancy firm Cambridge Analytica to unlock the psyche of voters, similarly attributing omniscience to data analytics tools, as previously critiqued by Robyn Caplan and colleagues in their discussion of platform determinism.[8] Another version of platform determinist election analysis insinuates that the Marcoses had organized bots[9] to control social media conversations at the press of a button.

Given the enormous growth of TikTok in the year leading up to the momentous presidential election, much handwringing also focused on the Filipino youth exposed to the mix of Marcos propaganda and dance crazes on TikTok,[10] while fearing their lack of direct experience of atrocities under Marcos Sr. and their miseducation about history.[11] TikTok media panics are part of a long history of stereotyping youth and policing the respectability of new media forms and technologies,[12] as media scholar Alice Marwick has pointed out.[13]

The day after the election, Nobel Peace Prize winner and antidisinformation advocate Maria Ressa posed the question to her viewers on alternative news outlet Rappler's live broadcast, "Did Filipinos vote with free will, or were they insidiously manipulated on social media?"[14] As a journalist who has been the target of legal harassment by former President Rodrigo Duterte, and also a frequent target of misogynist speech from Duterte and Marcos supporters on social media, Ressa has used her personal and professional experiences to draw international attention to, and support for, press freedom and platform accountability issues in the Philippines. While her international advocacy strategically draws resources to embattled journalists in the Philippines, locally, there is danger in how this same advocacy can perpetuate stereotypes of the "manipulable, uneducated voter" and deepen long-existing class divisions. This explanatory frame might be internationally resonant in the way it draws connection points between the Philippines and other liberal democracies struggling with angry populist formations and radicalization, yet locally, it dangerously fans the flames of class resentments given long histories of working-class revolt, oppression, and ridicule.[15]

These expressions are not new. They extend and reanimate long-held assumptions about the *bobotante*, which is a Filipino slang portmanteau of dumb (*bobo*) and voter (*botante*), often used to describe the political behaviors of people from low-income classes. Political scientist Frederic Schaffer (2005) has given helpful context about elections as "a source of frustration and anxiety" among the Filipino middle and upper classes because they fear that poor voters are "easily swayed by depraved, inept, and/or corrupt politicians."[16] In his analysis of voter education campaigns, Schaffer has exposed that poor communities find voter education and literacy campaigns insulting as they are often based on stereotypes that middle- and upper- class groups hold about poor people's political practices. Older versions of the "social media-brainwashed unruly poor" are the *jejemon*,[17] the *Dutertard*, and "the trolls."[18]

In recent years, under the Duterte administration, journalists, civil society, and academics have increasingly folded antidisinformation work into their voter education and literacy campaigns portfolio. Mainstream advocacies in the antidisinformation space are guilty of conceptual slippages of the problematic *bobotante* stereotype, where equivalences are made with the low-income Marcos or Duterte supporter with the paid troll or the "fake news peddler."

This is evident in liberal groups' investments into "troll-hunting," where pro-Duterte and pro-Marcos accounts on X (formerly Twitter) are shamed, unmasked, or mass reported. Rather than spotlighting political elites or savvy strategists as the chief architects of disinformation, liberal outrage and journalistic investigations have often been directed at anonymous trolls, fake accounts, or "bots" with low numbers of followers. Even high-level bipartisan senate investigations have focused energies on grilling Duterte's influencers and vloggers,[19] often focused on shaming the "crass" language of influencers and, occasionally, slut-shaming sexy microcelebrities who lack middle-class respectability.[20]

Liberal supporters on social media post online jokes and memes poking fun at Marcos and Duterte supporters for their bad English grammar and spelling in their tweets and posts. Even journalistic investigations of Marcos influencers focus their investigation on the educational backgrounds of popular YouTube pundits, asserting that their lack of college degrees has made them not only "vulnerable to disinformation" but that they have become disinformers themselves. For example, in one deep dive of YouTube influencers supporting Marcos, vloggers' social class identity as "poor" is spotlighted.[21]

Insofar as platform determinist discourses also fold in antipoor sentiments in blaming the less-educated, the low-income groups, and younger generations for their gullibility as audiences of disinformation and for their responsibility as producers of disinformation, then we argue that such expressions exacerbate the social divisiveness that populist leaders have stoked to their advantage. Worse, when journalists and civil society scapegoat "online trolls" as the newest version of the historically problematic "*bobotante*" trope, they affirm populist public perceptions of the progressive movement as elitist, hypocritical, and detached from everyday realities. When finger-pointing is too focused on external or technological villains, advocates might also miss asking the much tougher questions of how to penalize the local creative economies churning out attack memes for profit or how progressives might develop more satisfying narratives that directly speak to populist publics' grievances. For us, antidisinformation advocates have too often punched down when they should be punching up and assigning accountability to chief disinformation architects of dirty political campaigns who are part of the commercial and political elite.[22] Of course, politicians themselves have come to owe a debt of gratitude to the political strategists in advertising and public relations who have helped elect them into office, and so we assume they are complicit in keeping their regulatory attention and public indignations focused on denouncing the lower-class trolls.

In the next section, we illustrate how dominant antidisinformation interventions in the country have taken form and either overtly or inadvertently perpetuate reductive tropes about deficient and social media–manipulated voters without addressing structural features of disinformation economies and political systems.

The Weak Spots in Current Approaches

The *bobotante* trope instantiates elitist sentiments by portraying the lower classes as being unworthy of deliberative engagement and addressed only as objects of developmentalist and educational campaigns. Indeed, the more updated social media age version of the *bobotante* trope interconnects the identity of the mis-/less-educated voter with the manipulable social media user. We saw this new expression of the "social media *bobotante*" first emerge in 2016 in pundits' attempts to psychologize the roots of the "surprise" electoral victory of angry populist Rodrigo Duterte, followed by other global populist victories of Brexit and Donald Trump. Critical scholars Paula Chakravartty and Srirupa Roy have previously discussed the resurgence of the long-debunked hypodermic needle view of media effects[23] in global public discourse, which overstates how new media technologies and content have direct impacts on people's behaviors, especially when it comes to elections. In the Philippine context, where socioeconomic inequalities and resentments run deep, this discourse of media exerting direct effects takes an even more problematic turn when it overplays the vulnerabilities of the poor and the uneducated.

In the Philippines, pundits often cited Facebook's rollout of its Free Basics model as the starting point for "when they think the internet went wrong" in the country. While critical scholars of platform accountability have spotlighted Facebook's Free Basics as a specific problem of data extraction and data capitalism by Silicon Valley platforms expanding to new markets in the Global South,[24] Filipino antidisinformation advocates are likely to bring up Free Basics as the moment when "the Filipino masses" became exposed to social media manipulation and propaganda that they have come to accept as truth. For example:

> [I]n countries like the Philippines, Indonesia, Myanmar, when you get your cellphone, Facebook is automatically a default. That is your internet because it's free. So what happened in 2016 after the propaganda machine is fully formed is that they can so easily manipulate the people who are on Free Basics because all they see is the headline, and they can add anything on top of that headline. And when you click it, you have to pay, so Filipinos won't click it. They can't afford to. That then made it even easier to spread this information—forget it—to spread lies . . . Not just in the Philippines, in a lot of countries in South and East Asia, and a lot of countries in the global south, where the dangers are far greater than in the West because, in our countries, people are dying."[25]

Critical global scholars such as Toussaint Nothias have previously deployed anticolonial perspectives in the critique of Facebook's Free Basics, insofar as this digital innovation fits broader patterns of Western companies' experimentation on marginalized populations.[26] However, statements such as Maria Ressa's above more specifically express local liberal anxiety about how social media have expanded political expression of the lower classes in unpredictable ways. This anxiety is not new and is historically rooted in the upper and middle classes' feelings of "electoral powerlessness" as their votes do not decide electoral outcomes. This also applies to other contexts with similar social class inequalities.[27]

Platform determinist statements are strategic for attracting international support and activist indignation; they are useful for drawing foreign philanthropy, activist networks, and organizational resources to embattled local journalists and news outlets dealing with legal and digital forms of harassment. For instance, media freedom agencies such as Internews have helped fund large legacy media organizations that have been targeted by Duterte while supporting newer and smaller community media outlets under the broad frame of fact-checking or monitoring disinformation.[28]

However, we caution that adopting platform determinism as the umbrella framework to critique harmful disinformation campaigns is highly vulnerable to backlash. For one, local communities may feel detached, misrepresented, or scapegoated in such international-facing advocacies. Indeed, pro-Duterte and pro-Marcos pundits are quick to mobilize online around nationalist expressions that critique such international-facing advocacies as undermining Filipino interests and casting "shame" on their country. Second, and more closely aligned with our own ethnographic research, we argue that platform determinism lacks a nuanced framework on responsibility when it leaves unaccountable political and commercial elites primarily benefiting from disinformation campaigns. The Philippines is not unique here, and like many Global South contexts, disinformation campaigns are supported by a large digital workforce—some operating within corporate boardrooms, while others work in more precarious roles in a highly competitive race-to-the-bottom digital economy. A platform determinist frame often leaves out local creative industries and digital entrepreneurs from transparency and accountability debates about the media information ecosystem.[29] For example, our previous research exposed advertising and public relations professionals as the chief architects of disinformation campaigns, and they remain largely untouchable, even by investigative journalists, given that these corporate elites could withhold advertising money that the news agencies also depend on.[30]

We argue that platform determinist frameworks severely restrict the kinds of interventions that antidisinformation coalitions can imagine and develop. They harm the promise of multistakeholderism in a "whole-of-society approach" to misinformation. Platform determinist narratives lend themselves too easily to securitization frameworks that are also prone to authoritarian state capture, which has become the case for many Global South countries, despite the critical scholars' many warnings.[31] Also, the liberal advocates with platform determinist mindsets tend to be overly focused on content moderation and deplatforming. Finally, platform determinist narratives can themselves perpetuate colonial dependencies where Global South advocates come to rely on Western allies and their frameworks of platform governance to solve local political crises. We observe this defeatist and disempowering attitude from some antidisinformation advocates in the Philippines who await US or EU governance models of platform accountability as the central "solution," as we will discuss in the next section.

Anti-"Fake News" Laws and Other Legal Approaches

Unlike its neighboring countries in Southeast Asia and fellow Global South countries with illiberal governments, the Philippines does not (yet) have the kind of overbroad anti-"fake news" legislation granting executive overreach on social media content. Neighboring Singapore innovated the Protection from Online Falsehoods and Manipulation Act (POFMA), an "anti-fake news law" that granted the government the power to determine whether something is misinformation and punish its authors accordingly, and it has been critiqued as an example of using moral panics about fake news as "legislative opportunism."[32]

In the Philippines, antidisinformation advocates, including liberal opposition leaders, activist-lawyers, and journalists themselves, have surprisingly expressed interest in legislation that monitors and penalizes "fake news" online, despite the proximity of countries such as Singapore. We interpret liberals' and antidisinformation advocates' desire for top-down legislation that somehow catches and bans disinformation as expressive of real activist frustration and burnout under six years of Duterte's leadership and in the face of another six years under Marcos. In the face of Marcos' electoral victory in May, many journalists and activists have been at a loss as to how to regroup, how to "fight back," and whom exactly to blame for the electoral results. But fundamentally, legalistic approaches focused on the policing and banning of social media content extend from the same platform determinist mindset that has conceptualized the crisis in the Philippine information ecosystem as about failures of policing unruly so-called trolls run amok on social media. In conceptualizing the disinformation crisis as rooted in platforms, the Philippine liberal leaders ultimately see platforms as still holding the magic solution to this crisis.

As a result, even liberal politicians have started to author potentially dangerous legislation prone to abusive surveillance and censorship. For example, liberal opposition politicians critical of Duterte (and Marcos) advanced the SIM card registration bill,[33] which empowers law enforcement to use state surveillance to hunt down the actors behind anonymous SMS text scams, as well as anonymous accounts that might originate fake news on social media. Digital rights activists, presumably in the same camp as the liberal opposition, have had to publicly criticize this bill as abusing data privacy and posing a real threat to free speech and dissent. More progressive activists and scholars have had to remind liberal allies that overbroad legislation is especially dangerous in contexts where there is a culture of impunity; the Philippines is listed as one of the countries with the most retaliatory killings against journalists.[34]

We interpret that the SIM Card Registration Act primarily functioned as a tool for visibility and advocacy for liberal opposition politicians. The public ritual of senate hearings, mainstream news interviews, and engagement with academics and social media platforms, broadcast during the contentious election season, allowed embattled liberal opposition politicians to center themselves as victims of fake news and online hate speech that have benefited illiberal leaders. These public hearings, in effect, framed fake news as especially harmful content to opposition figures and sought to enlist platforms to be more sympathetic when addressing their particular requests for content takedowns as they present themselves as the primary victims of social media "trolls."

Crucially, the justifications for the SIM Card Registration Act instantiate the reductive platform determinist frameworks, narrowly focused on top-down solutions seeking more aggressive content takedowns. By spotlighting anonymous accounts as the main culprits of the whole mix of political disinformation, business scams, and hate speech—however vaguely defined by this legislation—the bill reveals the same underlying moral panics about the unruly masses[35] that have come to invade social media spaces.

Another problematic example of legal solutionism advanced by liberal opposition politicians and activists is the embrace of existing libel and cyberlibel laws to hunt down social media influencers. Fixation on libel laws as regulatory tools for disinformation hinges on the idea that the primary answer to disinformation rests on fixing the content. For example, the Movement Against Disinformation (MAD) issued a public statement proclaiming that the battle against disinformation will be fought mostly in courts. MAD stated that they will pursue a multi-pronged approach towards government officials, media establishments, social media platforms, that will allow them to "go after" these entities with civil or criminal cases should they espouse falsehoods.[36] Former Supreme Court justice and liberal leader Antonio Carpio had previously called for the amendment of the libel law to allow for the presumption of malice if remarks were made by "fake persons."[37] Carpio went on to say that "the use of fake or fictitious names also encourages the spread of disinformation in social media" and that the "use of fake or fictitious names in online platforms to libel a person is per se proof of malice and this should be written in the law."[38] These are more examples where disinformation production is displaced onto low-level anonymous accounts perceived to be the key culprits behind toxic online discourse. These frameworks continue to overlook the higher-level elite strategists, politicians, and wealthy bankrollers who have masterminded and profited from disinformation campaigns.

It is definitely disappointing that these sentiments come from key political personalities associated with principles and institutions of liberal democracy. By advocating for this law, these liberal leaders are, in effect, deeming libel laws acceptable democratic tools, but only when they are the ones using them.

Thus, we want to highlight the irony of using libel and defamation laws as a way of fighting disinformation, given that these laws are already widely abused, such as in the high-profile cases where Maria Ressa and Rappler journalists became targets of cyberlibel accusations. If journalists, activists, and legal experts recognize the unevenness of the political terrain in the Global South, it is risky to legitimize the state's tool for oppression by resorting to it when they benefit.

Legal approaches overly focused on policing social media content are highly dangerous and prone to authoritarian state capture, resulting in potential witch hunts[39] of dissenters, activists, and even academics. Journalists, lawyers, and activists have to be united in understanding that libel laws can harm more than they help, and, that ultimately, they do not dislodge the disinformation industry. While legal efforts at public accountability are well meaning, they are ultimately unsustainable and nearly impossible to scale up. Furthermore, it often targets the notorious social media influencers, while the political elites and chief disinformation architects are never penalized.

Finally, another strand of legal advocacy by mainstream antidisinformation advocates is playing the waiting game and relying on policy flows from the United States[40] and European legal frameworks of platform accountability to be adopted by the Global South. For example, Filipino antidisinformation advocates have pinned their hopes on the EU Code for Disinformation as a game changer for social media in the Philippines.[41] We do not dispute that global-/top-level solutions focused on accountability platforms are important, but they are not enough.[42] For example, European social platform accountability models have cultural roots and values expressive of ideological contexts specific to the area.[43] Thus, there is a question of whether mainstream legalist approaches and platform accountability initiatives are even transplantable, especially to countries in the Global South, where regulatory institutions lack specific expertise and act on political incumbents' whims.

Fact-Check Models and Their Shortcomings

By framing the disinformation crisis as primarily an issue of platform sanitation, platform determinist frameworks tend to support fact-checking as a key intervention. In many Global South countries, fact-checking start-ups have mushroomed and became a veritable "industry"[44] by attracting foreign philanthropy and organizing local liberal supporters to a practical intervention. Of course, the expansion of fact-checking models is accelerated by Big Tech platforms themselves who have supported local third-party partners to help with their content moderation decisions. From a global worker justice perspective, it is important to consider how emotionally distressing content moderation work has been outsourced to Global South countries such as the Philippines, which is known as a "content moderation capital" of the world, responsible for cleaning up gore and hate not only locally but also for international markets. Despite this, we observe that news agencies in the Philippines feel like they benefit from the additional financial support while they themselves are privately critical of the merit and efficacy of their third-party arrangement with platforms.[45]

Scholars have noted that publishing independent fact-checking is a rather recent phenomenon, first appearing in the United States in the form of Snopes and later FactCheck.org,[46] while in the 1990s, American news channels started broadcasting verifications of political campaign commercials with their AdWatch reports.[47] In the Philippines, fact-checking teams and independent organizations have expanded in recent years. In 2018, Facebook enlisted Rappler, Vera Files, and Agence France-Press as third-party fact checkers, where partner journalists have been provided special access to the platform CrowdTangle to observe viral content, produce fact-check reports on their independent news sites, and help Facebook determine which false content should be downvoted (but not banned) from the newsfeed.[48] Platforms' remuneration and incentive systems narrowly restrict their third-party fact-checkers to hunt rumors peddled by ordinary users and influencers, but fact-checking false claims by powerful politicians themselves are not rewarded in this specific arrangement.

Fact-checking is a model easily replicated and transposable, and this has been widely supported by foreign philanthropy. Government funders such as USAID and AusAID have partnered with various media freedom intermediaries to support local fact-checking incubators. For example, USAID and Internews have initiated TotooBa.Info, described on its website as a "disinformation reporting platform."[49] Other organizations include Break The Fake and the election coalition Facts First. All these organizations tend to focus their energy on hunting online rumors peddled by social media users and hunting down "anonymous trolls."

Global South journalism studies scholars have produced various analyses of fact-checking platforms, ranging from more positive assessments of these new digital innovations to those who are more critical in identifying their various weak spots. For example, Peter Cunliffe Jones, who is very positive about fact-checking, says that the Global North can learn from Africa's successful experiences with holistic fact-checking, engaging platforms to regulate content, and improving media literacy in schools.[50] However, critical scholars Chiaoning Su and Wei-Ping Li spotlight their specific limitation when they say in-depth political fact-checking demands extensive experience and institutional knowledge among journalists and civil society organizations,[51] which might not always be present in developing democracies. Third-party fact-checkers employed by platforms like Facebook are also incentivized to observe viral content online, which means that private messaging apps and misinformation expressed in local vernaculars could slip past monitors.[52]

Of course, in the Global North, the idea that fact-checking can inadvertently popularize false claims has been thoughtfully advanced by communications scholar Whitney Phillips, who advocates for the use of strategic silence, or quarantining dangerous speech in cases when reporting could inadvertently draw more visibility and clicks to extreme perspectives.[53]

Writing about India, media anthropologist Sahana Udupa raises concern that fact-checking as a practice is highly vulnerable to accusations of partisanship. She observes in the Indian context that fact-checking and "fake news busting" have become "weaponized" and hyper-partisan "following the patterns of political and ideological fissures" in the country.[54] We see warning signs in the Philippines, where fact-checking has been aggressively discredited as partisan, biased, and undermining national interests. Various conspiracies have accused foreign philanthropists of spreading a "Western agenda."[55] No less than President Ferdinand Marcos Jr. and his sister, Senator Imee Marcos, have accused Meta platforms of "bias" for their selection of third-party fact-checkers and raised questions about their procedures.[56]

Fact-checkers' corrections are also vulnerable to backlash when they spotlight erroneous expressions of low-level social media influencers and celebrities in a way that talks down to them as uneducated and illiterate. For example, a young celebrity who made an off-the-cuff comment that "history is like gossip" in a press conference about a Marcos biopic, in which she played the role of one of the Marcos children. She was met with journalistic fact-checks and academic webinars dedicated to fact-checking and history education. Marcos supporters savvily framed the incident in their own online talk shows as liberals acting like bullies.[57]

The popularity of fact-checking organizations and volunteer coalitions upholding "Facts First" represent that liberals are indeed highly engaged and protective of whatever spaces are left to defend historical truths. They assert the presence of a political opposition that continues to hold abusive and corrupt politicians and their enablers accountable.

But these practices are prone to backfire and invite backlash; they also fail to address the broader structural conditions that allow disinformation campaigns to be produced and organized in the first place. They also refuse to acknowledge the real feelings of grievances and anxieties of ordinary people, which political elites have stoked through savvy disinformation campaigns.

Manifesting a Truly "Whole-of-Society Approach"

As media sociologists, we offer a critique of antidisinformation advocacies that overly spotlight platform responsibility and platform-centric solutions that emphasize content takedowns and "troll hunting." Platform determinism not only flattens out the diverse possibilities for creative interventions that can connect with local communities; in its worst expression, it has functioned as a moral denialism for prodemocracy leaders to acknowledge their own failures of listening, coalition-building, and community organizing. Such a framework hurts liberal institutions and liberal values insofar as this explanatory framework only deepens long-existing social class divisions in a country with vast social inequalities. Historically, the middle and upper classes have asserted moral ascendancy in their display of "right" values and political education,[58] while they deny the lower classes any deliberative agency by addressing them only as subjects of voter and media literacy campaigns. While this chapter has discussed the specific perils of platform determinism in a Global South context, the lessons we offer here apply to advanced liberal democracies as well. Prodemocracy leaders need inclusive and hopeful frames that appeal to diverse communities rather than play into the same social divisions and festering resentments that populist leaders have masterfully stoked to serve their interests.

As engaged scholars involved in policy- and community-level interventions, we continue to emphasize the need to introduce accountability mechanisms targeting the local disinformation-for-hire industry and spotlighting the responsibility of chief disinformation architects who are the masterminds of campaigns. For us, this means moving away from hunting low-level anonymous accounts to shading in the layers of power, responsibility, and complicity in highly unregulated creative industries involved in political campaigning. Our experiences in the Philippines direct us to "assign the most culpability here to the chief architects who are at the top level of influence and benefit most from the architecture they have built."[59] Doing so means we ensure transparency and accountability in social media regulation while safeguarding liberal principles of free speech and tolerance.[60]

This applies to the Global South more broadly, where disinformation-for-hire mechanisms mean that there's a great need to develop new frameworks for ethics and accountability for creative workers, influencers, and content creators who are recruited for political campaigns.

Instead of "othering" the "trolls" or the "disinformers" as exceptional villains through gotcha journalism, libel battles, fact-check reports, and name-and-shame media literacy campaigns, we need to expose the ordinariness through which young people are routinely recruited to political campaigns. Our own modest contribution is to create worker support and legal protection mechanisms for potential whistleblowers keen to expose their organizations' and clients' responsibility or complicity in disinformation campaigns. One such public-facing collaboration was with investigative journalists in the start-up news agency PumaPodcast, an educational podcast that normalizes discussions of ethics and accountability in the advertising, public relations, and digital influencer industries. By recruiting former and current "paid trolls," influencers, and political strategists to anonymously speak about their experiences in our podcast, our aim has been to ground shocking or salacious stories of disinformation workers in ordinary realities of race-to-the-bottom work arrangements, moral compromises, and entrepreneurialism to prevent other young people from being recruited.[61]

Manifesting a whole-of-society approach means that we also need to trust in new voices rather than just the usual liberal leaders to solve the crisis from the top-down approaches. Rather than anticipate Global North-to-Global South policy flows in the disinformation space, we recommend that Filipino researchers and civil society actors build and participate in more South-to-South learning spaces that bring us in direct conversation with our counterparts in Brazil, India, Thailand, and Nigeria, among others. We invite new collaborators to take up space, and we join supportive international organizations to empower a more diverse roster of antidisinformation academics and civil society leaders.

Notes

1 Robyn Caplan, Meredith Clark, and Will Partin, "Against Platform Determinism. A Critical Orientation," Data & Society, October 13, 2020, available online: https://medium.com/datasociety-points/against-platform-determinism-899acdf88a3d.

2 Directorate-General for Communications Networks, "A Multi-Dimensional Approach to Disinformation: Report of the Independent High Level Group on Fake News and Online Disinformation," Publications Office of the European Union, April 30, 2018, available online: https://op.europa.eu/en/publication-detail/-/publication/6ef4df8b-4cea-11e8-be1d-01aa75ed71a1/language-en; Nyi Nyi Kyaw, "Facebooking in Myanmar: From Hate Speech to Fake News to Partisan Political Communication," Think Asia (ISEAS Yusof Ishak Institute, June 18, 2019), available online: https://mediawell.ssrc.org/citations/facebooking-in-myanmar-from-hate-speech-to-fake-news-to-partisan-political-communication/

3 Chinmayi Arun, "Facebook's Faces," *Harvard Law Review*, March 20, 2022, available online: https://harvardlawreview.org/2022/03/facebooks-faces/.

4 Evelyn Douek, "Facebook's 'Oversight Board': Move Fast with Stable Infrastructure and Humility," *North Carolina Journal of Law & Technology* (2019), available online: https://scholarship.law.unc.edu/ncjolt/vol21/iss1/2/; Kate Klonick, "The Facebook Oversight Board: Creating an Independent Institution to Adjudicate Online Free Expression," *Yale Law Journal* 129, no. 8 (2020), available online: https://yalelawjournal.org/feature/the-facebook-oversight-board.

5 Joan Donovan et al., "Mitigating Medical Misinformation: A Whole-of-Society Approach to Countering Spam, Scams, and Hoaxes," March 24, 2021, available online: https://doi.org/10.37016/tasc-2021-03.

6 Antidisinformation coalitions in the Philippines are most visibly led by journalists who have been targets of legal harassment under the Duterte administration. The common approach is usually personality-oriented reporting and naming-and-shaming of influencers associated with Duterte and, more recently, Marcos. In the past two years, liberal politicians critical of the Duterte administration have taken on antidisinformation work as part of their advocacy. Their "expert" opinion and public statements often center on their personal experiences of being victims of "fake news" and attributing these operations to the incumbent Duterte administration. That said, academics and other civil society groups, including those from the community media and human rights sector, have advanced different approaches. While we do not have the space to map out the many diverse groups creating distinct interventions, we find it crucial to highlight internal divides within antidisinformation coalitions and how they follow patterns of Left infighting, previously discussed in both the Philippines and other contexts such as Turkey. For internal divides in the Left, see Nathan Gilbert Quimpo, *Contested Democracy and the Left in the Philippines After Marcos*, vol. 58 (Yale University Southeast Asia Studies, 2008). For parallels in Turkey, see Zeynep Tufekci, *Twitter and Tear Gas: The Power and Fragility of Networked Protest* (Yale University Press, 2021).

7 Julio Teehankee, "Duterte Set Stage for Second Coming of Marcoses," ANC 24/7, YouTube, 2022, available online: https://www.youtube.com/watch?v=3FUGQG G10oY; Nicole Curato, "Strongmen Inc.: The Marcos Comeback," *Australian Foreign Affairs* no. 15 (2022): 50–69, available online: https://search.informit.org/doi/10.3316 /informit.633533988186376.

8 See Caplan et al., *Against Platform Determinism*; There is no hard evidence of any paid engagement. This theory emerged based on a photograph that captured Marcos' campaign team meeting with Alexander Nix back in 2016 when Marcos ran and lost the vice presidency race.

9 David Pierson, "Dictator's Son Uses TikTok to Lead in Philippine Election and Rewrite His Family's Past," *Los Angeles Times*, May 5, 2022, available online: https://www.latimes.com/world-nation/story/2022-05-05/dictators-son-uses-tiktok -to-lead-philippines-election-and-rewrite-his-familys-past.

10 Tim Culpan, "Bongbong Benefited from TikTok in Philippines Election. Watch out for Midterms," Bloomberg, June 28, 2022, available online: https://www.bloomberg .com/opinion/articles/2022-06-28/bongbong-benefited-from-tiktok-in-philippines -election-watch-out-for-midterms?leadSource=uverify+wall.

11 Chad de Guzman, "Philippines Election: How TikTok Is Helping Bongbong Marcos," *Time*, May 5, 2022, available online: https://time.com/6173757/bongbong-marcos -tiktok-philippines-election/.

12 Heidi Tworek, "Cambridge Analytica, Trump, and the New Old Fear of Manipulating the Masses," Nieman Lab, May 17, 2017, available online: https://www.niemanlab .org/2017/05/cambridge-analytica-trump-and-the-new-old-fear-of-manipulating-the -masses/.

13 Alice E. Marwick, "I Have Something to Say about This Batshit Crazy Story. Basically: The Media Loves a Teen Technopanic. The PR Firm Easily Exploited a Hundred-Year Old Moral Panic over Kids and Tech. Here's Why. Https://T.co /wy0y3kg64w," Twitter, March 30, 2022, available online: https://twitter.com /alicetiara/status/1509176562574413829.

14 "#WeDecide: Disinformation in the 2022 Philippine Elections," YouTube, Rappler, 2022, available online: https://www.youtube.com/watch?v=mUl5Cmcjf18.

15 Randolf S. David, *Understanding Philippine Society, Culture, and Politics* (Anvil, 2017).

16 Frederic Schaffer, "Clean Elections and the Great Unwashed: Vote Buying and Voter Education in the Philippines," April 2005, available online: https://www.ias.edu/sites /default/files/sss/papers/paper21.pdf.

17 Christian Tablazon, "The Jejemon as Symptom and Slippage: Notes on Issues of Power and Identity in Media Literacy and (Mass) Communication," in *Filipino Generations in a Changing Landscape*, ed. Amaryllis T. Torres, Laura L. Samson, and Manuel P. Diaz (Philippine Social Science Council, 2015), 271–6.

18 Jason Cabañes and Jayeel Cornelio, "The Rise of Trolls in the Philippines (and What We Can Do About It)," in *A Duterte Reader: Critical Essays on Rodrigo Duterte's Early Presidency*, ed. Nicole Curato (Ateneo de Manila University Press, 2017), 231–50.

19 Lara Tan, "Senators Urge Mocha Uson: Use Your Power Wisely," CNN, October 5, 2017, available online: https://www.cnnphilippines.com/news/2017/10/04/Mocha-Uson-fake-news.html.

20 Jonathan Corpus Ong and Jason Vincent A. Cabañes, "Architects of Networked Disinformation: Behind the Scenes of Troll Accounts and Fake News Production in the Philippines," ScholarWorks@UMass Amherst (Newton Tech4Dev Network, February 2018), available online: https://scholarworks.umass.edu/communication_faculty_pubs/74/.

21 Rambo Talabong, 2022. "Documentary: Ang Bagong Media Ng Bagong Lipunan," YouTube, Rappler, 2022, available online: https://www.youtube.com/watch?v=F9NeAvuaUQo.

22 Ong and Cabañes, "Architects of Networked Disinformation."

23 Paula Chakravartty and Srirupa Roy, "Mediatized Populisms: Inter-Asian Lineages," *International Journal of Communication* 11 (2017): 4073–92.

24 Toussaint Nothias, "Access Granted: Facebook's Free Basics in Africa," *Media, Culture & Society* 42, no. 3 (2020): 329–48, available online: https://doi.org/10.1177/0163443719890530.

25 Interview with Maria Ressa, *The Facebook Dilemma* (Public Broadcasting Service, 2018), available online: https://www.pbs.org/wgbh/frontline/interview/maria-ressa/.

26 Nothias, "Access Granted."

27 Schaffer, "Clean Elections."

28 "TotooBa.info." n.d. InterNews, available online: https://totooba.info/.

29 Jonathan Corpus Ong, Ross Tapsell, and Nicole Curato, "Tracking Digital Disinformation in the 2019 Philippine Midterm Election," New Mandala, August 2019, 41, available online: https://www.newmandala.org/wp-content/uploads/2019/08/Digital-Disinformation-2019-Midterms.pdf.

30 Jonathan Corpus and Jason Vincent A. Cabañes, "When Disinformation Studies Meets Production Studies: Social Identities and Moral Justifications in the Political Trolling Industry," *International Journal of Communication* 13 (2019): 5771–90.

31 Gabrielle Lim, "Securitize/Counter-Securitize: The Life and Death of Malaysia's Anti-Fake News Act," Data & Society, March 25, 2020, available online: https://datasociety.net/library/securitize-counter-securitize/.

32 Cherian George, "Disinformation: A Debate That Needs to Be Better Informed," Freedom From The Press, October 7, 2019, available online: https://blog.freedomfromthepress.info/2019/10/07/disinformation-2/.

33 Neil Jerome Morales, "Philippines Passes Law to Tackle Anonymous Social Media Abuse," Reuters, February 3, 2022, available online: https://www.reuters.com/world/asia-pacific/philippines-passes-law-tackle-anonymous-social-media-abuse-2022-02-03/.

34 Jennifer Dunham, "Murders of Journalists More than Double Worldwide," Committee to Protect Journalists, February 25, 2021, available online: https://cpj.org/reports/2020/12/murders-journalists-more-than-doubled-killed/.

35 Tworek, "Cambridge Analytica."

36 "Movement Against Disinformation' Wages War against Fake News," YouTube, One News PH, 2022, available online: https://www.youtube.com/watch?v=AMUik3JKzbs.

37 Christia Marie Ramos, "Carpio Wants Libel Law Amended; Presume Malice If Libelous Remark Made by 'Fictitious User,'" INQUIRER.net, December 15, 2021, available online: https://newsinfo.inquirer.net/1528001/carpio-wants-libel-law-amended-presume-malice-if-libelous-remark-made-by-fictitious-user.

38 Ramos, "Carpio Wants."

39 Alicia Wanless, "The Philippines Is Democracy's Dystopian Future," Carnegie Endowment for International Peace, June 24, 2020, available online: https://carnegieendowment.org/2020/06/24/philippines-is-democracy-s-dystopian-future-pub-82147.

40 Chico Q. Camargo and Felix M. Simon, "Mis- and Disinformation Studies Are Too Big to Fail: Six Suggestions for the Field's Future," 2022, available online: https://misinforeview.hks.harvard.edu/article/mis-and-disinformation-studies-are-too-big-to-fail-six-suggestions-for-the-fields-future/.

41 Maria Ressa, "Secretary Antony J. Blinken with Maria Ressa on Digital Diplomacy and Human Rights Online—United States Department of State," U.S. Department of State, June 7, 2022, available online: https://www.state.gov/secretary-antony-j-blinken-with-maria-ressa-on-digital-diplomacy-and-human-rights-online/.

42 Heidi Tworek, "Whose Democracy Counts When Global Social Media Rules Are Set?," Centre for International Governance Innovation, June 18, 2021, available online: https://www.cigionline.org/articles/whose-democracy-counts-when-global-social-media-rules-are-set/.

43 Emiliana De Blasio and Donatella Selva, "Who Is Responsible for Disinformation? European Approaches to Social Platforms' Accountability in the Post-Truth Era," *American Behavioral Scientist* 65, no. 6 (2021): 825–46, https://doi.org/10.1177/0002764221989784.

44 Sahana Udupa, "India Needs a Fresh Strategy to Tackle Online Extreme Speech," *Economic and Political Weekly*, September 11, 2019, available online: https://www.epw.in/engage/article/election-2019-india-needs-fresh-strategy-to-tackle-new-digital-tools.

45 Ong, Tapsell, and Curato, "Tracking Digital Disinformation," 32.

46 Anya Schiffrin and Peter Cuniffe-Jones, "Online Misinformation: Policy Lessons from the Global South," in *Disinformation in the Global South*, ed. Wasserman and Dani Madrid-Morales (Wiley Blackwell, 2022), 161–78.

47 Chiaoning Su and Wei-Ping Li, "Excavating Truth: Assessing Citizen-Led Fact-Checking Practices in Taiwan," in *Resistance in the Era of Nationalisms: Performing Identities in Taiwan and Hong Kong*, ed. Hsin-I Cheng and Hsin-I Sydney Yueh (Michigan State University Press, 2023); Lucas Graves, *Deciding What's True: The Rise of Political Fact-Checking in American Journalism* (Columbia University Press, 2016).

48 Manuel Mogato, "Philippines Complains Facebook Fact-Checkers Are Biased," Reuters, April 16, 2018, available online: https://www.reuters.com/article/us-philippines-facebook/philippines-complains-facebook-fact-checkers-are-biased-idUSKBN1HN1EN.

49 "About TotooBa.info." n.d., InterNews, available online: https://totooba.info/about.html.

50 Peter Cunliffe-Jones, "From Church and Mosque to WhatsApp—Africa Check's Holistic Approach to Countering 'Fake News,'" *The Political Quarterly* 91, no. 3 (2020): 596–9, https://doi.org/10.1111/1467-923x.12899.

51 Su and Li, "Excavating Truth."

52 Ong, Tapsell, and Curato, "Tracking Digital Disinformation."

53 Whitney Phillips, "The Oxygen of Amplification," Data & Society Research Institute, May 22, 2018, available online: https://datasociety.net/library/oxygen-of-amplification/.

54 Matti Pohjonen and Sahana Udupa, "Extreme Speech Online: An Anthropological Critique of Hate Speech Debates," *International Journal of Communication* 11 (2017): 1173–91.

55 Jonathan Corpus Ong et al., "Parallel Public Spheres: Influence Operations in the 2022 Philippine Elections," Media Manipulation Casebook, October 28, 2022, available online: https://mediamanipulation.org/research/unmasking-influence-operations-in-the-philippines.

56 Vanne Elaine Terrazola, "Sen. Marcos Questions FB Fact-Checkers in PH," *Manila Bulletin*, January 21, 2021, available online: https://mb.com.ph/2021/01/21/sen-marcos-questions-fb-fact-checkers-in-ph/.

57 Nicole Curato, "When It Comes to Historical Distortion, We Cannot Fight Fire with Fire," *New Mandala*, November 2, 2022, available online: https://www.newmandala.org/when-it-comes-to-historical-distortion-we-cannot-fight-fire-with-fire/.

58 Wataru Kusaka, *Moral Politics in the Philippines: Inequality, Democracy and the Urban Poor* (Ateneo de Manila University Press, 2019).

59 Ong and Cabañes, "Architects of Networked Disinformation" 64.

60 Ong, Tapsell, and Curato, "Tracking Digital Disinformation," 41.

61 Kat Ventura and Jonathan Corpus Ong, "Catch Me If You Can," PumaPodcast, available online: https://www.pumapodcast.com/podcasts/catch-me-if-you-can.

Bibliography

"About Totooba.info." TotooBa.info. Internews. Available online: https://totooba.info/about.html.

Arun, Chinmayi. "Facebook's Faces." *Harvard Law Review*, March 20, 2022. Available online: https://harvardlawreview.org/2022/03/facebooks-faces/.

Cabañes, Jason Vincent, and Jayeel Cornelio. "The Rise of Trolls in the Philippines (and What We Can Do About It)." Essay. In *A Duterte Reader: Critical Essays on Rodrigo Duterte's Early Presidency*, edited by Nicole Curato. Ateneo de Manila University Press, 2017.

Camargo, Chico Q., and Felix M. Simon. "Mis- and Disinformation Studies Are Too Big to Fail: Six Suggestions for the Field's Future." *Harvard Kennedy School Misinformation Review*, 2022. https://doi.org/10.37016/mr-2020-106.

Caplan, Robyn, Meredith Clark, and Will Partin. "Against Platform Determinism." Data & Society: Points, October 14, 2020. Available online: https://medium.com/datasociety-points/against-platform-determinism-899acdf88a3d.

Chakravartty, Paula, and Srirupa Roy. "Mediatized Populisms: Inter-Asian Lineages." *International Journal of Communication* 11 (2017): 4073–92.

Culpan, Tim. "Bongbong Benefited from TikTok in Philippines Election. Watch Out for Midterms." Bloomberg, June 28, 2022. Available online: https://www.bloomberg.com/opinion/articles/2022-06-28/bongbong-benefited-from-tiktok-in-philippines-election-watch-out-for-midterms?leadSource=uverify%2Bwall.

Cunliffe-Jones, Peter. "From Church and Mosque to WhatsApp—Africa Check's Holistic Approach to Countering 'Fake News.'" *The Political Quarterly* 91, no. 3 (2020): 596–9. https://doi.org/10.1111/1467-923x.12899.

Curato, Nicole. "Strongmen Inc.: The Marcos Comeback." *Australian Foreign Affairs* no. 15 (2022): 50–69.

Curato, Nicole. "When It Comes to Historical Distortion, We Cannot Fight Fire with Fire." New Mandala, November 2, 2022. Available online: https://www.newmandala.org/when-it-comes-to-historical-distortion-we-cannot-fight-fire-with-fire/.

David, Randolph. *Understanding Philippine Society, Culture, and Politics*. Edited by Laura L. Samson. Anvil, 2017.

De Blasio, Emiliana, and Donatella Selva. "Who Is Responsible for Disinformation? European Approaches to Social Platforms' Accountability in the Post-Truth Era." *American Behavioral Scientist* 65, no. 6 (2021): 825–46. https://doi.org/10.1177/0002764221989784.

de Guzman, Chad. "Philippines Election: How TikTok Is Helping Bongbong Marcos." *Time*, May 5, 2022. Available online: https://time.com/6173757/bongbong-marcos-tiktok-philippines-election/.

Directorate-General for Communications Networks. "A Multi-Dimensional Approach to Disinformation: Report of the Independent High Level Group on Fake News and Online Disinformation." Publications Office of the European Union, April 30, 2018. Available online: https://op.europa.eu/en/publication-detail/-/publication/6ef4df8b-4cea-11e8-be1d-01aa75ed71a1/language-en.

Donovan, Joan, Brian Friedberg, Gabrielle Lim, Nicole Leaver, Jennifer Nilsen, and Emily Dreyfuss. "Mitigating Medical Misinformation: A Whole-of-Society Approach to Countering Spam, Scams, and Hoaxes." Technology and Social Change Project, 2021. https://doi.org/10.37016/tasc-2021-03.

Douek, Evelyn. "Facebook's 'Oversight Board:' Move Fast with Stable Infrastructure and Humility." *North Carolina Journal of Law & Technology* 21, no. 1 (2019): 1–76.

Durham, Jennifer. "Murders of Journalists More than Double Worldwide." Committee to Protect Journalists, February 25, 2021. Available online: https://cpj.org/reports/2020/12/murders-journalists-more-than-doubled-killed/.

George, Cherian. "Disinformation: A Debate That Needs to Be Better Informed." Freedom From The Press (blog). October 7, 2019. Available online: https://blog.freedomfromthepress.info/2019/10/07/disinformation-2/.

Graves, Lucas. *Deciding What's True: The Rise of Political Fact-Checking in American Journalism*. Columbia University Press, 2016.

Internews. "TotooBa.Info." Internews. Available online: https://totooba.info/.

Klonick, Kate. "The Facebook Oversight Board: Creating an Independent Institution to Adjudicate Online Free Expression." *Yale Law Journal* 129, no. 8 (2020). Available online: https://yalelawjournal.org/feature/the-facebook-oversight-board.

Kusaka, Wataru. *Moral Politics in the Philippines: Inequality, Democracy, and the Urban Poor*. Ateneo de Manila University Press, 2019.

Kyaw, Nyi Nyi. "Facebooking in Myanmar: From Hate Speech to Fake News to Partisan Political Communication." Think Asia. ISEAS Yusof Ishak Institute, June 18, 2019.

Available online: https://mediawell.ssrc.org/citations/facebooking-in-myanmar-from-hate-speech-to-fake-news-to-partisan-political-communication/.

Lim, Gabrielle. "Securitize/Counter-Securitize." Data & Society, March 25, 2020. Available online: https://datasociety.net/library/securitize-counter-securitize/.

Marwick, Alice E. "I Have Something to Say About This Batshit Crazy Story. Basically: The Media Loves a Teen Technopanic. The PR Firm Easily Exploited a Hundred-Year Old Moral Panic over Kids and Tech. Here's Why. Https://T.co/wy0y3kg64w." Twitter, March 30, 2022. Available online: https://x.com/alicetiara/status/1509176562574413829.

Mogato, Manuel. "Philippines Complains Facebook Fact-Checkers Are Biased." Reuters. April 16, 2018. Available online: https://www.reuters.com/article/us-philippines-facebook-idUSKBN1HN1EN.

Morales, Neil Jerome. "Philippines Passes Law to Tackle Anonymous Social Media Abuse." Reuters, February 3, 2022. Available online: https://www.reuters.com/world/asia-pacific/philippines-passes-law-tackle-anonymous-social-media-abuse-2022-02-03/.

Nothias, Toussaint. "Access Granted: Facebook's Free Basics in Africa." *Media, Culture & Society* 42, no. 3 (2020): 329–48. https://doi.org/10.1177/0163443719890530.

One News PH. "'Movement Against Disinformation' Wages War Against Fake News." YouTube. One News PH, April 29, 2022. Available online: https://www.youtube.com/watch?v=AMUik3JKzbs.

Ong, Jonathan Corpus, and Jason Vincent A. Cabañes. *Architects of Networked Disinformation: Behind the Scenes of Troll Accounts and Fake News Production in the Philippines*. Newton Tech4Dev Network, February 2018. Available online: https://scholarworks.umass.edu/communication_faculty_pubs/74/.

Ong, Jonathan Corpus, and Jason Vincent A. Cabañes. "When Disinformation Studies Meets Production Studies: Social Identities and Moral Justifications in the Political Trolling Industry." *International Journal of Communication* 13 (2019): 5771–90.

Ong, Jonathan Corpus, Rossine Fallorina, Jose Mari Hall Lanuza, Ferdinand Sanchez, and Nicole Curato. "Parallel Public Spheres: Influence Operations in the 2022 Philippine Elections." Media Manipulation Casebook. Harvard Kennedy School Shorenstein Center for Media, Politics and Public Policy, October 28, 2022. Available online: https://mediamanipulation.org/research/unmasking-influence-operations-in-the-philippines.

Ong, Jonathan Corpus, Ross Tapsell, and Nicole Curato. Rep. *Tracking Digital Disinformation in the 2019 Philippine Midterm Election*. New Mandala, August 2019. Available online: https://www.newmandala.org/wp-content/uploads/2019/08/Digital-Disinformation-2019-Midterms.pdf.

Phillips, Whitney. "The Oxygen of Amplification." Data & Society Research Institute, May 22, 2018. Available online: https://datasociety.net/library/oxygen-of-amplification/.

Pierson, David. "Dictator's Son Uses TikTok to Lead in Philippine Election and Rewrite His Family's Past." *Los Angeles Times*, May 5, 2022. Available online: https://www.latimes.com/world-nation/story/2022-05-05/dictators-son-uses-tiktok-to-lead-philippines-election-and-rewrite-his-familys-past.

Pohjonen, Matti, and Sahana Udupa. "Extreme Speech Online: An Anthropological Critique of Hate Speech Debates." *International Journal of Communication* 11 (2017): 1173–91.

Quimpo, Nathan Gilbert. *Contested Democracy and the Left in the Philippines After Marcos*. Vol. 8. Yale University Southeast Asia Studies, 2008.

Ramos, Christia Marie. "Carpio Wants Libel Law Amended; Presume Malice If Libelous Remark Made by 'Fictitious User'." *Inquirer*, December 15, 2021. Available online:

https://newsinfo.inquirer.net/1528001/carpio-wants-libel-law-amended-presume-malice-if-libelous-remark-made-by-fictitious-user.

Rappler. "#Wedecide: Disinformation in the 2022 Philippine Elections." YouTube. Rappler, May 10, 2022. Available online: https://www.youtube.com/watch?v=mUI5Cmcjf18.

Ressa, Maria. "Secretary Antony J. Blinken with Maria Ressa on Digital Diplomacy and Human Rights Online—United States Department of State." Other. U.S. Department of State, June 7, 2022. Available online: https://2021-2025.state.gov/secretary-antony-j-blinken-with-maria-ressa-on-digital-diplomacy-and-human-rights-online/.

Ressa, Maria. "The Facebook Dilemma." Public Broadcasting Service, December 10, 2018. Available online: https://www.pbs.org/wgbh/frontline/interview/maria-ressa/.

Schaffer, Frederic. "Clean Elections and the Great Unwashed." Institute for Advanced Study, April 2005. Available online: https://www.ias.edu/sites/default/files/sss/papers/paper21.pdf.

Schiffrin, Anya, and Peter Cunliffe-Jones. "Online Misinformation: Policy Lessons from the Global South." Essay. In *Disinformation in the Global South*, edited by Herman Wasserman and Dani Madrid-Morales. Wiley Blackwell, 2022.

Su, Chiaoning, and Wei-Ping Li. "Excavating Truth: Assessing Citizen-Led Fact-Checking Practices in Taiwan." Essay. In *Resistance in the Era of Nationalism: (Per)Forming Identities in Taiwan and Hong Kong*, edited by Hsin-I Cheng and Hsin-I Sydney Yueh. Michigan State University Press, n.d.

Tablazon, Christian. "The Jejemon as Symptom and Slippage: Notes on Issues of Power and Identity in Media Literacy and (Mass) Communication." Essay. In *Filipino Generations in a Changing Landscape*, edited by Amaryllis Torres, Laura Samson, and Manuel Diaz. Philippine Social Science Council, 2015.

Talabong, Rambo. "Documentary: Ang Bagong Media Ng Bagong Lipunan." YouTube. Rappler, 2022. Available online: https://www.youtube.com/watch?v=F9NeAvuaUQo.

Tan, Lara. "Senators Urge Mocha Uson: Use Your Power Wisely." CNN Philippines, October 5, 2017.

Teehankee, Julio. "Duterte Set Stage for Second Coming of Marcoses." YouTube, 2022. Available online: https://www.youtube.com/watch?v=3FUGQGG10oY.

Terrazola, Vanne Elaine. "Sen. Marcos Questions FB Fact-Checkers in PH." *Manila Bulletin*, January 21, 2021. Available online: https://mb.com.ph/2021/01/21/sen-marcos-questions-fb-fact-checkers-in-ph/.

Tufekci, Zeynep. *Twitter and Tear Gas: The Power and Fragility of Networked Protest*. Yale University Press, 2021.

Tworek, Heidi. "Cambridge Analytica, Trump, and the New Old Fear of Manipulating the Masses." Nieman Lab, May 17, 2017. Available online: https://www.niemanlab.org/2017/05/cambridge-analytica-trump-and-the-new-old-fear-of-manipulating-the-masses/.

Tworek, Heidi. "Whose Democracy Counts When Global Social Media Rules Are Set?" Centre for International Governance Innovation, June 18, 2021. Available online: https://www.cigionline.org/articles/whose-democracy-counts-when-global-social-media-rules-are-set/.

Udupa, Sahana. "India Needs a Fresh Strategy to Tackle Online Extreme Speech." *Economic and Political Weekly*, September 11, 2019. Available online: https://subscription.epw.in/engage/article/election-2019-india-needs-fresh-strategy-to-tackle-new-digital-tools.

Ventura, Kat, and Jonathan Corpus Ong. "Catch Me If You Can." PumaPodcast, November 5, 2022. Available online: https://www.pumapodcast.com/podcasts/catch-me-if-you-can.

Wanless, Alicia. "The Philippines Is Democracy's Dystopian Future." Carnegie Endowment for International Peace, June 24, 2020. Available online: https://carnegieendowment.org/2020/06/24/philippines-is-democracy-s-dystopian-future-pub-82147.

PART TWO
DATA

5
UNDERSTANDING DATA THEATER THROUGH THE PERFORMATIVITY OF RATINGS IN PLATFORM WORK

Siddharth Peter de Souza

Introduction

In March 2021, a case of a conflict between a worker[1] and a customer from a popular food delivery company, Zomato, became feverish news on social media in India. The worker was accused of assaulting a customer and was subsequently arrested and suspended for it. However, a few days later, it emerged that the customer might have assaulted the worker first, and she, in turn, had issued a complaint against the worker. The company's founder stepped in, offering support to both parties, saying that the company wanted to get to the bottom of the case. In describing the worker, the founder said that the worker had made 5,000 deliveries so far and had a 4.75/5 rating on the platform after twenty-six months. The founder went on to say these are "facts not opinions or inferences."[2]

This statement attributes value to the existence of ratings to ascertain and provide testaments about the nature of relations between customers, workers, and platforms in platform work. Ratings consist of reviews through numerical responses (a one- to five-star rating) or descriptive responses by customers for the services they receive. Such ratings have become an important benchmark for the customer and the platform to evaluate the worker. It is a method to establish how certain tasks are carried out, how functions are executed, and how decisions are made.

In this chapter, I examine the life cycle of ratings as devices that are constructed, engaged with, and then acted upon. I also explore their ability to structure relations in the platform economy. Ratings are used as techniques to encode, define, and describe complex situations into standardized formats.[3] Through a process of quantification, ideas that may be conflicting, subjective, and value laden are provided with numeric values through which they are offered up as objective in nature.[4] Ratings provide the basis upon which things are classified, ordered, ranked, and even hierarchized, and the grounds upon which decisions are taken.[5] This takes place as ratings help create categories that make it possible to commodify, audit, and compare different experiences.[6] They also function as tools that become the basis for control, through which performance, behavior, and risk are ascertained.[7] Once developed, ratings are seen as uncontested facts and become an important criterion for what knowledge is seen as valuable and important.[8] As a result, knowledge generated through ratings acquires a life of its own without necessarily examining the methods through which these ratings have been arrived at and the fact that they have been layered with choices and decisions.[9]

Ratings create a series of effects based on their capacity to make certain interactions measurable. These effects also have material consequences that affect the livelihood of those who are evaluated by it.[10] This chapter examines the role of ratings in terms of workers' lives, including their capacities to build relationships with customers and the company, and in terms of their employment conditions.

The perception of ratings as incontrovertible facts has implications for those who are evaluated by them. To examine the impacts of ratings, I introduce the concept of "data theater," which manufactures a sense of data justice, enhances data violence, and embeds data silences. Subsequently, I define ratings and the idea of them as standards that are perceived to be objective and neutral. In the following section, I explore the impacts of ratings on workers through examining ratings as tools of evaluation, wherein they determine the nature of the behavior of workers. I also explore how ratings become tools of management and the basis for relations being formed in the platform economy, and, finally, as tools of marginalization for the dependencies they create in the lives of workers.

I further argue that reflecting on the role of ratings within platform work illustrates the ways in which a theater is emerging around data. This is the situation where the alleged objectivity of data is used as a basis to create justifications for decision-making that can have governance, knowledge, and material effects. I argue that data theater has three components. The first is that it manufactures a sense of fairness and justice by purporting to offer an objective and neutral basis for action. The second aspect is to borrow from the notion of data violence, where the life cycle of data has implications for how people can experience and access different spaces and services. The third is that, by virtue of data having a management function, it creates reactivity based on its narrative—experiences and contexts that are not part of its framing become silenced, and as a result, we have a phenomenon where only what is measured has value. I further develop this concept in the course of the paper by discussing the life cycle of ratings, the purposes with which they are introduced, and the aftereffects they have.

Ratings, Objectivity, and Evaluation

Ratings are a common way to define work and relationships in the platform economy. They are used as techniques to produce commensurability[11] and create categories and concepts that become the basis for conversations about a particular phenomenon.[12] Ratings provide ways to define ideas by creating benchmarks and standards in which complex social scenarios can be reduced to numerical functions.[13] By aggregating responses and comments into commensurable categories, ratings perform a governance function, whereby they become the basis for not just knowing phenomena but also for being able to control and act upon them.[14]

Ratings have been around for a long time. The impetus behind their development was to find ways to build trust between parties who were anonymous and strangers to each other in digital spaces. Many customers did not know the background of the provider, the quality of the services of products that were sold, and the general nature of the service. eBay pioneered seller feedback in the late 1990s to be able to address the anonymity of the parties who would enter transactions with one another.[15] Since then, several companies, including the likes of Uber, Airbnb, and Amazon, have used different versions of ratings as a means of building accountability between providers and consumers of products and services and ensuring that listings on their platforms are legitimate.

In the case of platform work, ratings are used as the means by which ideas of productivity, trustworthiness, and efficiency are constructed by platform companies. For instance, ride-sharing companies suggest that their drivers can keep their ratings up by maintaining good personal hygiene, being polite and courteous, accepting rides, and not canceling often.[16] These "suggestions" become the basis for evaluation and determine who is considered a good and professional driver because they are formats upon which standards are set, and codes of conduct are enforced. As a key aspect of the performance evaluation, and structuring relations between workers, customers, and the company, these ratings are seen as facts, suggesting a sense of neutrality to the numbers.[17] Since the ratings are seen as objective, platforms treat them as facts and are a means through which one can get a good idea of the performance of the workers.

In an interview to journalist Adi Renadi for *Rest of the World*, an Indonesian truck driver recounts his experiences of being a gig worker and talks about his perfect rating. He states, "My performance rating has never dropped below 5.0. I'm never late in picking up or delivering cargo. I've never canceled an order. The rating matters. If you go below 4.9, you don't get prioritized by the algorithm for orders."[18] In sharing his experiences, the truck driver elaborates upon the nature of permissible and impermissible behavior that is allowed by a platform. This includes ideas of punctuality, the importance of always being available, the nature of competition, and the notion that, without having a certain rating, there is a strong likelihood of harmful impacts.

Companies use ratings not only to encourage productivity, meet incentive targets, and create incentives but also to impose punishment.[19] Workers are also nudged into making sure they get the highest rating.[20] A recent study showed how Zomato used ratings to encourage competition between workers by sharing information and data wherein workers could find out how they fared compared to others within their location.[21]

These ratings assume the character of a social world[22] as they become a key consideration for determining how workers respond to ensure that they are well placed on the rating. Upon being evaluated by customers for their performance, ratings also become the basis upon which they continue to get future business, have work allocated to them, and the medium through which they are monitored and surveilled by companies.[23] Being monitored by these metrics produces a "rating game," where workers perform and react in certain ways and make decisions to maximize their ratings, accepting, thereby, not just a surveillance of their activities but also a standardization of accepted behavior and discipline through the ratings.[24]

As companies begin to regard ratings as neutral, the "inferences" and "opinions," which are the data that makes up the rating, are not questioned. There is less discussion about the metrics that influence ideas of professionalism or trustworthiness, as a result of which these notions assume a truth of their own because of the numerous times in which they are used and generated.[25]

There is a cognitive distance that numbers provide from the complexity of opinion, circumstance, and context.[26] This means that, rather than engaging with the reasons behind a particular rating, for instance, an unpleasant experience with a customer or feeling unwell on the job and having to cancel a request, the rating is treated like a technical device. The limitations of doing so are that what this maintains is a notion of ratings as technical tools, not as tools that are embedded in the social and political ways in which they are constructed.[27]

Ratings, Management, and Marginalization

Ratings affect the material lives of workers at multiple levels. They are the basis upon which workers can continue to work on the platform or risk being deplatformed. It is the basis upon which their profiles get greater attention. Those with higher ratings get more work. Ratings are also scrutinized in negotiations with platform companies. Very often, having one bad review attracts more attention from the company than having several good reviews on the platform.

An extract from an experience of a worker in Sri Lanka in a piece by journalist Dyna Rochmyaningsih, demonstrates the impacts that ratings have on reputation, future business, and decision-making possibilities.

> I can cancel up to two trips per day. If I cancel more than that, my rating goes down. The lower your rating is, the longer it takes for a request to show up. My rating is now 4.79 out of five. If you are rated lower than 4.5, you don't get many long-distance trips, which means you make less money. So, I have to be careful when I decline requests or cancel a trip.[28]

A product manager of a ride-hailing app provides a similar point of view from the perspective of the product company in a piece by researcher Pallavi Bansal stating:

> Apart from proximity, the algorithms keep in mind various parameters for assigning rides, such as past performance of the drivers, their loyalty towards the platform, feedback from the customers, if the drivers made enough money during the day etc. The weightage of these parameters keeps changing and hence cannot be revealed.[29]

These extracts demonstrate how ratings provide an understanding of otherwise contested notions of performance, loyalty, and quality by providing firm criteria of the ways in which workers are managed. This management system not only requires constant attention from the worker but also becomes the basis upon which freedom and opportunity to work within the sector is determined. The choice to take on a new task, for instance, is determined by the fear of a rating drop, as well as the concern of having the company question your loyalty. Therefore, oftentimes, even at the expense of personal well-being, workers are expected to constantly be on call.

In addition to being forms of evaluation and management, the ratings are also the basis of negotiation. They are the basis upon which workers need to engage and often interact with their customers and clients. Often, companies do not consider the ratings that the workers provide on the customer, and consequently, the workers are engaged in an unequal relationship with the customer, and their scope for complaint is almost negligible. In several platform companies, drivers or workers are deplatformed or deactivated from the system if their ratings are low. There is no scope for discussion, and in many instances, no termination notice. In these cases, the nature of the legal contract,[30] which is lopsided in favor of the company,[31] results in the marginalizing of workers who, once removed from the platform, find it hard to work independently due to price undercutting by platform companies.

The president of the Telangana Gig and Platform Worker Union in India, Shaik Salauddin, has argued how customers had the power to determine the nature of platform workers' lives because ratings carry punitive power. In a piece by Rohitha Naraharisetty he states, "I have to beg for each, and every rating and the customer demands extra services. If I say I can't do something, he says, 'Don't you want a rating?' He doesn't say tip, mind you; he is only talking about the ratings."[32]

Salauddin demonstrates how customers have begun not to use reviews as ways to offer objective or even truthful feedback but rather seek to exert power over workers. In this use of ratings and reviews, customers are taking on the roles of managers, where, through their reviews, they are able to discipline and determine the performance of workers.[33] Their reviews inform the ways in which companies act,[34] producing, thereby, an asymmetry in terms of the ways in which different stakeholders address each other.[35]

Ratings have become a self-referential system that companies, workers, and customers continue to adhere to because of their narrative power to influence different behaviors and functions.[36] There is a clear power differential between those who determine the terms upon which such ratings are developed and those who are evaluated by them.[37] For instance, in the making of ratings, how far would the conditions within which the worker is expected to complete a task be an issue, what are the ways in which the inequality between the customer and the worker are considered in mutual ratings, and, finally, while productivity is given prominence to ensure that workers complete as many trips as possible, how far is well-being accounted for?

The precarity of workers who are dependent on ratings in this way indicates the technocratic and managerial ways their work is evaluated. During the Diwali season in India, Amazon instituted a Delivery Premier League organized on the principles of the Indian Premier League, a popular cricket tournament. The idea of this feature was to encourage part-time workers to spend more time on the platform. The more time spent on the platform, and the more deliveries completed, resulted in "runs" (as in cricket) being collected. With a series of "guaranteed" prizes available, with further incentives to collect more runs, particularly during difficult times, for instance, during bad weather, workers were encouraged to put themselves in difficult situations to meet the incentives.[38]

In another case, an online grocery company in India named Blinkit (previously Grofers) offered to deliver products in less than ten minutes. When this marketing ploy was critiqued on social media for its lack of consideration of workers and their well-being, the founder justified the move by saying that it is disappointing that people are not celebrating the innovation of being able to offer more efficient services and instead are being cynical.[39] The connection between ratings, the incentive structure, and the marginalization it perpetuates is typified in the long working hours and occupational and health hazards that such work causes. The Indian Federation of App-Based Transport Workers (IFAT) and the International

Transport Workers' Federation (ITF), New Delhi office, which conducted over 2,200 surveys across six cities in India, found that drivers spent an average of sixteen to twenty hours per day in their cars, with less than six hours of sleep.[40] This resulted in assorted health issues, including neck pain, waist pain, constipation, liver issues, and backache, which were the five major health issues. Over 60.7 percent complained of back pain as a key concern from the work. Documenting the nature of ratings through the pain and suffering they have caused offers insights into the kinds of marginalization ratings produce. By focusing on pain, as researcher Laine Nooney argues, we are centering users, their bodies, and the ways in which they interact, rather than just the technology and the companies that provide these services.[41]

A Fairwork report in 2021 in Indonesia also demonstrated how the incentive structure and payment structure were such that only when workers worked over seventy hours and sometimes over a hundred hours would they be able to earn above the local and regional minimum income level.[42] With an emphasis on efficiency and scale, ratings support conditions to continuously reinvent how platform companies can enhance customer satisfaction, with the platforms designed to extract as much time as possible from the worker.[43] What ratings are doing, therefore, is creating systems, on account of being tools for evaluation, management, and marginalization that lead to a system of inclusion and exclusion that affects the capacity of workers to lead a dignified and flourishing life.

The capacity to engage with ratings and their methods is also further inhibited by the opacity with which ratings, which are seen as proprietary technologies, are developed. A lack of meaningful transparency in terms of how work is allocated, evaluated, and then paid further limits the capacity to be able to question and challenge conditions within platform work.[44]

Focusing on ratings is important because ratings build reactivity around them.[45] They impact not just the work that people are able to do but also their capacity to be able to organize, negotiate, and resist. This is already underway, where food delivery companies threaten to suspend workers from the app or cut commissions and payments when workers protest their payments and incentive structures.[46] In doing so, we are confronted with the fact that ratings also have the power of sanction, the power of punitive action, and the power of erasure.

Data Theater: Subverting Data Justice, Facilitating Data Violence, and Cementing Data Silence

Ratings, advanced as objective and neutral objects and tools, in fact, percolate and influence the very ways in which people are able to participate and engage in work. In this section, I reflect on the implications that ratings have for the life cycle of data in the platform economy by unpacking the notion of data theater. The notion of a theater is used here because of the ways in which data are used to project ideals that are meant to enhance agency, capacity, and freedoms of people, but rather end up creating only being a performance of these attributes. As a result, a theater offers opportunities to observe, to see, and to watch without there being real and material effects that come from it.[47]

There are three parts of a data theater. The first is the ways in which it, in actual effect, denies people the capacity to engage, interrogate, and negotiate with the data about them, thereby causing injustices. The second is facilitating violence by becoming a proxy gatekeeper to deny people the capacity to fully participate through affecting surveillance and control. The third is the ways in which it cements silences by valuing that which is measured and eliminating different considerations that are equally relevant.

At the first level, the standard argument is that ratings demonstrate fairness, transparency, and neutrality. However, as previous examples affirm, rather than ensuring justice, they manufacture an illusory sense of justice. To guarantee real justice would require engaging with the material effects of the ratings in such a data-driven economy. Data justice, as researcher Linnet Taylor advances is an approach that grounds questions of fairness, representation, and antidiscrimination in the analysis of the implications that data has on society.[48] It places an importance on the autonomy and capability of people to make choices to participate and act in a data-driven economy. In the case of ratings, there is a strong asymmetry between who is measuring and who is being measured, and hence, the agency of a platform worker to be able to take decisions is constantly controlled and surveilled. For instance, it was found that Uber drivers were often nudged to keep driving when they wanted to log off. This was done by mentioning to them that they were very close to driving targets, meeting competitor benchmarks, and achieving incentive targets, such that the decision to log off was often contrasted with rewards dangled before them.[49] These nudges cannot be seen as beneficial to drivers because they are also entangled with the threat of censure for not showing loyalty to the platform, canceling potential drives, and getting negative feedback from customers. Consequently, drivers are stripped of their ability to participate freely and are unable to make decisions based on their interest, but rather, based on the implications this will have for their future work.

In reflecting on her time as a Lyft driver, Sarah Mason discusses how the platform games you to engage with the ratings.

> Our rate of pay does not increase for being a highly rated driver. In fact, I was losing money trying to flatter customers with candy and keep my car scrupulously clean. And yet, I wanted to be a highly rated driver. And this is

> the thing that is so brilliant and awful about the gamification of Lyft and Uber: it preys on our desire to be of service, to be liked, to be good. On weeks that I am rated highly, I am more motivated to drive. On weeks that I am rated poorly, I am more motivated to drive. It works on me, even though I know better. To date, I have completed more than 2,200 rides.[50]

The ratings, thereby, also enhance data injustice because they deny workers the ability to control and determine the narratives of the data around them. They are not able to decide for what purposes the data about them is used, and the implications this may have. As a result, they have little control over the social relations that will result.[51]

The data injustice that emerges is also multifarious. It can be instrumental, meaning it can be gauged by the outcomes of the data, for instance, the lack of work, the lack of choice for particular rides, and the ways in which incentives are paid out. It can equally be procedural in terms of how the data is stored, processed, and handled and, thereby, in this case, also how the wealth of data has implications for the control that can be exercised over workers. It can also be distributive in nature, which determines how the allocation and sharing of resources has implications for how people are able to exercise their ownership and control over the data.[52]

Ratings can also produce data violence, particularly because they are portrayed as neutral and transparent. Data violence occurs where the collection of data has impacts not only in terms of bias and discrimination but also in terms of access to services.[53]

Ratings, while purported to be devices to increase incentives, efficiencies, and benefits for workers, are instead used as tools of oppression to monitor and control the lives of workers. Journalist Noam Scheiber describes how gamification and psychological manipulation are used by companies like Uber to keep their workers on the road. He argues that:

> In its messages to drivers, it included a graphic of an engine gauge with a needle that came tantalizingly close to, but was still short of, a dollar sign . . . At any moment, the app shows drivers how many trips they have taken in the current week, how much money they have made, how much time they have spent logged on and what their overall rating from passengers is. All of these metrics can stimulate the competitive juices that drive compulsive game-playing.[54]

As the example above shows, there is a clear attempt here to manipulate how workers make decisions while using the app. The design of these games to keep workers on the platform for well over what is healthy creates a danger because, as detailed previously, they are vulnerable as independent businesses. There are also real health consequences for these workers, who have no alternative but to stay on the platform due to a lack of social security benefits. The data violence of these platforms manifests because the ratings influence the ways in which workers can make choices, thereby limiting their agency; it can also have an impact by increasing the dependence that workers have on the platform by ensuring that the alternatives outside the platform are nonexistent; workers are also limited by the knowledge of the nature of work, for instance, on the length of the drive, and this limits their capacity to make an informed decision; and, finally, the fear of reputational consequences, which affect how subsequent work can be attained.[55]

At the heart of this is the fact that the control over the data and the ratings resides with the platform. An increasing number of voices have emerged that speak to the importance of having portability of ratings, because this will allow workers greater agency over their own ratings and evaluations. It will also mean they have more freedom to choose between different platforms.[56] While this will change the nature of power and control of the data, the unreliability and bias with ratings themselves, and the implications this causes on the life of the worker, remain.

This leads to the third aspect of the data theater—data silences, where companies only give value to what is measured with business implications. Data silences ask questions about what data is important to collect, what is important to share, and what can be ignored and made invisible, and in this sense, de-prioritized.[57] Data silences ask questions of ratings, including what their design motivations are, who they are aiming to evaluate, and what the implications of such ratings can be. Exploring data silences in thinking about ratings involves examining the power differentials that exist in the methods used in the lifecycle of data.

For instance, ratings have different implications for workers and customers, and as discussed before, customers have the power to determine the livelihoods of their drivers through becoming managers. In a piece in *Verge* by writer Josh Dzieza, Uber drivers spoke of this power asymmetry

> I went to go to work one day, got up, got dressed, headed out to the car, turned the app on, and it said you've been deactivated," said a Florida driver who guesses she was rated low for refusing to let people bring drinks in her car. "It's so horrible, have you ever been fired? You feel absolutely powerless. I'm trying to get Uber's attention, saying 'Wait don't fire me, I didn't do anything wrong, I'm following the rules, I won't let them bring alcohol in my car and you're firing me?' . . . "We're not just working for money," an Uber driver told me. "We're working for ratings, but ratings have no value. Ratings serve only to prevent you from getting fired. Only bad things can happen to you. We're scurrying like rats after these things with no value.[58]

These examples demonstrate the performativity that rankings encourage, where rather than being systems of objectivity and transparency as they are touted to be, they result in prioritizing of certain narratives over others, while rendering other narratives invisible. As a result, they create differences between who and what is being measured and why certain measurements have value over others.

Together, data injustice, data violence, and data silence emphasize the emergence of a data theater. This data theater is a technique that affords companies the capacity to hide behind numbers by arguing that these numbers have a foundation in fairness and objectivity. It perpetuates a license for platform companies to project that they have treated their workers fairly based on objective facts and systemic assessment, but it masquerades the way in which this theater marginalizes those being evaluated.

We need to pay attention to the theater around data to ensure that, rather than being swept up in the performance that data offers, we remain concerned with the aftereffects and implications that it has for people's lives. Focusing on the injustices, silences, and violence around data offers a way of centering the ways in which data can affect people's capacity to negotiate, dialogue, and oppose data that harms them, all of which are central to ensure that we are alive to the fact that data cannot be differentiated from the bodies, pains, and interactions that it affects.

Conclusion

This chapter examined how ratings have become an important form of communication and managing relations in platform work. It traced how ratings can be defined, the ways in which they are used, and the different implications they have had for the everyday lives of workers. Subsequently, drawing from an analysis of ratings and their performativity, the chapter introduced the idea of a data theater by examining different aspects of this phenomenon, including the injustices it perpetuates, the violence it manifests, and the silences it embeds through the ways in which it is used. The chapter argues that ratings need to be evaluated, not as tools of objective analysis but as tools that have far-reaching consequences because they diminish the rights of workers to participate, limit the ability of workers to organize and negotiate with platforms, and consign them to further precarity by not accounting for their material lives.

It is imperative that ratings are examined as contested tools that provide a limited and flawed understanding of complex realities, and further that we engage with the reactivities that ratings create to understand the lifeworld that they engineer. Finally, in thinking about data theater, as already advanced, this chapter has sought to advance a concept that provides a framework to examine where data becomes performance and when its use causes injustice, violence, and silence.

Notes

1 I will use worker instead of delivery agent/partner across this chapter.

2 *Indian Express*, "'Providing Support to Both Parties, Delivery Executive Had Highest Rating': Zomato on Alleged Attack in Bengaluru," | India News, *The Indian Express*, 2021, available online: https://indianexpress.com/article/india/providing-support-to-both-parties-zomato-on-alleged-attack-in-bengaluru-7224987/.

3 Steffen Mau, *The Metric Society: On the Quantification of the Social* (Polity Press, 2019).

4 Ibid.

5 Kevin Davis et al., *Governance by Indicators: Global Power Through Classification and Rankings* (Oxford University Press, 2012).

6 Michael Power, *The Audit Explosion* (Oxford University Press, 1999).

7 Dan Bouk, *How Our Days Became Numbered: Risk and the Rise of the Statistical Individual* (University of Chicago Press, 2018).

8 Ian Hacking, ed., "The Argument," in *The Taming of Chance*, Ideas in Context (Cambridge University Press, 1990), 1–10, https://doi.org/10.1017/CBO9780511819766.001.

9 Alain Desrosières, "Introduction: Arguing from Social Facts," in *The Politics of Large Numbers: A History of Statistical Reasoning* (Harvard University Press, 1998).

10 Timothy Graham and Aleesha Rodriguez, "The Sociomateriality of Rating and Ranking Devices on Social Media: A Case Study of Reddit's Voting Practices," *Social Media + Society* 7, no. 3 (2021): 20563051211047668, https://doi.org/10.1177/20563051211047667.

11 Wendy Nelson Espeland and Mitchell L. Stevens, "Commensuration as a Social Process," *Annual Review of Sociology* 24 (1998): 313–43, https://doi.org/10.1146/annurev.soc.24.1.313.

12 Sally Engle Merry, "Measuring the World: Indicators, Human Rights, and Global Governance," *Current Anthropology* 52, no. S3 (2011): S83–95, https://doi.org/10.1086/657241.

13 Kevin E. Davis et al., "Indicators as a Technology of Global Governance," *Law & Society Review* 46, no. 1 (2012): 71–104, https://doi.org/10.1111/j.1540-5893.2012.00473.x.

14 Bal Sokhi-Bulley, "Governing (Through) Rights: Statistics as Technologies of Governmentality," *Social & Legal Studies* 20, no. 2 (2011): 139–55, https://doi.org/10.1177/0964663910391520.

15 "How Seller Feedback Helped Build eBay, Uber and AirBnB," BBC News, September 17, 2017, sec. Business, available online: https://www.bbc.com/news/business-41188461.

16 Ola, "Improve Your Driver Rating," Ola Cabs, June 19, 2019, available online: https://ola.co.nz/blog/tips-to-improve-your-driver-rating/; Uber, "How the Uber Rating System Works," Uber Blog, November 22, 2018, available online: https://www.uber.com/blog/how-the-uber-rating-system-works/.

17 Theodore M. Porter, "Introduction: Cultures of Objectivity," in *Trust in Numbers: The Pursuit of Objectivity in Science and Public Life* (Princeton University Press, 1995).

18 Adi Renaldi, "5.0: What It's like to Be a Last-Mile Delivery Driver in Indonesia," Rest of World (blog), September 21, 2021, available online: https://restofworld.org/2021/global-gig-workers-truck-driver-indonesia/.

19 Dyna Rochmyaningsih, "On Gojek's Gamified Platform, the Rules Change, and the Drivers Lose," Rest of World (blog), May 18, 2021, available online: https://restofworld.org/2021/only-gojek-knows-this-mystery/.

20 Shruti Gupta and Sarayu Natarajan, "Futures of Workers" (Aapti Institute, 2020), available online: https://uploads.strikinglycdn.com/files/8689ec98-6ddd-48f3-a5f2-1eae96ad8e28/Future%20of%20Workers_Final_High%20Resolution.pdf.

21 Soumyarendra Barik, "When Algorithms Dictate Your Work: Life as a Food Delivery 'Partner,'" Entrackr (blog), August 20, 2021, available online: https://entrackr.com/2021/08/zomato-when-algorithms-dictate-your-work-life-as-a-food-delivery-partner/.

22 Wendy Nelson Espeland and Michael Sauder, "Rankings and Reactivity: How Public Measures Recreate Social Worlds," *American Journal of Sociology* 113, no. 1 (2007): 1–40, https://doi.org/10.1086/517897.

23 Gupta and Natarajan, "Futures of Workers."

24 Ngai Keung Chan, "The Rating Game: The Discipline of Uber's User-Generated Ratings," *Surveillance & Society* 17, no. 1–2 (2019): 183–90, https://doi.org/10.24908/ss.v17i1/2.12911.

25 Siddharth Peter de Souza, *Designing Indicators for a Plural Legal World*, vol. 1 (Cambridge University Press, 2022), available online: https://www.cambridge.org/core/books/designing-indicators-for-a-plural-legal-world/AA30C6193F42159FB0654A14D9670AAC.

26 Sally Engle Merry, *The Seductions of Quantification: Measuring Human Rights, Gender Violence, and Sex Trafficking* (University of Chicago Press, 2016).

27 Rochmyaningsih, "On Gojek's Gamified Platform, the Rules Change, and the Drivers Lose"; AnnJanette Rosga and Margaret L. Satterthwaite, "The Trust in Indicators: Measuring Human Rights," *Berkeley Journal of International Law* 27 (2009): 253.

28 Zinara Rathnayake, "25%: What It's Like Being a Woman Tuk-Tuk Driver in Sri Lanka," Rest of World (blog), September 21, 2021, available online: https://restofworld.org/2021/global-gig-workers-tuktuk-driver-srilanka/.

29 Pallavi Bansal, "Platform Drivers: From Algorithmizing Humans to Humanizing Algorithms," FemLab.Co (blog), October 2, 2020, available online: https://femlab.co/2020/10/02/platform-drivers-from-algorithmizing-humans-to-humanizing-algorithms/.

30 Siddharth de Souza, "Proactive Contracting for Platform Work: Making the Design of Terms and Conditions More Participatory," FemLab.Co (blog), October 23, 2020, available online: https://femlab.co/2020/10/23/proactive-contracting-for-platform-work-making-the-design-of-terms-and-conditions-more-participatory/.

31 Fairwork, "Principles," available online: https://fair.work/en/fw/principles/.

32 Rohitha Naraharisetty, "In the Gig Economy, Customers Are Complicit in Labor Exploitation," The Swaddle (blog), August 20, 2021, available online: https://theswaddle.com/swiggy-zomato-labor-exploitation/.

33 Joshua Sperber, *Customer Management in the Internet Age*, 2019, available online: https://academicworks.cuny.edu/cgi/viewcontent.cgi?article=2776&context=gc_etds.

34 Nora Cour, "Platform Capitalists Are Turning Customers into Managers in Disguise," 2021, available online: https://jacobinmag.com/2021/09/platform-capitalists-gig-economy-employee-ratings-reviews-yelp-doordash-uber-lyft-management-discipline-prosumption.

35 Max Kim, "Delivery Apps' Obsession with Star Ratings Is Ruining Lives," Rest of World (blog), March 8, 2022, available online: https://restofworld.org/2022/south-korea-star-ratings-trouble/.

36 Wendy Espeland, "Narrating Numbers," in *The World of Indicators: The Making of Governmental Knowledge through Quantification*, ed. Richard Rottenburg et al. (Cambridge University Press, 2015), https://doi.org/10.1017/CBO9781316091265.003.

37 Alex Rosenblat and Luke Stark, "Algorithmic Labor and Information Asymmetries: A Case Study of Uber's Drivers," SSRN Scholarly Paper (Social Science Research Network, July 30, 2016), https://doi.org/10.2139/ssrn.2686227.

38 Nilesh Christopher, "Amazon's 'Delivery Premier League' Gamifies Gig Work in India," Rest of World (blog), October 25, 2021, available online: https://restofworld.org/2021/amazons-delivery-premier-league-gamifies-gig-work-in-india/.

39 Livemint, "Grofers Founder Criticised for 10-Minute Grocery Delivery. His Reply," *mint*, August 28, 2021, available online: https://www.livemint.com/companies/news/grofers-founder-criticised-for-10-minute-grocery-delivery-his-reply-11630160621963.html.

40 IFAT and ITF, "Protecting Workers in the Digital Platform Economy: Investigating Ola and Uber Drivers' Occupational Health and Safety" (The Centre for Internet and Society, 2020), available online: https://cis-india.org/raw/ifat-itf-protecting-workers-in-digital-platform-economy-ola-uber-occupational-health-safety.

41 Laine Nooney, "How the Personal Computer Broke the Human Body," Vice (blog), May 12, 2021, available online: https://www.vice.com/en/article/y3dda7/how-the-personal-computer-broke-the-human-body.

42 Fairwork, "Fairwork Indonesia Ratings 2021: Labour Standards in the Gig Economy," 2021, available online: https://fair.work/en/fw/publications/fairwork-indonesia-ratings-2021-labour-standards-in-the-gig-economy/.

43 Kaushal Shroff, *Inside the Winter of Discontent for India's Gig Workers*, 2021, available online: https://thewire.in/labour/india-gig-workers-protests-pil.

44 Cansu Safak and James Farrar, "Managed by Bots: Data Driven Exploitation in the Gig Economy," available online: https://www.workerinfoexchange.org/wie-report-managed-by-bots.

45 Espeland and Sauder, "Rankings and Reactivity."

46 "Hyderabad: Threats, Cash Lures in Swiggy's Playbook to 'Break Strike,'" NewsClick, September 26, 2020, available online: https://www.newsclick.in/Hyderabad-Threats-Cash-Lures-Swiggy-Playbook-Break-Strike.

47 See generally Sean McDonald, "Technology Theatre," Centre for International Governance Innovation (blog), July 13, 2020, available online: https://www

.cigionline.org/articles/technology-theatre/; Stefania Milan et al., "Promises Made to Be Broken: Performance and Performativity in Digital Vaccine and Immunity Certification," *European Journal of Risk Regulation* 12, no. 2 (2021): 382–92, https://doi.org/10.1017/err.2021.26.

48 Linnet Taylor, "What Is Data Justice? The Case for Connecting Digital Rights and Freedoms Globally," *Big Data & Society* 4, no. 2 (2017): 1–14, https://doi.org/10.1177/2053951717736335.

49 Noam Scheiber, "How Uber Uses Psychological Tricks to Push Its Drivers' Buttons," *The New York Times*, April 2, 2017, sec. Technology, available online: https://www.nytimes.com/interactive/2017/04/02/technology/uber-drivers-psychological-tricks.html.

50 Sarah Mason, "High Score, Low Pay: Why the Gig Economy Loves Gamification," *The Guardian*, November 20, 2018, sec. Business, available online: https://www.theguardian.com/business/2018/nov/20/high-score-low-pay-gamification-lyft-uber-drivers-ride-hailing-gig-economy.

51 Lina Dencik et al., "Exploring Data Justice: Conceptions, Applications and Directions," *Information, Communication & Society* 22, no. 7 (2019): 873–81, https://doi.org/10.1080/1369118X.2019.1606268.

52 Richard Heeks and Jaco Renken, "Data Justice for Development: What Would It Mean?," *Information Development* 34, no. 1 (2018): 90–102, https://doi.org/10.1177/0266666916678282; Taylor, "What Is Data Justice?"

53 Anna Lauren Hoffmann, "Data Violence and How Bad Engineering Choices Can Damage Society," Medium (blog), April 30, 2018, available online: https://medium.com/s/story/data-violence-and-how-bad-engineering-choices-can-damage-society-39e44150e1d4.

54 Scheiber, "How Uber Uses Psychological Tricks to Push Its Drivers' Buttons."

55 Sangeet Paul Choudary, "Digital Manipulation: How Platforms Like Uber and Deliveroo Exploit Workers," Medium (blog), June 11, 2018, available online: https://medium.com/@sanguit/digital-manipulation-and-the-future-of-work-how-platforms-like-uber-and-deliveroo-exploit-workers-bc80339fc271.

56 Gavin Kelly, "Give Me My Reputation Back," Medium, October 12, 2017, available online: https://gavinkellyblog.com/give-me-my-reputation-back-c1fa5daca78c.

57 Siddharth Peter de Souza, "Invisibilising Migrant Distress in Times of COVID-19," Global Data Justice, 2020, available online: http://globaldatajustice.org/covid-19/data-silences-invisibility.

58 Josh Dzieza, "The Rating Game: How Uber and Its Peers Turned Us into Horrible Bosses," *The Verge*, October 28, 2015, available online: https://www.theverge.com/2015/10/28/9625968/rating-system-on-demand-economy-uber-olive-garden.

Bibliography

Bansal, Pallavi. "Platform Drivers: From Algorithmizing Humans to Humanizing Algorithms." FemLab.Co (blog), October 2, 2020. Available online: https://femlab.co/2020/10/02/platform-drivers-from-algorithmizing-humans-to-humanizing-algorithms/.

Barik, Soumyarendra. "When Algorithms Dictate Your Work: Life as a Food Delivery 'Partner.'" Entrackr (blog), August 20, 2021. Available online: https://entrackr.com/2021/08/zomato-when-algorithms-dictate-your-work-life-as-a-food-delivery-partner/.

BBC News. "How Seller Feedback Helped Build EBay, Uber and AirBnB," September 17, 2017, sec. Business. Available online: https://www.bbc.com/news/business-41188461.

Bouk, Dan. *How Our Days Became Numbered: Risk and the Rise of the Statistical Individual*. University of Chicago Press, 2018.

Chan, Ngai Keung. "The Rating Game: The Discipline of Uber's User-Generated Ratings." *Surveillance & Society* 17, no. 1–2 (2019): 183–90. https://doi.org/10.24908/ss.v17i1/2.12911.

Choudary, Sangeet Paul. "Digital Manipulation: How Platforms Like Uber and Deliveroo Exploit Workers." Medium (blog), June 11, 2018. Available online: https://medium.com/@sanguit/digital-manipulation-and-the-future-of-work-how-platforms-like-uber-and-deliveroo-exploit-workers-bc80339fc271.

Christopher, Nilesh. "Amazon's 'Delivery Premier League' Gamifies Gig Work in India." Rest of World (blog), October 25, 2021. Available online: https://restofworld.org/2021/amazons-delivery-premier-league-gamifies-gig-work-in-india/.

Cour, Nora. "Platform Capitalists Are Turning Customers into Managers in Disguise." 2021. Available online: https://jacobinmag.com/2021/09/platform-capitalists-gig-economy-employee-ratings-reviews-yelp-doordash-uber-lyft-management-discipline-prosumption.

Davis, Kevin, Angelina Fisher, Benedict Kingsbury, and Sally Engle Merry. *Governance by Indicators: Global Power Through Classification and Rankings*. Oxford University Press, 2012.

Davis, Kevin E., Benedict Kingsbury, and Sally Engle Merry. "Indicators as a Technology of Global Governance." *Law & Society Review* 46, no. 1 (2012): 71–104. https://doi.org/10.1111/j.1540-5893.2012.00473.x.

Dencik, Lina, Arne Hintz, Joanna Redden, and Emiliano Treré. "Exploring Data Justice: Conceptions, Applications and Directions." *Information, Communication & Society* 22, no. 7 (2019): 873–81. https://doi.org/10.1080/1369118X.2019.1606268.

de Souza, Siddharth Peter. "Invisibilising Migrant Distress in Times of COVID-19." Global Data Justice, 2020. Available online: http://globaldatajustice.org/covid-19/data-silences-invisibility.

Desrosières, Alain. "Introduction: Arguing from Social Facts." In *The Politics of Large Numbers: A History of Statistical Reasoning*, 1–15. Harvard University Press, 1998.

Dzieza, Josh. "The Rating Game: How Uber and Its Peers Turned Us into Horrible Bosses." *The Verge*, October 28, 2015. Available online: https://www.theverge.com/2015/10/28/9625968/rating-system-on-demand-economy-uber-olive-garden.

Espeland, Wendy. "Narrating Numbers." In *The World of Indicators: The Making of Governmental Knowledge Through Quantification*, edited by Richard Rottenburg, Sally Engle Merry, Sung-Joon Park, and Johanna Mugle. Cambridge University Press, 2015. https://doi.org/10.1017/CBO9781316091265.003.

Espeland, Wendy Nelson, and Michael Sauder. "Rankings and Reactivity: How Public Measures Recreate Social Worlds." *American Journal of Sociology* 113, no. 1 (2007): 1–40. https://doi.org/10.1086/517897.

Espeland, Wendy Nelson, and Mitchell L. Stevens. "Commensuration as a Social Process." *Annual Review of Sociology* 24 (1998): 313–43. https://doi.org/10.1146/annurev.soc.24.1.313.

Fairwork. "Fairwork Indonesia Ratings 2021: Labour Standards in the Gig Economy." 2021. Available online: https://fair.work/en/fw/publications/fairwork-indonesia-ratings-2021-labour-standards-in-the-gig-economy/.

Fairwork. "Principles." Available online: https://fair.work/en/fw/principles/.

Graham, Timothy, and Aleesha Rodriguez. "The Sociomateriality of Rating and Ranking Devices on Social Media: A Case Study of Reddit's Voting Practices." *Social Media + Society* 7, no. 3 (2021): 20563051211047668. https://doi.org/10.1177/20563051211047667.

Gupta, Shruti, and Sarayu Natarajan. "Futures of Workers." Aapti Institute, 2020. Available online: https://uploads.strikinglycdn.com/files/8689ec98-6ddd-48f3-a5f2-1eae96ad8e28/Future%20of%20Workers_Final_High%20Resolution.pdf.

Hacking, Ian, ed. "The Argument." In *The Taming of Chance*, 1–10. Ideas in Context. Cambridge University Press, 1990. https://doi.org/10.1017/CBO9780511819766.001.

Heeks, Richard, and Jaco Renken. "Data Justice for Development: What Would It Mean?" *Information Development* 34, no. 1 (2018): 90–102. https://doi.org/10.1177/0266666916678282.

Hoffmann, Anna Lauren. "Data Violence and How Bad Engineering Choices Can Damage Society." Medium (blog), April 30, 2018. Available online: https://medium.com/s/story/data-violence-and-how-bad-engineering-choices-can-damage-society-39e44150e1d4.

IFAT and ITF. "Protecting Workers in the Digital Platform Economy: Investigating Ola and Uber Drivers' Occupational Health and Safety." The Centre for Internet and Society, 2020. Available online: https://cis-india.org/raw/ifat-itf-protecting-workers-in-digital-platform-economy-ola-uber-occupational-health-safety.

Indian Express. "'Providing Support to Both Parties, Delivery Executive Had Highest Rating': Zomato on Alleged Attack in Bengaluru." | India News, *The Indian Express*, 2021. Available online: https://indianexpress.com/article/india/providing-support-to-both-parties-zomato-on-alleged-attack-in-bengaluru-7224987/.

Kelly, Gavin. "Give Me My Reputation Back." Medium, October 12, 2017. Available online: https://gavinkellyblog.com/give-me-my-reputation-back-c1fa5daca78c.

Kim, Max. "Delivery Apps' Obsession with Star Ratings Is Ruining Lives." Rest of World (blog), March 8, 2022. Available online: https://restofworld.org/2022/south-korea-star-ratings-trouble/.

Livemint. "Grofers Founder Criticised for 10-Minute Grocery Delivery. His Reply." mint, August 28, 2021. Available online: https://www.livemint.com/companies/news/grofers-founder-criticised-for-10-minute-grocery-delivery-his-reply-11630160621963.html.

Mason, Sarah. "High Score, Low Pay: Why the Gig Economy Loves Gamification." *The Guardian*, November 20, 2018, sec. Business. Available online: https://www.theguardian.com/business/2018/nov/20/high-score-low-pay-gamification-lyft-uber-drivers-ride-hailing-gig-economy.

Mau, Steffen. *The Metric Society: On the Quantification of the Social*. Polity Press, 2019.

McDonald, Sean. "Technology Theatre." Centre for International Governance Innovation (blog), July 13, 2020. Available online: https://www.cigionline.org/articles/technology-theatre/.

Merry, Sally Engle. "Measuring the World: Indicators, Human Rights, and Global Governance." *Current Anthropology* 52, no. S3 (2011): S83–95. https://doi.org/10.1086/657241.

Merry, Sally Engle. *The Seductions of Quantification: Measuring Human Rights, Gender Violence, and Sex Trafficking*. University of Chicago Press, 2016.

Milan, Stefania, Michael Veale, Linnet Taylor, and Seda Gürses. "Promises Made to Be Broken: Performance and Performativity in Digital Vaccine and Immunity Certification." *European Journal of Risk Regulation* 12, no. 2 (2021): 382–92. https://doi.org/10.1017/err.2021.26.

Naraharisetty, Rohitha. "In the Gig Economy, Customers Are Complicit in Labor Exploitation." The Swaddle (blog), August 20, 2021. Available online: https://theswaddle.com/swiggy-zomato-labor-exploitation/.

NewsClick. "Hyderabad: Threats, Cash Lures in Swiggy's Playbook to 'Break Strike.'" September 26, 2020. Available online: https://www.newsclick.in/Hyderabad-Threats-Cash-Lures-Swiggy-Playbook-Break-Strike.

Nooney, Laine. "How the Personal Computer Broke the Human Body." Vice (blog), May 12, 2021. Available online: https://www.vice.com/en/article/y3dda7/how-the-personal-computer-broke-the-human-body.

Ola. "Improve Your Driver Rating." Ola Cabs, June 19, 2019. Available online: https://ola.co.nz/blog/tips-to-improve-your-driver-rating/.

Porter, Theodore M. "Introduction: Cultures of Objectivity." In *Trust in Numbers: The Pursuit of Objectivity in Science and Public Life*, 3–8. Princeton University Press, 1995.

Power, Michael. *The Audit Explosion*. Oxford University Press, 1999.

Rathnayake, Zinara. "25%: What It's Like Being a Woman Tuk-Tuk Driver in Sri Lanka." Rest of World (blog), September 21, 2021. Available online: https://restofworld.org/2021/global-gig-workers-tuktuk-driver-srilanka/.

Renaldi, Adi. "5.0: What It's Like to Be a Last-Mile Delivery Driver in Indonesia." Rest of World (blog), September 21, 2021. Available online: https://restofworld.org/2021/global-gig-workers-truck-driver-indonesia/.

Rochmyaningsih, Dyna. "On Gojek's Gamified Platform, the Rules Change, and the Drivers Lose." Rest of World (blog), May 18, 2021. Available online: https://restofworld.org/2021/only-gojek-knows-this-mystery/.

Rosenblat, Alex, and Luke Stark. "Algorithmic Labor and Information Asymmetries: A Case Study of Uber's Drivers." SSRN Scholarly Paper. Social Science Research Network, July 30, 2016. https://doi.org/10.2139/ssrn.2686227.

Rosga, AnnJanette, and Margaret L. Satterthwaite. "The Trust in Indicators: Measuring Human Rights." *Berkeley Journal of International Law* 27 (2009): 253.

Safak, Cansu, and James Farrar. "Managed by Bots: Data Driven Exploitation in the Gig Economy." Available online: https://www.workerinfoexchange.org/wie-report-managed-by-bots.

Scheiber, Noam. "How Uber Uses Psychological Tricks to Push Its Drivers' Buttons." *The New York Times*, April 2, 2017, sec. Technology. Available online: https://www.nytimes.com/interactive/2017/04/02/technology/uber-drivers-psychological-tricks.html.

Shroff, Kaushal. "Inside the Winter of Discontent for India's Gig Workers." The Wire, 2021. Available online: https://thewire.in/labour/india-gig-workers-protests-pil.

Sokhi-Bulley, Bal. "Governing (Through) Rights: Statistics as Technologies of Governmentality." *Social & Legal Studies* 20, no. 2 (2011): 139–55. https://doi.org/10.1177/0964663910391520.

Souza, Siddharth de. "Proactive Contracting for Platform Work: Making the Design of Terms and Conditions More Participatory." FemLab.Co (blog), October 23, 2020. Available online: https://femlab.co/2020/10/23/proactive-contracting-for-platform-work-making-the-design-of-terms-and-conditions-more-participatory/.

Souza, Siddharth Peter de. *Designing Indicators for a Plural Legal World*. Vol. 1. Cambridge University Press, 2022. Available online: https://www.cambridge.org/core/books/designing-indicators-for-a-plural-legal-world/AA30C6103F42150FB0654A14D9670AAC.

Sperber, Joshua. *Customer Management in the Internet Age*, 2019. Available online: https://academicworks.cuny.edu/cgi/viewcontent.cgi?article=2776&context=gc_etds.

Taylor, Linnet. "What Is Data Justice? The Case for Connecting Digital Rights and Freedoms Globally." *Big Data & Society* 4, no. 2 (2017): 1–14. https://doi.org/10.1177/2053951717736335.

Uber. "How the Uber Rating System Works." Uber Blog, November 22, 2018. Available online: https://www.uber.com/blog/how-the-uber-rating-system-works/.

6
DATA ARCHITECTURE OF THE EUROPEAN SMART BORDER AND ITS DISCONTENT

Amin Parsa

Introduction

In a poem titled *Jawaz al-safar* (passport), the renowned Palestinian poet Mahmoud Darwish points to a contradiction that resides at the heart of the modern states' attempt to control human mobility through recording, surveilling, and leveraging personal identification data. He writes:

> They did not recognize me in the shadows/ That suck away my color in this Passport/ . . . / They did not recognize me,/ Ah . . . Don't leave/ The palm of my hand without the sun/ Because the trees recognize me/ Don't leave me pale like the moon!/ All the birds that followed my palm/ To the door of the distant airport/ All the wheatfields/ All the prisons/ All the white tombstones/ All the barbed Boundaries/ All the waving handkerchiefs/ All the eyes were with me,/ But they dropped them from my passport/ Stripped of my name and identity?/ On soil I nourished with my own hands?/ . . . / Oh, gentlemen,/ Prophets,/ Don't ask the trees for their names/ Don't ask the valleys who their mother is/ From my forehead bursts the sward of light/ And from my hand springs the water of the river/ All the hearts of the people are my identity/ So take away my passport!

I understand this poem to be pointing out that any attempt to capture personal identities is destined to isolate the said identity from the complex social context that gives it multiple, complex meanings in the first place. Such attempts inevitably produce an incomplete, eschewed, and inaccurate image of what they try to identify.

Jawaz al-safar, like most of Darwish's poems, is a reflection on the specific perils faced by Palestinian refugees. Yet, as will be shown later in this chapter, the question of identity, its constant evolution, and its in-capturability is central to his larger critique of powers that subjugate refugees all across the world. In this chapter, I aim to bring this point, made so poetically by Darwish, into a critique of the European personal data architecture of smart borders, all the while not losing sight of the human aspect of cross-border travel, which all too often hides behind dry, technical language.

Traveling across international borders is a data-intensive practice. To receive a passport and a travel visa today entails enrollment in comprehensive biometric data collection processes, in which different authorities at every port of entry register, measure, describe, photograph, authenticate, record, and verify a person. For some, notably citizens of the Global South, these processes are more intrusive than for others. Traveling irregularly across international borders is designed to be an even more data-intensive process. The term *undocumented* suggests that people who travel across borders without valid travel documents are subjected to less scrutiny. Yet, in reality, they are subjected to intense and unregulated data collection operations at every stage of their movement. States systematically document, track, trace, assess, and analyze people on the move and, if arrested, interview and biometrically enroll them to produce a biometrically verifiable identity.

This chapter specifically looks at the context of the European border control practices, exploring the central role of personal identity data and its interoperation in the European smart border architecture. The chapter first introduces European smart border architecture while critically investigating the origin and logic of the smart border back to the US war on terror, a turning point in the deployment of digital personal data technologies for large-scale surveillance. It then highlights two significant and inherent flaws in this technological apparatus of border control. The chapter argues that as technologies of personal data processing found their way into the context of migration control, situational awareness emerged as a strategic necessity for exploiting the technological promise of efficiency. Yet embedded in the desire for situational awareness is an expansionist logic of bulk data collection, which inevitably amplifies rights violations against those crossing borders.

Scholarship on migration and technology has already engaged with different forms of violence that smart border technologies impose on people on the move. In practice, "digital gatekeeping,"[1] through machine-acquired situational awareness, leads to institutionalization of a proactive prohibitory impetus within the European border control operation.[2] Proactive border controlling, in turn, goes hand in hand with a desire to control people's movement beyond the actual European borders—specifically under the guise of early and efficient risk identification and increased reaction capabilities.[3] A long-term consequence of proactive border control is the replacement of legal procedures with that of risk management logic, where risk is no longer a matter to be avoided but a logic of governance in itself.[4] A more immediate consequence of such proactive and preemptory intervention is the scaling up of what migration scholarship refers to as *externalization*. Externalization refers to the increasing outsourcing of oppressive and policing operations, as well as the dumping of any international and human rights responsibilities that may arise from border rejections and mistreatments upon partnering third countries, such as Libya, Turkey, and Rwanda, which carry out border policing on behalf of the European states.[5] Furthermore, proactive intervention amounts to an effective expansion of the geographical area of influence of the European Union (EU) migratory apparatus and laws, which is, in effect, a rearticulation, if not the expansion, of European borders and, with it, a severe undermining of the international legal structure upon which international refugee law obligations are built.[6]

More specifically, bulk data governance of borders has been criticized for violating the privacy rights of the people on the move. For instance, Cristina Blasi Casagran, assistant professor in law, points out that the turn to interoperability of personal data of travelers in Europe violates basic requirements of the EU's own General Data Protection Regulation (GDPR). She argues that the current interoperability of personal information databases violates the requirements of fairness, transparency, limited purpose, and proportionality of Article 5 of the GDPR by sharing the personal data of travelers with numerous authorities across various countries, with different purposes and mandates.[7] Concerns over privacy rights and breaches of other principles of international law, such as *the non-refoulement principle*, have also been expressed by the EU Fundamental Rights Agency.[8] Yet, most notably, data governance of border crossing exacerbates the racial logic of mobility control. The racial and colonial pedigree of personal data technologies and their use as a means of mobility limitation, the systematic misreading, flagging, and mismatching of racialized bodies by these technologies, the routinization of technological data extraction *from* and technological experimentation *upon* racialized travelers, as well as the automation of intolerance and prejudice are among the reasons that Tendayi Achiume, the UN Special Rapporteur on contemporary forms of racism, has warned against the use of digital border technologies.[9]

Acknowledging these rich and diverse critiques, this chapter questions the basic assumption underlying the smart border project altogether, namely, the "knowability" of travelers' identities. I argue that predicating the technological control of borders upon verification of personal identity is essentially a flawed practice. Personal identities are not fixed but contested and negotiable. In fact, the contestability of identities is most often the very reason people flee from their homelands in search of protection. Under such conditions, then, to build a system of border control upon the idea of fixed and verifiable identity is no less than a sinister move to preemptively diminish the possibility of seeking protection for people on the move.

The Architecture of the European Smart Border

The project of the European smart border—that is, leveraging advanced digital technology as a means of border control—began in 2008.[10] By then, advanced digital technologies, including bulk data collection, data analytics, algorithmic decision-support technologies, automated pattern recognition, and data visualization technologies, as well as remote surveillance mechanisms, were already commonplace in high-intensity security contexts, mainly within the US armed conflicts in the Middle East. These technologies largely included real-time drone surveillance and biometric data registration tools, such as fingerprint and iris scanners, facial and pattern recognition systems, and predictive and risk evaluation technologies. To understand the operation and pitfalls of these technologies, it is important to understand that they entered border control operations across the Global North from the so-called war on terror and the global US counterinsurgency in the Middle East and North Africa.

The European smart border project involves various technological solutions, the "smartness" of which, like similar contexts, comes from their reliance on the extraction, processing, storage, and analysis of large amounts of data. Despite the implications of its name, smart border technology is in no way limited to technologies that operate at the border sites or in their immediate vicinity. These technologies are spread out both temporally and spatially at all stages of cross-border travel. Traditionally, when speaking of smart borders, we might think of automated machine-readable travel documents such as biometric passports—passports embedded with RFID chips storing personal, biographical, and biometric data of their owner[11]—and the digital infrastructure of smart airports that read and authenticate said smart documents. These authentication infrastructures, in turn, typically involve Automated Border Control gates (ABC gates), self-service document authentication kiosks (at preborder checks and airports), as well as surveillance systems, facial recognition, fingerprints, and iris pattern scanners.[12] The reach of smart border technologies, however, goes far beyond the limited site of the airports or border crossing points. Indeed, a general critique of the real-time surveillance technologies, as well as predictive and pattern analysis technologies, is that the European border site and border operation extend far beyond Member State borders and well into the territories of third countries, some of which don't even share borders with the so-called European external borders.[13] The expansionist nature of situational awareness, as a necessity of digitalized border control, manifests itself in the ways in which the European Union enforces its exclusionary desires and methods onto various African countries. One example is the criminalization of the domestic movement of international travelers from the city of Agadez in Niger, northbound toward the Algerian or Libyan borders. In May 2015, the Nigerien government, under pressure from its European partners, passed the Law Against Illicit Smuggling of Migrants (36/2015).[14] This law criminalizes *internal* transportation of international travelers within the country of Niger, northbound from the city of Agadez. This law effectively reflects a version of the EU's own carrier sanction directive imposed upon third countries.[15] Technological tools and their accompanying legal and political mechanisms have allowed the EU Member States to project their preventive and punitive powers beyond their national territory, on a scale and intensity that would otherwise not be possible.

The EU smart borders also include the development and use of AI-enhanced automated lie-detection technologies—scanning the facial demeanor of third-country national travelers at the border entry point and comparing it with similar data gathered earlier from the same traveler during a visa interview.[16] Beyond the actual entry points, the asylum procedure deploys similar data-driven automated technologies, such as natural language processing, age assessment, and decision-support technologies, throughout, particularly during the credibility assessment phase, to algorithmically determine the country of origin, estimated age, and validity of the asylum seekers' claims. When adding to this list the real-time video surveillance of border zones and beyond by drones, AI-enhanced thermal surveillance cameras, and CO_2 and heartbeat detectors for cargo vehicles at borders,[17] we are confronted with an extensive apparatus of data-driven border technology that goes well beyond the geographical location of borders or the actual moment of crossing them.

Operating these technologies requires vast amounts of data stored in databases against which the newly extracted personal data are examined, verified, and authenticated. Today, such data collection is routinized as part of international travel. That is the case with biometric data collection during passport or visa applications in one's home country. At other times, such data are taken forcibly, illegally, and illegitimately. For instance, German, UK, Danish, and Belgian border guards infamously confiscate smart devices from irregularized travelers to use them as a gateway to personal and/or social network data that, in turn, might reveal a traveler's country of origin or their route of travel—invaluable information for later deportation of the said people.[18]

Data technologies have permeated every facet of the European integrated border management because the achievement of situational awareness is set not only as a strategic objective but also as a prerequisite of the smart border project.[19] The regulation establishing the European Border Surveillance system (EUROSUR)—the European border surveillance system operated by Frontex—defines situational awareness as "the ability to monitor, detect, identify, track and understand illegal cross-border activities in order to find reasoned grounds for reaction measures on the basis of combining new information with existing knowledge, and to be better able to reduce loss of lives of migrants at, along or in the proximity of, the external borders."[20]

A more elusive side of technologically acquired situational awareness is the promise of preemptive and predictive interventions against cross-border travel of the undesired population.[21] This strategic ambition of the EU's external border, in turn, depends upon an interoperable architecture of data and information sharing between numerous repositories of travelers' personal data. The current European architecture of travelers' data management came into force on June 11, 2019, and overhauled the European border data strategy by establishing an interoperability framework for nine separate personal databases pertaining to cross-border travel across and beyond the Union. The data in question includes, but is not limited to, biometric and biographical data, travel history, criminal record, identification, and identity document history of travelers who appear of interest to the European border control authorities. This interoperable system includes Schengen Information System (SIS), Visa Information System (VIS), Eurodac (European fingerprint database of asylum seekers and "irregular migrants"), European Travel Information and Authorisation System (ETIAS), Entry/Exit Information System (EES), the European Criminal Records Information System for Third Country Nationals (ECRIS-TCN), Interpol's Stolen and Lost Travel and Identity Document (STLD), Interpol's Travel Documents Associated With Notices (TDAWN), and the Europol database (as far as it is relevant for the functioning of the ETIAS). The interoperation of such a diverse mix of authorities, types of data, competencies, and legal mandates is, in turn, enabled by three new components in the EU's border data architecture: Shared Biometric Matching Service (sBMS), Common Identity Repository (CIR), and Multiple Identity Detector (MID).

The result is an assumed increase in effectiveness, efficiency, and reaction capability of the Union's border authorities while enabling the mobilization of its resources—legal and material—from criminal and judicial apparatuses as part and parcel of the migration control regime. While most of this technological structure applies to all travelers across European borders, it does not apply so evenly to all subjects or produce uniform subjectivities. For passengers with valid travel documents, a smart border is an enhancement of the seamless travel experience, whereas for travelers from the Global South, travelers without such documents, asylum seekers, and other migrants, this architecture solidifies a global hierarchy of travel.[22] The following two sections will spell out some of the more consequential critiques of smart border technologies that pertain to the ever more restrictive regime of cross-border travel as they concern asylum seekers and refugees.

The Slippery Slope of Data-Induced Situational Awareness

This multilayered surveillance mechanism subjects primarily refugees and asylum seekers to continuous data extraction with little-to-no regard for their rights. It remains controversial. The European border sites are now a testing ground for the newest technologies of surveillance and policing on the most vulnerable border crossers: asylum seekers and refugees.[23] Professor Nicholas De Genova refers to the European borders as "a transnational and intercontinental laboratory for the regimentation and subordination of human powers and freedoms in relation to the space of the plant."[24] In her examination of the Greek asylum process' reliance upon Skype interviews and an Asylum Service app, Professor Claudia Aradau pushes this point further and argues that experimentation and improvisation with technology at the border have become a governing rationality of the control of borders.[25] She argues that technological apparatuses expose the relations between refugees, their legal rights, and the state's responsibilities to continuous decomposition and reconfiguration by introducing different categories and classifications, and also by constantly introducing new affordances or glitches that come with the use of each technology.[26] This constant reconfiguration of legal/administrative processes of identification and processing of asylum applicants through technological innovations destabilizes status categories, as well as increases unpredictability and even illegibility of regulations (including access to rights). It does not resolve border violence but rather changes its expressions.

Reformulating the problems instead of providing answers is, in fact, a feature of techno-solutionism as such. As Philippe Bonditti, teacher, researcher, and author, puts it, "the excessive resorting to technology effectively hides the political character of problems that technology is intended to solve."[27] In the context of the European data architecture of borders, the absurdity of the current model of national borders, its inhumanity,[28] and its colonial pedigree[29] are continuously reframed as a mere problem of efficiency of control measures and protection mechanisms. Efficiency then arises by relying on acquiring swift, comprehensive knowledge of all relevant migratory events to increase reaction ability. This, however, brings us to the slippery slope, namely, data collection for the purpose of situational awareness.

Just as technologies of wartime surveillance found their way into the EU's border operations, so too did the operational logics and practices, as well as their associated pitfalls. Data-driven techno-solutionism is predicated on the idea that the key to preventing risks and vulnerability is hidden in patterns of relations that could be discovered by sifting through the bulk of available and collectible data. This belief was at the core of the US military's turn to develop and use data surveillance technologies in large-scale security operations. The US Joint Inquiry into the Terrorist Attacks of September 11, 2001, claims that "on September 11, enough relevant data was resident in existing databases" that "had the dots [been] connected," the attacks could have been "exposed and stopped."[30] This belief, that the unknown risks are readily available if we "connect the dots," has been invoked almost verbatim in another report that justifies the US National Security Agency's (NSA) international scandal of bulk and secretive collection of personal data.[31]

At the EU border security level, a similar rationale motivated the development of the interoperable databases, as well as data communication systems such as EUROSUR. The official communications and feasibility studies of European border technologies repeatedly point to the necessity of fostering information and data-sharing environments because data that might be useless for one Member State can very well be critical to control the operations of another.[32] These data can include anything from a person's travel route, history of travel, documents, and biometrics/biographical data of a person to climate conditions at a border site or a travel route, pattern, number, or origin of a confiscated forged passport at a specific port of entry or any event that could have a bearing on border control operations.

Yet any security technology that leverages situational awareness through data gathering to achieve preemptive, predictive, and preventive reaction capabilities must sooner or later face the inherent contradictions between, on the one hand, the large-scale violation of the privacy rights of its data subjects and, on the other, the necessity of bulk data collection. In this regard, the European smart border project is on the same path as its technological predecessor in the United States' national security context. The problem of systematic rights violations increases here as refugees are often excluded from data protection regulations at the EU level.[33] One example, reflected in a report by the UN Special Rapporteur on contemporary forms of racism, points out that EU border technologies already systematically disregard the legal protections of refugees, asylum seekers, and undocumented persons. In Germany, undocumented persons benefit from the same health-care rights as asylum seekers. However, under section 87 of the Residence Act, health-care authorities are required to share personal data with migration authorities, effectively tying the right to access to health care to violation of privacy rights and, in turn, to an even more vulnerable migratory condition. Similar practices exist in many European countries, including Denmark, Belgium, Italy, the Czech Republic, Finland, and the Netherlands.[34]

Such proactive tendencies in collecting data through expanding policing practices of public authorities are also reflected in the gradual expansion of Eurodac's mandate since 2003. This European repository of asylum seekers' fingerprints was initially established to operationalize the Dublin Regulation (i.e., the allocation of asylum cases to the country that first registered said fingerprints). In 2013, the law enforcement authorities of Member States and Europol acquired direct access to this database, effectively expanding its operation beyond enforcing the Dublin Regulation. More recently and under the new recast of the Eurodac regulation in 2020, this databank was overhauled to store biometric and biographical data, beyond fingerprints, for a longer period (five years instead of eighteen months) and from persons as young as six years old (previously fourteen).[35] Most alarming, however, is the proposed expansion of Eurodac to include data from undocumented persons who already live inside Member States (allowing for active police search and collection of personal data), as well as the introduction of a new migratory status called "persons disembarked following a search and rescue operation" in order to target them for speedy processing and deportation.[36]

The slippery slope of rights violation that data-driven situational awareness demands reflects a strong example of what media scholar Mirca Madianou calls technocolonialism: "the constitutive role that data and digital innovation play in entrenching inequalities between refugees and humanitarian agencies and, ultimately, inequalities in the global context."[37] A particular implication of this analysis, one that is evident from the trajectory of the ever-expanding grip of digital technologies over the personal data of people on the move, is the gradual but ensured expansion of such extralegal disregard for the integrity of data subjects to include more and more people. Hence, a feature that met its eventual end point in the NSA leaks is currently in force within the European smart border data architecture.

Situatedness of Data and the Inaccuracy of Personal Identity

The problem with data technologies as border control mechanisms far supersedes their expansionist or extractive ambitions. A second foundational flaw of the European smart border project resides in understanding individual personal identities as unchangeable and, hence, holding an objective truth about people. One that, if reordered, allows for the tracing and identification of people at any time and any place. The renowned Palestinian poet Mahmoud Darwish, in a poem dedicated to his friend, the Palestinian American literary critic and political activist Edward Said, captures a significant point in the form of a dialogue between the two of them:

> What about identity? / I asked/ He said: It's self-defense . . . / Identity is the child of birth, but/ at the end, it is self-invention, and not/ an inheritance of

> the past. I am multiple . . . / Within me an ever new exterior/ And I belong to the question of the victim.[38]

The question of identity and its construction through partial representations of the onlooking agents of colonial power was a significant part of Edward Said's scholarship. To him, identities are inseparable from histories, as well as the social and political context of their representation, construction, and contestation.[39] His well-known work *Orientalism* was concerned with scrutinizing the temporally and spatially ungrounded construction of the identity of the people of the East by European colonizers. In a passage in *Orientalism,* he writes: "Far from a static thing then, identity of self or of 'other' is a much worked-over historical, social, intellectual, and political process that takes place as a contest involving individuals and institutions in all societies."[40]

Such meditations over the contested and constructed nature of identities, Said wrote in his 1995 Afterword to *Orientalism*, are "anything but mere academic wool-gathering," they are "urgent social contests involving such concrete political issues as immigration laws," because, after all, "the construction of identity is bound up with the disposition of power and powerlessness in each society."[41]

Other scholars have further built on Said's argument that identities are fluid, unfixed, and constantly renegotiated to point out the role of state bureaucratic practices, as well as the material world of technologies in this construction. In an exploration of the historical emergence of specific material practices of identification, author Mahmoud Keshavarz traces the design politics of passports as documents of travel and shows that personal identities, as constructed in and through the passport, are historically contingent, socially constructed, and materially maintained. Part and parcel of the verified self, he shows, is the unique and specific material and/or operational affordances that inscription, documentation, and authentication offer.[42]

To bring this point home, Keshavarz explores how the supposed verification of identities based on the technological certainty of documents such as passports is always contextually negotiated between individual subjects. This example is narrated by an Iranian traveling on a forged Israeli passport. At the border crossing, a suspicious border guard attempts to verify this traveler's identity—in other words, match the person with the document of identification. The guard turns and shouts at the line of passengers:

> "[I]s there anyone from Israel here?" Another friend of mine who had also obtained an Israeli passport was in the line. He stepped out and replied: "I am from Israel." The guard asked him to come closer and talk to me in Hebrew to see if we understand each other. We started speaking in Farsi for few seconds. The border guard asked him if I knew Hebrew and my friend confirmed it. We both crossed the border.[43]

Said's point regarding the social construction of personal identities has direct implications for the utility of the technological means of border control that base their efficiency claims upon rapid and seamless verification of personal identities. If identity itself is not fixed and instead constantly negotiable, then what can be achieved by gathering and mobilizing digital personal data en masse for border security purposes?

This contradiction sits at the core of the European digital architecture of border control, yet ironically, it is praised as a novel component of the system. At the center of the interoperable personal data architecture of the EU border regime is a Multiple Identity Detector (MID) tool. This tool aims "to enable correct identification of persons and the discovery of identity fraud and multiple identities."[44] While identity fraud is a plausible feature of a hierarchical global regime of travel, these technologies overlook the basic fact that multiplicity of identity is not an anomaly of social life but a feature of it.

During the second US war in Iraq, *The New York Times* reported that many Iraqi people carry multiple ID cards at all times,[45] with each card coupling the same personal biometric data with a different name, religion, and tribal affiliation. In a warzone with an intensified sectarian animosity, possessing *multiple identities*, far from being a fraudulent act, is a measure of safety and self-protection. Similarly, issuing biometric ID cards to produce national identities in Afghanistan has faced decades of popular resistance. The reason here was a general aversion among people to self-identify as a particular religion or affiliate with the limiting identity of being an "Afghan," which in turn mainly invokes the ethnicity of the majority Pashtun population.[46]

Contested identity, at times, is the very reason people travel across borders for protection. By March 2019, around 909,000 Rohingya refugees had fled the ongoing genocide in Myanmar.[47] The majority of Rohingya refugees sought protection in Bangladesh, where, in collaboration with the United Nations High Commissioner for Refugees (UNHCR), they have been biometrically identified and registered.[48] But this identification system not only did not offer "Rohingya" as an identity but also imposed upon them the identity of "Myanmar nationals," the very identity that the Myanmar regime denied the Rohingya people, and a gross misrepresentation of their legal identity as stateless people.[49] Examples such as these should crystallize that what is assumed to be fixed and traceable identity is nothing but a fiction. Individuals' identities are constantly contested, negotiated, and denied, yet at no point can they be represented as a comprehensive whole. As Edward Said writes:

> No one today is purely one thing. Labels like Indian, or woman, or Muslim, or American are not more than starting points . . . . Imperialism consolidated the mixture of cultures and identities on a global scale. But its worst and most paradoxical gift was to allow people to believe that they were only, mainly,

> exclusively, white, or Black, or Western, or Oriental. Yet just as human beings make their own history, they also make their cultures and ethnic identities.[50]

Data are always local and bound to the relations of force available on the ground but also depend upon the manners and conditions of interactions between individuals and the machines.[51] It is by now a well-cited fact that biometric data collection machines systematically misread, misidentify, or altogether do not identify people with darker skin color, darker eye color, or eyes with cataracts, etc.[52] Moreover, people on the move, when confronting this complicated apparatus of surveillance that deploys a "truth" of their bodies against their own tactics of self-preservation, often interact with these technologies in ways that reduce their reliability. This can be illustrated by those who burn their fingertips to leverage their personal truth against biometric machine unreadability.[53]

Contestability, negotiability, and multiplicity of identities are both mechanisms of survival for those fleeing from violence and, at times, the very reason why people take refuge elsewhere. Mobilizing this specific feature of social life as a mechanism for hunting and rejecting the very people for whom protections of asylum are imagined in the first place is simply cruel.

Conclusion

To ask again, if identity is not fixed and instead constantly negotiated, then what can be achieved by gathering and mobilizing digital personal data en masse for border security purposes?

In her study of the social functions of technologies, Sheila Jasanoff argues that technologies, far from being objective tools developed to carry out a limited practical purpose, are also mechanisms of coproducing the context in which they are deployed:

> Knowledge and its material embodiments [technologies] are at once products of social work and constitutive of forms of social life; society cannot function without knowledge any more than knowledge can exist without appropriate social supports.[54]

As much as the interoperable data infrastructure of the European Union is a mechanism of border control, they are also tools for producing the borders of Europe and the social world of mobility that they seek to regulate. In this view, the various personal identity databanks and their associated tools are conditions of possibility of a world in which people in search of refuge are forced to inflict violence on themselves, be it in the forms of the removal of biometric markers with acid, fire, and razor or picking an ever more dangerous route for crossing borders. In other words, if the data technologies of the border cannot achieve an objective, incontestable, and generalizable truth of personal identity, they certainly can contribute to producing a world in which cross-border travel of people in search of protection is pushed toward terrains in which the geography would do the dirty work.[55]

Notes

1 M. I. Franklin, "Refugees and the (Digital) Gatekeepers of 'Fortress Europe,'" *State Crime* 7, no. 1 (2018): 77–99.

2 Julien Jeandesboz, "Beyond the Tartar Steppe: EUROSUR and the Ethics of European Border Control Practices," in *Europe Under Threat? Security, Migration and Integration*, ed. J. Peter Burgess and Serge Gutwirth (VUB Press, 2011).

3 See European Commission, "Annex to the Commission Recommendation: Adopting the Practical Handbook for Implementing and Managing the European Border Surveillance System (EUROSUR Handbook)," Strasbourg, C(2015) 9206, 2015.

4 Dimitri Van Den Meerssche, "Virtual Borders–International Law and the Elusive Inequalities of Algorithmic Association," *European Journal of International Law* 33, no. 1 (2021): 171–204.

5 Victoria Adelmant, "Pilots, Pushbacks, and the Panopticon: Digital Technologies at the EU's Borders," Center for Human Rights and Justice, NYU School of Law, available online: https://chrgj.org/2021/11/23/pilots-pushbacks-and-the-panopticon-digital-technologies-at-the-eus-borders/; Mark Akkerman, *Expanding the Fortress: The Policies, the Profiteers and the People Shaped by the EU's Border Externalisation Programme* (Transnational Institute and Stop Wapenhandel, 2018), and Ruben Zaiotti, "Mapping Remote Control: The Externalization of Migration Management in the 21st Century," in *Externalizing Migration Management*, ed. Ruben Zaiotti (Routledge, 2016), 3–30.

6 Sabrina Ellebrecht, "The European Border Surveillance System EUROSUR: The Computerization, Standardization, and Virtualization of Border Management in Europe," in *Yearbook on the Organization for Security and Co-operation in Europe (OSCE)* (2014), https://doi.org/10.5771/9783845252698_231.

7 Blasi Casagran, "Fundamental Rights Implications of Interconnecting Migration and Policing Databases in the EU," *Human Rights Law Review* 21, no. 2 (2021): 445.

8 European Union Agency for Fundamental Rights, *How the EUROSUR Regulation Affects Fundamental Rights* (Office of the European Union, 2018).

9 The UN Office of the High Commissioner for Human Rights, Racial and Xenophobic discrimination and the use of digital technologies in border and immigration enforcement—Report of the Special Rapporteur on contemporary forms of racism, racial discrimination, xenophobia and related intolerance (A/HRC/48/76), September 22, 2021. For a more detailed exploration of technological violence of borders and racialization of border crossers as a result of the deployment of such technologies, see Petra Molnar, *The Walls Have Eyes: Surviving Migration in the Age of Artificial Intelligence* (New Press, 2024).

10 The European Commission, "Communication of 13 February 2008 from the Commission to the European Parliament, the Council, the European Economic and Social Committee and the Committee of the Regions: Preparing the next steps in border management in the European Union," COM(2008) 69 (The European Commission, 2008).

11 European Commission Decision 18/VI/2006 on establishing the technical specifications on the standards for security features and biometrics in passports and travel documents issued by Member State.

12 See The European Agency for the operational management of large-scale IT systems (EU-LISA, *Smart Borders Pilot Project Report on the technical conclusions of the Pilot (Volume 1)* (Publication Offices of the European Union, 2015).

13 Sabrina Ellebrecht, *Mediated Bordering: Eurosur, the Refugee Boat, and the Construction of an External EU Border* (Transcript Verlag, 2020).

14 For an analysis of the Law 36/2015, see Mattea Weihe, Lea Müller-Funk, and Mounkaila Abdou, "How EU Pressure Hampers Circular Migration Between Niger and Libya," *GiGa Focus Middle East* no. 5 (2021): 1–12.

15 The European carrier sanction directive turns anyone involved in cross-border transportation into de facto border police. Accordingly, transport companies, travel agents, airport staff, aircraft personnel, truck drivers, and so on will be punished and fined if they transport any improperly documented individual into the Union.

16 A smart lie-detection system is part of the iBorderCtrl project with a budget of 4.5 million Euros. For more information, see https://ec.europa.eu/research-and-innovation/en/projects/success-stories/all/smart-lie-detection-system-tighten-eus-busy-borders.

17 Andrei Popoviciu, "'They Can See Us in the Dark': Migrants Grapple with Hi-Tech Fortress EU," *The Guardian,* 2021, available online: https://www.theguardian.com/global-development/2021/mar/26/eu-borders-migrants-hitech-surveillance-asylum-seekers.

18 Morgan Meaker, "Europe Is Using Smartphone Data as a Weapon to Deport Refugees," *WIRED UK,* 2018, available online: https://www.wired.co.uk/article/europe-immigration-refugees-smartphone-metadata-deportations.

19 Frontex, *Technical and Operational Strategy for European Integrated Border Management* (Frontex–European Border and Coast Guard Agency, 2019), 27.

20 Article 3(a), European Union, "Regulation (EU) No 1052/2013 of the European Parliament and of the Council of 22 October 2013 establishing the European Border Surveillance System (Eurosur)," ed. European Parliament (2013), available online: https://eur-lex.europa.eu/eli/reg/2013/1052/oj/eng.

21 Frontex, *Technical and Operational Strategy for European Integrated Border Management*, 27.

22 For an exploration of passports as a technology of limiting movement along racial, class, and gender hierarchies, see Mira Siegelberg, *Statelessness: A Modern History* (Harvard University Press, 2020), also Mahmoud Keshavarz, *The Design Politics of the Passport: Materiality, Immobility, and Dissent* (Bloomsbury, 2020).

23 Petra Molnar, *Technological Testing Grounds: Migration Management Experiments and Reflections from the Ground Up* (EDRi; and The Refugee Law Lab, 2020).

24 Nicholas De Genova, "The Border of 'Europe' and the European Question," in *The Borders of 'Europe': Autonomy of Migration, Tactics of Bordering*, ed. Nicholas De Genova (Duke University Press, 2017), 24.

25 Claudia Aradau, "Experimentality, Surplus Data and the Politics of Debilitation in Borderzones," *Geopolitics* 27, no. 1 (2022): 26–46.

26 Ibid.

27 Philippe Bonditti, "From Territorial Space to Networks: A Foucaldian Approach to the Implementation of Biometry," *Alternatives: Global, Local, Political* 29, no. 4 (2004): 466.

28 For questioning the existing deportation regime as a potential crime against humanity, see Vincent Chetail, "Is There Any Blood on My Hands? Deportation as a Crime of International Law," *Leiden Journal of International Law* 29 (2016): 917–43.

29 See Radhika Mongia, *Indian Migration and Empire: A Colonial Genealogy of the Modern State* (Duke University Press, 2018); Nandita Sharma, *Home Rule: National Sovereignty and the Separation of Natives and Migrants* (Duke University Press, 2020); Lucy Mayblin, *Asylum After Empire: Colonial Legacies in the Politics of Asylum Seeking* (Rowman & Littlefield, 2017).

30 House Permanent Select Committee on Intelligence (HPSCI) and Senate Select Committee on Intelligence (SSCI), "Report of the Joint Inquiry into the Terrorist Attacks of September 11, 2001," December 20, 2002, 14.

31 US National Research Council Computer Science and Telecommunications Board, *Bulk Collection of Signals Intelligence: Technical Options* (The National Academies Press, 2015), 16.

32 The European Commission, "Examining the Creation of a European Border Surveillance System (EUROSUR)" (European Commission, 2008).

33 European Union Agency for Fundamental Rights, *How the Eurosur Regulation Affects Fundamental Rights*, European Union Agency for Fundamental Rights (Publications Office of the European Union, 2018).

34 The Special Rapporteur on contemporary forms of racism, racial discrimination, xenophobia and related intolerance, *Racial and Xenophobic Discrimination and the Use of Digital Technologies in Border and Immigration Enforcement (A/HRC/48/76)* (2021): 13–14. For examination of similar practices, see Annika Lindberg, "The Production of Precarity in Denmark's Asylum Regime," *Zeitschrift für Sozialreform* 66, no. 4 (2020): 413–39. Similar examples include Article 29 of the Belgian Code of Criminal Procedure and Article 361 of the Italian Criminal Code, which require every authority or civil servant to report any crime with which they encounter as a result of their profession. Similarly, Article 37 (2) and 40 of the Greek Code of Criminal Procedure, Article 8 of the Czech Code of Criminal Procedure, Article 304 of the Polish Code of Criminal, Article 3 of the Slovak Code of Criminal Procedure, and Article 145 of the Slovenian Code of Criminal Procedure. See European Union Agency for Fundamental Rights, *Fundamental Rights of Migrants in an Irregular Situation in the European Union* (Office of the European Union, 2011), 42–4.

35 Niovi Vavoula, "Transforming Eurodac from 2016 to the New Pact: From the Dublin System's Sidekick to a Database in Support of EU Policies on Asylum, Resettlement and Irregular Migration," ECRE Working Paper, ECRE, Brussels.

36 The European Commission, "Amended Proposal for a Regulation of the European Parliament and of the Council on the Establishment of 'Eurodac' for the Comparison of Biometric Data for the Effective Application of Regulation (EU) XXX/XXX, 2018 /1240 and (EU) 2019/818" (European Commission, 2020).

37 Mirca Madianou, "Technocolonialism: Digital Innovation and Data Practices in the Humanitarian Response to the Refugee Crisis," *Social Media + Society* (2019): 4.

38 Mahmoud Darwish, "Edward Said: A Contrapuntal Reading," *Cultural Critique* 67 (2007): 175–82.

39 Natasha Afrin, "Edward Said on the Identity Question," *Journal of the Asiatic Society of Bangladesh* 63, no. 1 (2018): 117–33.

40 Edward Said, *Orientalism: Western Conception of the Orient* (Penguin Classics, 2003 [1995]), 332.

41 Ibid.

42 Keshavarz, *The Design Politics of the Passport*.

43 Ibid., 94.

44 Katrien Luyten and Sofija Voronova, *Interoperability between EU Border and Security Information Systems* (European Parliament, 2019), 5.

45 Edward Wong, "To Stay Alive, Iraqis Change their Names," *The New York Times*, September 6, 2006.

46 Jeffrey E. Stern, "Afghanistan's Growing Identity (Card) Crisis," *Foreign Policy*, January 21, 2014.

47 See UNHCR page on Rohingya Refugee Crisis, available online: https://www.unocha.org/rohingya-refugee-crisis.

48 See UNHCR on Rohingya emergency, available online: https://www.unhcr.org/en-us/rohingya-emergency.html.

49 See Mirca Madianou, "Technocolonialism: Digital Innovation and Data Practices in the Humanitarian Response to the Refugee Crisis," *Social Media + Society* (2019): 1–13.

50 Edward Said, *Culture and Imperialism* (Vintage Books, 1993), 336.

51 See Yanni Loukissas, *All Data Are Local: Thinking Critically in a Data-Driven Society* (MIT Press, 2019).

52 Colleen Bell, "Grey's Anatomy Goes South: Global Racism and Suspect Identities in the Colonial Present," *Canadian Journal of Sociology* 38, no. 4 (2013): 465–86. Also Shoshana Magnet, *When Biometrics Fail: Gender, Race, and the Technology of Identity* (Duke University Press, 2011), 11, 25–8, and 29.

53 Amade M'charek, "Harraga: Burning Borders, Navigating Colonialism," *The Sociological Review* 68, no. 2 (2020): 418–34.

54 Sheila Jasanoff, "Future Imperfect: Science, Technology, and the Imaginations of Modernity," in *Dreamscapes of Modernity: Sociotechnical Imaginaries and the Fabrication of Power*, ed. Sheila Jasanoff and Sang-Hyun Kim (University of Chicago Press, 2015), 3.

55 This phrase is a reworking of the infamous quote from the former commissioner of the US Immigration and Naturalization Service, Doris Meissner: "geography would do the rest." For more on this, see Leti Volpp, "Signs of Law," in *Looking for Law in All the Wrong Places: Justice Beyond and Between*, ed. Marianne Constable, Leti Volpp, and Bryan Wagner (University of California, 2019), 105.

Bibliography

Adelmant, Victoria. "Pilots, Pushbacks, and the Panopticon: Digital Technologies at the EU's Borders." Center for Human Rights and Justice, NYU School of Law. Available online: https://chrgj.org/2021/11/23/pilots-pushbacks-and-the-panopticon-digital-technologies-at-the-eus-borders/.

Afrin, Natasha. "Edward Said on the Identity Question." *Journal of the Asiatic Society of Bangladesh* 63, no. 1 (2018): 117–33.

Akkerman, Mark. *Expanding the Fortress: The Policies, the Profiteers and the People Shaped by the EU's Border Externalisation Programme*. Transnational Institute and Stop Wapenhandel, 2018.

Aradau, Claudia. "Experimentality, Surplus Data and the Politics of Debilitation in Borderzones." *Geopolitics* 27, no. 1 (2022): 26–46. https://doi.org/10.1080/14650045.2020.1853103.

Bell, Colleen D. "Grey's Anatomy Goes South: Global Racism and Suspect Identities in the Colonial Present." *Canadian Journal of Sociology* 38, no. 4 (2013): 465–86. Available online: http://www.jstor.org/stable/canajsocicahican.38.4.465.

Blasi Casagran, Cristina. "Fundamental Rights Implications of Interconnecting Migration and Policing Databases in the EU." *Human Rights Law Review* 21, no. 2 (2021): 433–57.

Bonditti, Philippe. "From Territorial Space to Networks: A Foucaldian Approach to the Implementation of Biometry." *Alternatives: Global, Local, Political* 29, no. 4 (2004): 465–82.

Chetail, Vincent. "Is There Any Blood on My Hands? Deportation as a Crime of International Law." *Leiden Journal of International Law* 29 (2016): 917–43.

Darwish, Mahmoud. "Edward Said: A Contrapuntal Reading." *Cultural Critique* 67 (2007): 175–82.

De Genova, Nicholas. "The Border of 'Europe' and the European Question." In *The Borders of 'Europe': Autonomy of Migration, Tactics of Bordering*, edited by Nicholas De Genova. Duke University Press, 2017.

Ellebrecht, Sabrina. "The European Border Surveillance System EUROSUR: The Computerization, Standardization, and Virtualization of Border Management in Europe." In *Yearbook on the Organization for Security and Co-operation in Europe (OSCE)*, 2014. https://doi.org/10.5771/9783845252698_231.

Ellebrecht, Sabrina. *Mediated Bordering: Eurosur, the Refugee Boat, and the Construction of an External EU Border*. Transcript Verlag, 2020.

European Agency for the Operational Management of Large-Scale IT Systems (EU-LISA. *Smart Borders Pilot Project Report on the Technical Conclusions of the Pilot (Volume 1)*. Publication Offices of the European Union, 2015.

European Commission. "Amended Proposal for a Regulation of the European Parliament and of the Council on the Establishment of 'Eurodac' for the Comparison of Biometric Data for the Effective Application of Regulation (Eu) Xxx/Xxx [Regulation on Asylum and Migration Management] and of Regulation (Eu) Xxx/Xxx [Resettlement

Regulation], for Identifying an Illegally Staying Third-Country National or Stateless Person and on Requests for the Comparison with Eurodac Data by Member States' Law Enforcement Authorities and Europol for Law Enforcement Purposes and Amending Regulations (Eu) 2018/1240 and (Eu) 2019/818." Brussels, 2020.

European Commission. "Annex to the Commission Recommendation: Adopting the Practical Handbook for Implementing and Managing the European Border Surveillance System (EUROSUR Handbook) C(2015) 9206." Strasbourg, 2015.

European Commission. "Communication of 13 February 2008 from the Commission to the European Parliament, the Council, the European Economic and Social Committee and the Committee of the Regions: Preparing the Next Steps in Border Management in the European Union, COM(2008) 69." Strasbourg, 2008.

European Commission. "Examining the Creation of a European Border Surveillance System (Eurosur)." Brussels, 2008.

European Union. "Regulation (Eu) No 1052/2013 of the European Parliament and of the Council of 22 October 2013 Establishing the European Border Surveillance System (Eurosur)." Edited by European Parliament. 2013. Available online: https://eur-lex.europa.eu/eli/reg/2013/1052/oj/eng.

European Union Agency for Fundamental Rights. *Fundamental Rights of Migrants in an Irregular Situation in the European Union*. Office of the European Union, 2011. Available online: https://fra.europa.eu/en/publication/2012/fundamental-rights-migrants-irregular-situation-european-union.

European Union Agency for Fundamental Rights. *How the EUROSUR Regulation Affects Fundamental Rights*. Office of the European Union, 2018. Available online: https://fra.europa.eu/en/publication/2018/how-eurosur-regulation-affects-fundamental-rights.

Feroz, Emran. "After 20 Years of Drone Strikes, It's Time to Admit They've Failed." *MIT Technology Review*, 2021. Available online: https://www.technologyreview.com/2021/10/07/1036456/opinion-afghanistan-drone-strike-warfare-failed/.

Franklin, M. I. "Refugees and the (Digital) Gatekeepers of 'Fortress Europe'." *State Crime* 7, no. 1 (2018): 77–99.

Frontex. *Technical and Operational Strategy for European Integrated Border Management*. Frontex–European Border and Coast Guard Agency, 2019.

House Permanent Select Committee on Intelligence (HPSCI), and Senate Select Committee on Intelligence (SSCI). "Report of the Joint Inquiry into the Terrorist Attacks of September 11, 2011." December 20, 2002. Available online: https://fas.org/irp/congress/2002_rpt/911rept.pdf.

Jasanoff, Sheila. "Future Imperfect: Science, Technology, and the Imaginations of Modernity." In *Dreamscapes of Modernity: Sociotechnical Imaginaries and the Fabrication of Power*, edited by Sheila Jasanoff and Sang-Hyun Kim. University of Chicago Press, 2015.

Jeandesboz, Julien. "Beyond the Tartar Steppe: EUROSUR and the Ethics of European Border Control Practices." In *Europe Under Threat? Security, Migration and Integration*, edited by J. Peter Burgess and Serge Gutwirth. VUB Press, 2011.

Keshavarz, Mahmoud. *The Design Politics of the Passport: Materiality, Immobility, and Dissent*. Bloomsbury, 2020.

Latonero, Mark. "Stop Surveillance Humanitarianism." 2019. Available online: https://www.nytimes.com/2019/07/11/opinion/data-humanitarian-aid.html.

Lindberg, Annika. "The Production of Precarity in Denmark's Asylum Regime." *Zeitschrift für Sozialreform* 66, no. 4 (2020): 413–39. https://doi.org/10.1515/zsr-2020-0018.

Loukissas, Yanni Alexander. *All Data Are Local: Thinking Critically in a Data-Driven Society*. MIT Press, 2019.

Luyten, Katrien, and Sofija Voronova. *Interoperability Between EU Border and Security Information Systems*. European Parliament, 2019. Available online: https://www.ouroparl.ouropa.ou/RogData/otudoo/BRIE/2018/628267/EPRS_BRI(2018)628267_EN.pdf.

Madianou, Mirca. "Technocolonialism: Digital Innovation and Data Practices in the Humanitarian Response to the Refugee Crisis." *Social Media + Society* (2019): 1–13. https://doi.org/10.1177/2056305119863146.

Magnet, Shoshana Amielle. *When Biometrics Fail: Gender, Race, and the Technology of Identity*. Duke University Press, 2011.

Mayblin, Lucy. *Asylum after Empire: Colonial Legacies in the Politics of Asylum Seeking*. Rowman & Littlefield, 2017.

M'charek, Amade. "Harraga: Burning Borders, Navigating Colonialism." *The Sociological Review* 68, no. 2 (2020): 418–34.

Meaker, Morgan. "Europe Is Using Smartphone Data as a Weapon to Deport Refugees." *WIRED UK*, 2018. Available online: https://www.wired.co.uk/article/europe-immigration-refugees-smartphone-metadata-deportations.

Molnar, Petra. *Technological Testing Grounds: Migration Management Experiments and Reflections from the Ground Up*. EDRi; and The Refugee Law Lab, 2020.

Molnar, Petra. *The Walls Have Eyes: Surviving Migration in the Age of Artificial Intelligence*. New Press, 2024.

Mongia, Radhika. *Indian Migration and Empire: A Colonial Genealogy of the Modern State*. Duke University Press, 2018.

Popoviciu, Andrei. "'They Can See Us in the Dark': Migrants Grapple with Hi-Tech Fortress EU." *The Guardian*, 2021. Available online: https://www.theguardian.com/global-development/2021/mar/26/eu-borders-migrants-hitech-surveillance-asylum-seekers.

Said, Edward W. *Culture and Imperialism*. Vintage Books, 1993.

Said, Edward W. *Orientalism: Western Conception of the Orient*. Penguin Classics, 2003 (1995).

Sharma, Nandita. *Home Rule: National Sovereignty and the Separation of Natives and Migrants*. Duke University Press, 2020.

Siegelberg, Mira L. *Statelessness: A Modern History*. Harvard University Press, 2020.

Special Rapporteur on Contemporary Forms of Racism, Racial Discrimination, Xenophobia and Related Intolerance. *Racial and Xenophobic Discrimination and the Use of Digital Technologies in Border and Immigration Enforcement (A/HRC/48/76)*. 2021. Available online: https://www.ohchr.org/en/documents/thematic-reports/ahrc4876-racial-and-xenophobic-discrimination-and-use-digital.

Stern, Jeffrey E. "Afghanistan's Growing Identity (Card) Crisis." Foreign Policy, January 21, 2014. Available online: http://foreignpolicy.com/2014/01/21/afghanistans-growing-identity-card-crisis/.

US Department of the Army/US Marine Corps. *The US Army/Marine Corps Counterinsurgency Field Manual, FM 3–24*. Edited by US Department of Defense. University of Chicago Press, 2006.

US National Research Council Computer Science and Telecommunications Board. *Bulk Collection of Signals Intelligence: Technical Options*. National Academies Press, 2015.

Van Den Meerssche, Dimitri. "Virtual Borders: International Law and the Elusive Inequalities of Algorithmic Association." *European Journal of International Law* 33, no. 1 (2020): 171–204.

Vavoula, Niovi. "Transforming Eurodac from 2016 to the New Pact: From the Dublin System's Sidekick to a Database in Support of EU Policies on Asylum, Resettlement and Irregular Migration." ECRE Working Paper. ECRE, Brussels.

Volpp, Leti. "Signs of Law." In *Looking for Law in All the Wrong Places: Justice Beyond and Between*, edited by Marianne Constable, Leti Volpp, and Bryan Wagner. University of California, 2019.

Weihe, Mattea, Müller-Funk, Lea, and Mounkaila Abdou. "How EU Pressure Hampers Circular Migration Between Niger and Libya." *GiGa Focus Middle East* no. 5 (2021). Available online: https://pure.giga-hamburg.de/ws/files/28664119/web_Nahost_2021_05_en.pdf.

Wong, Edward. "To Stay Alive, Iraqis Change Their Names." *New York Times*, September 6, 2006. Available online: http://www.nytimes.com/2006/09/06/world/middleeast/06identity.html?ex=1315195200&en=2dd07d4416997e50&ei=5088&partner=rssnyt&emc=rss&_r=0.

Zaiotti, Ruben. "Mapping Remote Control: The Externalization of Migration Management in the 21st Century." In *Externalizing Migration Management*, edited by Ruben Zaiotti. Routledge, 2016.

7

MLOps: A PRIMER FOR POLICYMAKERS ON A NEW FRONTIER IN MACHINE LEARNING

An Explainer of Tools for Bias Mitigation in the MLOps Life Cycle

Jazmia Henry

Introduction

Whether AI will help us reach our aspirations or reinforce the unjust inequalities is ultimately up to us.

—JOY BUOLAMWINI[1]

Whether you're driving your car using a GPS system, ask Alexa or Siri to turn on your favorite tune, go on social media to perform a well-earned scroll down memory lane, or go to Google Search to find a gift for a friend, you have encountered a machine learning (ML) model. These models collect data to make predictions that can make our lives easier, or harder, depending on the care taken during the machine learning life cycle process. The machine learning life cycle refers to the multistep process that begins with understanding project objectives and ends with model deployment and maintainability. Each step in the process is as follows: define project objectives; acquire and explore data; model the data; interpret and communicate; and implement, document, deploy, and maintain the model.[2] The reason it is referred to as a life cycle is simple: At each step of the process, the ML practitioner is likely to go back a step or two to validate results by adjusting original project objectives, retrieving more or different data, tuning the model, or documenting their process for model maintenance. In artificial intelligence (AI) ethics, researchers focus heavily on the first three steps in the process to find ways to mitigate bias downstream. This work focuses on the last step of the life cycle: implementing, documenting, and maintaining the model. This step is also referred to as machine learning operations, or MLOps, in this chapter. Before getting into my argument as to why a focus on MLOps is an important addition to the AI ethical lexicon, I will first discuss past work and then examine the importance of bias mitigation in the MLOps step of the ML life cycle.

Professors Batya Friedman and Alan Borning and psychologist Peter Kahn Jr. take a particular interest in part 1 of the cycle, defining project objectives, in their article "Value Sensitive Design: Theories and Methods."[3] Within the article, Friedman et al. propose a tripartite method for designing a system that keeps human values in mind. This system can be an application that makes decisions that affect the public, and for the purposes of this chapter, readers can think of machine learning as a type of system. The tripartite method considers the conceptual, empirical, and technical components of a system's design to formulate its main objectives and the way practitioners should model success. Conceptual considerations involve the values that are being supported or perpetuated in the model's build. The empirical method considers the trade-offs of what can often be competing values and seeks to understand the desired outcome of the model. Here, practitioners should consider the difference between intent and impact. Just because a model intends to do good does not mean it will, and if it commits harm, the impact should outweigh the intent of the model builder, and the decision-makers of the model must go back to the drawing board for realignment. The last method, technological investigations, looks into how technologies have been used in the past and if these technologies "have hindered or supported human values."[4]

In both *Algorithms of Oppression* by Safiya Noble and *Weapons of Math Destruction* by Cathy O'Neil, they perform a technological investigation and examine how technologies have been used to perpetuate harms in the past.[5] They investigate where efforts to automate processes have been placed and question the validity of model use, leaning on the side of using simpler technical solutions over ones that learn, adapt, and exploit biases. Noble goes so far as to suggest that a model's values have been, at its core, biased, and these biases are amplified in the overall technology by design.[6]

Joy Buolamwini, Timnit Gebru, and Ruha Benjamin have work that focuses on part 2 of the machine learning life cycle—acquire and explore data. Opposed to focusing on what technologies have done in the past, these researchers take what computer scientist Andrew Ng refers to as the "data-centric" approach to close the gap between model performance and model values.[7] Their work comes after an instance of bias showing up in a model built by Google to label people and animals.

On June 29, 2015, Twitter (now X) user Jacky Alciné tweeted: "Google Photos, y'all [expletive] up. My friend's not a gorilla."[8] The post went viral, with people around the world criticizing Google's latest classification algorithm.[9] Scholarship on algorithmic fairness soon followed, with AI ethicists and researchers from around the world highlighting bias perpetuated by machine learning models. Subsequently, Joy Buolamwini and Timnit Gebru released the article "Gender Shades: Intersectional Accuracy Disparities in Commercial Gender Classification," exposing the misclassification of Black women in large classification models. They set out to supplement the lack of image data of Black women, using their own facial analysis dataset and incorporating it into three commercial classification models—IBM, Microsoft, and Face++. What they found was an outsized error rate when classifying Black women compared to lighter complexioned men (8 percent compared to 34.7 percent). While supplementation improved performance in Black women, the classifier was still a long way from being equitable. Buolamwini and Gebru conclude their work by advocating for transparency and accountability through "inclusive benchmark datasets and subgroup accuracy reports."[10]

In *Race after Technology*, Ruha Benjamin suggests a similar approach to the one prescribed by Gebru and Buolamwini, increasing transparency using, what she calls, a dataset nutrition label. Much like a nutrition label on the back of packaged food, the dataset nutrition label will describe the contents of each model and its performance for tasks across subgroups.[11] If Google had had a dataset nutrition label and been more transparent in its data collection process, solutions to the Google misclassification problem might have been found more quickly. Unfortunately, instead of finding a solution to the problem, three years later, Google simply deleted "Gorilla" and "Chimpanzee" tags from the offending model completely.[12] While dataset transparency is an important step in mitigating bias in the ML life cycle, it forgets a very important reality of deploying AI in the real world: AI, by its nature, is built to adapt to new situations and, many times, can cover its biased assumptions, creating far-reaching problems down the line. This takes us into a common tension in model building observed by ML practitioners in industry: the difference between the work done in part 3 of the life cycle, model building, and part 5 of the life cycle, deploying and maintaining the model.

An example of this is discussed in *You Look Like a Thing and I Love You* by Janelle Shane. In it, she gives the example of AI being trained in a "dream world," with the skills acquired there transferred to the "real world."[13] Unfortunately, the rules that bind us in reality are not present in the "dream world," and the AI was able to exploit the glitches it learned in the dream world and tried to apply them in the real world. This caused the model to subsequently fail. If you change the term "dream world" and replace it with "training environment," you quickly see how models can perpetuate biased reasoning even with balanced training data.

AI can adapt to cover its mistakes by learning to exploit gaps in the training set for higher reward in the real world.

Microsoft learned this firsthand in 2016 when it unveiled "Tay"—a conversational AI bot deployed on Twitter. Made to mine public data and incorporate the data it gathers from conversations with people online to become more conversational, the chatbot quickly picked up racist and homophobic attitudes, even going so far as to praise Hitler in one of its tweets within twenty-four hours of being online.[14] Microsoft never trained its bot on such divisive language. The bot was trained in a dream world, where the interactions it had and the data it collected were upbeat and positive. Once deployed, it was no longer within the confines of its dreamlike training environment and, like a new bowler bowling without guardrails, the bot's language quickly went into the gutter. While the details of the bot's training environment were not made public, the bot seemed to be rewarded through its learning of new ways of interacting with human respondents. This led to the bot exploiting a gap between its training and what it was observing in the real world to gain maximal reward by engaging in divisive behavior—behavior that, undoubtedly, had more reactions online than positive ones based on the popularity it gained after sending hateful tweets.[15] Dataset nutrition labels and data transparency may have helped in Google's case, but they would not have helped fix Tay. Tay would have needed tools put in place during the deployment step of ML life cycle management to ensure that poor behavior is not exploited for the model to receive greater reward.

MLOps is the final line of defense between the model and the user interacting with the model. MLOps covers the last step in the ML life cycle: implementation, deployment, and model maintenance.[16] By creating a path to bias mitigation within the MLOps function of the ML life cycle, we can better ensure that the work that has been done to mitigate bias in parts 1 to 3 of the life cycle is fortified and continued in the real world through a robust framework created, with the last step of the ML life cycle prioritized.

Models in the Wild, Wild West

Algorithms work very differently once they have been deployed than they do in a practitioner's notebook or local machine. Veterans refer to models that have been deployed into production as models "in the wild" because once a model has been deployed and users are able to interact with it, it behaves very differently than it did when going through training. Also, the practitioner who built the model may have underestimated the sample and has much less control over exogenous variables that may affect the model's performance. Because of this, bias mitigation techniques that ignore the deployment portion of the machine learning life cycle are at risk of augmenting bias in the model once it has been put into production. There are many strategies that have been introduced to get models "in the wild" under control, with a specific emphasis on practitioners monitoring deployed models for concept or data drift in traditional MLOps methods. This method can be extended as a bias mitigation technique in the model deployment.

Concept and Data Drift as Clues

Both concept and data drift can cover biases showing up in a model that has been deployed and should be looked at from a perspective of not only model performance but also bias mitigation. Data drift occurs when the distribution of some input within the model is different in the wild than during model training. Concept drift occurs when the relationship between the model's input and output is different during model training than when it is deployed. Both concept and data drift can occur when a model has biased results against a group. This can hold true even if a practitioner goes above and beyond to mitigate bias in model building. It is important to understand the fundamentals of how this might happen before discussing its implications and how it can be addressed.

A simple example develops the point. Imagine a model is trying to identify people with comorbidities who took the COVID-19 vaccine last year and tries to predict if a person belongs to one of two populations within a relatively wealthy coastal city in the United States. In this case, each population is decided by the labels "does not have a comorbidity" or "has a comorbidity." Let's say population A (*does not have comorbidity*) is 95 percent of a model's training dataset and population B (*has comorbidity*) is 5 percent of the training dataset. A data scientist aware of the imbalance in the dataset decides to run a synthetic minority oversampling technique (SMOTE), a method to equalize extremely imbalanced data by synthetically overestimating the minority population to match that of the major population. Once that is done, the data scientist trains the newly balanced dataset with the knowledge that doing so may result in a reduction in model performance, but they want to prioritize equal observations over maximized performance. After model deployment, however, the ML practitioner finds that the population of people interacting with the model has a different distribution. Population A accounts for 89 percent of interacting users, and population B accounts for 11 percent.

To be clear, depending on the overall size of the population and the targeted confidence interval, this change in percentage of the population may not be noticeable enough for a practitioner to change it. Every modeler has some margin of error that they deem acceptable once a model is in production, as long as the model does not go outside of those bounds. On its face, this may not appear to be something of concern, but for practitioners tasked with model deployment, taking a closer look can yield some important results.

While data drift has been identified in the aforementioned model by the change in model input, practitioners benefit from looking at the distribution within each label and the features shared by each label and judge the variance of each population within the sample to establish true model confidence. If training data from population A does a good job of generalizing to predict "in the wild" population A but does a poor job of predicting population B, one should stratify the sample to understand if there is variance between groups. Here is where demographic data can be used to overcome bias by allowing an ML practitioner to break the data into groups and examining the variance in performance between them. I will discuss this technique within the "Statistical Methods in Model Monitoring" section.

Now, let's take the same example above, but instead of the proportion of the population's distribution in deployment differing from the training dataset, let's assume that the reason for the outcome is misunderstood in the dataset, so the model is unable to adapt. Say there is a campaign in the area to get more people with comorbidities to get vaccinated. This causes population A to increase in training data share and population B to decrease. Not only this, but say, due to a lack of resources, people from less affluent areas with comorbidities come to the more affluent area to get vaccinated, causing population A to decrease and population B's share to increase. During the model interpretation process, practitioners unaware of the campaign believe that people in less affluent areas with comorbidities are less likely to get vaccinated than people with comorbidities in affluent areas. The model they created then uses the share of the population with comorbidities who are getting the vaccine to allocate more resources to the affluent area, causing the cycle of people with comorbidities from less affluent areas to get the vaccine in the more wealthy town to continue. Assumptions being made about this group based on model prediction may lend themselves to bias simply because of this exogenous effect. This would be an example of concept drift occurring due to the introduction of bias in a model.

Identify the Source of the Problem

When concept or data drift occurs, it is important for practitioners to make adjustments to the model through the strategic collection of more data. There are many ways that practitioners can search for where to begin to find more data and what sources of data would be most reliable. There are two main avenues to consider when trying to identify how to get to the bottom of this problem: (1) internal data leakage and (2) external variable capture.

Internal data leakage is when the data source, data pipeline, query, model, dashboard, or other data-based process has broken down. There are many stages at which this can happen and show up in model output as concept drift, so be sure to thoroughly examine each one. Unless you have reason to believe otherwise, looking for signs of internal data leakage is the best place to start, as this is normally the most likely cause of changes in model performance and is a much easier thing to prove and rectify. The second avenue to consider is external variable capture. This was shown in the example above: When an exogenous variable affects model performance, it is up to the practitioner to find data that supports the premise of an exogenous effect.

Statistical Methods in Model Monitoring

There are more techniques the ML practitioner can take advantage of beyond monitoring for concept and data drift that use statistical analysis.

Stratified Sampling

In the setup of a model monitoring dashboard, ML practitioners could add a plot monitoring the scores of each group within a sample through a process called stratified sampling. Stratified sampling is defined by taking an overall sample and dividing it into subgroups for further analysis. In the case of making predictions on any population of people, creating subgroups around demographic factors can, at best, help lead to overall parity between groups and, at least, can allow business leaders and practitioners to see the difference in model performance across groups for further analysis downstream.

Here's what it would look like in practice. Consider an example of a data practitioner monitoring the performance of a model that has been deployed on a simple prediction model that is attempting to predict who would be more or less likely to place a bet. The labels are divided into two populations: population A, which does not place bets, and population B, which does place bets. Within each population is a distribution of subgroups according to demographics. Perhaps, during model training, the data scientist notices that gender is a strong predicting factor of who would be likely to place bets, so the ML practitioner monitoring the model may stratify model output by gender to see if there is a divergence of scores by that feature. This can allow observers to gain extra confidence in the model as strong features may cause model performance to be favored in the direction of one subgroup over another, causing overall scores to be an incomplete picture of true model performance.

Imbalanced Classification/Model Weighting

The idea of using imbalanced classification techniques to improve classification models is not new. In fact, data scientists frequently use imbalanced classification techniques when these problems arise. Popular techniques such as SMOTE and Near-Miss are frequently used to improve performance in cases of predictive algorithms. For the purposes of this chapter, I will focus on using imbalanced classification techniques to assist with instances of bias in model training and model performance.

When working on a machine learning model that is meant to be used by the general population, it is important for the data scientist to identify ways in which some groups may have biased results over others. This can be done with the stratified sampling technique I discussed above. Once they have identified that there is an imbalance within the groups, however, they have the ability to use demographics as a label and then apply SMOTE or Near-Miss (or some other imbalanced classification method) to increase model performance for the underrepresented group.

Experiments and Analytics

In the case of experimentation, it is very important for the ML practitioner to make sure that they separate out the experimentation groups based on subgroups. After they have done so, it is important to judge the efficiency of an experiment, not simply based on the mean or median scoring but on the overall performance of each subgroup.

This is where the data analyst and the ML practitioner can collaborate on the best way of gauging experimentation performance optimality. The data analyst can then analyze the results coming from the experiment to use as extra data that can be fed back into the model in future versioning and model tuning.

Experimentation is an important tool in the ML practitioner's toolbox. Experiments can be used to prove model efficiency in the wild, to compare the performance of multiple models applied to the same problem, or even to prove if a model is a superior solution over a simple technical solution. Practitioners should take care of separating users into treatment and control groups, stratify each group into subgroups based on historically marginalized groups, and compare the performance of the ML model when serving predictions to people versus a simple tech solution that gives people offerings based on explicit user selections. The practitioners should then monitor observations and judge model efficiency on how well it performs on marginalized groups compared to the simple tech solution.

Model Parity Using the Confusion Matrix

Model parity is a technique commonly discussed among circles of ethicists and policymakers during discussions about fairness in machine learning models. There are different types of parity metrics that can be used to mitigate bias in a model and a modeling dashboard for machine learning practitioners to monitor model performance.

The first type of parity metric we are going to discuss is one that is quite familiar to most: demographic parity. Demographic parity requires that the positive rates of the underrepresented subgroup be equal to the percentage of the positive rate of the overrepresented class. The probability equation of the outcome is defined as follows:

$$P(\hat{Y} \mid A = 0) = P(\hat{Y} \mid A = 1)$$

Such that the positive rate of the overrepresented subgroup $A = 0$ is the same as the positive rate of the underrepresented subgroup $A = 1$. An ML practitioner can simply use a confusion matrix to demonstrate if each subgroup has the same positive rate.

The second type of parity is called the equal opportunity parity metric. This parity metric takes things a step further and says that, assuming all things are equal, the underrepresented subgroup should receive some prediction at the same rate as the overrepresented group. In this case, the ML practitioner would use the true positive rate within the confusion matrix for each subgroup to identify if the outcomes are equal. The formula for this probability is as follows:

$$P(\hat{Y} = 1 \mid A = 0, Y = 1) = P(\hat{Y} = 1 \mid A = 1, Y = 1)$$

Such that the true positive rate of the overrepresented subgroup $A = 0$ is the same as the positive rate of the underrepresented subgroup $A = 1$.

The last type of parity I will discuss within this chapter is the equalized odds parity metric. This metric is one that suggests not only that outcomes should be equal, suggesting known factors remain constant, but also that false positives across subgroups must be equal. To get the equalized odds parity rate, the ML practitioner would need to divide the true positive rate of each subgroup by the false positive rate for each subgroup. The goal is to make the percentage of the equalized odds parity metric as close to zero as possible. The probability formula is as follows:

$$P(\hat{Y} = 1 \mid A = 0, Y = \mathrm{y}) = P(\hat{Y} = 1 \mid A = 1, Y = 1), \mathrm{y} \in \{0,1\}$$

Such that the true positive rate of the overrepresented group $A = 0$ is equal to the true positive rate of the underrepresented subgroup $A = 1$, and the false positive rate of the overrepresented group $A = 0$ is equal to the false positive rate of the underrepresented subgroup $A = 1$.

Deployment Methods for Bias Mitigation

Of all the deployment methods in a machine learning operative's arsenal, there are two that can be used specifically for the purpose of bias mitigation that I will talk about in this chapter. The first one is canary deployment, and the second is blue/green deployment.

Canary Deployment

Canary deployment is aptly named based on an old mining strategy. If you ever heard of the "canary in the coal mine" saying, you are somewhat familiar with the heart of this process. When coal miners would approach a new mine, they would release a canary into the coal mine to test if harmful gases were present. If the canary was able to survive entering and leaving the coal mine, the coal miners felt assured that the coal mine was safe to enter. If not, the coal miners would go back to step one and apply methods to reduce the toxic gases until the coal mine was safe to enter.

Bias in a model is a type of toxic gas. When a model is making predictions that unjustly discriminate against a historically marginalized group, it is to the detriment of the performance of the model, and, in some cases, to society as a whole. When the ML practitioner uses canary deployment, they have the ability to test if model performance degradation has occurred as a result of bias that has been introduced to the model "in the wild."

This process can be used after stratified sampling techniques that separate a population set into subgroups based on demographics and/or analyze the variance between said subgroups. The ML practitioner can schedule a staggered release of the model to an equitable sample of people in the entire population through the process of canary deployment. In practice, this will look like taking a representative sample of some percentage N of a population and unveiling the model to this group over some T time and testing the interactions of the model across each group while analyzing model parity. If the model performs up to an acceptable standard, the ML practitioner can safely extend the deployed model to a larger population $N + 1$ until model stability has been achieved.

Blue/Green Deployment

The second deployment strategy is called blue/green deployment. This is a process where the ML practitioner can slowly move people from one production environment to another. Here, applications of experimentation can be employed for further model testing. ML practitioners can test the efficiency of model 1 versus model 2 and examine how much bias is present in each model as a key performance indicator (KPI) and then move forward with the model that has the best parity performance. They can also compare the status quo to the introduction of a new machine learning production environment and compare the parity of the model over time. Either way, this method allows an ML practitioner to compare the efficiency of model performance through the lens of bias mitigation. They can then work with their team after some *T* time to examine model efficiency.

Human in the Loop

A wonderful way to reduce bias, either picked up by a model in the wild or covered up in model training by exploitative decision-making by the model, is returning observations picked up by the model for retraining purposes to a database for human approval. This can be done in a couple of ways:

Flagging: ML practitioners can initiate a flagging mechanism that causes the model to err on the side of human deferment. This can be done by tracking scoring per observation in a database that tracks predicted observations and marking predicted observations that do not score high enough. The definition of adequate scoring should be based on the originating error rate identified during the training process and tracked in the dataset nutrition label. So, for example, if a classifier has an F1 score of 88 percent for Black women within the training environment, based on overall variance between training and deployed performance, practitioners may decide to flag all observations with F1 scores outside of the range of acceptability and find a questionable score to be 84 percent or lower. These observations can be flagged for further review by practitioners and logged for model transparency.

Pruning: This is when a practitioner removes an observation for model retraining. Practitioners can decide to do this as a way of erecting guardrails that mitigate bias being introduced by the model exploiting a gap between its training environment and the real world.

Nudging: Observations flagged in the retraining set can be returned to the human for the human to hardcode the appropriate response for the model to learn from.

Reinforcement Learning for Model Alignment

The bias mitigation techniques covered in previous sections of this chapter focus primarily on identifying and addressing bias during the traditional steps of the

ML life cycle. However, there's an emerging class of approaches that takes bias mitigation and model alignment a step further by using reinforcement learning (RL) methods to continuously align model behavior with human values and preferences post deployment.

For practitioners working with large language models (LLMs) and interactive AI systems, these approaches offer new tools for ensuring models behave appropriately even as they encounter novel situations in production. This section examines two approaches that show particular promise for integration into MLOps pipelines: reflexion, which uses verbal RL for iterative self-improvement, and reinforcement learning from human feedback (RLHF), including its more practical variant, direct preference optimization (DPO).

Reflexion: Teaching Models to Learn from Their Mistakes

How Reflexion Works

Reflexion takes a fundamentally different approach to model improvement compared to traditional methods.[17] Instead of requiring expensive model retraining every time performance degrades, reflexion enables models to improve through self-reflection and memory—much like humans learn from experience.

The framework operates through three components that work together in a continuous feedback loop:

The actor: This is your primary model for making decisions and generating outputs in production. It takes into account both the current situation and its accumulated experience from previous interactions.

The evaluator: This component determines whether the actor's performance meets your defined criteria. The evaluation can be as simple as binary success/failure or as complex as multidimensional scoring based on your specific requirements.

The self-reflection component: When the actor fails, this component analyzes what went wrong and generates specific, actionable feedback that gets stored in the model's memory for future reference.

What makes this particularly attractive for practitioners is that it doesn't require the computational overhead of traditional RL. There's no gradient descent, no weight updates, and no expensive retraining cycles. Instead, the model learns through linguistic feedback that becomes part of its decision-making context.

Practical Implementation in MLOps

The beauty of reflexion is that it can be layered onto existing MLOps infrastructure without requiring major architectural changes. You can think of it as adding a feedback and memory system to your current deployment pipeline.

Here's how it might work in practice: Let's say your deployed model consistently struggles with requests from users in a specific demographic group. Traditional approaches would require you to identify the bias, collect additional training data, retrain the model, and redeploy—a process that could take weeks or months. With reflexion, when the model encounters a failure, it generates a reflection about what went wrong and stores that insight in its episodic memory. The next time it encounters a similar situation, it can reference that experience and adjust its approach accordingly.

This approach proved effective across several domains relevant to production systems. In sequential decision-making tasks, reflexion improved performance by 22 percent over baseline approaches. For code generation, it achieved 91 percent pass@1 accuracy on HumanEval—a substantial improvement over GPT-4's 80 percent performance. In complex reasoning tasks, it showed 20 percent improvements on HotpotQA.[18]

But reflexion isn't a silver bullet. The approach struggles with tasks that require extremely diverse exploration strategies. In experiments with WebShop—an e-commerce navigation benchmark—reflexion failed to show meaningful improvement over baseline methods, with performance plateauing at around a 35 percent success rate compared to React's baseline performance.[19] This suggests that while reflexion excels at learning from specific types of failures, it may not be suitable for tasks requiring highly creative or diverse problem-solving approaches.

RLHF

Understanding the RLHF Process

RLHF has become the go-to method for aligning large language models with human preferences, and it's the technique behind models such as ChatGPT and GPT-4.[20] For practitioners, understanding RLHF is crucial because it represents one of the most effective ways to ensure your deployed models behave according to your organization's values and user expectations.

The traditional RLHF process works in three stages:

1 **Supervised fine-tuning:** Start with a pretrained model and fine-tune it on high-quality demonstrations of the behavior you want. This establishes a baseline level of performance.

2. **Reward model training:** Collect human preferences by having annotators compare pairs of model outputs and indicate which response is better. Use these comparisons to train a reward model that can predict human preferences.
3. **Policy optimization:** Use RL (typically Proximal Policy Optimization [PPO]) to fine-tune your original model to maximize the learned reward while preventing it from deviating too far from the original behavior.[21]

The Problem with Traditional RLHF

While RLHF has proven effective, it creates significant challenges for practitioners trying to implement it in production.

1. **Computational overhead:** Traditional RLHF requires training and maintaining multiple models. The RL phase involves extensive sampling from the policy during training, making the whole process computationally expensive and difficult to scale.
2. **Training instability:** PPO-based training can be unstable and highly sensitive to hyperparameter settings. Small changes in configuration can lead to drastically different results, making it difficult to achieve consistent performance across training runs.
3. **Infrastructure complexity:** The need to coordinate multiple models, manage extensive sampling processes, and tune numerous hyperparameters creates significant operational overhead for teams trying to deploy these systems.

These challenges have made traditional RLHF impractical for many organizations, despite its effectiveness in research settings.[22]

DPO: RLHF Made Practical

DPO solves many of RLHF's practical problems by eliminating the need for explicit reward modeling and RL training altogether.[23] This is a game changer for practitioners because it makes preference-based training accessible without the computational and operational overheads of traditional RLHF.[24]

The key insight behind DPO is that you can directly optimize the policy using preference data without going through the intermediate step of training a reward model. Instead of the complex three-stage RLHF pipeline, DPO transforms the preference learning problem into a simple classification task.

Why This Matters for Practitioners

- **Simplified training:** DPO uses a straightforward binary cross-entropy loss instead of complex RL algorithms.
- **Reduced computational requirements:** There is no need for multiple models or extensive sampling during training.
- **Improved stability:** It involves more predictable training behavior with fewer hyperparameters to manage.
- **Easy integration:** It can be integrated into existing supervised learning pipelines with minimal changes.

Integrating RL Approaches with Existing Bias Mitigation

Building on Traditional Techniques

The RL approaches discussed here don't replace the bias mitigation techniques covered earlier in this chapter, although they do extend them. The most effective MLOps pipelines will combine both approaches to create comprehensive bias mitigation systems.

The stratified sampling techniques discussed earlier become even more critical when working with aligned models. You need to ensure that improvements in alignment don't come at the cost of equitable performance across different demographic groups. This means applying the same demographic parity and equalized odds metrics we discussed, but now in the context of preference-based evaluation.

You can and should incorporate explicit fairness constraints into your alignment objectives. The confusion matrix analysis and parity metrics from earlier sections can be integrated into both reflexion's evaluation criteria and RLHF's reward modeling process.

Both reflexion and RLHF naturally support human oversight mechanisms.[25] This creates opportunities to implement the human-in-the-loop strategies we discussed (flagging, pruning, and nudging) within the alignment framework.

Practical Implementation Considerations

Aligned models require evaluation frameworks that go beyond traditional metrics. You're no longer just measuring accuracy or F1 scores; you're measuring alignment with human preferences, which can be subjective and context-dependent.

Traditional concept and data drift detection must be augmented with alignment-specific monitoring. Your model might maintain its technical performance while exhibiting subtle behavioral shifts that violate your intended alignment objectives. Production systems often need to balance preferences from multiple stakeholders who may have conflicting objectives. This requires careful consideration of how to weigh different preference signals and resolve conflicts between them.

Deployment Strategies

Given the complexity of alignment objectives, these models should be deployed using canary strategies with careful monitoring for alignment degradation across different user populations. Alignment failures may not be immediately apparent through traditional performance metrics.

Traditional A/B testing frameworks need to be adapted to compare models based on preference-based metrics rather than simple performance indicators. This requires developing evaluation frameworks that can capture human preferences at scale.

The complexity of alignment objectives makes robust rollback mechanisms essential. When aligned models exhibit unexpected behaviors, you need the ability to quickly revert to previous versions while investigating the root cause.

Limitations and Practical Considerations

Scalability Challenges

1. **Preference collection:** Human preference collection remains expensive and can be biased toward certain demographics or viewpoints. Scaling this process while maintaining quality and representativeness is an ongoing challenge that practitioners need to address.
2. **Computational resources:** Even simplified approaches, such as DPO, require significant computational resources for large models. Organizations need to carefully balance alignment benefits against computational costs.
3. **Multiobjective optimization:** Real-world deployments often require balancing multiple, potentially conflicting alignment objectives. Developing frameworks that can handle these trade-offs effectively remains challenging.

Safety and Robustness Issues

1. **Reward hacking:** Models optimized for human preferences may learn to exploit weaknesses in evaluation metrics or human feedback rather than genuinely improving their behavior. This is particularly concerning in high-stakes applications.
2. **Distribution shift:** Aligned behavior demonstrated during training may not generalize to deployment scenarios, especially when the deployment environment differs significantly from the training environment.
3. **Adversarial robustness:** Aligned models must maintain their desired behaviors even when exposed to inputs designed to elicit problematic responses.

Moving Forward with RL-Based Alignment

The integration of RL approaches into MLOps pipelines represents a significant step forward in our ability to deploy AI systems that remain aligned with human values throughout their life cycles. Reflexion offers an interpretable and computationally efficient approach for scenarios where understanding failure modes is critical. RLHF and DPO provide robust frameworks for incorporating human preferences directly into model behavior.[26]

However, these approaches require careful integration with existing MLOps practices. The traditional bias mitigation techniques discussed throughout this chapter, such as stratified sampling, fairness metrics, and human-in-the-loop processes, become even more important when working with aligned models. Success requires extending these established practices to work alongside RL approaches while developing new methods for evaluating model behavior against subjective human preferences.

For practitioners, the key is to start small and build expertise gradually. Begin by implementing DPO for preference-based fine-tuning in controlled environments before scaling to full production deployments. Experiment with reflexion for specific use cases where interpretable failure analysis is valuable. Most importantly, ensure that your existing bias mitigation infrastructure is robust enough to support these more complex alignment objectives.

Conclusion

What would have happened to Microsoft if, instead of simply releasing Tay without taking proper care to mitigate bias during the MLOps cycle, they had employed some of the techniques discussed in this chapter? Using concept drift, practitioners would begin to notice that the environment that Tay had been deployed into was drastically different from the environment in which they trained her. They would begin to see a preponderance of data being ingested that was not present in their training environment using data drift and could have adapted accordingly. Using a canary deployment approach, they could have tested Tay in a real-world environment with fewer people and segmented the people using Tay into test and control groups using experimentation. They could have compared Tay's performance as a conversational AI bot to a bot with hardcoded responses and seen how well each bot performed in the real world. Finally, practitioners could have flagged new words introduced into Tay's training lexicon, removed profanity and divisive words using pruning, and nudged the dataset by replacing the inappropriate words with more appropriate ones.

From defining project objectives to model deployment, every step of the ML life cycle should include bias mitigation techniques. If we focus on steps 1 to 3 and do not take care to understand step 5 and how it contributes to bias as well, we will not be able to have the equitable and value-driven models that are good for society. While this chapter serves as an overview of a few techniques that machine learning practitioners can use to mitigate bias in a model during the MLOps life cycle, there are more techniques that can and should be explored by people passionate about making ML models more equitable for those who have been historically marginalized.

Notes

1 Barbican Centre, "Joy Buolamwini: Examining Racial and Gender Bias in Facial Analysis Software," Google Arts & Culture, available online: https://artsandculture.google.com/story/joy-buolamwini-examining-racial-and-gender-bias-in-facial-analysis-software-barbican-centre/BQWBaNKAVWQPJg?hl=en.

2 DataRobot, "Machine Learning Lifecycle Is the Process That Derives Practical Business Value," available online: https://www.datarobot.com/wiki/machine-learning-life-cycle/#:~:text=The%20machine%20learning%20life%20cycle%20is%20the%20cyclical%20process%20that,to%20derive%20practical%20business%20value.

3 Batya Friedman, Peter Kahn Jr., and Alan Borning, "Value Sensitive Design: Theory and Methods," UW CSE Technical Report 02-12-01 (2002): 1–8.

4 Ibid., 6–8.

5 Safiya Umoja Noble, *Algorithms of Oppression: How Search Engines Reinforce Racism* (New York University Press, 2018); Cathy O'Neil, *Weapons of Math Destruction: How Big Data Increases Inequality and Threatens Democracy* (Penguin Books, 2018).

6 Noble, *Algorithms of Oppression*, 25–9.

7 Deeplearning.ai, "MLOps: From Model-centric to Data-Centric AI," available online: https://www.slideshare.net/slideshow/mlops-from-model-centric-to-data-centric-ai-pdf/271328668.

8 Jacky Alciné, @jackyalcine, "Google Photos, Y'all [Expletive] Up. My Friend's Not a Gorilla," Twitter (now X.com), June 29, 2015, available online: https://x.com/jackyalcine.

9 Tom Simonite, "When It Comes to Gorillas, Google Photos Remains Blind," *WIRED*, January 11, 2018, available online: https://www.wired.com/story/when-it-comes-to-gorillas-google-photos-remains-blind/.

10 Joy Buolamwini and Timnit Gebru, "Gender Shades: Intersectional Accuracy Disparities in Commercial Gender Classification," *Proceedings of Machine Learning Research* 81 (2018): 12.

11 Ruha Benjamin, *Race After Technology: Abolitionist Tools for the New Jim Code* (Polity, 2019), 175.

12 Simonite, "When It Comes to Gorillas."

13 Janelle Shane, *You Look Like a Thing and I Love You: How Artificial Intelligence Works and Why It's Making the World a Weirder Place* (Voracious/Little, Brown, 2019), 125–9.

14 Rob Price, "Microsoft Deletes Racist Genocidal Tweets from AI Chatbot Tay," *Business Insider*, March 24, 2016, available online: https://www.businessinsider.com/microsoft-deletes-racist-genocidal-tweets-from-ai-chatbot-tay-2016-3.

15 James Vincent, "Microsoft Chatbot Racist," *The Verge*, March 24, 2016, available online: https://www.theverge.com/2016/3/24/11297050/tay-microsoft-chatbot-racist.

16 DataRobot, "Machine Learning Lifecycle Is the Process That Derives Practical Business Value," available online: https://www.datarobot.com/wiki/machine-learning-life-cycle/#:~:text=The%20machine%20learning%20life%20cycle%20is%20the%20cyclical%20process%20that,to%20derive%20practical%20business%20value.

17 Long Ouyang et al., "Training Language Models to Follow Instructions with Human Feedback," *Advances in Neural Information Processing Systems* 35 (2022): 27730–44.

18 Noah Shinn, "Reflexion: Language Agents with Verbal Reinforcement Learning," *arXiv* preprint arXiv:2303.11366 (2023): 3–8.

19 Ouyang et al., "Training Language Models."

20 Ibid.; Daniel Ziegler et al., "Fine-Tuning Language Models from Human Preferences," *arXiv* preprint arXiv:2010.01967 (2020): 2–20.

21 Ziegler et al., "Fine-Tuning Language Models."

22 Rafael Rafailov et al., "Direct Preference Optimization: Your Language Model Is Secretly a Reward Model," *arXiv* preprint arXiv:2305.18290 (2023): 4–10.

23 Ibid.

24 Ibid.

25 Ouyang et al., "Training Language Models"; Ziegler et al., "Fine-Tuning Language Models."

26 Ouyang et al., "Training Language Models"; Rafailov et al., "Direct Preference Optimization."

Bibliography

Alciné, Jacky @jackyalcine. "Google Photos, Y'all [Expletive] Up. My Friend's Not a Gorilla." Twitter (now X.com), June 29, 2015. Available online: https://x.com/jackyalcine.

Barbican Centre. "Joy Buolamwini: Examining Racial and Gender Bias in Facial Analysis Software." Google Arts & Culture. Available online: https://artsandculture.google.com/story/joy-buolamwini-examining-racial-and-gender-bias-in-facial-analysis-software-barbican-centre/BQWBaNKAVWQPJg?hl=en.

Benjamin, Ruha. *Race after Technology: Abolitionist Tools for the New Jim Code*. Polity, 2019.

Buolamwini, Joy, and Timnit Gebru. "Gender Shades: Intersectional Accuracy Disparities in Commercial Gender Classification." *Proceedings of Machine Learning Research* 81 (2018): 1–15.

DataRobot. "Machine Learning Lifecycle Is the Process That Derives Practical Business Value." Available online: https://www.datarobot.com/wiki/machine-learning-life-cycle/#:~:text=The%20machine%20learning%20life%20cycle%20is%20the%20cyclical%20process%20that,to%20derive%20practical%20business%20value.

Deeplearning.ai. "MLOps: From Model-Centric to Data-centric AI." Available online: https://www.slideshare.net/slideshow/mlops-from-model-centric-to-data-centric-ai-pdf/271328668.

Friedman, Batya, Peter Kahn Jr., and Alan Borning. "Value Sensitive Design: Theory and Methods." UW CSE Technical Report 02-12-01 (2002): 1–8.

Noble, Safiya Umoja. *Algorithms of Oppression: How Search Engines Reinforce Racism*. New York University Press, 2018.

O'Neil, Cathy. *Weapons of Math Destruction: How Big Data Increases Inequality and Threatens Democracy*. Penguin, 2018.

Ouyang, Long, et al. "Training Language Models to Follow Instructions with Human Feedback." *Advances in Neural Information Processing Systems* 35 (2022): 27730–44.

Price, Rob. "Microsoft Deletes Racist Genocidal Tweets from AI Chatbot Tay." *Business Insider*, March 24, 2016. Available online: https://www.businessinsider.com/microsoft-deletes-racist-genocidal-tweets-from-ai-chatbot-tay-2016-3.

Rafailov, Rafael, Archit Sharma, Eric Mitchell, Stefano Ermon, Christopher D. Manning, and Chelsea Finn. "Direct Preference Optimization: Your Language Model Is Secretly a Reward Model." *arXiv* preprint arXiv:2305.18290 (2023): 4–10.

Shane, Janelle. *You Look Like a Thing and I Love You: How Artificial Intelligence Works and Why It's Making the World a Weirder Place*. Voracious/Little, Brown, 2019.

Shinn, Noah, Federico Cassano, Edward Berman, Ashwin Gopinath, Karthik Narasimhan, and Shunyu Yao. "Reflexion: Language Agents with Verbal Reinforcement Learning." *arXiv* preprint arXiv:2303.11366 (2023): 3–8.

Simonite, Tom. "When It Comes to Gorillas, Google Photos Remains Blind." *WIRED*, January 11, 2018. Available online: https://www.wired.com/story/when-it-comes-to-gorillas-google-photos-remains-blind/.

Vincent, James. "Microsoft Chatbot Racist." *The Verge*, March 24, 2016. Available online: https://www.theverge.com/2016/3/24/11297050/tay-microsoft-chatbot-racist.

Ziegler, Daniel, Nisan Stiennon, Jeffrey Wu, Tom B. Brown, Alec Radford, Dario Amodei, Paul Christiano, and Geoffrey Irving. "Fine-Tuning Language Models from Human Preferences." *arXiv* preprint arXiv:2010.01967 (2020): 2–20.

PART THREE
COMPETITION

8

SELF-REGULATING PLATFORMS AND ANTITRUST JUSTICE

Elettra Bietti

Introduction

What is a market? Historian Karl Polanyi defined it as "a meeting place for the purpose of barter or buying and selling."[1] He viewed one specific market form, the self-regulating market, as central to contemporary market societies. Self-regulating markets are markets ideally governed by price equilibrium, that is, the meeting of offer and demand for a product or service. The laws and institutions of market societies aim to create and promote efficient self-regulating price mechanisms by keeping these mechanisms at arm's length from political and legal pressures. This imaginary division of labor between the private sphere of price equilibrium and individual choice, and the public sphere of politics and democratic rule has come at a cost for humans and the natural world.

Self-regulating markets are constructed through law.[2] In the words of historian Quinn Slobodian, markets are "encased," made less prone to political pressures.[3] The tendency to separate self-regulating markets from politics, immunizing individual choices and market-derived advantages from democratic rule, is characteristic of the law and policy of many developed market economies, including in the United States and the European Union. The more a culture values markets as efficient modes of allocation, the more it tries to keep its economic processes artificially separate from the pressures of social life.

In digital market societies around the world, digital platforms, such as Facebook/Meta, Google/Alphabet, or Amazon, have become a new market form that extends across jurisdictional and regional boundaries and whose continued integrity and growth increasingly conflicts with national democratic pressures. Framing platforms as sovereigns, governors, or constitutional spaces[4] reflects a long history of seeing the internet as a self-governing space independent from the law of states.[5] Such framing entrenches the markets–politics divide and immunizes digital platforms from the pressures of democratic law.

This chapter focuses on antitrust law. It shows that platforms are neither autonomous sovereigns nor self-regulating marketplaces, and that antitrust must reconnect digital platform markets to their social and democratic roots and implications. Platforms are political spaces that construct and affect societies and are subject to the pressures of state law. The problem is that much of EU and US digital law, including antitrust, envisions platforms primarily as self-regulating marketplaces where individual choices are sovereign. This approach undermines democratic representation and distributive justice in platform spaces. Not all hope is lost, however. The United States has until recently seen the rise of an antimonopoly "spring"[6]: Progressive leaders were appointed to positions of power, important lawsuits were started against big tech companies,[7] and reform bills were introduced in Congress.[8] In Europe, the Digital Services and Digital Markets Acts introduced a fresh structural approach to digital markets combining traditional antitrust rules and new ex ante investigatory and remedial powers in tech markets.[9] An important question is whether this Progressive wave of change can be understood as being in continuity with the perception of digital platform markets as self-regulating spaces or if we are witnessing a new turn and the beginning of a new Era for antitrust and digital regulation.

The chapter proceeds as follows. It first introduces the current antitrust law approach to digital platform markets, which advances an ideal of autonomous efficient market processes immune from political and normative concerns. It shows that legal enforcement must be minimal, is particularly pervasive in antitrust law, and manifests in the form of a focus on low prices, efficiencies, and the consumer welfare standard. It then discusses how to reintroduce normative and distributive justice considerations in the regulation of digital platform markets. It argues that we must prefer a "predistributive" structural approach to fairness and justice considerations in markets over a focus on after-the-fact "redistribution" through taxation or other means that do not interfere with markets.

Digital Platforms as Self-Regulating Marketplaces: Efficiency and Welfare

This section shows that digital platforms, such as Facebook/Meta, Google/Alphabet, and Amazon, can be viewed simultaneously as monopolies and as market makers, and that their dual nature raises important conundrums that have yet to be resolved. It then argues that the apparent intractability of these conundrums can be traced to neoliberal approaches to antitrust.

Digital Platforms as Monopolies and Market Makers

Platforms as Monopolies

It is well accepted that companies such as Facebook, Google, or Amazon are dominant in their respective fields of operation. In 2019, Google's total revenues were as high as Hungary's GDP that same year, according to the World Bank indicator,[10] and these revenues continue to grow in 2021. The COVID-19 pandemic made Amazon's founder and former CEO, Jeff Bezos, break a historical record of personal wealth.[11] And more than a fourth of the people alive in 2020 are active daily users of at least one of Facebook's family of social platforms (Facebook, Instagram, WhatsApp, or Messenger).[12] As noted by the US House Judiciary Committee in its Antitrust Report in October 2020:

> Over the past decade, the digital economy has become highly concentrated and prone to monopolization. Several markets investigated by the Subcommittee—such as social networking, general online search, and online advertising—are dominated by just one or two firms. (. . .) Amazon, Apple, Facebook, and Google—have captured control over key channels of distribution and have come to function as gatekeepers. Just a decade into the future, 30% of the world's gross economic output may lie with these firms, and just a handful of others.[13]

Courts and regulators have found these companies to be dominant bottlenecks in a number of industries. The US House Judiciary Committee and Germany's antitrust regulator, among other authorities, have found Facebook dominant in the market for social networking services in their respective jurisdictions.[14] Google's dominance in the markets for general search, search advertising, and online advertising intermediation was confirmed in several EU and US cases since the *Google/DoubleClick* merger investigations.[15] Most notably, Google has been declared a monopoly in two important antitrust decisions in the United States.[16] Google is dominant in a number of other market segments, including an 80 percent market share in the market for navigation mapping services in the United States.[17] Amazon has "significant and durable market power in the US online retail market," with an approximate share of 50 percent of online retail sales.[18]

Findings of dominance or durable market power, that is, of the long-term ability to set prices or market conditions and exclude competitors, also tend to rely on definitions of markets, i.e., of supply and demand substitutability, unsuited to digital contexts. They frequently presume large markets and rely on price instead of nonprice indicators to infer market definition and market competitors. Current analytical methods provide weak guidance in digital environments, where prices are not always the best signals for market power, and where questions of access and infrastructural and network power require different measurements.[19] Courts also frequently define antitrust harms in terms of price increases, output reductions, and a reduction in the number of options available, instead of looking to more subtle digital indicators of harm, such as dark patterns, the inability to leave a platform, the opacity of terms of service, and the indiscriminate nature of surveillance and manipulation on the platform.[20] The markets that Google, Facebook, or Amazon operate in are poorly competitive, not only in the loose sense that other competitors that would "enter" them find it difficult to do so but also because these markets are hierarchically constructed in ways that disadvantage competitors and lock-in users and customers by default. They are dominated and shaped by the infrastructural and informational advantages of platform gatekeepers.[21] Competition in the digital economy occurs through the creation of alternative marketplaces (competition for the platform market), not through competing in the same market (competition in the platform market).[22]

Platforms as Market Makers

Platforms are not just monopolies; they also are and make markets. In legal scholar Julie Cohen's words, platforms are "information intermediar[ies] that use . . . data-driven, algorithmic methods and standardized, modular interconnection protocols to facilitate digitally networked interactions and transactions."[23] They "replace (and rematerialize)" markets.[24] They are, therefore, market *makers* at the same time as they are market players. Professor Maurice Stucke and author Ariel Ezrachi refer to digital platform companies as "gamemakers," borrowing the term from the *Hunger Games*.[25] They argue that digital platforms control the digital game, design and manipulate preferences, dictate the terms of competition for the market actors that operate within their ecosystems, and exploit users. Before being anyone's competitors, these entities intermediate and infrastructurally enable access and repeated transactions between diversified groups of customers and users.

An illustrative example is how digital platforms have contributed to shifting contemporary patterns of consumption from physical ownership of goods to the purchase of access rights and subscription-based goods and services.[26] Airbnb intermediates between homeowners and temporary travelers, replacing and reimagining hospitality[27]; Netflix and YouTube offer video on-demand services,[28] replacing VRs, DVDs, and the traditional content production and distribution industries. Amazon and eBay have reinvented retail consumption, and Facebook and Twitter have changed social interaction, public discourse, and political life. Together, these platforms have transformed owned goods or social experiences into consumerist lifestyles accessible at any point in time from anywhere but entirely dependent on access to a platform controlled by a platform gatekeeper. They do not merely compete with supermarkets, hotels, and other analog services. They contribute to creatively disrupting many of these markets, advancing new forms of consumerism on steroids.

The economic literature focuses on two connected aspects of platform business models: their multisidedness and the network effects they give rise to. A market is multisided if three conditions are present.[29] First, there must be two or more distinct groups of customers. Second, coordinating and connecting these groups of customers must be costly, and third, an intermediary platform must be able to internalize some of these costs. Amazon, for example, makes it cheaper for buyers of books to find sellers of books and for sellers to find buyers. This translates into the possibility that books sold through Amazon are less expensive to buy and sell than they would be otherwise. Shopping malls, credit cards, the stock exchange, newspapers, the farmer's market, and the auction house are all multisided markets. The second concept, network effects, reflects the positive effect that an additional user of a good or service has on the value of that product for others.[30]

Attempts to understand and theorize digital platform markets through traditional economic concepts have not been successful.[31] In the United States, neoliberal antitrust influences have oriented antitrust law toward productive efficiencies and "perfect competition" and obscured a myriad of digital harms.[32] Such influence has contributed to a conception of platform markets as self-regulating spaces immune from significant legal and regulatory pressures.

Antitrust Law in Digital Markets

American antitrust law has progressive roots that date back to the 1890s, when antitrust emerged as an apparatus for tackling abuses of market power and anticompetitive commercial conduct, particularly in the railway and electricity industries.[33] The Sherman Antitrust Act came into force in 1890, and the Supreme Court first declared a merger unlawful in 1904.[34] Strong regulatory enforcement began at the turn of the century, and the antitrust toolbox was used quite aggressively until the 1980s. In the 1911 landmark case of *Standard Oil,* the Supreme Court ordered the oil monopoly's breakup into thirty-four segments.[35] In 1982, the AT&T monopoly was similarly broken up.[36] By the time it was Microsoft's turn in the 1990s, the context had changed.[37] Although the District Court in that case also ordered a breakup of Microsoft,[38] the company was able to reverse the ruling and to settle the case instead.[39] Despite its importance and length, the *Microsoft* trial showcased antitrust enforcers' reluctance to intervene aggressively in innovative markets, preferring instead

Judge Easterbrook's famous *error cost* underenforcement approach.[40] The more recent rulings in the *FTC v. Meta* and *U.S. v. Google (Search)* cases continue to demonstrate such reluctance, despite changed circumstances and significant clarity on Google and Meta's dominance in tech markets.[41]

In the 1890s, antitrust law was understood as a vehicle for ensuring representation in productive and economic matters.[42] It was understood that markets were structured by antitrust law, and other branches of law and regulation. Political institutions had the power to rectify economic inequalities and restructure markets in the public interest, and antitrust was one source of such power. However, the political nature of antitrust and its role in furthering the public interest have, at various moments in its history, been obscured by the emphasis on "competitiveness," "efficiency," or "consumer welfare."

The 1970s marked a shift toward a Chicago School, and a Harvard School approach aimed explicitly at encasing markets from politics, promoting self-regulating markets, efficiency, and consumer welfare. Judge Robert Bork contributed to popularizing and transposing the neoclassical and Chicago School approach to economics into antitrust policy in his classic review of the goals of antitrust law published in 1978.[43] In it, he reinvented the history of antitrust law, arguing that it should be understood as a history concerned with the promotion of consumer welfare,[44] the maximization of productive and allocative efficiencies, that is, of outputs.[45] This approach became consciously tolerant of, and friendly to, monopolies, favoring large (and purportedly efficient) conglomerates of economic power, including digital power, over the fairness of markets and the well-being of consumers, workers, and other actors.[46] Chicago School antitrust, alongside other dominant schools of antitrust, favored deregulation over intervention in digital markets. This approach is likely to have contributed to the growth of digital monopolies, such as Google/Alphabet, Facebook/Meta, and Amazon, through mergers and acquisitions, as well as exclusionary prices or other dealings. For long, Big Tech's exclusionary conduct failed to attract Section 2 of the Sherman Antitrust Act scrutiny. Another salient Chicago School symptom has been the generous approach to mergers in the digital sector. Bork's legacy has profoundly shaped contemporary US antitrust law and digital markets to this day.[47] It has contributed to naturalizing a vision of digital platforms as efficient self-regulating spaces that do not require political, legal, or regulatory intervention.

The recent Supreme Court judgment in *Ohio v. American Express* ("Amex") illustrates the many limitations of dominant antitrust thinking on platform markets and its deregulatory effects.[48] The case examined the credit card market, and the Supreme Court, for the first time, looked at the question of anticompetitive behavior in two-sided markets. Credit card provider American Express had imposed antisteering provisions in its agreements with merchants, prohibiting merchants from steering consumers away from *Amex* cards. The court found that Amex's effort to limit merchants' ability to choose other payment methods was not anticompetitive because its overall effect was to incentivize consumers to engage in more transactions beneficial to them. The result of such antisteering measures was indeed an increase in the volume of transactions and, therefore, an overall increase in consumer welfare. According to the dominant conception of antitrust, this meant that antisteering was not a problem, even if it resulted in American Express charging merchants more in a unilateral manner.[49]

The case illustrates some confusion on the basic pillars of antitrust analysis in platform and multisided markets. Together with other cases such as *United States v. Sabre Corp.*,[50] Amex casts doubts on the nature of digital platform markets and how antitrust law should address harm in those markets. It was unclear in the court's reasoning how one should define digital platform markets, let alone market power in the digital economy. Contrary to judges' assertions, multisidedness is not clearly indicative of how anticompetitive behavior plays out on these markets.[51] In some cases, two-sidedness means that platforms can engage in anticompetitive behavior by cross-subsidizing between platform sides or engaging in opaque behavior. In other cases, two-sided markets behave like any other market. In response to these doubts, John Newman has argued that focusing on two-sided or multisided markets obscures the fact that many platform markets are best described as traditional distribution chains where natural persons are suppliers of attention or data, platforms and intermediaries are distributors, and advertisers or merchants are consumers of attention, data, and more.[52] Legal scholar Thomas Nachbar has also argued that anticompetitive effects in platform markets require a case-by-case analysis of what he calls "platform effects," defined as the ability of platforms to cross-subsidize between customer groups.[53]

Importantly, platforms price-discriminate and personalize pricing to different customers and subgroups based on algorithmic and infrastructural control. Leveraging infrastructural capability maximizes their revenues and ensures that customers on various sides of the platform do not switch to other competitors. Price discrimination, personalization, and cross-subsidization of pricing to different customers and subgroups is a clear characteristic of market power in digital platform markets, one that dominant antitrust approaches, including the court in the Amex case, have struggled to capture. Recently, courts and antitrust experts' understanding of tech markets has grown more sophisticated. In the antitrust complaint against Google alleging Section 2 violations in AdTech markets, a senior Google employee is quoted as saying that:

> . . . by charging non-transparently on both sides, we give ourselves some flexibility to react and counteract market changes. If we face tons of pricing pressure on the buy-side, we can fall back on the sell-side, and vice versa.[54]

What matters in a (digital) platform context is how platforms structure their marketplaces, that is, the terms they impose on different categories of merchants, customers, workers, and users, the opacity that allows platforms to nudge customers toward certain prices and outputs to avoid switching and to maintain dominance. Antitrust in platform markets thus requires a radically different approach and raises foundational issues about the relationship between efficiency and justice and between markets, politics, and law. Importantly, it prompts us to think more closely about the interdependencies between markets and productive systems on the one hand, and their social and political effects on the other.

Distributive Justice

Chicago School antitrust is premised on the idea that efficient markets can be guided by consumer welfare maximization rationales and can remain separate from and immune to justice and distributive considerations. This belief in the separability of justice and efficiency is both a symptom and part of a more general belief that markets should follow logics that are distinct and separable from politics and the whims of states or polities, a belief that applies to antitrust in digital markets and beyond. In this section, I show that belief in the separability of efficiency maximization from questions of justice has led to a "division of labor" between legal branches and to a redistributive approach to justice that carries several blind spots. I argue that shifting toward a predistributive justice focus, that is, a focus that embeds distributive concerns in the structure of markets in a durable way, can shed light on the limits of the current approach to digital markets. It is imperative to move from views of markets and politics as separate to Neo-Polanyian views that embed political justice into the regulation of digital economies.

Efficiency and Redistribution

Mainstream antitrust thinking, as it emerged in the 1980s, believes that antitrust law's primary function is to minimize state interference in markets and maximize total welfare (i.e., Kaldor–Hicks allocative efficiency). It assumes that other branches of the law, including taxation, can perform a redistributive function, that of compensating consumers and ensuring a fair reallocation of the resulting economic surplus.[55]

The "Separability Thesis"

The move to elevate efficiency and wealth maximization to the status of a normative value[56] and to isolate efficiency considerations from justice and distribution[57] are recognized features of law and economic thinking in US law, as discussed by Jedediah Purdy and others in their *Law and Political Economy Manifesto*.[58] They identify a tendency to isolate and elevate efficiency across a range of legal areas, including antitrust:

> Efficiency itself is typically defined—in practice if not always in theory—as a kind of "wealth maximization" that works to structurally prioritize the interests of those with more resources. This methodological approach offers no framework for thinking systematically about the interrelationships between political and economic power.[59]

The tendency is indeed to isolate economic and efficiency considerations from distributive, social, and structural considerations. This shields what happens in markets from democratic and political decision-making. It also leads to a view of justice that favors *ex post* redistribution (increasing the size of the pie first) rather than structural predistribution (ensuring the shares of the pie are proportionate first).[60] As they put it:

> Elevating efficiency as a value . . . marginalize[s] questions of distribution, so that the law of economic exchange [is] itself "encased," protected from distributive or other political demands beyond the demand for efficiency itself.[61]

In antitrust law, the so-called separability thesis posits that all distributive and social justice considerations fall outside the remit of antitrust law and must be handled outside competitive markets by other branches of law (such as tax law).[62] The idea is that consumers benefit from an increase in the size of the pie, even if that size increase is not immediately beneficial to them in the form of a bigger share. That is because, in theory, when a transaction or market decision maximizes total welfare (the size of the pie), it makes transfers of wealth from those with larger shares to those with smaller shares of the pie possible. The problem is that, in practice, welfare-maximizing decisions in antitrust, such as tolerance toward monopoly profits, are not followed by actual redistribution through taxation. These decisions more often than not result in long-term inequality that favors some people, for example, shareholders or CEOs, and disfavors others, for example, certain classes of consumers.

The Limits of Redistribution

Not interfering in the business affairs of efficient digital monopolies such as Amazon or Google is often motivated by the belief that these monopolies, if left to operate autonomously, contribute to improving society and creating wealth,

wealth that allegedly can be redistributed to the least well-off through more jobs or taxes. The function of antitrust and economic law, according to this view, must thus be to increase the size of the economic pie, not to ensure that everyone gets a fair share of it: A bigger pie, even if unevenly divided, makes everyone better off than a smaller evenly divided one.[63] The imperative is to avoid a system where antitrust regulators prohibit efficient monopolies, leading to less wealth creation.

Applied to digital markets, the separability thesis roughly implies that it is legitimate for tech monopolies such as Amazon, Facebook, Google, or Apple to keep accumulating monopolistic profits without raising their employees' wages or sharing profits with users, as long as some branch of the law other than antitrust or private law is capable of taxing the company and its excessively wealthy (former) CEO, forcing a redistribution of monopolistic profits. The view goes hand in hand with approaches that seek to enable greater "redistribution" in digital environments without directly interfering with or restructuring productive processes themselves. Proposals to treat data as labor exchangeable at an auction, to create data dividends, or to consider data as property and a tradeable commodity could arguably fall within this category, depending on how one interprets them.[64] These views all assume that redistribution, for example, through taxation, is sufficient to ensure justice, and that a division of tasks amongst legal branches is acceptable and fair.

Departing from these conceptions of separability and redistribution in digital platform markets, I argue that healthy and just digital political economies require that efficiency not be separated from justice and political considerations. They must be considered as part of a unified methodology. The separability of efficiency from justice is questionable for empirical and normative reasons. Empirically, scholars have demonstrated a causal connection between the consumer welfare approach in antitrust, the separation of wealth maximization from distribution, and income inequality.[65] Legal scholars Lina Khan and Sandeep Vaheesan have shown, for example, that current US antitrust enforcement does not have progressive effects on income and on the position of the least well-off in society.[66] Under current economic arrangements, market power legitimates transfers of wealth from ordinary Americans to affluent executives and shareholders.[67] These executives are all in the top 1 to 10 percent of the population and, in 2014, concentrated about 70 percent of the nation's wealth.[68] Rory Van Loo has shown that consumer and antitrust law have regressive effects, leading to wealth transfers from consumers to wealthy corporations, executives, and shareholders of more than a trillion dollars every year.[69] Economist John Kwoka has demonstrated that over 75 percent of merger transactions since 2000 have led to price increases for consumers.[70]

Further, the separation of efficiency from justice considerations legitimates unchecked levels of surveillance, allowing opaque data practices to be governed by manipulative nudging and notice and consent on the grounds that these practices contribute to high levels of growth and innovation.[71] It creates an information ecosystem that promotes scale, attention hoarding, polarizing, and manipulative and harmful speech because such practices benefit shareholders even when they perniciously affect democracy.[72] The separation of welfare maximization from justice considerations also creates incentives to personalize, price-discriminate, or differentiate access, as well as creating incentives to pursue unfair market practices that have differential impacts on vulnerable populations on the grounds that these are the most immediate ways of maximizing overall welfare.[73]

These empirical and normative findings suggest that a moral approach to antitrust requires moving in a new direction beyond a redistributive understanding of how economic institutions allocate fundamental protections, wealth, and social advantages. What critiques of the separability of justice and efficiency reveal, in fact, is that neither redistribution through taxation nor trickle-down economics incorporate considerations of justice and equality into market processes. As the rise of digital monopolies such as Amazon, Google/Alphabet, and Facebook/Meta shows, consumer welfare approaches have tended to favor business decisions that maximize production and consumption and that favor the interests of large investors and business owners, often to the detriment of privacy, equality, environmental justice, and the opportunities of smaller firms and market actors.[74]

Predistributive Justice in Digital Platform Markets

A methodological shift is in order for antitrust in digital markets. By separating questions of justice from questions of efficiency and welfare maximization, the Chicago School and neoliberal ideologies have made it harder to question preexisting marketplaces, their structure, their guiding logics, and their negative effects on society. Current Big Tech business models emerged from contingent political, legal, and regulatory choices that are traceable to a long neoliberal tradition. Alternative infrastructures, managed through very different procedures, corporate structures, and incentives, are possible. Beginning to imagine these possibilities requires moving beyond current assumptions, viewing digital markets as political spaces that cannot be isolated from considerations of justice or democratic politics. This requires a vision that embeds predistributive justice in digital markets. At its inception, it requires starting from three pillars: a historical revival of the progressive antimonopoly tradition, a philosophical renewal, and a methodological shift.

Historical Revival

Historically, the consumer welfare focus on antitrust law is relatively recent.[75] Early progressive antitrust focused to a much greater extent on justice and on the close ties between market regulation, democracy, and distributive justice.[76] In lawyer and judge Louis Brandeis's words, democracy requires "not merely political and religious liberty, but industrial liberty also."[77] The 1980s' severing of ties between competition and distributive justice was somewhat exceptional. Pre-Chicago School, antitrust law was concerned with the need to diffuse and predistribute private power in the economy. A particular focus was on the need to ensure political equality and prevent concentrations of power, as captured by Justice William Douglas in his 1948 dissent in the case of *Columbia Steel Co*[78]:

> . . . all power tends to develop into a government in itself. Power that controls the economy should be in the hands of elected representatives of the people, not in the hands of an industrial oligarchy. Industrial power should be decentralized. It should be scattered into many hands so that the fortunes of the people will not be dependent on the whim or caprice, the political prejudices, the emotional stability of a few self-appointed men. . . . That is the philosophy and the command of the Sherman Act.[79]

Drawing from the lessons of early Progressivism in antimonopoly is a key starting point.[80] This is indeed what "Neo-Brandeisian"[81] scholars and policymakers have attempted to do: united around a legal and political agenda that seeks to revive the proactive antimonopoly roots of the past. These scholars and activists aimed to promote decentralization, distributive justice, equality, self-determination, and democracy through antimonopoly law. Reform proposals include strong presumptions against the lawfulness of certain mergers and acquisitions, an offense of abuse of dominance, stronger remedies against digital monopolies, greater powers to the Federal Trade Commission, and emphasis on interoperability and data portability in digital markets.[82] Many of these proposals have begun to see the light of day, but their future remains uncertain at a time of political change.

Philosophical Renewal

Philosophically, the imperative is to move beyond formalist and utilitarian conceptions that focus on uniform and acontextual goals such as efficiency or total welfare maximization and to instead foreground social values, justice, and contextuality in antimonopoly regulation.[83] Neo-Brandeisian reform tends to align with republican ideals of economic and political equality: a wide dispersion of ownership, monopoly breakups, structural separation remedies, and democratic equality. Regardless of the exact tradition one attributes to new antitrust developments, a philosophical reinvention is underway. Renewal should start from an ideal of "predistribution," a tentative word used to capture three core moves as part of a rich vision of political and economic equality in markets: cooperation, reciprocity, and collective empowerment.

The first move is to extend the grammar of cooperation to contemporary (digital) markets. Economist Elinor Ostrom has famously theorized the value of cooperation and collective management of collectively owned resources.[84] Author Yochai Benkler and others have extended these ideas to digital markets, demonstrating that digital networked economies could sustain themselves effectively on the basis of cooperation and altruism—the examples of Wikipedia or Linux are very salient in this context.[85] In antitrust, authors Maurice Stucke and Ariel Ezrachi have additionally advocated for a platonic ideal of noble competition or cooperation between competitors, aimed at "help[ing] . . . rivals achieve their full potential."[86] For them, large tech platforms, such as Amazon, should be incentivized to help small competitors, such as eBay or local bookstores, flourish. Nonprofits and for-profits should be able to coexist, and the bigger players should enable the smaller ones to exist. From a pragmatic policy standpoint, this means making it so expensive for giants to pursue monopoly gains that competitive cooperation and market diversity would pay off.

The second move goes further. It grounds the (digital) political economy not only in principles of cooperation but also in the ideal of social and economic reciprocity between citizens. In his late work *Justice as Fairness: A Restatement,* John Rawls offers a few suggestions on how to envision such an economy.[87] He recognizes that welfare-state capitalism is unjust because it allows "very large inequalities in the ownership of real property."[88] Instead, he prefers two noncapitalist forms of economic governance that can ensure broad predistribution of control over productive resources: property-owning democracy and liberal democratic socialism. Both models favor bottom-up economic democracy and are based on the idea of the coexistence of smaller units of production that are either owned by the state, or collectively owned, or owned by private individuals who are not allowed to accumulate levels of social and economic advantages that would undermine overall reciprocity between citizens.

The third move is to enhance social and collective empowerment in productive processes. Here, the imperative is collective self-determination in markets, not only in the form of renewed patterns of empowered consumption but also in the form of a stronger power to shape and reorient productive and labor processes in the public interest. In the current economy, decisions on what products are produced, how much and what labor is employed, and what choices consumers have tend to depend on the private whims of entrepreneurs or the atomistic choices of individualized consumers in decentralized marketplaces. Instead, these decisions should become matters for collective or public decision-making, more closely aligned with the public interest.

Methodological Shift

The historical revival and philosophical renewal must go hand in hand with a methodological shift. Since 2020, a number of lawsuits have been started against big tech companies, alleging anticompetitive conduct. In December 2020, two complaints were issued against Facebook, one by more than forty states[89] and one by the Federal Trade Commission (FTC),[90] and two other lawsuits were started against Google.[91] Some of these lawsuits have been dropped or repleaded, while new lawsuits against Amazon and Apple have begun. Some lawsuits were won by the Department of Justice (DOJ).[92] One characteristic of these lawsuits is an attempt to shift regulatory priorities while maintaining dominant methodologies in place (e.g., the role of efficiency and consumer welfare). In the first FTC complaint against Facebook, for example, harms to users were described as questions of lack of choice: the inability to walk away or make choices regarding[93]

> personal social networking provider[s] that more closely suits their preferences, including, but not limited to, preferences regarding the amount and nature of advertising, and the availability, quality, and variety of data protection privacy options for users, including, but not limited to, options regarding data gathering and data usage practices.[94]

While these lawsuits are generally symptomatic of a wind change in US antitrust, values such as equality, privacy, and justice continue to have little salience in antitrust discourse. Efficiency and welfare concerns take priority, eluding the complexities discussed in this chapter and the myriad of ways in which power manifests online, infrastructurally, and epistemically, among other things affecting distributive justice, reciprocity, and the ability of people to collectively self-determine in markets. Renewed thinking is needed, therefore, in both legal and economic scholarship.

Conclusion

At a time of great change in politics and in digital markets, market regulation is still pervaded by neoliberal roots. These present digital platform markets as efficient and autonomous processes that regulators must try not to interfere with. These visions tend to shield digital markets from political processes and from collective decision-making, and often do so by prioritizing concerns about efficiency and welfare maximization. In doing so, they neglect concerns about privacy, dignity, equality, and collective self-determination in digital and economic spaces. In the last few years, new winds have started blowing in antimonopoly and platform regulation circles, which have begun to see political and economic processes as more inseparable and interdependent. In the United States, lawsuits and reforms clearly aimed at curbing big tech power suggest an appetite for a radically different vision of regulation and justice in the political economy. The Trump Era is also pioneering new forms of oligarchic government-tech relations that shadow prior neoliberal understandings of the market. In Europe, reform including the Digital Services and Digital Markets Acts shifted regulatory priorities from *ex post* to *ex ante* and more "structural" regulation. The success of these efforts remains uncertain, but the end of self-regulating markets and of self-regulating platforms ideals seems near. Regardless of short-term effects and successes, it is of utmost urgency to begin or continue building the historical, philosophical, and methodological pillars to construct more just and equal digital markets that are embedded in law and politics yet do not tend toward oligarchy.

Notes

1 Karl Polanyi, *Great Transformation: The Political and Economic Origins of Our Time* (Beacon Press, 2001, orig. ed. 1944), 59.

2 Richard R. John, "Bringing Political Economy Back In," *Enterprise & Society* 9, no. 3 (2008): 487.

3 Quinn Slobodian, *Globalists: The End of Empire and the Birth of Neoliberalism* (Harvard University Press, 2018), 5–7, 13.

4 Kate Klonick, "The New Governors: The People, Rules, and Processes Governing Online Speech," *Harvard Law Review* 131 (2018): 598–670; David Pozen, "Authoritarian Constitutionalism in Facebookland," Knight First Amendment Institute Essay, October 18, 2018, available online: https://knightcolumbia.org/content/authoritarian-constitutionalism-facebookland; Clifford Maxwell and Scott D. Kominers, "What Makes an Online Marketplace Disruptive?," *Harvard Business Review,* May 24, 2021, available online: https://hbr.org/2021/05/what-makes-an-online-marketplace-disruptive.

5 See John Perry Barlow, "A Declaration of Independence of Cyberspace," Electronic Frontier Foundation, 1996, available online: https://www.eff.org/cyberspace-independence; David R. Johnson and David Post, "Law and Borders: The Rise of Law in Cyberspace," *Stanford Law Review* 48, no. 5 (1996): 1367.

6 House Committee on the Judiciary, "Investigation of Competition in the Digital Marketplace: Majority Staff Report and Recommendations," October 6, 2020, available online: https://judiciary.house.gov/news/documentsingle.aspx?DocumentID=3429 (hereafter "House Report"). Maurice E. Stucke, "Antitrust Spring," Institute for New Economic Thinking, December 18, 2020, available online: https://www.ineteconomics.org/perspectives/blog/antitrust-spring.

7 State of New York et al. v. Facebook Inc., No. 1:2020cv03589 (US District Court for the District of Columbia, filed December 9th, 2020); FTC v. Facebook Inc., No. 1:2020cv03590 (US District Court for the District of Columbia, filed December 9, 2020); United States of America v. Google LLC, No. DC/1:20-cv-03010 (US District

Court for the District of Columbia, filed October 20, 2020); State of Colorado et al. v. Google LLC, No. 1:2020cv03715 (US District Court for the District of Columbia, filed December 17, 2020); The State of Texas, et al. v. Google, LLC, No. 4:2020cv00957 (US District Court for the Eastern District of Texas, filed December 16, 2020). More generally, see Rachel Kraus, "A Running List of American Antitrust Lawsuits against Google and Facebook," *Mashable*, December 17, 2020, available online: https://mashable.com/article/antitrust-lawsuits-facebook-google/.

8 See, for example, Rebecca Klar, "Amazon Hit with Antitrust Lawsuit Alleging E-Book Price Fixing," *The Hill*, January 14, 2021, available online: https://thehill.com/policy/technology/534364-amazon-hit-with-class-action-lawsuit-alleging-e-book-price-fixing; Chris M. Rodrigo, "Klobuchar to Introduce Omnibus Antitrust Bill," *The Hill*, February 4, 2021, available online: https://thehill.com/policy/technology/537279-klobuchar-to-intro-omnibus-antitrust-bill; American Economic Liberties Project, "The Courage to Learn: A Retrospective on Antitrust and Competition Policy During the Obama Administration and Framework for a New Structuralist Approach," Report, January 12, 2021, available online: https://www.economicliberties.us/our-work/courage-to-learn/.

9 Commission Proposal for a Regulation on a Single Market for Digital Services (Digital Services Act) COM/2020/825 final, available online: https://eur-lex.europa.eu/legal-content/en/TXT/?qid=1608117147218&uri=COM%3A2020%3A825%3AFIN; Commission Proposal for a Regulation on contestable and fair markets in the digital sector (Digital Markets Act), COM/2020/842 final, available online: https://ec.europa.eu/info/sites/info/files/proposal-regulation-single-market-digital-services-digital-services-act_en.pdf.

10 See the World Bank Indicator here: https://data.worldbank.org/indicator/NY.GDP.MKTP.CD?year_high_desc=true.

11 Tom Maloney, "Jeff Bezos Is Stepping Back with Wealth Near All-Time High," Bloomberg, February 2, 2021, available online: https://www.msn.com/en-us/money/companies/jeff-bezos-is-stepping-back-with-wealth-near-all-time-high/ar-BB1dkxdK.

12 Facebook, Inc., Quarterly Report (Form 10-Q) 29 (July 31, 2020), available online: https://investor.fb.com/financials/sec-filings-details/default.aspx?FilingId=14302237.

13 House Report, 11.

14 House Report, 12; and see Press Release, "Bundeskartellamt Prohibits Facebook from Combining User Data from Different Sources," February 7, 2019, available online: https://www.bundeskartellamt.de/SharedDocs/Meldung/EN/Pressemitteilungen/2019/07_02_2019_Facebook.html.

15 See, for example, Commission decision of June 27, 2017, in case 39740 Google Search (Shopping), available online: https://ec.europa.eu/competition/elojade/isef/case_details.cfm?proc_code=1_39740; Case AT. 40411 Google Search (AdSense), European Commission Decision of March 30, 2019, available online: https://ec.europa.eu/competition/elojade/isef/case_details.cfm?proc_code=1_40411; European Commission decision of March 11, 2008 in Case COMP M.4731—Google / DoubleClick, available online: http://ec.europa.eu/competition/mergers/cases/decisions/m4731_20080311_20682_en.pdf; Statement of the Federal Trade Commission Concerning Google/DoubleClick, FTC File No. 071-0170 (December 20, 2007), available online: https://www.ftc.gov/system/files/documents/public_statements/418081/071220googledc-commstmt.pdf.

16 United States v. Google LLC, Case No. 1:23-cv-00108 [2025]; United States v. Google LLC, Case No. 20-cv-3010 (APM), Case No. 20-cv-3715 (APM) [2024].

17 House Report, 15.

18 Ibid.

19 See John M. Newman, "Antitrust in Attention Markets: Definition, Power, Harm," *Santa Clara Law Review* 59, no. 2 (2020): 743–69. On the notion of power in networks, see Manuel Castells, "A Network Theory of Power," *International Journal of Communication* 5 (2011): 773–87.

20 Johanna Gunawan, Amogh Pradeep, David Choffnes, Woodrow Hartzog, and Christo Wilson, "A Comparative Study of Dark Patterns Across Mobile and Web Modalities," *Proceedings of the ACM on Human-Computer Interaction* 5 (2021): 1–29.

21 Marshall Steinbaum, "Establishing Market and Monopoly Power in Tech Platform Antitrust Cases," *Antitrust Bulletin* 67, no. 1 (2022): 130–45.

22 On this, see, for example, Peter Thiel with Blake Masters, *Zero to One: Notes on Startups, or How to Build the Future* (Crown Currency, 2014).

23 Julie E. Cohen, "Tailoring Election Regulation: The Platform Is the Frame," *Georgetown Law Technology Review* 4 (2020): 641, 656.

24 Julie E. Cohen, *Between Truth and Power* (Oxford University Press, 2019), 42.

25 Maurice E. Stucke and Ariel Ezrachi, *Competition Overdose: How Free Market Mythology Transformed Us from Citizen Kings to Market Servants* (Harper Business, 2020), chapter 8.

26 See Shelly Kreiczer-Levy, "Share, Own, Access," *Yale Law & Policy Review* 36 (2017): 155–218.

27 Available online: https://www.airbnb.com/.

28 Available online: www.netflix.com; www.youtube.com.

29 See David Evans, "The Antitrust Economics of Multi-Sided Platform Markets," *Yale Journal on Regulation* 20 (2003): 325–81.

30 Carl Shapiro and Hal R. Varian, *Information Rules: A Strategic Guide to the Network Economy* (Harvard Business Press Review, 1999).

31 *Ohio v. American Express*, 585 U.S. ___ (2018).

32 On the inadequate treatment of Amazon's monopoly position under current antitrust law, see, for example, Lina M. Khan, "Amazon's Antitrust Paradox," *Yale Law Journal* 126 (2017): 710–805; in particular, her discussion of predatory pricing and *Brooke Group* at 756.

33 William J. Novak, "Institutional Economics and the Progressive Movement for the Social Control of American Business," *Business History Review* 93, no. 4 (2019): 665–96.

34 Northern Securities Co. v. United States, 193 U.S. 197 (1904).

35 Standard Oil Co. v. United States, 221 U.S. 1, 52–5 (1911).

36 AT&T, 552 F. Supp. 131 (D.D.C. 1982).

37 US v Microsoft, 253 F.3d 34 (D.C. Cir. 2001).

38 United States v. Microsoft Corp., 97 F. Supp. 2d 59, 64–65 (D.D.C. 2000) (the District Court for the District of Columbia issued an order requiring Microsoft to submit a proposed plan of divestiture, with the company to be split into an operating systems business and an applications business).

39 *Microsoft* (2001). Department of Justice, "Reach Effective Settlement on Antitrust Lawsuit," Press Release, November 2, 2001, available online: https://www.justice.gov/archive/atr/public/press_releases/2001/9463.htm; US v Microsoft Corporation Information on the Settlement, November 6, 2001, available online: https://www.justice.gov/atr/usdoj-antitrust-division-us-v-microsoft-corporation-information-settlement.

40 Frank H. Easterbrook, "The Limits of Antitrust," *Texas Law Review* 63, no. 1 (1984): 1–40.

41 *United States et al. v. Google LLC*, Case No. 20-cv-3010 (APM) (D.D.C. Sep. 2, 2025), both parties appealed the case in January and February 2026; *Fed. Trade Comm'n v. Meta Platforms, Inc.*, Case No. 1:20-cv-03590 (D.D.C. 2025), notice of appeal filed Jan. 20, 2026.

42 William Novak, *New Democracy: The Creation of the Modern American State* (Harvard University Press, 2022).

43 Robert Bork, *The Antitrust Paradox* (Free Press, 1978).

44 For progressive accounts of this history, see Sanjukta Paul, "Recovering the Moral Economy Foundations of the Sherman Act," *Yale Law Journal* 131, no. 1 (2021): 175–255; Novak, *New Democracy*; Tim Wu, *The Curse of Bigness: Antitrust in the New Gilded Age* (Columbia Global Reports, 2018); Khan, "Amazon's Antitrust Paradox."

45 See Bork, *The Antitrust Paradox*; Herbert J. Hovenkamp, "Distributive Justice and Consumer Welfare in Antitrust," *All Faculty Scholarship* 1868 (2013): 1–23, available online: https://scholarship.law.upenn.edu/faculty_scholarship/1868; Alan J. Meese, "Debunking the Purchaser Welfare Account of Section 2 of the Sherman Act: How Harvard Brought us a Total Welfare Standard and Why We Should Keep It," *NYU Law Review* 85 (2010): 659, 690–8; and see Reiter v. Sonotone Corp., 442 U.S. 330, 343 (1979) (where the court found that antitrust should pursue the consumer welfare standard and that consumers could sue price fixers directly for an overcharge). Also see Ioannis Lianos, "Some Reflections on the Question of the Goals of EU Competition Law," CLES Working Paper Series 3/2013 (January 2013), 4–13. For a normative discussion of the place of efficiency in the consumer welfare driven understanding of market regulation Richard A. Posner, "The Ethical and Political Basis of the Efficiency Norm in Common Law Adjudication," *Hofstra Law Review* 8 (1980): 487–507; Richard A. Posner, "Utilitarianism, Economics, Legal Theory," *Journal of Legal Studies* 8, no. 1 (1979): 103–40.

46 See David Harvey's overview of the way neoliberalism became part of the political agenda in the United States during the Reagan Era, and its ties to business interests, in David Harvey, *A Brief History of Neoliberalism* (Oxford University Press, 2005), 64.

47 Richard A. Posner, "The Chicago School of Antitrust Analysis," *University of Pennsylvania Law Review* 127 (1978): 925–48.

48 *Ohio v. American Express*, 585 U.S. ___ (2018).

49 See Standard Oil (1911).

50 United States v. Sabre Corp., 452 F. Supp. 3d 97 (D. Del. 2020) (holding that one-sided and two-sided firms could not be competitors).

51 Caio Mario da Silva Pereira Neto and Filippo Lancieri, "Revisiting Ohio vs. American Express: It's Time for a More Nuanced Approach to Market Definition," Promarket, March 31, 2021, available online: https://promarket.org/2021/03/31/ohio-vs-american-express-market-definition-antitrust/; also see House Report, 399, and Thomas Nachbar, "Platform Effects," *Jurimetrics* 62, no. 1 (2021): 1–48.

52 Nachbar, "Platform Effects," 17.

53 Nachbar, "Platform Effects."

54 In re Google Digital Advertising Antitrust Litigation, State of Texas AG et al. v Google LLC, Second Amended Complaint, No. 1:21-md-03010-PKC (US District Court of Southern District of New York), September 9, 2021, at 93.

55 See the detailed discussion in Lianos, "Some Reflections," 8 ("The implicit assumption is that the tax system is a more efficient way of engaging in redistribution than the regulatory system.").

56 Richard A. Posner, "The Ethical and Political Basis of the Efficiency Norm," 502–7, (arguing that the common law is efficient and that this is normatively desirable); Louis Kaplow and Steven Shavell, *Fairness versus Welfare* (Harvard University Press, 2002), 5; Richard A. Posner, "Law and Economics Is Moral," *Valparaiso University Law Review* 24 (1990): 163, 166 ("the minimum state defined by the economic analysis of market failure is the state that works best to achieve the common goals of most people in the world ").

57 See, for example, Steven Shavell, *Foundations of Economic Analysis of Law* (Belknap Press of Harvard University Press, 2004), 2–3 (focusing attention on efficiency and excluding distributive concerns); Louis Kaplow and Steven Shavell, "Why the Legal System Is Less Efficient Than the Income Tax in Redistributing Income," *The Journal of Legal Studies* 23, no. 2 (1994): 667–81.

58 See Jedediah Britton-Purdy et al., "Building a Law-and-Political-Economy Framework: Beyond the Twentieth-Century Synthesis," *Yale Law Journal* 129, no. 6 (2020): 1784, 1790.

59 Also see Zachary Liscow, "Is Efficiency Biased?," *University of Chicago Law Review* 85, no. 7 (2018): 1649–718.

60 Britton-Purdy et al., "Building a Law-and-Political-Economy Framework," 1795.

61 Ibid., 1797. For a connected use of the term "encasing," see Slobodian, *Globalists*, 5–7, 13.

62 Lianos, "Some Reflections," 4–13; Posner, "Ethical and Political Basis of the Efficiency Norm;" Posner, "Utilitarianism, Economics, Legal Theory."

63 But see Ronald Dworkin's critique of theories that assume the increase or maximization of wealth in society to be valuable *per se* in Ronald M. Dworkin, "Is Wealth a Value?," *The Journal of Legal Studies* 9 (1980): 191–226. Also see Lawrence E. Mitchell, *Corporate Irresponsibility: America's Newest Export* (Yale University Press, 2001), 84–94.

64 See Eric A. Posner and E. Glen Weyl, *Radical Markets: Uprooting Democracy for a Just Society* (Princeton University Press, 2018), chap. 5; Imanol Arrieta-Ibarra, Leonard Goff, Diego Jiménez-Hernández, Jaron Lanier, and E. Glen Weyl, "Should We Treat Data as Labor? Moving Beyond 'Free,'" *AEA Papers and Proceedings* 108 (2018): 38–42; Will.I.Am, "We Need to Own Our Data as a Human Right—And Be Compensated for It," *The Economist*, January 1, 2019, available online: https://www

.economist.com/open-future/2019/01/21/we-need-to-own-our-data-as-a-human-right-and-be-compensated-for-it; Yang 2020 Campaign, Data as a Property Right, available online: https://2020.yang2020.com/policies/data-property-right/; David Floyd, "Blockchain Could Make You—Not Equifax—The Owner of Your Data," *Investopedia*, June 25, 2019, available online: https://www.investopedia.com/news/blockchain-could-make-you-owner-data-privacy-selling-purchase-history/; Laura Hautala, "California Wants Silicon Valley to Share the Wealth with You. Here's How," CNET, February 25, 2019, available online: https://www.cnet.com/news/california-wants-silicon-valley-to-pay-you-a-data-dividend/. Also see https://www.radicalxchange.org/about/; and https://www.datadividends.org/.

65 But see Daniel A. Crane, "Antitrust and Wealth Inequality," *Cornell Law Review* 101, no. 5 (2016): 1171–228 (arguing that there is no connection between a consumer welfare approach and income inequality).

66 Lina Khan and Sandeep Vaheesan, "Market Power and Inequality: The Antitrust Counterrevolution and Its Discontents," *Harvard Law & Policy Review* 11 (2017): 235–94.

67 Khan and Vaheesan, "Market Power and Inequality."

68 See Emmanuel Saez and Gabriel Zucman, "Wealth Inequality in the United States Since 1913: Evidence from Capitalized Income Tax Data," *The Quarterly Journal of Economics* 131, no. 2 (2016): 519–78. Also see Thomas Piketty, Emmanuel Saez, and Gabriel Zucman, "Distributional National Accounts: Methods and Estimates for the United States," *The Quarterly Journal of Economics* 133, no. 2 (2018): 553–609.

69 Rory Van Loo, "Broadening Consumer Law: Competition, Protection and Distribution," *Notre Dame Law Review* 95, no. 1 (2019): 211, 214.

70 See John E. Kwoka, "Does Merger Control Work? A Retrospective on US Enforcement Actions and Merger Outcomes," *Antitrust Law Journal* 78, no. 3 (2013): 619, 631–2; John E. Kwoka, *Mergers, Merger Control, and Remedies: A Retrospective Analysis of U.S. Policy* (MIT Press, 2014). For further evidence of price increases and wealth transfers to the detriment of consumers in the United States in the last decade or more, see Thomas Philippon, *The Great Reversal: How America Gave Up on Free Markets* (Harvard University Press, 2019).

71 Julie E. Cohen, "Turning Privacy Inside Out," *Theoretical Inquiries in Law* 20, no. 1 (2019):1–31; Elettra Bietti, "Consent as a Free Pass: Platform Power and the Limits of the Informational Turn," *Pace Law Review* 40, no. 1 (2020): 310–98; Elettra Bietti, "The Discourse of Control and Consent Over Data in EU Data Protection Law and Beyond," Aegis Paper Series no. 2001. Hoover Institution. January 10, 2020, available online: https://ssrn.com/abstract=3759329.

72 Cohen, *Truth and Power*, chap. 3; W. Lance Bennett and Steven Livingston, eds., *The Disinformation Age: Politics, Technology, and Disruptive Communication in the United States* (Cambridge University Press, 2020).

73 Ramsi Woodcock, "Big Data, Price Discrimination, and Antitrust," *Hastings Law Journal* 68, no. 6 (2017): 1371–420; Ariel Ezrachi and Maurice E. Stucke, "Online Platforms and the EU Digital Single Market," Submission to the UK House of Lords, Internal Market Sub-Committee (October 2015); Akiva Miller, "What Do We Worry About When We Worry About Price Discrimination? The Law and Ethics of Using Personal Information for Pricing," *Journal of Technology Law & Policy* 19, no. 1 (2014): 41–104.

74 Khan, "Amazon's Antitrust Paradox;" Dina Srinivasan, "The Antitrust Case Against Facebook," *Berkeley Business Law Journal* 16, no. 1 (2018): 39–76; Ariel Ezrachi and Maurice Stucke, *Virtual Competition, the Promise and Perils of the Algorithm-Driven Economy* (Harvard University Press, 2016); Stucke, "Antitrust Spring;" Reuben Binns and Elettra Bietti, "Dissolving Privacy, One Merger at a time: Competition, Data and Third Party Tracking," *Computer Law & Security Review* 36 (2020): 1–19.

75 Paul, "Recovering the Moral Economy Foundations."

76 See, for example, Louis B. Schwartz, "'Justice' and Other Non-Economic Goals of Antitrust," *University of Pennsylvania Law Review* 127 (1979): 1076–81. See early accounts such as John B. Kirkwood and Robert H. Lande, "The Fundamental Goal of Antitrust: Protecting Consumers, Not Increasing Efficiency," *Notre Dame Law Review* 84, no. 1 (2008): 191–244. For a more recent account informed by a richer account of political economy, see Paul, "Recovering the Moral Economy Foundation."

77 Louis Brandeis, Address to the Economic Club of New York, November 1, 1912.

78 United States v. Columbia Steel Company, 334 U.S. 495 (1948).

79 Ibid.

80 William J. Novak, "Institutional Economics and the Progressive Movement for the Social Control of American Business," *Business History Review* 93, no. 4 (2019): 665–96.

81 Novak, *New Democracy*; William J. Novak, "The Public Utility Idea and the Origins of Modern Business Regulation," in *The Corporation and American Democracy*, ed. Naomi R. Lamoreaux and W. J. Novak (Harvard University Press, 2017). But see Daniel A. Crane, "How Much Brandeis Do the Neo-Brandeisians Want?," *Antitrust Bulletin* 64 (2019): 531–9.

82 House Report, 19.

83 See, for example, Maurice Stucke, "Reconsidering Antitrust's Goals," *Boston College Law Review* 53 (2012): 551–629; Marshall Steinbaum and Maurice E. Stucke, "The Effective Competition Standard: A New Standard for Antitrust," *University of Chicago Law Review* 86 (2019): 595–623.

84 See, for example, Elinor Ostrom, *Governing the Commons: The Evolution of Institutions for Collective Action* (Cambridge University Press, 1990).

85 Yochai Benkler, *The Wealth of Networks: How Social Production Transforms Markets and Freedom* (Yale University Press, 2006); Yochai Benkler, *The Penguin and the Leviathan: How Cooperation Triumphs Over Self-Interest* (Penguin Random House, 2011).

86 Stucke and Ezrachi, *Competition Overdose*, 225.

87 John Rawls, *Justice as Fairness: A Restatement,* ed. Erin Kelly (The Belknap Press of Harvard University Press, 2001).

88 Rawls, *Justice as Fairness*, at para. 41. Also *see* William A. Edmundson, *John Rawls: Reticent Socialist* (Cambridge University Press, 2017), 5.

89 State of New York et al. v. Facebook Inc., No. 1:2020cv03589 (US District Court for the District of Columbia, filed December 9, 2020).

90 FTC v. Facebook Inc., No. 1:2020cv03590 (US District Court for the District of Columbia, complaint filed December 9, 2020).

91 More generally, see Kraus, "A Running List of American Antitrust Lawsuits against Google and Facebook."

92 US v Google search and AdTech opinions.

93 Facebook complaint.

94 Facebook complaint, at page 48.

Bibliography

Referenced Policy and Court Documents

American Economic Liberties Project. "The Courage to Learn: A Retrospective on Antitrust and Competition Policy During the Obama Administration and Framework for a New Structuralist Approach." Report, January 12, 2021. Available online: https://www.economicliberties.us/our-work/courage-to-learn/.

Ariel, Ezrachi, and Maurice E. Stucke. "Online Platforms and the EU Digital Single Market." Submission to the UK House of Lords, Internal Market Sub-Committee, October 2015. Available online: http://dx.doi.org/10.2139/ssrn.2677267.

Case AT. 40411 Google Search (AdSense), European Commission Decision of March 30, 2019. Available online: https://ec.europa.eu/competition/elojade/isef/case_details.cfm?proc_code=1_40411.

Commission decision of 27 June 2017 in case 39740 *Google Search (Shopping)*. Available online: https://ec.europa.eu/competition/elojade/isef/case_details.cfm?proc_code=1_39740.

Commission Proposal for a Regulation on a Single Market for Digital Services (Digital Services Act) COM/2020/825 final. Available online: https://eur-lex.europa.eu/legal-content/en/TXT/?qid=1608117147218&uri=COM%3A2020%3A825%3AFIN.

Commission Proposal for a Regulation on Contestable and Fair Markets in the Digital Sector (Digital Markets Act), COM/2020/842 final. Available online: https://ec.europa.eu/info/sites/info/files/proposal-regulation-single-market-digital-services-digital-services-act_en.pdf.

Department of Justice. "Reach Effective Settlement on Antitrust Lawsuit." Press Release, November 2, 2001. Available online: https://www.justice.gov/archive/atr/public/press_releases/2001/9463.htm.

European Commission Decision of 11 March 2008 in Case COMP M.4731—Google/DoubleClick. Available online: http://ec.europa.eu/competition/mergers/cases/decisions/m4731_20080311_20682_en.pdf.

Facebook, Inc., Quarterly Report (Form 10-Q) 29 (July 31, 2020). Available online: https://investor.fb.com/financials/sec-filings-details/default.aspx?FilingId=14302237.

FTC v. Facebook Inc., No. 1:2020cv03590 (US District Court for the District of Columbia, complaint filed December 9, 2020).

House Committee on the Judiciary. "Investigation of Competition in the Digital Marketplace: Majority Staff Report and Recommendations." October 6, 2020. Available online: https://judiciary.house.gov/news/documentsingle.aspx?DocumentID=3429.

Northern Securities Co. v. United States, 193 U.S. 197 (1904).

Ohio v. American Express, 585 U.S. ___ (2018).

Press Release. "Bundeskartellamt Prohibits Facebook from Combining User Data from Different Sources." February 7, 2019. Available online: https://www.bundeskartellamt.de/SharedDocs/Meldung/EN/Pressemitteilungen/2019/07_02_2019_Facebook.html.

Reiter v. Sonotone Corp., 442 U.S. 330, 343 (1979).

Standard Oil Co. v. United States, 221 U.S. 1 (1911).

State of Colorado et al v. Google LLC, No. 1:2020cv03715 (US District Court for the District of Columbia, filed December 17, 2020).

State of New York et al. v. Facebook Inc., No. 1:2020cv03589 (US District Court for the District of Columbia, filed December 9, 2020).

The State of Texas, et al v. Google, LLC, No. 4:2020cv00957 (US District Court for the Eastern District of Texas, filed December 16, 2020).

Statement of the Federal Trade Commission Concerning Google/DoubleClick, FTC File No. 071-0170 (December 20, 2007). Available online: https://www.ftc.gov/system/files/documents/public_statements/418081/071220googledc-commstmt.pdf.

United States of America v. Google LLC, No. DC/1:20-cv-03010 (US District Court for the District of Columbia, filed October 20, 2020).

United States v. Google LLC, Case No. 1:23-cv-00108 (2025).

United States v. Columbia Steel Company, 334 U.S. 495 (1948).

United States v. Microsoft Corp., 97 F. Supp. 2d 59, 64–5 (D.D.C. 2000).

United States v. Sabre Corp., 452 F. Supp. 3d 97 (D. Del. 2020) (holding that one-sided and two-sided firms could not be competitors).

US v AT&T, 552 F. Supp. 131 (D.D.C. 1982).

US v Microsoft, 253 F.3d 34 (D.C. Cir. 2001).

US v Microsoft Corporation Information on the Settlement, November 6, 2001. Available online: https://www.justice.gov/atr/usdoj-antitrust-division-us-v-microsoft-corporation-information-settlement.

World Bank Indicator. Available online: https://data.worldbank.org/indicator/NY.GDP.MKTP.CD?year_high_desc=true.

Yang 2020 Campaign, Data as a Property Right. Available online: https://2020.yang2020.com/policies/data-property-right/.

Other References

Arrieta-Ibarra, Imanol, Leonard Goff, Diego Jiménez-Hernández, Jaron Lanier, and E. Glen Weyl. "Should We Treat Data as Labor? Moving beyond 'Free'." *AEA Papers and Proceedings* 108 (2018): 38–42.

Barlow, John Perry. "A Declaration of Independence of Cyberspace." Electronic Frontier Foundation, 1996. Available online: https://www.eff.org/cyberspace-independence.

Benkler, Yochai. *The Penguin and the Leviathan: How Cooperation Triumphs over Self-Interest*. Penguin, 2011.

Benkler, Yochai. *The Wealth of Networks: How Social Production Transforms Markets and Freedom*. Yale University Press, 2006.

Bennett, W. Lance, and Steven Livingston. *The Disinformation Age: Politics, Technology, and Disruptive Communication in the United States*. Cambridge University Press, 2020.

Bietti, Elettra. "Consent as a Free Pass: Platform Power and the Limits of the Informational Turn." *Pace Law Review* 40, no. 1 (2020): 310–98.

Bietti, Elettra. "The Discourse of Control and Consent over Data in EU Data Protection Law and Beyond." Aegis Paper Series no. 2001. Hoover Institution, January 10, 2020. Available online: https://ssrn.com/abstract=3759329.

Bork, Robert. *The Antitrust Paradox*. Free Press, 1978.

Brandeis, Louis. Address to the Economic Club of New York. November 1, 1912. Available online: https://www.econclubny.org/legacyarchive?p_p_id=33&p_p_lifecycle=0&p_p_state=normal&p_p_mode=view&p_p_col_id=column-4&p_p_col_count=1&p_r_p_564233524_tag=louis+brandeis.

Britton-Purdy, Jedidiah, David Singh Grewal, Amy Kapczynski, and K. Sabeel Rahman. "Building a Law-and-Political-Economy Framework: Beyond the Twentieth-Century Synthesis." *Yale Law Journal* 129, no. 6 (2020): 1784–835.

Castells, Manuel. "A Network Theory of Power." *International Journal of Communication* 5 (2011): 773–87.

Cohen, Julie E. *Between Truth and Power*. Oxford University Press, 2019.

Cohen, Julie E. "Tailoring Election Regulation: The Platform Is the Frame." *Georgetown Law Technology Review* 4 (2020): 641–63.

Cohen, Julie E. "Turning Privacy Inside Out." *Theoretical Inquiries in Law* 20, no. 1 (2019): 1–31.

Crane, Daniel A. "Antitrust and Wealth Inequality." *Cornell Law Review* 101, no. 5 (2016): 1171–228.

Crane, Daniel A. "How Much Brandeis Do the Neo-Brandeisians Want?" *Antitrust Bulletin* 64 (2019): 531–9.

da Silva Pereira Neto, Caio Mario, and Filippo Lancieri. "Revisiting Ohio vs. American Express: It's Time for a More Nuanced Approach to Market Definition." Promarket, March 31, 2021. Available online: https://promarket.org/2021/03/31/ohio-vs-american-express-market-definition-antitrust/.

Dworkin, Ronald M. "Is Wealth a Value?" *Journal of Legal Studies* 9, no. 2 (1980): 191–226.

Easterbrook, Frank H. "The Limits of Antitrust." *Texas Law Review* 63, no. 1 (1984): 1–40.

Edmundson, William A. *John Rawls: Reticent Socialist*. Cambridge University Press, 2017.

Evans, David. "The Antitrust Economics of Multi-Sided Platform Markets." *Yale Journal on Regulation* 20 (2003): 325–81.

Ezrachi, Ariel, and Maurice Stucke. *Virtual Competition: The Promise and Perils of the Algorithm-Driven Economy*. Harvard University Press, 2019.

Floyd, David. "Blockchain Could Make You—Not Equifax—The Owner of Your Data." *Investopedia*, June 25, 2019. Available online: https://www.investopedia.com/news/blockchain-could-make-you-owner-data-privacy-selling-purchase-history/.

Gunawan, Johanna, Amogh Pradeep, David Choffnes, Woodrow Hartzog, and Christo Wilson. "A Comparative Study of Dark Patterns Across Mobile and Web Modalities." *Proceedings of the ACM on Human-Computer Interaction* 5 (2021): 1–29.

Harvey, David. *A Brief History of Neoliberalism*. Oxford University Press, 2005.

Hautala, Laura. "California Wants Silicon Valley to Share the Wealth with You. Here's How." CNET, February 25, 2019. Available online: https://www.cnet.com/news/california-wants-silicon-valley-to-pay-you-a-data-dividend/.

Hovenkamp, Herbert J. "Distributive Justice and Consumer Welfare in Antitrust." *All Faculty Scholarship* 1868 (2013): 1–23. Available online: https://scholarship.law.upenn.edu/faculty_scholarship/1868.

John, Richard R. "Bringing Political Economy Back In." *Enterprise & Society* 9, no. 3 (2008): 487–90.

Johnson, David R., and David Post. "Law and Borders: The Rise of Law in Cyberspace." *Stanford Law Review* 48, no. 5 (1996): 1367–402.

Kaplow, Louis, and Steven Shavell. *Fairness versus Welfare*. Harvard University Press, 2002.

Kaplow, Louis, and Steven Shavell. "Why the Legal System Is Less Efficient than the Income Tax in Redistributing Income." *The Journal of Legal Studies* 23, no. 2 (1994): 667–81.

Khan, Lina M. "Amazon's Antitrust Paradox." *Yale Law Journal* 126 (2017): 710–805.

Khan, Lina M., and Sandeep Vaheesan. "Market Power and Inequality: The Antitrust Counterrevolution and Its Discontents." *Harvard Law & Policy Review* 11 (2017): 235–94.

Kirkwood, John B., and Robert H. Lande. "The Fundamental Goal of Antitrust: Protecting Consumers, Not Increasing Efficiency." *Notre Dame Law Review* 84, no. 1 (2008): 191–244.

Klar, Rebecca. "Amazon Hit with Antitrust Lawsuit Alleging E-Book Price Fixing." *The Hill*, January 14, 2021. Available online: https://thehill.com/policy/technology/534364-amazon-hit-with-class-action-lawsuit-alleging-e-book-price-fixing.

Klonick, Kate. "The New Governors: The People, Rules, and Processes Governing Online Speech." *Harvard Law Review* 131 (2018): 1598–670.

Kraus, Rachel. "A Running List of American Antitrust Lawsuits Against Google and Facebook." *Mashable*, December 17, 2020. Available online: https://mashable.com/article/antitrust-lawsuits-facebook-google/.

Kreiczer-Levy, Shelly. "Share, Own, Access." *Yale Law & Policy Review* 36 (2017): 155–218.

Kwoka, John E. "Does Merger Control Work? A Retrospective on US Enforcement Actions and Merger Outcomes." *Antitrust Law Journal* 78, no. 3 (2013): 619–50.

Kwoka, John E. *Mergers, Merger Control, and Remedies: A Retrospective Analysis of U.S. Policy*. MIT Press, 2014.

Lianos, Ioannis. "Some Reflections on the Question of the Goals of EU Competition Law." CLES Working Paper Series 3/2013 (January 2013): 1–65.

Liscow, Zachary. "Is Efficiency Biased?" *University of Chicago Law Review* 85, no. 7 (2018): 1649–718.

Maloney, Tom. "Jeff Bezos Is Stepping Back with Wealth Near All-Time High." Bloomberg, February 2, 2021. Available online: https://www.msn.com/en-us/money/companies/jeff-bezos-is-stepping-back-with-wealth-near-all-time-high/ar-BB1dkxdK.

Maxwell, Clifford, and Scott D. Kominers. "What Makes an Online Marketplace Disruptive?" *Harvard Business Review*, May 24, 2021. Available online: https://hbr.org/2021/05/what-makes-an-online-marketplace-disruptive.

Meese, Alan J. "Debunking the Purchaser Welfare Account of Section 2 of the Sherman Act: How Harvard Brought Us a Total Welfare Standard and Why We Should Keep It." *NYU Law Review* 85 (2010): 659–737.

Miller, Akiva. "What Do We Worry About When We Worry About Price Discrimination? The Law and Ethics of Using Personal Information for Pricing." *Journal of Technology Law & Policy* 19, no. 1 (2014): 41–104.

Mitchell, Lawrence E. *Corporate Irresponsibility: America's Newest Export*. Yale University Press, 2001.

Nachbar, Thomas. "Platform Effects." *Jurimetrics* 62, no. 1 (2021): 1–48.

Newman, John M. "Antitrust in Attention Markets: Definition, Power, Harm." *Santa Clara Law Review* 59, no. 2 (2020): 743–69.

Novak, William J. "Institutional Economics and the Progressive Movement for the Social Control of American Business." *Business History Review* 93, no. 4 (2019): 665–96.

Novak, William J. *New Democracy: The Creation of the Modern American State*. Harvard University Press, 2022.

Novak, William J. "The Public Utility Idea and the Origins of Modern Business Regulation." In *The Corporation and American Democracy*, edited by Naomi R. Lamoreaux and William J. Novak. *Harvard University Press*, 2017.

Ostrom, Elinor. *Governing the Commons: The Evolution of Institutions for Collective Action*. Cambridge University Press, 1990.

Paul, Sanjukta. "Recovering the Moral Economy Foundations of the Sherman Act." *Yale Law Journal* 131, no. 1 (2021): 175–255.

Philippon, Thomas. *The Great Reversal: How America Gave Up on Free Markets*. Harvard University Press, 2019.

Piketty, Thomas, Emmanuel Saez, and Gabriel Zucman. "Distributional National Accounts: Methods and Estimates for the United States." *The Quarterly Journal of Economics* 133, no. 2 (2018): 553–609.

Polanyi, Karl. *Great Transformation: The Political and Economic Origins of Our Time*. Beacon Press, 2001, orig. publ. 1944.

Posner, Eric A., and E. Glen Weyl. *Radical Markets: Uprooting Democracy for a Just Society*. Princeton University Press, 2018.

Posner, Richard A. "The Chicago School of Antitrust Analysis." *University of Pennsylvania Law Review* 127 (1978): 925–48.

Posner, Richard A. "The Ethical and Political Basis of the Efficiency Norm in Common Law Adjudication." *Hofstra Law Review* 8 (1980): 487–507.

Posner, Richard A. "Law and Economics Is Moral." *Valparaiso University Law Review* 24 (1990): 163–74.

Posner, Richard A. "Utilitarianism, Economics, Legal Theory." *Journal of Legal Studies* 8, no. 1 (1979): 103–40.

Pozen, David. "Authoritarian Constitutionalism in Facebookland." Knight First Amendment Institute Essay, October 18, 2018. Available online: https://knightcolumbia.org/content/authoritarian-constitutionalism-facebookland.

Rawls, John. *Justice as Fairness: A Restatement*. Edited by Erin Kelly. The Belknap Press of Harvard University Press, 2001.

Rodrigo, Chris M. "Klobuchar to Introduce Omnibus Antitrust Bill." *The Hill*, February 4, 2021. Available online: https://thehill.com/policy/technology/537279-klobuchar-to-intro-omnibus-antitrust-bill.

Saez, Emmanuel, and Gabriel Zucman. "Wealth Inequality in the United States Since 1913: Evidence from Capitalized Income Tax Data." *The Quarterly Journal of Economics* 131, no. 2 (2016): 519–78.

Schwartz, Louis B. "'Justice' and Other Non-Economic Goals of Antitrust." *University of Pennsylvania Law Review* 127 (1979): 1076–81.

Shapiro, Carl, and Hal R. Varian. *Information Rules: A Strategic Guide to the Network Economy*. Harvard Business Review Press, 1999.

Shavell, Steven. *Foundations of Economic Analysis of Law*. The Belknap Press of Harvard University Press, 2004.

Slobodian, Quinn. *Globalists: The End of Empire and the Birth of Neoliberalism*. Harvard University Press, 2018.

Srinivasan, Dina. "The Antitrust Case against Facebook." *Berkeley Business Law Journal* 16, no. 1 (2018): 39–76.

Steinbaum, Marshall. "Establishing Market and Monopoly Power in Tech Platform Antitrust Cases." *Antitrust Bulletin* 67, no. 1 (2022): 130–45.

Steinbaum, Marshall, and Maurice E. Stucke. "The Effective Competition Standard: A New Standard for Antitrust." *University of Chicago Law Review* 86 (2019): 595–623.

Stucke, Maurice E. "Antitrust Spring." Institute for New Economic Thinking, December 18, 2020. Available online: https://www.ineteconomics.org/perspectives/blog/antitrust-spring.

Stucke, Maurice E. "Reconsidering Antitrust's Goals." *Boston College Law Review* 53 (2012): 551–629.

Stucke, Maurice E., and Ariel Ezrachi. *Competition Overdose: How Free Market Mythology Transformed Us from Citizen Kings to Market Servants*. Harper Business, 2020.

Thiel, Peter, with Blake Masters. *Zero to One: Notes on Startups, or How to Build the Future*. Crown Currency, 2014.

Van Loo, Rory. "Broadening Consumer Law: Competition, Protection and Distribution." *Notre Dame Law Review* 95, no. 1 (2019): 211–61.

Will.I.Am. "We Need to Own Our Data as a Human Right—And Be Compensated for It." *The Economist*, January 1, 2019. Available online: https://www.economist.com/open-future/2019/01/21/we-need-to-own-our-data-as-a-human-right-and-be-compensated-for-it.

Woodcock, Ramsi. "Big Data, Price Discrimination, and Antitrust." *Hastings Law Journal* 68, no. 6 (2017): 1371–420.

Wu, Tim. *The Curse of Bigness: Antitrust in the New Gilded Age*. Columbia Global Reports, 2018.

9

COMPETITION LAW, DIGITALIZATION, AND PLATFORMS

Separating the Old Challenges from the New

Pınar Akman*

Introduction

There is a frenzy around so-called digital markets in competition law and policy (antitrust) circles throughout the world. The frenzy results, first and foremost, from a desire to "do something about the big tech," but also more generally from a perceived enforcement gap in relation to online platform markets. These concerns have led to calls for reforming and/or amending competition laws and/or their enforcement mechanisms in leading antitrust jurisdictions, such as the United States and the European Union (EU). Besides amending competition laws and/or enforcement mechanisms, lawmakers and policymakers around the world are also exploring ex ante regulations to complement or substitute competition laws, establishing new regulators for "digital markets," and introducing soft or hard laws applicable exclusively to a subset of online platforms ("gatekeepers") that are deemed particularly important for access to parts of the digital economy.

The growing discourse in the current competition law, policy, and regulation debate is that the digitalization of markets and the conduct and position of some market players, such as online platforms have thrown up new problems for competition law, economics, and policy, and that none of these (or the enforcers)

---

* Professor of Law, University of Leeds and Senior Advisor, White & Case LLP. The cutoff date for the research underlying this chapter is March 1, 2022.

have risen up to the challenge.[1] As one commentator puts it, "Antitrust stands accused of failure."[2] Hence, the need to do something different and new, such as introducing novel and different rules for the digital economy or specific rules for the incumbent "gatekeepers," has come to the fore of numerous policy debates.

Most of the current policy proposals, such as the EU's Digital Markets Act,[3] proceed on the basis that competition law has failed to deliver what was expected of it in the digital economy, and, thus, it must be reimagined, rewritten, in part or in full, and/or be superseded or complemented by ex ante regulation where needed. Hence, it is now commonly argued that there is a need for ex ante regulation of the relevant markets. Ex ante regulation, however, stands in stark contrast to the traditional approach of competition law, which only intervenes in markets ex post and case by case to impose penalties and remedies where competition on the market has been distorted or prevented through a violation of the rules.[4] Whereas competition law proceeds on the assumption that *competition* is the premise on which free markets should operate, regulation proceeds on the assumption that the operation of a given market should take place based on the specific rules set in advance by the regulator. Resorting to ex ante regulation to compensate for the failures or inadequacies of competition law signifies that the "market," "competition," and competition law enforcement are all perceived to have failed in these markets.

At a time of such wide-ranging reform, it is important to take a step back to separate the old challenges from the new. The core argument of this chapter is that *many* of the challenges sought to be tackled by the recent antitrust policy proposals are *not* new challenges. Rather, they are challenges that predate digitalization and the rise to prominence of digital platforms. Challenges arising out of fundamental questions about competition law and economics and their application to different business practices in different contexts, as well as fundamental questions about what competition law does and/or should aim to achieve, are as old as competition law itself. The questions were unanswered—and some are probably unanswerable in the way policymakers seem to want them to be answered—long before "big tech" or digital markets became a competition concern. Thus, many of the current challenges are *not* the outcome of digitalization, nor are they specific to digital platforms and, therefore, should not be attributed to either of these modern phenomena. What appears to be happening is that some of the questions have become *unavoidable* for policymakers due to the economic power of the digital platforms concerned and due to the societal, political, and economic importance of the various practices of these large digital platforms and of the power they hold.

The problem with attributing the challenges and the cause for reforming competition laws and rules to digitalization and/or to the practices of certain digital platforms is that it misguides the policy discourse and undermines the complexity and difficulty of finding answers to some of the pertinent questions. Attributing the perceived legal or economic problems to digitalization and/or to practices of powerful digital platforms without recognizing that some of these issues have always been around in different shapes and forms and resolved under the existing competition laws through a case-by-case approach[5] causes a further problem. It turns a debate that has to be had first at the technical level—from at least the legal and economics perspectives—into one that is heavily politicized and driven by vested interests of various stakeholders. That state of affairs makes it difficult, if not impossible, to distinguish self-serving rhetoric from informed discourse that should guide policymaking.[6] That approach also conceals the fact that some of the questions that have become particularly pertinent in digital markets, albeit not new, are technically complex. For example, what the "relevant market" is in a competition case with multisided platforms or what constitutes "market power" in markets with network effects or where the limits of "competitive" business conduct lie in case of platforms that serve and also compete with their customers, and so on, are hardly questions that can be answered with straightforward answers that can be translated into straightforward policy solutions, positive or negative legal obligations, or simple fixes. Consequently, crafting a narrative that competition law must change or must be superseded by ex ante regulation because it fails to deal appropriately with big tech underplays the real importance of what is at stake if antitrust shifts to a new paradigm without new technical tools and new analytical methods that can appropriately replace the existing ones to actually resolve some long-standing challenges.

This chapter first elaborates on the challenges of applying existing competition law rules in digital markets. In doing so, it identifies which of these challenges represent *new* challenges to traditional competition law. It then discusses some of the major, long-standing challenges of competition law and economics—challenges that concern the objectives of competition law, the role of economics, and the ambiguities and technicalities involved in applying competition law and economics. Such questions are neither new nor unique to digital platform markets. The chapter concludes by offering some final observations on the relevance and importance of separating the old challenges from the new.

The Challenges of Applying Competition Law in Digital Markets

Recent years have seen growing and intense global scrutiny of some online platform markets and, in particular, the practices of the large digital service providers, most notably the big tech companies such as Alphabet, Amazon, Apple, and Meta. The scrutiny has been driven by various concerns, some of which are rooted in economic and competition-related concerns (e.g., exclusion of competitors and exploitation of market power) and many of which are rooted in broader societal concerns around myriad issues such as content moderation, protection of minors, misinformation, and disinformation. At the time of writing, a clear international trend can be observed toward adopting new (ex ante) rules and/or revising existing legal frameworks, such as competition law frameworks, to tackle a variety of issues observed on these markets, including, for example, the ranking of results on certain platforms, acquisition of startups by big tech platforms, exclusion of platforms' customer competitors from relevant markets through discrimination, and so on.[7] The jurisdictions that are searching for and/or establishing the (new) rules of the game in the context of antitrust include the United States, the EU, the UK, Japan, Germany, France, Australia, and many more.

In the antitrust context, the "mobilization" of policymakers around the world has been accompanied—and perhaps to some extent led—by a small number of expert reports that have studied existing knowledge and reported features of the leading platforms and the primary markets in which these platforms are active.[8] These expert reports, emanating mainly from Europe and North America, have come to broadly similar—but certainly not identical—conclusions about the perceived state of competition in some "digital markets" and have proposed a variety of policy changes, such as the introduction of specific ex ante rules of conduct for gatekeepers.[9] Notably, these expert reports did *not* carry out empirical (or de novo) studies of the markets in question. Such market studies were undertaken by a small number of authorities to study closely some specific platform markets and the practices of the platform providers in these markets.[10] Alongside the expert reports and market studies, certain notable antitrust jurisdictions, such as the EU, continued to make considerable use of their available competition enforcement tools under existing competition laws in their pursuit of numerous investigations against numerous large online platform providers.[11]

The main factors that triggered a variety of new policy proposals since 2019 in the context of digital markets include both issues arising from a wide range of concerns related to the "power" held by some very large online platforms and issues resulting directly from some specific features of these digital markets. The first set of issues that have triggered an avalanche of policy proposals regarding digital markets around the world has to do with the perceived power—economic, political, and societal—of the very large online platforms such as big tech. This set of concerns is more complicated than the second set in terms of "solutions" that may alleviate them because the debate around these concerns is increasingly more political and politicized than technical. It is, thus, not surprising that it is in this context that antitrust made it to presidential campaigns in the United States, as well as into Presidential Orders.[12] Against this backdrop, calls have been made to, for example, "break up" big tech, nationalize big tech, or regulate the services of gatekeeper platforms as utilities.[13] This strand of concerns is driven by a wide array of concerns, ranging from increasing market concentration in the economy, labor's falling share of income, increasing income inequalities, censorship (e.g., of Republican views in the United States) to, more recently, rising inflation.[14] Most of these calls at the more radical end of the spectrum of policy options are not based on an accumulation of *antitrust* expertise. For example, subjecting a market to utility-style regulation in the absence of a natural monopoly lacks theoretical and empirical underpinnings. The breadth of these concerns, all of which, according to some, can be resolved by the magic touch (or sledgehammer) of antitrust, suggests that there is a possibility that the debate has been hijacked by a myriad of stakeholders seeking to use antitrust for various purposes for which it is not fit. It is in this first set of concerns that it becomes most apparent that policy "solutions" may be reached by reverse engineering particular political, societal, or economic outcomes that are desirable rather than by following the accumulation of evidence and expertise to reach solutions.

The second set of issues relates to the specific features of platform markets. First and foremost, online platforms differ from one another in important ways, such as how they generate income and their size and profitability.[15] For example, the Google search engine and the Amazon marketplace differ significantly from one another in terms of business model and profitability, and they both differ substantially from Airbnb or Uber in terms of size, even though they are all online platforms. These differences mean that one-size-fits-all solutions, as currently conceived, regulatory or otherwise, are unlikely to be effective in terms of policymaking.[16] However, platforms also share many common features; some of these features have raised concerns about whether existing competition laws can effectively prevent distortions of competition in platform markets. Some of these pertinent features are discussed next.

Platforms can be viewed as "matchmakers" that reduce transaction costs for parties who have something valuable to exchange with one another.[17] This means that platforms need to attract at least two different groups of customers who will interact with each other.[18] In contrast to traditional firms, platforms first need to create value through these interactions, then achieve critical mass and network effects before they can capture a share of that value for monetization purposes.[19] This multisided nature of platforms implies that the participation of one group of customers generates (indirect) network effects (externalities) on the other side of the platform.[20] Platforms may also benefit from (direct) network effects, where the utility a user receives from a service directly increases with the number of other users of the same service (e.g., social networks).[21] Network effects imply that the efficiency and user benefits of platforms increase with their size.[22] Thus, a platform that is successful in generating positive network effects can grow substantially, creating a virtuous cycle. Network effects will also be reflected in the pricing *structure* (i.e., the relationship between the prices charged to different sides of the platform).[23] Subsequently, in platform markets, unlike in most other markets, price *levels* do not matter as much as the price structure, hence the frequent occurrence of zero prices to users on one side subsidized by payment on the other side of the platform.

Further, economies of scale are typical in multisided markets due to the relatively high proportion of fixed costs (e.g., for R&D) and relatively low variable costs in these markets.[24] These particular features of multisided platform businesses and network effects can lead to "winner-takes-all" dynamics and put businesses in a situation where competition takes place on the basis of "ecosystems."[25] The prevalence of network effects also means that in platform markets, competition may be *for* the market rather than *in* the market.[26] This factor increases the importance of the threat exerted by smaller market players and entrants, rendering, for example, mergers and acquisitions that target such threats, particularly important in such markets for removing their behavior-disciplining effect.[27]

Having said that, not all markets with online platforms are "winner-takes-all" or "winner-takes-most" markets because these require strong network effects, high switching costs, and multihoming to be undesirable or difficult for users.[28] In turn, multihoming by users will depend on, among others, the nature of the alternative platforms (i.e., substitutes vs complements), switching costs between platforms, and the pricing policy of the platform.[29] In fact, although positive network effects and economies of scale and scope (particularly when coupled with strong first-mover advantages and high switching costs) may stifle competition by entrenching the market position of incumbents and deterring entry, other features of such markets can make it easier for entrants to displace incumbents quickly.[30] These include network effects, scale without mass, and the nonrivalrous nature of digital information.[31] For example, the nonrivalrous nature of digital information can facilitate multihoming by users as they can share their information (e.g., social connections) with competing platforms.

Some features of multisided platforms elaborated on above lead to challenges with respect to existing, traditional competition law rules and their application in digital markets. These *new* challenges are unique to platform markets or to digital platform services and derive from the inherent features of these markets or business models. Existing competition laws are sufficiently broad to cover many of these new challenges presented by digital markets. But the existing tools and methods used in enforcing competition laws may not be adequate in dealing with some of these challenges. One such difficulty is, for example, "market definition" and deciding which sides of a multisided business—digital or traditional—to include in the competitive assessment of a given business practice adopted by platforms.[32] Namely, whether a single market or multiple markets should be defined (i.e., whether two sides of the platform are in the same "relevant market" or are in different markets) and in which circumstances.[33]

Another new challenge is that many of the platforms' services are offered at zero price to consumers, which makes the traditional tools used in competition law and economics to define the relevant market unsuitable due to their reliance on a positive price point. The growing prevalence of digital platforms also raises new questions around whether and, if so, when online and traditional markets should be considered part of the same market. How these questions are answered has direct implications for the assessment of the competitive effects of a given practice and, therefore, the lawfulness or otherwise of the practice in question.

Likewise, some previous enforcement decisions have been criticized for underestimating the potential anticompetitive effect of some mergers.[34] The implication would be allowing mergers and acquisitions to take place when they should not be allowed to do so to protect competition in the relevant markets. There has been particular concern about the new challenge of "killer acquisitions," where a large platform (e.g., Facebook) arguably acquires a startup (e.g., Instagram) to kill the potential competition that the startup's products and services may pose to the products and services of the large platform.[35] Existing competition laws may not be adept at catching such mergers due to the laws' focus on turnover thresholds, and so on, and, thus, may need to be revised.

Another challenge for competition authorities in digital platform cases is establishing the extent of market power held by the relevant firms.[36] The multisided nature of platforms creates challenges (albeit not all new) in this context, too, because focusing on one side of the market in establishing market power can overestimate or underestimate the degree of market power by failing to assess the influence of competitive conditions on the other side of the platform.[37] As noted by commentators, the "traditional framework" for measuring market power, based on prices, may be inadequate in multisided markets.[38]

Similarly, in the digital economy context, access to consumer data can play a key role. Although the use of data by businesses is certainly not new, the scope and scale of data used by some online platforms may throw up new challenges for antitrust, for example, regarding whether and how data creates a competitive advantage and the value of data. The theoretical arguments and empirical evidence around the potential competitive advantages from data are scarce and equivocal.[39] The disruption of markets by entrants without existing data, such as TikTok, Airbnb, Uber, Spotify, Snapchat, Tinder, and WhatsApp, suggests that entry is possible, at least in some market segments, without a data advantage.

A further set of potential and new challenges for the application of competition law arises from the increasing development and deployment of machine learning and artificial intelligence by platform businesses (and nonplatform businesses). Use of algorithms and big data throws up substantive and enforcement-related legal questions regarding, for example, algorithmic collusion and "individualized pricing."

Finally, a genuine but not new challenge is that competition law enforcement is necessarily slow due to the fact-intensive and economic inquiries involved and the numerous stages of analysis required. The speed of antitrust enforcement contrasts starkly with how quickly digital markets move and may "tip" to the winner in the competition *for* the market. Thus, there is a danger that by the time competition law enforcement takes place using the existing rules and tools, competition in a market will have been irrecoverably eliminated.

Long-Standing Challenges of Competition Law and Economics

Objectives

Competition laws around the world generally comprise a very small number of codified, broadly worded, general provisions. This phenomenon is not surprising given that the same situation occurs in the two key jurisdictions that have influenced these competition laws specifically, namely, the United States and the EU. The core of antitrust law in the United States and the EU comprises *two* legal provisions that apply to all economic activity in all sectors of the entire economy.[40] Broadly speaking, one of these provisions concerns collusion and the other, the (ab)use of market power/monopolization. Crucially, neither the US nor the EU competition rules stipulate their objectives. Although that state of affairs may not cause a problem in every area of law, when the legal provisions are so flexible, broad, and applicable to all types of business practices in all types of different economic and legal contexts, the absence of clear objectives leads to alternative interpretations of the law.

Different schools of thought posit different objectives for antitrust law, reflecting not just the established technical expertise of the relevant time but, potentially, also broader contemporary economic, societal, and political currents. This can be observed most clearly in the development of the US antitrust law, where schools of thought, such as the Harvard, Chicago, post-Chicago, and, most recently, the neo-Brandeisian, attribute to the same law—which has remained the same on paper for over a century—a wide range of objectives and aims, some of which are mutually exclusive and all of which supposedly reflect the "true" goals of the US antitrust law.[41] The goals range from structural ones, focusing on, for example, the number of competitors and preserving a particular market structure to protect competition, to outcome-oriented ones, focusing on, for example, the level of prices or output in a given market to process-driven ones, focusing on, for example, the prohibition of practices impeding rivals' market access.

Digitalization and the rising economic prominence of large, incumbent technology platforms, coupled with a global pandemic and its economic consequences, have taken the disagreement on the objectives of antitrust to a new level.[42] Competition policymakers and enforcers find themselves called to act against the power of technology platforms in the face of falling wages, failing firms in traditional industries, online harms, rising inflation, and so on, juxtaposed against unprecedented levels of market capitalization and profitability accruing to a small few. Thus, antitrust, which can break up even the most powerful businesses, levy headline-grabbing fines on them, issue them the new rules of how they must conduct their business, and potentially send their CEOs to jail, becomes a highly versatile tool that could be sought to be used to achieve a myriad of goals for a variety of ends.

A pertinent example of endeavors to move antitrust toward a new set of goals is the recent call by commentators to abandon the "consumer welfare" approach as the dominant paradigm guiding the application of competition rules. Commentators, mostly from the United States and subscribing to what has been dubbed the "new Brandeis School," argue that the consumer welfare objective of antitrust should be abandoned.[43] They take issue with the enforcement of the antitrust laws pursuing the consumer welfare standard, which focuses on outcomes (such as efficiency and low prices) as opposed to focusing on market structures and processes of competition.[44] In the digital economy, one of the central concerns of those arguing for abandoning consumer welfare is the fact that many digital services are provided at a price of zero to consumers. Where price is zero and consumers are "paying" with their attention or data for the service, and quality is difficult to observe, consumers may not be appreciative of their "surplus" and the economics of their transaction.[45] Another shortcoming of the standard has been noted to be the possibility of overlooking anticompetitive predatory strategies aimed at excluding rivals with low prices to consumers.[46] While the consumer welfare approach is by no means perfect,[47] what is missing from the calls for abandoning consumer welfare is a realistic and feasible alternative to it that would guide antitrust enforcement and policy and that would improve upon the status quo.

Agreement on *the* goal(s) of antitrust is unlikely to be forthcoming. It is also unlikely that antitrust can effectively deliver on many objectives that policymakers may wish to use it for beyond lowering prices, increasing quality or choice, and so on. In fact, some of the objectives sought by some recent approaches under the umbrella of "antitrust," such as those propagated by the neo-Brandeisians, are anathema to what may be expected of rigorous competition in a given market, such as low consumer prices or increased efficiency.[48] This particular take on objectives is specifically important in the context of digital platforms because a major impact of large platforms, such as online marketplaces, has been to disrupt established markets and established market operators and reduce prices through fierce (perhaps ruthless) "competition." Thus, there is currently a fight for the soul of antitrust and a search for a new paradigm for competition law and what the application of the law should be seeking to achieve.[49] This search has been aggravated most recently by the question of what to do about large online platforms, but some of the ways in which antitrust is sought to be used may not coincide with what competition, competition law, or competition policy could realistically achieve. Indeed, focusing on, for example, the process of competition and market structure as neo-Brandeisians posit can lead to worse outcomes than a status quo for consumers, including higher prices.[50] Yet there is currently no credible new, alternative paradigm that would justify, for example, worsened outcomes for consumers in pursuit of other more "appropriate" objectives, whatever they might be.

It is at least debatable whether there is robust evidence that indicates that antitrust is the best or most appropriate policy to achieve some of the goals recently sought to be attributed to it. It is also unclear which (other) objectives should be pursued and in which priority order and *why* under any new paradigm of competition law. The question of, for example, *why* it is acceptable or desirable to pursue a competition policy aimed at ensuring a particular structure in the market is "competitive" when that structure may lead to higher prices or lower quality services for the consumers is unanswered. In fact, it is well established that a focus on the structure of a market as indicative of how competitive the market is constitutes a flawed approach.[51] Thus, the search for the goals of antitrust is an old one that is here to stay and is simply exaggerated by virtue of the size and importance of the perceived issues that the large online platforms pose for policymakers and enforcers. It is not a digitally born or new challenge, nor should it be treated as such when devising new policies in search of solutions.

The Role of Economics

Economics occupies a central point in the debate on what competition law or policy could or should aim to achieve and deliver.[52] Arguably, the "mainstream" model of competition law disregards questions that current methods and tools of economics and, particularly, of neoclassical price theory cannot integrate or analytically process.[53] Although the extent to which competition law adopts an economic approach in any given jurisdiction varies and is open to debate, the fundamental concepts underlying or informing the current approach in jurisdictions such as the United States and the EU are indeed rooted in industrial organization economics. Such economic concepts that inform the application and enforcement of competition law include market power, competitive price, perfect competition, oligopoly, monopoly, collusion, foreclosure, and market failure. Besides the role that these concepts occupy in informing the law, economic analysis is also the dominant approach to the case-by-case assessment of the competitive effects of given practices and relevant "theories of harm."[54] Thus, perhaps unlike any other area of law, economics and economists play a central role in the application of competition law by providing a framework of assessment and a methodology for it. However, the role of economics and economists has been subject to debate in antitrust circles for decades preceding the rise of digital markets or digital platforms on policy agendas.[55] The debate has simply taken a new turn in the context of digital markets, platforms, and competition.

The current search for the soul of antitrust, amplified in the context of what to do about competition in digital markets, includes calls for adopting objectives and goals that go beyond economic outcomes. This movement promulgates the pursuit of political or noneconomic objectives by competition law and enforcement.[56] What may be easily overlooked is that such propositions also include calls *against* the *use of economics* as the dominant methodology of interpretation, application, and enforcement.[57] However, what *would* or *should* replace economics or economic tools in the assessment of different business practices and their effects on competition under this alternative approach to competition law and enforcement is unclear and unspecified. These questions are relevant in the process of instituting a new paradigm for antitrust, not just in online platform markets but across the board—antitrust is applicable to *all* economic activity. Yet it is unclear whether the proponents of a paradigm shift for antitrust, the narrative for which is mainly crafted in the context of digital platform competition, have identified the new, general method of application and the tools of antitrust under this new paradigm. When economics is abandoned as the method of analysis in favor of, for example, politically motivated resolutions to assess the *acceptability* of business practices and market outcomes from a competition perspective, there is no real analytical toolset with which to reach consistent, predictable, and coherent resolutions regarding business conduct by an application of competition law.

Ambiguities and Technicalities

On the one hand, the unspecified list of objectives of competition law and the myriad ways in which business conduct may or may not harm competition in a given market lead to ambiguities in the application of the competition rules in a given case. On the other hand, economics as the dominant methodology of applying competition law and the somewhat misleading image of the categorical nature of economics with apparent mathematical force lead to competition law's being a highly technical discipline. As articulated by the Competition Appeal Tribunal of the UK, "competition law is not an area of law in which there is much scope for absolute concepts or sharp edges."[58] It could be said that it is precisely the ambiguity and vagueness of the law that have *allowed* economics to take on the role that it has in competition analysis because, without the discipline imposed by economics, competition law lacks a framework of systematic analysis and a robust method of application. Whatever the reasons, the current state of affairs means that competition law is highly technical and uses a framework that encompasses technical constructs and concepts such as "market definition," "market power," "anticompetitive effects," "procompetitive effects," "efficiency analysis," "oligopolistic competition," and "barriers to entry." The current debate regarding the effectiveness of competition on some platform markets and how to apply competition law in these markets has revealed discontent and dissatisfaction with the law, partly because of its reliance on such economic and technical models and tools. There are indeed specific ways in which digital markets and, in particular, some platform business practices demonstrate the theoretical and practical (and perhaps, inherent) *limitations* of these established concepts and tools and the challenges of using them to apply competition law in these markets. This is not helped by the fact that the prohibition against the abuse of dominance (monopolization), which is perhaps the most relevant part of competition law in relation to digital platform markets, is also the least consistently enforced area of competition law globally, as things stand.[59] There is indeed considerable disagreement on what constitutes anticompetitive conduct in the context of the unilateral exercise of market power.[60] This is not specific to multisided markets.[61] Notably, the EU (and its Member States) and the United States have historically diverged on the assessment of unilateral conduct, whereby the former adopts a more interventionist approach than the latter.[62] Yet these are not novel revelations nor novel challenges or unique to digital markets.

Economists and lawyers have been debating for decades the role and relevance of many of the tools used in competition law and enforcement, such as market definition, market power, abuse of market power, and consumer welfare.[63] None of these questions will disappear if competition law adopts a radically different approach and, for example, abandons the economic approach altogether: Any alternative approach or paradigm will still need to put in place operational rules to underlie and inform the application of competition law in different market contexts to different business practices in a way that will both respect due process, rule of law, and fundamental principles, such as legal certainty, and preserve and protect competition in the market.

There is simply no way of avoiding some long-standing and difficult questions of interpretation and application of competition law rules, given the vagueness of the law, be it in relation to digital markets or traditional markets. Thus, although the pressing need to find the appropriate means of applying competition law—including by introducing new rules and regulations—means that the previously academic, technical questions now need to be tackled as a matter of priority, urgency does not render the relevant questions nontechnical or simple to answer.

Conclusion

There is a growing trend toward more competition enforcement action against some of the big tech companies, including in jurisdictions such as the United

States.[64] There have been several high-profile cases concerning digital platforms in the last couple of years. The EU and its Member States (most notably Germany) have been particularly active in this space. The divergence of the US and the EU approach in the context of applying competition law to firms with market power appears to be over for digital markets. The EU and the United States may—at least at face value—be converging more than ever before, driven by the desire to tame the power of "big tech."[65] The full extent of the irony in the US approach moving closer to that of the EU in curtailing the competitive positions of some of the biggest American entrepreneurial success stories will only be revealed in the years to come. Until that future arrives, there are numerous ongoing enforcement and judicial proceedings, as well as legislative initiatives, around the world concerning the largest online platforms, which will shape the future landscape of global digital competition.[66]

This chapter has demonstrated that many challenges currently sought to be resolved by an apparent shift to a new paradigm for antitrust, driven by the need to intervene in digital markets, are not new or unique to digital markets. This is not to say that there are no new or unique challenges. There are indeed many such challenges spanning from the use of big data to algorithms to enforcement capabilities. None of these new challenges, however, justifies an overhaul of the expertise and experience that accumulated over the decades, which sought to make antitrust more "scientific" or more "objective" and less politicized and arbitrary. The current movement in favor of adopting broader objectives and unidentified methodologies, while abandoning economics as the method of analysis on the premise that digital markets pose new challenges that must be overcome, has the potential to lead to *also* abandoning the role of expertise and experts in decision-making. Yet once the current technical framework carrying competition law is pulled from underneath it, there will be nothing in its place to sustain the subject as a discipline. The ramifications of that shift to such a new paradigm for antitrust without supporting technical tools and methods—which would make the law less predictable and potentially less coherent—will not be limited to digital markets or the "gatekeepers" as it entails an overhaul of antitrust. As things stand, there is no reason to expect that such a shift to a nontechnical (some may say populist) paradigm for antitrust will lead to an improved state of affairs in comparison to the status quo.

Notes

1 For the argument that competition law has been under-enforced, see Jason Furman et al., "Unlocking Digital Competition: Report of the Digital Competition Expert Panel," March 2019, 91, available online: https://assets.publishing.service.gov.uk/media/5c88150ee5274a230219c35f/unlocking_digital_competition_furman_review_web.pdf in relation to mergers; Jacques Crémer, Yves-Alexandre de Montjoye, and

Heike Schweitzer, "Competition Policy for the Digital Era," Directorate-General for Competition, European Commission, 2019, 3, 4, available online: https://euagenda.eu/upload/publications/untitled-257961-ea.pdf in relation to unilateral exercise of market power; Stigler Center for the Study of the Economy and the State, Markets Structure and Antitrust Subcommittee Report, "Report of the Committee for the Study of Digital Platforms," University of Chicago Booth School of Business, 2019, 63–4, 74, available online: https://publicknowledge.org/wp-content/uploads/2021/11/Stigler-Committee-on-Digital-Platforms-Final-Report.pdf in relation to mergers and monopolization. Calling for sweeping changes to antitrust law as currently applied due to its failure to control the power of the "big tech" platforms, and so on, see, for example, the US House of Representatives, Subcommittee on Antitrust, Commercial and Administrative Law of the Committee on the Judiciary, Majority Staff Report and Recommendations, Investigation of Competition in Digital Markets 2020, available online: https://www.govinfo.gov/content/pkg/CPRT-117HPRT47832/pdf/CPRT-117HPRT47832.pdf; Tim Wu, *The Curse of Bigness* (Columbia Global Reports, 2018).

2 Alan J. Devlin, *Reforming Antitrust* (Cambridge University Press, 2021), 9.

3 E.U. Commission, Proposal for a Regulation of the European Parliament and of the Council on Contestable and Fair Markets in the Digital Sector (Digital Markets Act) (15 Dec. 2020), available online: https://eur-lex.europa.eu/legal-content/EN/TXT/PDF/?uri=CELEX:52020PC0842.

4 This is with the exception of merger control, which operates, in many jurisdictions in ex ante fashion, whereby competition enforcers can disallow certain mergers and acquisitions from taking place, in the first place, due to their potential harm to competition.

5 Existing competition laws have historically been applied to many markets and practices that are "new" at the time, such as computer operating systems, credit card networks, and telecommunications monopoly breakups. For a discussion of the historical evolution of US antitrust in response to technological developments, economic shocks, and "predominant economic wisdom," see Laura Phillips Sawyer, "U.S. Antitrust Law and Policy in Historical Perspective," Harvard Business School Working Paper No. 19-110, May 2019, available online: https://www.hbs.edu/faculty/Pages/item.aspx?num=56116.

6 For a study demonstrating how traditional market actors in certain sectors such as media use "strategic institutionalization" by actively pushing for new laws to resist changes to the industry posed by online platforms such as news aggregators and to consolidate their traditional business models, see Heidi J. S. Tworek and Christopher Buschow, "Changing the Rules of the Game: Strategic Institutionalization and Legacy Companies' Resistance to New Media," *International Journal of Communication* 10 (2016): 2119–39.

7 Examples of legislative initiatives include, for example, Digital Markets Act (n 3); American Choice and Innovation Online Act, 117th Congress, H.R. 3816, June 24, 2021 (US); Ending Platform Monopolies Act, 117th Congress, H.R. 3825, June 11, 2021 (US); Competition and Antitrust Law Enforcement Reform Act of 2021, 116th Congress, SIL21191 6C1, February 4, 2021 (US); *Gesetz zur Änderung des Gesetzes gegen Wettbewerbsbeschränkungen fuer ein fokussiertes, proaktives und digitales Wettbewerbsrecht 4.0 und anderer Bestimmungen* (*GWB-Digitalisierungsgesetz*), January 18, 2021 ("Act Amending the Act against Restraints of Competition for a focused, proactive, and digital competition law 4.0 and amending other competition law provisions") (GWB-Digitalisation Act) (Germany); Act on Improving Transparency and Fairness of Digital Platforms, May 27, 2020 (Japan); Treasury Laws Amendment (News Media and Digital Platforms Mandatory Bargaining Code) Bill 2020, February 15, 2021 (Australia).

8 See, in particular, Cremer, de Montjoye and Schweitzer, "Competition Policy for the Digital Era"; Stigler Center, "Report of the Committee for the Study of Digital Platforms"; Furman et al., "Unlocking Digital Competition."

9 For an overview of the reports, see Filippo Lancieri and Patricia Morita Sakowski, "Competition in Digital Markets: A Review of Expert Reports," *Stanford Journal of Law, Business & Finance* 26, no. 1 (2021): 65–170. "Digital markets" can be defined as those in which companies develop and apply new technologies to existing businesses or create new services using digital capabilities; see Competition and Markets Authority (CMA), "The CMA's Digital Markets Strategy," June 2019, available online: https://www.gov.uk/government/publications/competition-and-markets-authoritys-digital-markets-strategy/the-cmas-digital-markets-strategy [1.1]. The term "digital markets" is somewhat of a misnomer because of the pervasive nature of digital technologies across different "sectors" of the economy. Thus, as digitalization continues to transform the economy, and the line between offline and online businesses becomes further blurred, concepts such as "digital markets" and "digital economy" may become redundant; see World Economic Forum, "Competition Policy in a Globalized, Digitalized Economy: Platform for Shaping the Future of Trade and Global Economic Interdependence," 2019, 5, available online: https://www3.weforum.org/docs/WEF_Competition_Policy_in_a_Globalized_Digitalized_Economy_Report.pdf.

10 These include, for example, the UK and Australia, where the competition authorities have conducted extensive studies of some of the relevant markets. See CMA, "Mobile Ecosystems Market Study," 2021, available online: https://www.gov.uk/cma-cases/mobile-ecosystems-market-study; Australian Competition and Consumer Commission (ACCC), "Digital Platform Services Inquiry 2020–2025," available online: https://www.accc.gov.au/publications/serial-publications/digital-platform-services-inquiry-2020-2025.

11 At the time of writing, these include three infringement decisions taken against Google in the EU (Case COMP/AT.40411—*Google Search (AdSense)*, March 20, 2019, currently on appeal in Case T-334/19, *Google and Alphabet v Commission* [2019] OJ C255/46; Case COMP/AT.40099—*Google Android*, July 18, 2018, currently on appeal in Case T-604/18, *Google and Alphabet v Commission* [2018] OJ C445/21; Case COMP/AT.39740—*Google Search (Shopping)*, June 27, 2017, an appeal against which was largely dismissed in Case T-612/17 *Google and Alphabet v Commission (Google Shopping)* ECLI:EU:T:2021:763. *Google Search (Shopping)* is now on further appeal in Case C-48/22 P—*Google and Alphabet v Commission (Google Shopping)*. Other ongoing investigations include those against Apple, Amazon, Facebook, and so on. See Case COMP/AT.40716 *Apple—App Store Practices*, June 16, 2020 (Opening of Proceedings); Case COMP/AT.40462 *Amazon Marketplace*, July 17, 2019 (Opening of Proceedings), November 10, 2020 (Statement of Objections); Case AT.40684 *Facebook Leveraging*, June 6, 2021 (Opening of Proceedings). Likewise, there are several cases against "big tech" in the United States, such as *FTC v. Facebook, Inc.*, December 9, 2020; *U.S. and Plaintiff States v. Google LLC*, October 20, 2020, and so on.

12 See Sheelah Kolhatkar, "Can Elizabeth Warren Win It All?," *The New Yorker*, June 14, 2019, available online: https://www.newyorker.com/magazine/2019/06/24/can-elizabeth-warren-win-it-all; Elizabeth Warren, "Reigniting Competition in the American Economy," Keynote Remarks at New America's Open Markets Program Event, June 29, 2016, available online: https://www.openmarketsinstitute.org/publications/senator-elizabeth-warrens-keynote-remarks-at-new-americas-open-markets-program-event-reigniting-competition-in-the-american-economy; US President Joseph R. Biden Jr., "Executive Order on Promoting Competition in the American Economy," July 9, 2021, available online: https://bidenwhitehouse.archives.gov/briefing-room/presidential-actions/2021/07/09/executive-order-on-promoting-competition-in-the-american-economy/.

13 See Nick Srnicek, "We Need to Nationalise Google, Facebook and Amazon. Here's Why," *The Guardian*, August 30, 2017, available online: https://www.theguardian.com/commentisfree/2017/aug/30/nationalise-google-facebook-amazon-data-monopoly-platform-public-interest; Colin Lecher, "Elizabeth Warren Says She Wants to Break Up Amazon, Google, and Facebook: A Proposal to Unwind Big Tech," *The Verge*, March 8, 2019, available online: https://www.theverge.com/2019/3/8/18256032/elizabeth-warren-antitrust-google-amazon-facebook-break-up; Vicente Bagnoli, "Digital Platforms as Public Utilities," *IIC—International Review of Intellectual Property and Competition Law* 51, no. 8, (2020): 903–5.

14 See Hal Singer, "Antitrust Should Be Used to Fight Inflation," *The American Prospect*, February 2, 2022, available online: https://prospect.org/economy/antitrust-should-be-used-to-fight-inflation/; Rep. Ken Buck, "The Third Way: Antitrust Enforcement in Big Tech," US House of Representatives, Judiciary Committee Subcommittee on Antitrust, Commercial, and Administrative Law, October 6, 2020, available online: https://www.politico.com/f/?id=00000174-fa7f-db77-abfe-fe7f5d740000; OECD, *Competition in Labour Markets*, 2020, available online: http://www.oecd.org/daf/competition/competition-concerns-in-labour-markets.htm; Wenjie Chen et al., *Rising Corporate Market Power: Emerging Policy Issues* (International Monetary Fund [IMF], March 15, 2021), available online: https://www.elibrary.imf.org/view/journals/006/2021/001/006.2021.issue-001-en.xml.

15 OECD, *An Introduction to Online Platforms and their Role in the Digital Transformation* (2019), 72, available online: https://www.oecd.org/en/publications/an-introduction-to-online-platforms-and-their-role-in-the-digital-transformation_53e5f593-en.html.

16 For a detailed discussion of the importance of *not* adopting a one-size-fits-all approach in the context of the EU's DMA, see Pınar Akman, "Regulating Competition in Digital Platform Markets: A Critical Assessment of the Framework and Approach of the EU Digital Markets Act," *European Law Review* 47, no. 1 (2022): 85–114.

17 David S. Evans and Richard Schmalensee, *Matchmakers: The New Economics of Multisided Platforms* (Harvard Business Review Press, 2016), 8.

18 Ibid., 15.

19 Michael G. Jacobides, Arun Sundararajan, and Marshall Van Alstyne in collaboration with Deloitte, *Platforms and Ecosystems: Enabling the Digital Economy* (World Economic Forum, 2019), 11, available online: https://www3.weforum.org/docs/WEF_Digital_Platforms_and_Ecosystems_2019.pdf.

20 OECD, "Latin American and Caribbean Competition Forum—Session III: Practical Approaches to Assessing Digital Platform Markets for Competition Law

Enforcement. Background Note," August 5, 2019, 6, available online: https://www.oecd.org/content/dam/oecd/en/publications/reports/2019/08/practical-approaches-to-assessing-digital-platform-markets-for-competition-law-enforcement_a5768dd8/938ffd20-en.pdf. Where these cross-network (indirect) externalities exist, demand on one side of the platform depends on participation on the other side; ibid.

21 Michael L. Katz and Carl Shapiro, "Network Externalities, Competition, and Compatibility," *American Economic Review* 75, no. 3 (1985), 424–40, 424.

22 Néstor Duch-Brown, "The Competitive Landscape of Online Platforms," JRC Digital Economy Working Paper 2017-04, European Commission Joint Research Centre, Seville, 2017, 4.

23 OECD, "Latin American and Caribbean Competition Forum," 9; Duch-Brown, "The Competitive Landscape of Online Platforms," 5.

24 Duch-Brown, "The Competitive Landscape of Online Platforms," 5.

25 Jacobides et al., *Platforms and Ecosystems*, 16. "Ecosystems" refer to new ways of organizing complementary goods and services that involve many companies collaborating and competing to offer a complex good or service; Jacobides et al., *Platforms and Ecosystems*, 14.

26 LEAR, "Ex-Post Assessment of Merger Control Decisions in Digital Markets: Final Report," May 9, 2019, I.47, available online: https://assets.publishing.service.gov.uk/media/5ce54e9aed915d2475aca875/CMA_past_digital_mergers_GOV.UK_version.pdf.

27 Ibid.

28 OECD, "Latin American and Caribbean Competition Forum," 25.

29 Duch-Brown, "The Competitive Landscape of Online Platforms," 6.

30 OECD, "Latin American and Caribbean Competition Forum," 24–5.

31 Ibid., 25.

32 See *Ohio v. American Express Co.*, 138 S. Ct. 2274 (2018); Case C-67/13 P *Groupement des cartes bancaires (CB) v. EU Commission*, ECLI:EU:C:2014:2204. "Market definition" is an exercise that involves determining the substitutes that are alternatives to and thus exert competitive pressure on the products/services of the company in question and is a preliminary step toward establishing the "market power" of the company.

33 OECD, "Latin American and Caribbean Competition Forum," 17.

34 LEAR, "Ex-Post Assessment of Merger Control Decisions," I.155.

35 For a discussion of killer acquisitions, see Colleen Cunningham, Florian Ederer, and Song Ma, "Killer Acquisitions," *Journal of Political Economy* 129, no. 3 (2021): 649–702.

36 OECD, "Latin American and Caribbean Competition Forum," 21.

37 Ibid.

38 See, for example, Emilio Calvano and Michele Polo, "Market Power, Competition and Innovation in Digital Markets: A Survey," *Information Economics and Policy* 54 (2021): 1–18.

39 LEAR, "Ex-Post Assessment of Merger Control Decisions," A.4 139.

40 These are Articles 101 and 102 TFEU and Sherman Antitrust Act Sections I and II.

41 For a detailed discussion of how the US antitrust jurisprudence has been historically shaped by schools of thought, see William E. Kovacic, "The Intellectual DNA of Modern U.S. Competition Law for Dominant Firm Conduct: The Chicago/Harvard Double Helix," *Columbia Business Law Review* 2007, no. 1 (2007): 1–82. On the range of goals attributed to antitrust and their relevance, see Barak Orbach, "Foreword: Antitrust's Pursuit of Purpose," *Fordham Law Review* 81 (2013): 2151–6. For the argument that the "consumer welfare" approach has taken antitrust away from its intended purposes, see Tim Wu, "The 'Protection of the Competitive Process' Standard," Columbia Public Law Research Paper No. 14-612, 2018, available online: https://scholarship.law.columbia.edu/faculty_scholarship/2290.

42 Most recently, for example, commentators have posited that competition law can be used for the goal of combating inflation. See Robert Reich, "We Need to Talk About the Real Reason Behind US Inflation," *The Guardian*, November 11, 2021, available online: https://www.theguardian.com/commentisfree/2021/nov/11/us-inflation-market-power-america-antitrust-robert-reich#:~:text=But%20there's%20a%20deeper%20structural,the%20power%20to%20raise%20prices. *Cf* Massimo Motta, *Competition Policy: Theory and Practice* (Cambridge University Press, 2004), 24; Edward Longe, "Antitrust Will Not Fix Inflation," *The Hill*, February 2, 2022, available online: https://thehill.com/opinion/finance/592502-antitrust-will-not-fix-inflation/.

43 See Wu, *The Curse of Bigness*, 135–6; Lina M. Khan, "The New Brandeis Movement: America's Antimonopoly Debate," *Journal of European Competition Law and Practice* 9, no. 3 (2018): 131–2, 132.

44 Ibid., 132.

45 Stigler Centre, "Report of the Committee for the Study of Digital Platforms," 45.

46 See Lina M. Khan, "Amazon's Antitrust Paradox," *Yale Law Journal* 126 (2017): 710–805.

47 On some of the imperfections of the approach, see Orbach, "Foreword," Pınar Akman, "'Consumer' versus 'Customer': The Devil in the Detail," *Journal of Law and Society* 37, no. 2 (2010): 315–44; Motta, *Competition Policy*, 21–2. On some of the advantages of the "consumer welfare" approach in comparison to alternatives such as its administrability and efficiency, see Herbert Hovenkamp, "Implementing Antitrust's Welfare Goals," *Fordham Law Review* 81, no. 5 (2013): 2471–96. Discussing both the strengths and deficiencies of the approach, see Devlin, *Reforming Antitrust*, 254–68.

48 See Khan, noting that the proposed "separations approach," whereby integrated operations of platforms would be structurally separated, can lead to higher prices and lost efficiencies; Lina M. Khan, "The Separation of Platforms and Commerce," *Columbia Law Review* 119 (2019): 973–1098, 1085. For a discussion of the neo-Brandeisian vision for antitrust, see Devlin, *Reforming Antitrust*, 174ff.

49 For a discussion of this new paradigm and an in-depth study of the current approach to competition law and policy, see Oles Andriychuk, "Between Microeconomics and Geopolitics: On the Reasonable Application of Competition Law," *Modern Law Review* 85, no. 3 (2022): 598–634. See also Motta, *Competition Policy*, 28, noting that "whenever competition policy is used for other purposes than efficiency, one has to wonder whether this is the optimal solution."

50 See Khan, "The Separation of Platforms and Commerce," 1085. See also Herbert Hovenkamp, "The Warren Campaign's Antitrust Proposals," University of

Pennsylvania Law School, Institute for Law and Economics, Research Paper No 19-14, 2019, available online: https://ssrn.com/abstract=3353716.

51 See the discussion in Simon Bishop and Mike Walker, *The Economics of EC Competition Law: Concepts, Application and Measurement*, 3rd ed. (Sweet & Maxwell, 2010), 63–7. See also Motta, *Competition Policy*, 39.

52 See Andriychuk, "Between Microeconomics and Geopolitics," Ioannis Lianos, "Lost in Translation? Towards a Theory of Economic Transplants," *Current Legal Problems* 62, no. 1 (2009): 346–404.

53 Ioannis Lianos, "Polycentric Competition Law," *Current Legal Problems* 71, no. 1 (2018): 161–213, 162.

54 For a discussion of how economic theory informs an understanding of the effects of common business practices that regularly become the subject matter of competition law inquiries, see Niels, Gunnar, Helen Jenkins, and James Kavanagh, *Economics for Competition Lawyers* (Oxford University Press, 2011), 2–5. "Theory of harm" in a competition inquiry sets out how conceptually and empirically the practice under scrutiny (actually or potentially) harms effective competition and, thereby, violates competition law. As noted by commentators, the "requirement to present a theory of harm imposes a logically consistent approach to the assessment of anticompetitive behaviour"; Hans Zenger and Mike Walker, "Theories of Harm in European Competition Law: A Progress Report," in *Ten Years of Effects-Based Approach in EU Competition Law*, ed. Jacques Bourgeois and Denis Waelbroeck (Bruylant, 2012), 185–209, 185.

55 See Lianos, "Lost in Translation?"; Damien Neven, "Competition Economics and Antitrust in Europe," *Economic Policy* 21, no. 48 (2006): 741–91; Oliver Budzinski, "Modern Industrial Economics: Open Problems and Possible Limits," in *Competition Policy and the Economic Approach: Foundations and Limitations*, ed. Josef Drexl, Wolfgang Kerber, and Rupprecht Podszun (Edward Elgar, 2011), 111–38.

56 See the "Utah Statement" expressing the principles of the neo-Brandeisian approach; Tim Wu, "The Utah Statement: Reviving Antimonopoly Traditions for the Era of Big Tech," November 18, 2019, available online: https://onezero.medium.com/the-utah-statement-reviving-antimonopoly-traditions-for-the-era-of-big-tech-e6be198012d7. See also Wu, *The Curse of Bigness*, 18; Lina Khan and Sandeep Vaheesan, "Market Power and Inequality: The Antitrust Counterrevolution and Its Discontents," *Harvard Law & Policy Review* 11 (2017): 235–94. For a study of the historical relation in Germany between economic concentration and Nazism, see Daniel Crane, "Fascism and Monopoly," *Michigan Law Review* 118 (2020): 1315–70.

57 See the discussion of the implications of so-called hipster antitrust in Joshua D. Wright, Elyse Dorsey, Jonathan Klick, and Jan M. Rybnicek, "Requiem for a Paradox: The Dubious Rise and Inevitable Fall of Hipster Antitrust," *Arizona State Law Journal* 51 (2019): 293–369.

58 *The Racecourse Association and others v Office of Fair Trading and The British Horseracing Board v Office of Fair Trading* [2005] CAT 29, [167].

59 World Economic Forum, "Competition Policy in a Globalized, Digitalized Economy," 5.

60 Michael L. Katz, "Exclusionary Conduct in Multi-Sided Markets," in *Rethinking Antitrust Tools for Multi-Sided Platforms* (OECD, 2018), 103–30, 103, available online: https://doi.org/10.1787/a013f740-en.

61 Ibid., 103.

62 Contrast, for example, perhaps most recently, the finding of an infringement by the EU Commission in *Google Shopping (Search)* (n 11) with the opposite outcome in *In the Matter of Google Inc*. FTC File Number 111-0163, January 3, 2013.

63 For example, in the context of market definition, compare Louis Kaplow, "Why (Ever) Define Markets?," *Harvard Law Review* 124 (2010): 437–517 with Greg Werden, "Why (Ever) Define Markets? An Answer to Professor Kaplow," *Antitrust Law Journal* 78, no. 3 (2013): 729–46. For further examples of the general debate, see notes 50 and 55.

64 See *US v Google* (n 11); *FTC v Facebook* (n 11). Other authorities are also closely watching this space, such as Australia, the UK, Japan, and so on.

65 See note 12. See also "EU-U.S. Joint Technology Competition Policy Dialogue, Inaugural Joint Statement between the European Commission, the United States Department of Justice Antitrust Division, and the United States Federal Trade Commission," December 7, 2021, available online: https://ec.europa.eu/competition-policy/system/files/2021-12/EU-US_Joint_Dialogue_Statement_12.6.21_1.pdf.

66 For a discussion of how the current legislative proposals in the United States will "punish success" and play into the hands of Chinese and European technology companies by weakening US technology platforms, see American Chamber of Commerce, "U.S. Antitrust Legislative Proposals: A Global Perspective," February 2022, available online: https://www.uschamber.com/assets/documents/U.S.-ANTITRUST-LEGISLATIVE-PROPOSALS-A-GLOBAL-PERSPECTIVE-FINAL-LOCKED-2.16.22.pdf. See note above for some of the most notable ongoing examples of litigation.

Bibliography

Akman, Pınar. "'Consumer' Versus 'Customer': The Devil in the Detail." *Journal of Law and Society* 37, no. 2 (2010): 315–44.

Akman, Pınar. "Regulating Competition in Digital Platform Markets: A Critical Assessment of the Framework and Approach of the EU Digital Markets Act." *European Law Review* 47, no. 1 (2022): 85–114.

American Chamber of Commerce. "U.S. Antitrust Legislative Proposals: A Global Perspective." February 2022. Available online: https://www.uschamber.com/assets/documents/U.S.-ANTITRUST-LEGISLATIVE-PROPOSALS-A-GLOBAL-PERSPECTIVE-FINAL-LOCKED-2.16.22.pdf.

Andriychuk, Oles. "Between Microeconomics and Geopolitics: On the Reasonable Application of Competition Law." *Modern Law Review* 85, no. 3 (2022): 598–634.

Bagnoli, Vicente. "Digital Platforms as Public Utilities." *IIC—International Review of Intellectual Property and Competition Law* 51, no. 8 (2020): 903–5.

Biden, Joseph R., Jr. "Executive Order on Promoting Competition in the American Economy." July 9, 2021. Available online: https://bidenwhitehouse.archives.gov/briefing-room/presidential-actions/2021/07/09/executive-order-on-promoting-competition-in-the-american-economy/.

Bishop, Simon, and Mike Walker. *The Economics of EC Competition Law: Concepts, Application and Measurement*. 3rd ed. Sweet & Maxwell, 2010.

Buck, Ken. "The Third Way: Antitrust Enforcement in Big Tech." US House of Representatives, Judiciary Committee Subcommittee on Antitrust, Commercial, and Administrative Law, October 6, 2020. Available online: https://www.politico.com/f/?id=00000174-fa7f-db77-abfe-fe7f5d740000.

Budzinski, Oliver. "Modern Industrial Economics: Open Problems and Possible Limits." In *Competition Policy and the Economic Approach: Foundations and Limitations*, edited by Josef Drexl, Wolfgang Kerber, and Rupprecht Podszun. Edward Elgar, 2011.

Calvano, Emilio, and Michele Polo. "Market Power, Competition and Innovation in Digital Markets: A Survey." *Information Economics and Policy* 54 (2021): 1–18.

Chen, Wenjie, Federico J. Diez, Romain A. Duval, Philipp Engler, Jiayue Fan, Chiara Maggi, Marina Mendes Tavares, Daniel A. Schwarz, Ippei Shibata, and Carolina Villegas-Sánchez. *Rising Corporate Market Power: Emerging Policy Issues*. International Monetary Fund (IMF), March 15, 2021. Available online: https://www.elibrary.imf.org/view/journals/006/2021/001/006.2021.issue-001-en.xml.

Competition and Markets Authority (CMA). "The CMA's Digital Markets Strategy: June 2019." 2019. Available online: https://www.gov.uk/government/publications/competition-and-markets-authoritys-digital-markets-strategy/the-cmas-digital-markets-strategy.

Crane, Daniel. "Fascism and Monopoly." *Michigan Law Review* 118 (2020): 1315–70.

Crémer, Jacques, Yves-Alexandre de Montjoye, and Heike Schweitzer. "Competition Policy for the Digital Era." Directorate-General for Competition, European Commission, 2019. Available online: https://euagenda.eu/upload/publications/untitled-257961-ea.pdf.

Cunningham, Colleen, Florian Ederer, and Song Ma. "Killer Acquisitions." *Journal of Political Economy* 129, no. 3 (2021): 649–702.

Devlin, Alan J. *Reforming Antitrust*. Cambridge University Press, 2021.

Duch-Brown, Néstor. "The Competitive Landscape of Online Platforms." JRC Digital Economy Working Paper 2017-04. European Commission Joint Research Centre, Seville, 2017.

EU Commission. "Proposal for a Regulation of The European Parliament and of the Council on Contestable and Fair Markets in the Digital Sector (Digital Markets Act)." December 15, 2020. Available online: https://eur-lex.europa.eu/legal-content/EN/TXT/PDF/?uri=CELEX:52020PC0842.

"EU-U.S. Joint Technology Competition Policy Dialogue, Inaugural Joint Statement between the European Commission, the United States Department of Justice Antitrust Division and the United States Federal Trade Commission." December 7, 2021. Available online: https://ec.europa.eu/competition-policy/system/files/2021-12/EU-US_Joint_Dialogue_Statement_12.6.21_1.pdf.

Evans, David S., and Richard Schmalensee. *Matchmakers: The New Economics of Multisided Platforms*. Harvard Business Review Press, 2016.

Furman, Jason, Diane Coyle, Amelia Fletcher, Derek McAuley, and Philip Marsden. *Unlocking Digital Competition: Report of the Digital Competition Expert Panel*. March 2019. Available online: https://assets.publishing.service.gov.uk/media/5c88150ee5274a230219c35f/unlocking_digital_competition_furman_review_web.pdf.

Hovenkamp, Herbert. "Implementing Antitrust's Welfare Goals." *Fordham Law Review* 81, no. 5 (2013): 2471–96.

Hovenkamp, Herbert. "The Warren Campaign's Antitrust Proposals." University of Pennsylvania Law School, Institute for Law and Economics, Research Paper No. 19-14 (2019). Available online: https://ssrn.com/abstract=3353716.

Jacobides, Michael G., Arun Sundararajan, and Marshall Van Alstyne in collaboration with Deloitte. *Platforms and Ecosystems: Enabling the Digital Economy*. World

Economic Forum, 2019. Available online: https://www3.weforum.org/docs/WEF_Digital_Platforms_and_Ecosystems_2019.pdf.

Kaplow, Louis. "Why (Ever) Define Markets?" *Harvard Law Review* 124 (2010): 437–517.

Katz, Michael L. "Exclusionary Conduct in Multi-Sided Markets." In *Rethinking Antitrust Tools for Multi-Sided Platforms*. OECD, 2018.

Katz, Michael L., and Carl Shapiro. "Network Externalities, Competition, and Compatibility." *American Economic Review* 75, no. 3 (1985): 424–40.

Khan, Lina M. "Amazon's Antitrust Paradox." *Yale Law Journal* 126 (2017): 710–805.

Khan, Lina M. "The New Brandeis Movement: America's Antimonopoly Debate." *Journal of European Competition Law and Practice* 9, no. 3 (2018): 131–2.

Khan, Lina M. "The Separation of Platforms and Commerce." *Columbia Law Review* 119 (2019): 973–1098.

Khan, Lina M., and Sandeep Vaheesan. "Market Power and Inequality: The Antitrust Counterrevolution and Its Discontents." *Harvard Law & Policy Review* 11 (2017): 235–94.

Kolhatkar, Sheelah. "Can Elizabeth Warren Win It All?" *The New Yorker*, June 14, 2019. Available online: https://www.newyorker.com/magazine/2019/06/24/can-elizabeth-warren-win-it-all.

Kovacic, William E. "The Intellectual DNA of Modern U.S. Competition Law for Dominant Firm Conduct: The Chicago/Harvard Double Helix." *Columbia Business Law Review* 2007, no. 1 (2007): 1–82.

Lancieri, Filippo, and Patricia Morita Sakowski. "Competition in Digital Markets: A Review of Expert Reports." *Stanford Journal of Law, Business & Finance* 26, no. 1 (Winter 2021): 65–170.

LEAR. "Ex-Post Assessment of Merger Control Decisions in Digital Markets: Final Report." May 9, 2019. Available online: https://assets.publishing.service.gov.uk/media/5ce54e9aed915d2475aca875/CMA_past_digital_mergers_GOV.UK_version.pdf.

Lecher, Colin. "Elizabeth Warren Says She Wants to Break Up Amazon, Google, and Facebook: A Proposal to Unwind Big Tech." *The Verge*, March 8, 2019. Available online: https://www.theverge.com/2019/3/8/18256032/elizabeth-warren-antitrust-google-amazon-facebook-break-up.

Lianos, Ioannis. "Lost in Translation? Towards a Theory of Economic Transplants." *Current Legal Problems* 62, no. 1 (2009): 346–404.

Lianos, Ioannis. "Polycentric Competition Law." *Current Legal Problems* 71, no. 1 (2018): 161–213.

Longe, Edward. "Antitrust Will Not Fix Inflation." *The Hill*, February 2, 2022. Available online: https://thehill.com/opinion/finance/592502-antitrust-will-not-fix-inflation/.

Motta, Massimo. *Competition Policy: Theory and Practice*. Cambridge University Press, 2004.

Neven, Damien. "Competition Economics and Antitrust in Europe." *Economic Policy* 21, no. 48 (2006): 741–91.

Niels, Gunnar, Helen Jenkins, and James Kavanagh. *Economics for Competition Lawyers*. Oxford University Press, 2011.

OECD. *Competition in Labour Markets*. 2020. Available online: https://www.oecd.org/content/dam/oecd/en/publications/reports/2020/03/competition-issues-in-labour-markets_02ec78ba/66980788-en.pdf.

OECD. *An Introduction to Online Platforms and their Role in the Digital Transformation*. 2019, 72. Available online: https://www.oecd.org/en/publications/an-introduction-to-online-platforms-and-their-role-in-the-digital-transformation_53e5f593-en.html.

OECD. "Latin American and Caribbean Competition Forum—Session III: Practical Approaches to Assessing Digital Platform Markets for Competition Law Enforcement. Background Note." August 5, 2019, 6. Available online: https://www.oecd.org/content/dam/oecd/en/publications/reports/2019/08/practical-approaches-to-assessing-digital-platform-markets-for-competition-law-enforcement_a5768dd6/938ffd20-en.pdf.

Orbach, Barak. "Foreword: Antitrust's Pursuit of Purpose." *Fordham Law Review* 81 (2013): 2151–6.

Phillips Sawyer, Laura. "U.S. Antitrust Law and Policy in Historical Perspective." Harvard Business School Working Paper No. 19-110, May 2019 (Revised September 2019). Available online: https://www.hbs.edu/faculty/Pages/item.aspx?num=56116.

Reich, Robert. "We Need to Talk about the Real Reason Behind US Inflation." *The Guardian*, November 11, 2021. Available online: https://www.theguardian.com/commentisfree/2021/nov/11/us-inflation-market-power-america-antitrust-robert-reich#:~:text=But%20there's%20a%20deeper%20structural,the%20power%20to%20raise%20prices.

Singer, Hal. "Antitrust Should Be Used to Fight Inflation." *The American Prospect*, February 2, 2022. Available online: https://prospect.org/economy/antitrust-should-be-used-to-fight-inflation.

Srnicek, Nick. "We Need to Nationalise Google, Facebook and Amazon. Here's Why." *The Guardian*, August 30, 2017. Available online: https://www.theguardian.com/commentisfree/2017/aug/30/nationalise-google-facebook-amazon-data-monopoly-platform-public-interest.

Stigler Center for the Study of the Economy and the State. "Report of the Committee for the Study of Digital Platforms." University of Chicago Booth School of Business, 2019. Available online: https://publicknowledge.org/wp-content/uploads/2021/11/Stigler-Committee-on-Digital-Platforms-Final-Report.pdf.

Tworek, Heidi J. S., and Christopher Buschow. "Changing the Rules of the Game: Strategic Institutionalization and Legacy Companies' Resistance to New Media." *International Journal of Communication* 10 (2016): 2119–39.

US House of Representatives, Subcommittee on Antitrust, Commercial and Administrative Law of the Committee on the Judiciary, Majority Staff Report and Recommendations, Investigation of Competition in Digital Markets (2020). Available online: https://www.govinfo.gov/content/pkg/CPRT-117HPRT47832/pdf/CPRT-117HPRT47832.pdf.

Warren, Elizabeth. "Reigniting Competition in the American Economy." Keynote Remarks at New America's Open Markets Program Event, June 29, 2016. Available online: https://www.openmarketsinstitute.org/publications/senator-elizabeth-warrens-keynote-remarks-at-new-americas-open-markets-program-event-reigniting-competition-in-the-american-economy.

Werden, Greg. "Why (Ever) Define Markets? An Answer to Professor Kaplow." *Antitrust Law Journal* 78, no. 3 (2013): 729–46.

World Economic Forum. "Competition Policy in a Globalized, Digitalized Economy: Platform for Shaping the Future of Trade and Global Economic Interdependence." 2019. Available online: https://www3.weforum.org/docs/WEF_Competition_Policy_in_a_Globalized_Digitalized_Economy_Report.pdf.

Wright, Joshua D., Elyse Dorsey, Jonathan Klick, and Jan M. Rybnicek. "Requiem for a Paradox: The Dubious Rise and Inevitable Fall of Hipster Antitrust." *Arizona State Law Journal* 51 (2019): 293–369.

Wu, Tim. *The Curse of Bigness*. Columbia Global Reports, 2018.

Wu, Tim. "The 'Protection of the Competitive Process' Standard." Columbia Public Law Research Paper No. 14-612 (2018). Available online: https://scholarship.law.columbia.edu/faculty_scholarship/2290.

Wu, Tim. "The Utah Statement: Reviving Antimonopoly Traditions for the Era of Big Tech." November 18, 2019. Available online: https://onezero.medium.com/the-utah-statement-reviving-antimonopoly-traditions-for-the-era-of-big-tech-e6be198012d7.

Zenger, Hans, and Mike Walker. "Theories of Harm in European Competition Law: A Progress Report." In *Ten Years of Effects-Based Approach in EU Competition Law*, edited by Jacques Bourgeois and Denis Waelbroeck. Bruylant, 2012.

10
TECHNOLOGY POLICYMAKING AND MARKET DOMINANCE
The Case of Safaricom in Kenya

Grace Mutung'u

In May 2021, the Ethiopian prime minister announced that a telecommunications license would be awarded to the Global Partnership for Ethiopia, a consortium led by Kenyan mobile network operator Safaricom, with partners Sumitomo (Japan), Vodacom (South Africa), Vodafone (Britain), and British development finance agency CDC Group.[1] The consortium had paid US$850 million for the license, the highest sum paid for such a contract on the continent yet. As the prime minister put it, "This will be Ethiopia's largest foreign direct investment deal yet, and the consortium intends to invest about US $85 billion dollars in the country."[2]

The entry of the consortium into Ethiopia is reminiscent of the late 1990s, when many of Africa's large mobile network operators (MNOs) were formed. They were licensed in various countries as part of economic liberalization policies, where the countries awarded limited MNO licenses and privatized state telecommunication monopolies. Unlike many other African countries, Ethiopia did not liberalize its telecommunications sector. The country's state monopoly—Ethiotel—has been solely providing mobile telecommunication, mobile money, and related services in the country. While Ethiotel is a successful company in its own right and considered among the government's big five, human rights activists have faulted it for centralizing government interests over those of its consumers and the public.[3]

The lead company in the consortium, Kenyan mobile giant Safaricom, is a similarly successful company in many measures. It has, in over a decade, made "super profits" from its large market share in various segments of the telecommunications market—voice, SMS, and mobile money.[4] The company has also been among the top contributors to Kenya's exchequer, as the government owns 35 percent equity in the company. Safaricom is also among the country's highest taxpayers and is often compared to a large bank due to the volume of transactions conducted on its mobile money platform, M-Pesa.[5] Its infrastructure network is the most spread out in the country, making it a key player in national functions from elections to payment for e-government services and collection of taxes.[6]

But as Safaricom expanded into Ethiopia, it faced competition-based regulatory actions at home. The company was protesting the communication regulator's directive to reduce mobile termination rates (MTR)—the fees the company charges other MNOs for calls completing outgoing calls over its network.[7] The MTR directive followed recommendations from a 2019 parliamentary report on competition in Kenya's telecommunications market.[8] More regulatory actions targeting various aspects of Safaricom's business are expected. However, pundits, as well as competitors, will not be surprised if the actions do not result in a significant reduction in Safaricom's market share. This is partly because the regulation was not timely, and Safaricom already has such significant market share and network effects that are difficult to overcome.[9] Moreover, even if the market share in these segments were to be reduced, Safaricom is actively creating new markets in areas such as home internet, on-demand content, internet of things, and integrated business services.[10] Should Safaricom become as successful in these new ventures, it is likely to expand its significant market share, thereby keeping regulators and policymakers in unending cycles of regulatory action aimed at correcting those market segments.

The Safaricom-led venture was, however, given a green light by two regional competition authorities: the Common Market for East and Southern Africa (COMESA) and the European Commission.[11] This is despite the history of telecommunications markets in Africa revealing that most countries lack healthy market competition. The markets are also not organic, but the outcome of deliberate international and local policies, where there are many considerations besides competitive markets.

In Ethiopia's case, liberalization follows a 2018 change of administration that heralded the opening up of democratic processes. However, ongoing conflict among the regional governments of Amhara, Afar, and Tigray has dampened economic growth in the country.[12] Safaricom's entry into Ethiopia is therefore not purely economic. The company has and will engage with the broader political and social environment. From a competitive perspective, Safaricom's actions are relevant when its engagement results in a more favorable market share or creates barriers to entry for other players.

This chapter takes a historical look at the role of Safaricom's social and political engagement in its market dominance. Using a nonmarket strategy lens, we consider how the company influenced the market from its creation in the late 1990s to date. We zone in on three policy aspects—convergence, mobile money, and data—to argue that Safaricom has not achieved market concentration by outdoing its competitors, but that it has taken advantage of social and political relations to co-opt new markets and avoid regulation. As a result of these actions, Safaricom has evolved into a platform with multiple and integrated uses. The article points out the risks of such behavior for consumers, competitors, and the public, concluding with a call for competition regulators to consider the role of nonmarket strategies in market shaping.

Platforms, Market Shaping, and Nonmarket Strategies

Platformization may be defined as the permeation of infrastructures, economic processes, and government frameworks into various spheres of life.[13] Globally, telecommunications companies are integrating their services to provide services for various groups—consumers, producers, and governments.[14] Technology corporation Huawei views the future MNOs transforming into internet of things (IoT) platforms. In this vision, MNOs begin by supplying IoT SIM cards, incrementally add services, and finally provide an integrated suite of services.[15] Similarly, industry players are promoting the concept of digital service providers (DSPs). DSP refers to the movement from MNOs offering core communication services to providing more integrated services—internet, add-on services, content, and apps, all sold directly from the device.[16] The multiple and integrated uses of Safaricom's services by individuals, organizations, and the government show that Safaricom is already a platform and it is further platformizing.[17]

Platformization of MNOs raises regulatory issues for competition. MNOs are already regulated under telecommunications, competition, and, in countries such as Kenya, under financial and data laws. However, the regulation is often siloed and has largely ignored practices such as the integration of various businesses and the creation of new business areas. Historically, questions of when and how to regulate novel business ideas labeled as innovation have resulted in delayed or soft regulation. It is such regulatory gaps that companies such as Safaricom exploit to shape the market and enjoy a competitive advantage before regulatory action is taken.

Market Shaping

Market shaping refers to deliberate activities of market actors aimed at creating certain market outcomes. These activities range from influencing regulation and institutions to filling in voids in the market.[18] The outcomes can broadly be summarized as disrupting, widening, maintaining, or reducing a market.[19] Market shaping, particularly when undertaken by competitors, is at odds with competition law, which seeks to level the market and open it to new entrants. While competition law generally targets the existing market, market shaping takes place in the broader social and political environment.

Telecommunications markets such as Kenya's are a classic case of market shaping by local and international policies. In the late 1990s, there was an economic downturn in much of Africa, triggered in part by the end of the Cold War and the subsequent collapse of major streams of economic support, as well as austerity measures imposed by multilateral financial institutions. Politically, there was also a decline in democracy in the postindependence nations. International policymaking bodies, the World Bank and the International Monetary Fund (IMF), prescribed the so-called Structural Adjustment Programs (SAPs)—conditions for countries to access loans. The conditions involved privatization of government entities, trade liberalization, and balancing of government deficit.[20] It was in this context that many African countries opened their telecommunications markets.

In Safaricom's case, its legacy as a former state-owned enterprise, followed by acquisition by a multinational company, gave it certain advantages in shaping the market. Prior to liberalization, telecommunication services consisted of landlines and an international gateway operated by Kenya Posts and Telecommunications Corporation (KPTC). In 1998, KPTC was converted into three entities—Telkom for telecommunications, Posta for postal services, and Communications Authority as the regulator. Telkom Kenya formed a subsidiary, Safaricom, for cellular (mobile) services. A year later, UK company Vodacom bought a 40 percent stake in Safaricom, but the government retained a majority stake in the company, even when its shares were further divested. To date, a representative from the treasury sits on Safaricom's board, and the treasury is deeply involved in the company's succession planning.[21] Safaricom's historical and current relationship with the government gives Safaricom the opportunity to participate in shaping markets.

Nonmarket Strategy

Nonmarket strategy refers to how a firm relates to not just its direct marketplace but also other stakeholders in the wider ecosystem—the public, regulators, and policymakers. It can broadly be categorized as public policy work, such as lobbying and engaging with regulators, and private strategies, such as engaging with activists.[22]

While competition law traditionally focuses on market issues such as price, product, and service, nonmarket strategy considers a firm's relationships in the broader social and political environment. It, therefore, goes beyond the market's primary stakeholders—businesses, employees, and consumers—to all stakeholders in public policy. Competition aims to keep the market open so that new competitors can set up business, increasing consumer choice.[23] Market failure occurs when there is a lack of sufficient information for consumers and regulators to make informed choices, when a few players have concentrated market power, or where users do not pay for public goods and externalities such as costs or benefits to third parties.[24] With a nonmarket strategy lens, competition policy would consider how a company has used its relationships with public and private actors to shape its operating environment.

Nonmarket strategy is relevant in the era of digital disruption, where many new products are being created, and companies such as MNOs consolidate their markets through platformization. It can help competition regulators imagine markets as they evolve and anticipate regulatory issues. Taking a historical look at dominant MNOs is therefore useful in understanding how companies can consolidate their dominance.

Safaricom has used "commercial nationalism" to promote itself as an Indigenous company that is closely intertwined in the social and economic development of Kenya.[25] This is achieved through public and private strategies that vary from charitable work, commitments to global processes such as the sustainable development goals, as well as lobbying directly and through industry associations.[26] In its formative years, it directly benefited by lobbying government agents with whom it was closely connected or who were in its management.[27]

Besides regulators, the company also engages with activists in the field. This has happened when the company's positions converge with those of civil society organizations (CSOs). An example is in the company's resistance to direct access to its network by state agencies or the regulation of information and communications technology (ICT) professionals. In both instances, Safaricom and CSOs resisted the policies, albeit from different perspectives—protection of business interests and human rights, respectively.[28]

This relationship between MNOs and CSOs extends to MNOs supporting CSOs through project funding, travel support, and appearance at events.[29] While more research is required to establish the impact of corporate funding on CSO advocacy, CSOs' lack of participation in competition-related policy processes is cause for concern. In the parliamentary inquiry on the legal and regulatory gaps in the telecommunications sector, digital rights CSOs did not submit memoranda or appear for hearings. This is despite there being a group of well-organized digital rights CSOs that have previously submitted memoranda and even been invited for hearings before the committee.

Safaricom continues to benefit from its relationship with the government, including through exemptions from being categorized as dominant, which would affect many of its business practices. This was the object of the parliamentary inquiry of 2018, which considered gaps that hinder competition in the Kenyan telecommunications subsector. The sector regulator, Communications Authority

(CA), had also previously commissioned a report along similar lines.[30] Both reports shy away from declaring Safaricom a dominant operator, instead calling for a better delineation of what constitutes market share. This could be attributed to the method used in the processes, where the narrative was framed as "breaking up of Safaricom." In turn, Safaricom and its allies put up a spirited defense, arguing that it should not be punished for its success.

Perhaps as a result of this framing, the debate did not sufficiently address Safaricom's emerging businesses. While the CA's report mentions the need to consider media content as a regulatory issue, the two reports fail to conceptualize the role of MNOs as DSPs. As Kenya grapples with correcting the telecommunications market, a historical look at how the market was shaped provides insights into the role of various actors.

Convergence as the Origin of MNO as a Platform

In Western countries such as the United States, telecommunication companies are advocating for convergence to enable them to provide full-suite services.[31] Convergence refers to the provision of mobile, voice, and data services within a single network.[32] It is a form of platformization that allows multidimensional services to be built on a mobile network. Kenya's experience with convergence is different from that of the United States. While in the United States and other Western markets, the various telecommunications services were provided separately, convergence was adopted several years after liberalization in Kenya.[33]

The policy process through which convergence was adopted, together with the broader political environment at the time, explains the genesis of Safaricom's dominance. At the point of liberalization, the Kenyan market was conceptualized from the perspective of existing services—the landline network operated by Telkom Kenya and cellular services operated by Telkom's subsidiary, Safaricom. During that time, the internet was also being internationalized and commercialized. Literature from this period shows that even with the very limited internet access, its impacts were already being felt in functions such as communications with the adoption of email, websites, and online repositories.[34]

A reflection by Kenya's former permanent secretary (PS) in the Ministry of Information and Communications, Professor Bitange Ndemo, demonstrates Safaricom's role in policy changes that took place at the time. The PS was appointed in 2005, a few years after formal liberalization. By then, there were only two MNOs—Safaricom and Celtel (now Airtel). While he links the failure of the market to launch to the political environment, he also recounts events in which Safaricom was pulled into opportunities that have defined its market share to date.[35]

One such process was the development of a submarine cable known as the East African Marine Systems (TEAMS). The cable was constructed under the "build it and they will come" policy despite there being very limited last-mile infrastructure or local content.[36] In circumstances that appeared like a public–private partnership, local internet service providers (ISPs) were invited to take up ownership of the cable. Per the PS's account, getting the TEAMS project off the ground was a huge task at a time when trust in government was very low after the highly contested 2007 elections. He, however, benefited from relationships with the companies' leadership through which he was able to sell to them the idea of investing in submarine cable.[37] Curiously, the two state-owned entities, Safaricom and Telkom, not only invested in the cable but also took up higher equity than the ISPs. While local ISPs took between 1 and 10 percent, Safaricom and Telkom took up 20 percent each.

The two companies' investment in TEAMS gave them the ability to integrate their businesses, effectively becoming not just ISPs but also traders in both wholesale and retail internet. The convergence of mobile and internet also gave Safaricom a competitive advantage. Shortly after the TEAMS venture took off, the new convergence-inspired licensing framework was introduced. Known as the unified licensing framework (ULF), operators are licensed under three broad categories—networks (physical infrastructure), applications, and content. Through these broad licenses, ULF enables platformized business since one operator can engage in a broad range of activities.[38]

During the ULF policy development process, concern about the impact of the broad licenses on competition was raised. Recalling that this was the same time that the government was in the process of seeking a third national operator, would ULF not enable Safaricom to integrate its services in ways that would make it difficult for future MNOs to offer competitive services? To allay fears that ULF would create an unhealthy market, the regulator added a requirement of the separation of business accounts for firms with more than one license.[39]

Statistics published by the communications regulator indicate that under the ULF, Safaricom accumulated a lead in all market segments. In the latest numbers, for example, the company has more than 60 percent of the market share in SIM subscriptions, voice, SMS, and mobile broadband. Since the introduction of home fiber, the company has overtaken internet service providers, commanding 37 percent of the market.[40] Under the ULF license, Safaricom not only serves subscribers directly but also acts as a platform for third parties to deliver content to subscribers. Examples of this are in its bulk SMS services, as well as its call ringback tone service, popularly known as *Skiza* tunes. For these services, Safaricom allows content service providers and artiste's representatives to deliver text messages and audio content over its network. These services are lucrative for the MNO. In 2020, for example, Safaricom reported over KSh5 billion revenue from bulk SMS, while about KSh200 million was paid to artistes under the *Skiza* program.[41]

One effect of Safaricom operating such a large multidimensional market is that Safaricom has acquired rulemaking power. On the issue of SMS, for example, in the 2007 election, Safaricom successfully lobbied against a government request to switch off its SMS network to curb the spread of hate messages via SMS. The company instead argued that it could use its SMS platform to send messages of peace.[42] With the benefit of that experience, the company made rules for political messages in the subsequent 2013 elections. These included blocking out foreign bulk SMS, which Safaricom argued were not licensed and would therefore be difficult to moderate.[43] While the actions taken by Safaricom were an important response to hate speech online, they also protected its position as the main bulk SMS provider since political actors could only send bulk SMS through local providers, and Safaricom is the main bulk SMS provider. Thereafter, the rule was adopted as a guideline by the communications regulator and later in a national cybercrimes law.[44]

Another example of rulemaking is in the Skiza tunes platform. Safaricom has been unilaterally deciding artistes' revenue share for the program. The payout was 7.5 percent at inception in 2009 and was only raised to the current 40 percent after long advocacy by artistes.[45] The Copyright Act was amended in 2022 to increase the artiste's revenue share to 52 percent.[46] By the time the law was passed, Safaricom had had adequate time to reap from the program and, today, is able to pay the prescribed payout to artistes, while companies that have not had such exclusivity will struggle to compete.

The concentrated market also has an impact on the political environment. Geographically, Safaricom has the most widely distributed network in Kenya. The firm has therefore become central in the delivery of the government's objectives. During the 2017 general elections, for example, Safaricom was relied upon for the transmission of results in over 90 percent of polling stations in the country.[47] In the subsequent 2022 elections, over 40 percent of the budget for the transmission of results was paid to Safaricom.[48] This meant that had there been a network failure, there would have been a delay in the transmission of results in a highly contested election. In turn, the sensitivity of the results could mean that network resources were dedicated to the election project. With Safaricom also serving over 90 percent of internet users in the country, it would therefore not be surprising if other network users were deprioritized and, in some cases, even denied access to the internet.[49]

The vastness of Safaricom's network, together with its surveillance capabilities, intersects with information control and national security interests. While laws protect against the intrusion of privacy, research has linked extrajudicial killings to targeted surveillance by law enforcement using Safaricom's network.[50] In

2014, the government awarded Safaricom a contract to construct a surveillance security system for two cities—Nairobi and Mombasa.[51] Around the same time, Safaricom was allocated additional frequency spectrum, sparking concerns of favoritism. While the regulator later allocated additional frequencies to competitor Airtel, Airtel still complained that the frequency band was expensive to operate in compared to that allocated to Safaricom. In this instance, Safaricom got an advantage and was able to better deploy its 4G network.[52]

As Safaricom establishes itself in Ethiopia, there are similarities with its genesis in Kenya. Just like in Kenya, it is the first licensee in the vast country. Similarly, Safaricom has the financial backing of governments such as the UK and the United States, through which the company can execute nonmarket strategies to shape the Ethiopian market. One early indicator of such strategies is Safaricom's negotiation to expand its license to include mobile money services.[53] With a long experience of mobile money in Kenya and beyond, the license to operate in Ethiopia could herald the beginnings of a pan-African payment platform.

As seen from Safaricom's history in Kenya, actors in a joint venture can be greatly influential in policymaking in ways that result in anticompetitive markets. Competition policy should therefore be alive to the power of actors in ventures such as Ethiopia's liberalization. Policymakers should analyze and mitigate the power of actors venturing into the country. In addition, the evolving nature of the digital sector calls for competition regulators to be proactive in anticipating competition issues even as markets are being invented. Mobile money, which is a classic case of market shaping, provides some lessons on cross-sector regulation.

Mobile Money

The 2020 FinAccess Survey, a report by the Central Bank of Kenya in collaboration with partners, indicates that about 35 percent of Kenyan adults access financial services through mobile money.[54] Safaricom commands over 97 percent of the mobile money market through its product M-Pesa.[55] From the onset, mobile money services were offered as part of mobile subscription, and this helped to consolidate Safaricom's market power.[56] This happened partly because M-Pesa was framed as a driver for financial inclusion in a country with a significant population of unbanked people, effectively bypassing banks in its initial deployment.[57]

However, policy discussions on M-Pesa began in the financial sector. M-Pesa's history can be traced to microfinance institutions experimenting on how to scale a social practice where Kenyans were trading using mobile money airtime.[58] However, the finance, as well as the telecommunications regulator, delayed the regulation of M-Pesa, and, in turn, competition regulation was also put on hold.

Among the reasons for the delay of regulation is the linking of M-Pesa to development goals and the framing of M-Pesa as innovation. Providing financial inclusion to the unbanked was seen as more important than creating a competitive market for mobile money services. And with M-Pesa being seen as an innovation that seemingly appeared in a void, regulators took a "test and learn" approach.[59]

Accounts by policymakers from the period support this thesis. The then permanent secretary in ICT, Ndemo, recounts personally intervening with fellow policymakers to permit the innovation.[60] The then Central Bank governor explains the government's delay of regulation from a ripeness perspective. He views M-Pesa's evolution in six dimensions: financial inclusion, linkage with financial institutions, digital loans, credit scores, international remittances, fintech, and, finally, impact on monetary policy.[61] Competition regulation would have been applied after Safaricom expanded beyond financial inclusion.

During this evolution, Safaricom shaped the market through collaboration with the government, as well as other actors in the political environment. Its first digital loan product, M-Shwari, for example, was with Kenya's top bank, KCB. Its overdraft facility, known as Fuliza, is a collaboration with NCBA, a bank whose ownership is linked to the first family.

In the absence of regulation, Safaricom assumed rulemaking power in ways that have helped the company expand M-Pesa from a means of sending and receiving money to a platform with multiple functions. Fifteen years after the system began commercial operations, Safaricom has several advantages that are difficult for any other MNO to replicate. These include the product's infrastructure, which, in 2022, was declared critical infrastructure that is now accorded protection under the cybercrimes law.[62] Another is the integration of M-Pesa with other services, such as payment systems and banking systems. Considered alongside other services that Safaricom has recently launched in integrated support to individuals and businesses, it would be difficult for another MNO to catch up.[63] For example, Safaricom has a service, such as separate wallets and accounting for individuals and businesses, which enables them to separate personal and business accounts and automate their bookkeeping.[64] Coupled with the fact that such businesses have many customers who pay for goods and services using M-Pesa, it naturally follows that Safaricom would maintain its market share unless a rival developed similarly convenient products.

These strengths of M-Pesa make it an asset for the implementation of government policies such as digital ID and tax collection. Kenya has a mandatory SIM card registration law, as well as know-your-customer requirements, which companies such as Safaricom implement when they provide services to subscribers. These requirements, while important for national security and antimoney laundering, have been implemented in ways that increase datafication of transactions, in the process creating what researchers refer to as financial reputation profiles.[65] It has been argued that Safaricom pushed for digital ID in pursuit of a credit information sharing system.[66] In 2022, Safaricom unilaterally added facial photographs as a requirement for M-Pesa registration.[67] Despite public complaints on the privacy implications of the project, Safaricom insisted that the photographs were important for its facial recognition technology that had been built to prevent M-Pesa fraud.[68]

With government-issued digital IDs, Safaricom is able to uniquely identify every subscriber and tag their transactions for analysis of their financial behavior. Such profiles are used to predict a person's credit rating and, therefore, create new products such as digital loans. This is lauded as financial inclusion since people can access credit even when they do not have the customary collateral—property documents. However, emerging research shows that digital financial services can be punitive to the same populations who need financial inclusion most. This is because data-based decisions favor those with a lot of data, for example, longer credit histories, as well as capacities such as digital literacy.[69] Therefore, for one to get a favorable credit rating, they need to make more transactions over the network, have a smartphone, and so on. Such requirements, in turn, keep people locked on the network as they pursue a positive rating, eventually resulting in market concentration.

M-Pesa's market concentration intersects with government targets such as fiscal transparency and e-payments.[70] In 2024, for example, over KSh8.7 trillion was transacted over mobile money, with about 93 percent of the transactions taking place on M-Pesa.[71] This represents over half of the country's GDP.[72] While not all the money is income, it indicates "where the money is," attracting the interest of the tax collector. Since 2018, in every budget cycle, the government has introduced new digital taxes, such as digital service tax (DST), as well as value-added tax (VAT) and excise duty on digital services. A presentation by the Kenya Revenue Authority (KRA) confirms the important role played by Safaricom in digital tax payments.[73] As KRA introduced DST in 2020, payment services providers such as Safaricom were exempted. Arguably, it could have been because Safaricom had already illustrated the potential for digital taxes from its remittance of taxes on its products. On *Skiza* tunes, for instance, Safaricom deducts and remits taxes to the government as it sends artistes' dues to their collection agents. While simplified tax administration is a positive benefit to society, the magnitude of rulemaking by Safaricom, coupled with opacity on the processes of rulemaking, as well as a lack of mechanisms for redress for those aggrieved by the rules, shows the dangers of a private entity taking up public roles.

The case of M-Pesa demonstrates the need to strike a balance between allowing innovation and the protection of public interest. The initial goal of M-Pesa—financial inclusion—has been swallowed by state interest to collect revenue and private interest to make a profit. M-Pesa's evolution is also a case of platformization, and it demonstrates the need for competition regulators to not only look at market issues but also nonmarket strategies that shape the market.

M-Pesa illustrates the gaps that can occur where there are multiple regulators, as well as the risk of the "test and learn" approach. This was repeated during the COVID-19 pandemic when the finance regulator, Central Bank of Kenya (CBK), directed a reduction of M-Pesa fees to encourage cashless transactions. While Safaricom was initially supportive of this move, it complained when the move was extended beyond the first three months. The company successfully lobbied for market-based pricing issued as principles on mobile money pricing by CBK.[74] While the principles apply to all MNOs, they are advantageous to Safaricom, which gained a significant number of users during the period when transaction fees were greatly reduced. Safaricom reverted to previous tariffs in the following year.[75]

The lack of involvement of the competition regulator in test regulation is a missed learning opportunity, as there is no monitoring of the effect of test regulations on competition. The approaches are also detrimental to the public interest, such as financial inclusion. Countries adopting disruptive ideas such as mobile money should therefore create avenues for coregulation among sectors and competition regulators. Even where an issue may not be ripe for regulation, the competition regulator should monitor the effects of various policies and mitigate competition issues.[76] They should intervene to halt or modify rules made by players where those rules have an anticompetitive effect.

Data

In January 2020, Safaricom published a request for expression of interest seeking to prequalify location tracking and intelligence platform providers.[77] Although the notice was subsequently taken down, it signified Safaricom's clearest intention to monetize the vast and unique data in its custody. This is despite Kenya enacting the Data Protection Act (DPA) in 2019. This law closely mirrors the European Union's General Data Protection Regulation (GDPR), which restricts commercial use of personal data. The DPA puts Safaricom in an interesting position, where it has unique and comprehensive data on the communication and financial behavior of Kenyan subscribers but is restricted from trading in the data. In this way, the DPA may be pushing companies that hold vast data, such as Safaricom, to build more services based on the data, thereby becoming digital service providers.

Safaricom participated in the policy development process of the DPA. Among the recommendations that the company successfully argued for was the removal of financial data from the definition of sensitive personal data.[78] While the DPA provides guidance on the processing of personal data, it restricts the processing of sensitive personal data to very limited grounds. Commercial processing is not included in these grounds.[79] Had the law included personal financial data in the definition of sensitive data, Safaricom would not have been able to exploit aspects of M-Pesa data since M-Pesa is widely used for personal finance. Although restricting M-Pesa to achieve data protection is restrictive, the data protection law could have been used to regulate aspects of M-Pesa, for example, restricting profiling or giving principles for access to M-Pesa data.

Safaricom has already begun making rules on M-Pesa data. For example, in 2021, the company announced that it would start hiding the identity of "*lipa na* M-Pesa" users from merchants.[80] Prior to this, merchants who used M-Pesa to receive payments from customers would get the phone number of the sender, among other details. There had been complaints that such data had been used to send unsolicited messages to customers. By hiding the phone numbers, Safaricom was therefore making a rule to resolve the practice of repurposing data collected during payment. In this instance, however, the rulemaking was not because of a legal vacuum. The DPA already addresses the issue of the repurposing of data. Data protection principles prohibit the processing of data, as happens with unsolicited marketing messages, without the consent of the data subject.

While Safaricom's move is laudable from a privacy perspective, it contributes to market concentration and creates barriers to entry. It also means that merchants who are part of Safaricom's ecosystem cannot exploit data in the same way Safaricom can. Should they need such data, they would need to seek it from Safaricom. Their need can result in a new business line for Safaricom, yet in using M-Pesa, the merchants also contribute to the data. This case demonstrates the need for competition regulation to engage with data protection law in the face of the platformization of data.

Safaricom introduced anonymization of *lipa na* M-Pesa data in the aftermath of the COVID-19 pandemic, when there was an increase in M-Pesa transactions. The rise was attributed to a cashless payment policy by the Central Bank, which Safaricom had initially supported by waiving M-Pesa fees for certain transactions.[81] The waiver was among seemingly corporate social responsibility (CSR) announcements made by the company at the onset of the pandemic. These included the doubling of home fiber speeds to support working from home, as well as donations in the form of internet credit to students.[82] With the benefit of hindsight, it appears that these measures, which have now been removed, were a test for new market areas. Since then, Safaricom has developed or advanced products in areas such as digital agriculture, education information, on-demand content, and health information. These products are an indication of the ongoing evolution of the company to a digital services provider and platform.

MNO data is of interest to many actors for functions ranging from personalized advertising and political campaigning to research. As illustrated by cooperation between governments and MNOs at the onset of the COVID-19 pandemic, the data can also be used for tracking specific people, mass surveillance, and general population control. The growth of an MNO that offers converged services should therefore be a concern not only from a market competition perspective but also for the whole of society. Competition regulators have an important role in checking this emerging power, but they cannot do it alone. They need to be supported by other institutions that check power.

Conclusion

Safaricom's entry into Ethiopia is a continuum from its origins as a state-owned enterprise to a dominant national MNO. The company is moving in many dimensions. Locally, it is becoming a digital platform that is beyond what was envisioned under the converged license, while beyond Kenya, its entry into Ethiopia could be the beginning of its regionalization. The company's exploitation of a nonmarket strategy to dominate in Kenya may also be replicated in Ethiopia. Such power has effects on competition, as well as broader social and political issues, such as the rule of law, human rights, and social justice. While competition alone cannot sufficiently address all the issues in the broader environment, competition policy can be more alive to how power is created through nonmarket strategies. From our analysis, areas that competition regulators should pay attention to when considering nonmarket strategy include rulemaking by dominant players in emerging market segments and coregulation with sector regulators, as well as other institutions that check power in society.

Notes

1 Abiy Ahmed, "The Council of Ministers Has Unanimously Made a Historic Decision Today Allowing Ethiopian Communications Authority to Grant a New Nationwide Telecom License to the Global Partnership for Ethiopia Which Offered the Highest Licensing Fee and a Very Solid Investment Case. 1/2 Https://T.Co/Ht6z95BHzZ," Tweet, @AbiyAhmedAli (blog), May 22, 2021, available online: https://twitter.com/AbiyAhmedAli/status/1396060475184533505.

2 Ibid.

3 Committee to Protect Journalists, "Ethiopian Law Criminalizes Independent Telecom Use," Committee to Protect Journalists, June 15, 2012, available online: https://cpj.org/2012/06/ethiopian-law-criminalizes-independent-telecom-use/.

4 Safaricom, "Condensed Unaudited Results for the Six Months Ended 30 September 2020," 2021, available online: https://www.safaricom.co.ke/images/Downloads/Resources_Downloads/H1_FY21_Press_Release.pdf.

5 Safaricom, "Safaricom Receives Award for the Top Taxpayer in the Country by the Kenya Revenue Authority," Safaricom Newsroom, March 17, 2021, available online: https://www.safaricom.co.ke/about/media-center/publications/press-releases/release/1037.

6 Independent Electoral and Boundaries Commission, "The Post Election Evaluation Report for the 8 August 2017 General Election and 26 October 2017 Fresh Presidential Election," IEBC, 2018, available online: https://www.iebc.or.ke/uploads/resources/V9UUoGqVBK.pdf.

7 Victor Juma, "Why Safaricom, Airtel Are Fighting over Call Rate Cuts," *Business Daily*, December 29, 2021, available online: https://www.businessdailyafrica.com/bd/corporate/companies/why-safaricom-airtel-are-fighting-over-call-rate-cuts-3667010.

8 Departmental Committee on Communication, Information and Innovation, "Report on the Inquiry into Legislative and Regulatory Gaps Affecting Competition in the Telecommunications Sub-Sector," Departmental paper, National Assembly, Kenya, March 2019, available online: http://www.parliament.go.ke/sites/default/files/2019-03/ICT%20Report%20on%20Inquiry%20on%20Competition%20in%20Telcom%20subsector.pdf.

9 Ibid., 73.

10 Safaricom, "Innovation," 2021, available online: https://www.safaricom.co.ke/sustainabilityreport_2019/our-material-topics/innovation/.

11 Brian Ngugi, "Comesa Watchdog to Review Safaricom Ethiopia Entry Deal," *Business Daily*, September 30, 2021, available online: https://www.businessdailyafrica.com/bd/markets/market-news/comesa-watchdog-safaricom-ethiopia-entry-deal-3568512; Brian Ngugi, "EU Watchdog Clears Vodafone, Safaricom Venture for Ethiopia Entry," *The East African,* September 8, 2021, available online: https://www.theeastafrican.co.ke/tea/business/eu-watchdog-clears-vodafone-safaricom-ethiopia-entry-3542540.

12 Maggie Fick and Duncan Miriri, "A Year of War in Ethiopia Batters Investors and Citizens," Reuters, December 16, 2021, sec. European Markets, available online: https://www.reuters.com/markets/europe/year-war-ethiopia-batters-investors-citizens-2021-12-16/.

13 Robert Gorwa, "What Is Platform Governance?," *Information, Communication & Society* 22, no. 6 (2019): 854–71, available online: https://doi.org/10.1080/1369118X.2019.1573914.

14 Tarleton Gillespie, "The Politics of 'Platforms,'" *New Media & Society* 12, no. 3 (2010): 347–64, available online: https://doi.org/10.1177/1461444809342738.

15 Cheng Qingjun, "Six IoT Models: Which Should Telcos Choose?" (Huawei Publications, 2018), available online: https://www.huawei.com/it/technology-insights/publications/huawei-tech/84/iot-business-models-telcos.

16 Kaveh Hushyar, Harald Braun, and Hossein Eslambolchi, *Telecom Extreme Transformation: The Road to a Digital Service Provider* (CRC Press, 2021), available online: https://www.routledge.com/Telecom-Extreme-Transformation-The-Road-to-a-Digital-Service-Provider/Hushyar-Braun-Eslambolchi/p/book/9780367750138.

17 Safaricom, "Innovation."

18 Christian Kabengele and Rüdiger Hahn, "Institutional and Firm-Level Factors for Mobile Money Adoption in Emerging Markets—A Configurational Analysis," *Technological Forecasting and Social Change* 171 (2021): 120934, available online: https://doi.org/10.1016/j.techfore.2021.120934.

19 Alexander Flaig, Daniel Kindström, and Mikael Ottosson, "Market-Shaping Strategies: A Conceptual Framework for Generating Market Outcomes," *Industrial Marketing*

Management 96 (2021): 254–66, available online: https://doi.org/10.1016/j.indmarman.2021.06.004; Ron Adner, "Ecosystem as Structure: An Actionable Construct for Strategy," *Journal of Management* 43, no. 1 (2017): 39–58, available online: https://doi.org/10.1177/0149206316678451.

20 Sylvia Wairimu Kang'ara, "When the Pendulum Swings Too Far: Structural Adjustment Programs in Kenya," *Third World Legal Studies* 15, no. 1 (2000): 109–51.

21 Safaricom, "Safaricom Board Charter" (Safaricom PLC, 2022), available online: https://www.safaricom.co.ke/images/directors/Safaricom-PLC-Board-Charter.pdf; Charles Mwaniki, "Who Will Take Over at Kenya's Most Profitable Firm?," *Business Daily,* September 24, 2020, available online: https://www.businessdailyafrica.com/bd/news/who-will-take-over-at-kenya-s-most-profitable-firm--2255900.

22 Adner, "Ecosystem as Structure"; Dylan Minor, "The Organization of Non-Market Strategy," in *Strategy Beyond Markets*, ed. John de Figueiredo et al. (Emerald Publishing, 2016), 431.

23 Simon Roberts, "Competition Law Prescriptions and Competitive Outcomes: Insight from Southern and East Africa," Centre for Competition, Regulation & Economic Development Working Paper No. 14/2017, 2017, available online: https://dx.doi.org/10.2139/ssrn.2982387.

24 Departmental Committee on Communication, Information and Innovation, "ICT Committee Report"; Rafe Mazer and Philip Rowan, "Competition in Mobile Financial Services: Lessons from Kenya and Tanzania," *African Journal of Information and Communication* no. 17 (2016): 39–59, available online: https://doi.org/10.23962/10539/21629.

25 David Tuwei and Melissa Tully, "Producing Communities and Commodities: Safaricom and Commercial Nationalism in Kenya," *Global Media and Communication* 13, no. 1 (2017): 21–39, available online: https://doi.org/10.1177/1742766517694471; Emma Park, "Intimacy and Estrangement: Safaricom, Divisibility, and the Making of the Corporate Nation-State," *Comparative Studies of South Asia, Africa and the Middle East* 41, no. 3 (2021), 423–40, available online: https://doi.org/10.1215/1089201X-9407975.

26 Safaricom, "Safaricom Foundation," 2022, available online: https://www.safaricomfoundation.org/; Safaricom, "M-PESA Foundation," 2022, available online: https://m-pesafoundation.org/; Safaricom, "Safaricom Sustainability Report," 2020, available online: https://www.safaricom.co.ke/sustainabilityreport_2020/stakeholder-engagement/employees/.

27 Bitange Ndemo, "Inside a Policymaker's Mind: An Entrepreneurial Approach to Policy Development and Implementation," in *Digital Kenya—An Entrepreneurial Revolution in the Making*, ed. Bitange Ndemo and Tim Weiss (Palgrave Macmillan, 2017), 339–62, available online: https://www.palgrave.com/gp/book/9781137578808.

28 N.A., "Safaricom Rejects KRA Bid for Free Access to Taxpayers M-Pesa Accounts," *Business Daily*, December 22, 2020, available online: https://www.businessdailyafrica.com/bd/economy/safaricom-rejects-kra-bid-for-free-access-to-taxpayers-m-pesa-accounts-2118628; Mwendwa Kivuva, "Memorandum on the ICT Practitioner's Bill 2020, Submitted to The National Assembly," KICTANet, February 26, 2021, available online: https://www.kictanet.or.ke/mdocs-posts/memorandum-on-the-ict-practitioners-bill-2020-submitted-to-the-national-assembly; KEPSA, "ICT Sector

Board Engages Senate Standing Committee on Legislative Issues in the Sector," KEPSA, March 15, 2021, available online: https://kepsa.or.ke/ict-sector-board-engages-senate-standing-committee-on-legislative-issues-in-the-sector/.

29 An example is an engagement dubbed "Talk to Safaricom," where the company appeared on a local ICT policy discussion list to address multiple issues of interest to civil society. See KICTANet (Kenya ICT Action Network), "Talk to Safaricom Stakeholder Engagement 2017," July 19, 2019, available online: https://www.kictanet.or.ke/mdocs-posts/talk-to-safaricom-stakeholder-engagement-2017/.

30 Stéphane Piot, Philip Bates, and Kerron Edmunson, "Telecommunication Competition Market Study in Kenya" (Communications Authority, 2018), available online: https://www.ca.go.ke/sites/default/files/2023-06/Presentation-on-Telecommunication-Competition-Study-to-Stakeholders-.pdf.

31 See, for example, the argument by leaders of America's largest telecommunications company, AT&T, Kaveh Hushyar, Harald Braun, and Hossein Eslambolchi, *Telecom Extreme Transformation: The Road to a Digital Service Provider* (CRC Press, 2021).

32 Monica Kerretts, "ICT Regulation and Policy at a Crossroads: A Case Study of the Licensing Process in Kenya," *South African Journal of Information and Communication* no. 5 (2004): 49–63, available online: https://doi.org/10.23962/10539/19816.

33 Timothy Mwololo Waema, "A Brief History of the Development of an ICT Policy in Kenya," in *At the Crossroads: ICT Policy Making in East Africa*, ed. Florence E. Etta and Laurent Elder (East African Educational Publishers/International Development Research Centre, 2005), 42.

34 Ibid.

35 Ndemo, "Inside a Policymaker's Mind."

36 Mandla Msimang, "Broadband in Kenya: Build It and They Will Come," Technical Report, InfoDev World Bank, 2011, available online: https://documents1.worldbank.org/curated/pt/617221468331457281/pdf/691800ESW0P120000Broadband0in0Kenya.pdf.

37 Ndemo, "Inside a Policymaker's Mind."

38 The network facilities provider license enables MNOs to deploy mobile communication services using any technology. MNOs that are licensed as national facilities providers are also guaranteed national spectrum reservation and allocation. The application service provider license gives licensees the freedom to provide noncontent services on the network. These include "voice, data, Internet, mobile virtual network operator, vehicle tracking service." The third category is the content service provider license, which allows the delivery of content to a subscriber.

39 Bowmans, "Telecom Regulation: Kenya Introduces a Unified Licensing Framework," Bowmans, 2012, available online: https://www.bowmanslaw.com/insights/technology-media-and-telecommunications/telecom-regulation-kenya-introduces-a-unified-licensing-framework/.

40 Communications Authority, "First Quarter Sector Statistics Report for the Financial Year 2021/22," 2021, available online: https://www.ca.go.ke/consumers/industry-research-statistics/statistics/.

41 Safaricom, "Condensed Unaudited Results for the Six Months Ended 30 September 2020"; Patrick Alushula, "New Skiza Tune 40pc Earnings Sweet Music to Artistes'

Ears," *Business Daily*, August 2, 2021, available online: https://www.businessdailyafrica.com/bd/corporate/companies/new-skiza-40pc-earnings-sweet-music-to-artistes-ears-3496346.

42 Joshua Goldstein and Juliana Rotich, "Digitally Networked Technology in Kenya's 2007–2008 Post-Election Crisis," *Wajibu* 24, no. 2 (2009): 5–13, available online: https://hdl.handle.net/10520/AJA10169717_364.

43 Institute for Human Rights and Business, "Digital Dangers: Corporate Responses to Hate Speech in the 2013 Kenya Presidential Elections," Case study (London, 2014), 16, available online: https://www.ihrb.org/pdf/DD-Safaricom-Case-Study.pdf.

44 Communications Authority and National Cohesion and Integration Commission, "Guidelines on Prevention of Dissemination of Undesirable Bulk and Premium Rate Political Messages and Political Social Media Content Via Electronic Networks," Guidelines on Prevention of Dissemination of Undesirable Bulk and Premium Rate Political Messages and Political Social Media Content Via Electronic Networks § (2017), available online: https://ca.go.ke/wp-content/uploads/2018/02/Guidelines-on-Prevention-of-Dissemination-of-Undesirable-Bulk-and-Premium-Rate-Political-Messages-and-Political-Social-Media-Content-Via-Electronic-Networks-1.pdf; Computer Misuse and Cybercrimes Act (2018), available online: https://kenyalaw.org/kl/fileadmin/pdfdownloads/Acts/ComputerMisuseandCybercrimesActNo5of2018.pdf.

45 Alushula, "New Skiza Tune 40pc Earnings Sweet Music to Artists' Ears."

46 Republic of Kenya, The Copyright (Amendment) Act No. 14 of 2022, available online: http://kenyalaw.org/kl/fileadmin/pdfdownloads/Acts/2022/TheCopyright_Amendment_Act_2022.pdf.

47 Independent Electoral and Boundaries Commission, "The Post Election Evaluation Report for the 8 August 2017 General Election and 26 October 2017 Fresh Presidential Election," 147.

48 "IEBC Spent Sh939m for 2022 Polls Results Transmission," *The Star*, March 15, 2023.

49 Robert Muthuri, "Internet Speed Throttling Surrounding Repeat Election?," *Centre for Intellectual Property and Information Technology Law* (2017), available online: https://cipit.strathmore.edu/internet-speed-throttling-surrounding-repeat-election/.

50 Privacy International, "Track, Capture, Kill: Inside Communications Surveillance and Counterterrorism in Kenya," NGO Report, 2017, available online: https://privacyinternational.org/sites/default/files/2017-10/track_capture_final.pdf.

51 "Safaricom Signs Security Contract with Kenya's Government," Reuters, November 25, 2014, sec. Telecommunications Services, available online: https://www.reuters.com/article/kenya-security-safaricom-idUSL6N0TF1A520141125.

52 Juma, "Why Safaricom, Airtel Are Fighting over Call Rate Cuts."

53 Otiato Guguyu, "Ethiopia Shields M-Pesa from Licence Freeze," *Business Daily*, February 7, 2022, available online: https://www.businessdailyafrica.com/bd/corporate/industry/ethiopia-shield-m-pesa-from-licence-freeze-3707294.

54 Central Bank of Kenya and FSD Kenya, "FinAccess Survey Report," 2021, available online: https://www.fsdkenya.org/wp-content/uploads/2019/04/21-12-15-FinAccess-launch-FSD-Kenya-CEO-remarks.pdf.

55 Communications Authority, "Fourth Quarter Sector Statistics Report for the Financial Year 2024/25," available online: https://www.ca.go.ke/sites/default/files/2025-09/Sector%20Statistics%20Report%20Q4%202024-2025_1.pdf; Edna Mwenda,

"Number of Mobile Money Accounts Rise to 80.8 Million," *Business Daily*, January 26, 2025, available online: https://www.businessdailyafrica.com/bd/corporate/companies/number-of-mobile-money-accounts-rise-to-80-8-million-4902514#:~:text=M%2DPesa%20is%20the%20dominant%20mobile%20money%20platform,with%20T%2Dkash%20of%20Telkom%20Kenya%20and%20Equitel.&text=In%20the%20half%20year%20that%20ended%20in,Kenyan%20market%20grew%2016.6%20percent%20to%20Sh77.

56 Simphiwe Nojiyeza and Jocelyn Muthoka, "Barriers to Entry of Kenya's Telecommunication Industry: Is There a Market Slice for New Entrants?," *Journal of Management & Administration* 11, no. 1 (2013): 136–96, available online: https://hdl.handle.net/10520/EJC141733.

57 Central Bank of Kenya and FSD Kenya, "FinAccess Survey Report."

58 Njuguna S. Ndung'u, "A Digital Financial Services Revolution in Kenya: The M-Pesa Case Study," African Economic Research Consortium, 2021, available online: https://aercafrica.org/old-website/wp-content/uploads/2021/03/AERC-MPesa-Case-Study.pdf.

59 For example, M-Pesa depends on Safaricom's nationwide network of agents who, until 2014, could only work exclusively for Safaricom. Exclusivity ended in 2014 after intervention by the regulator, but according to the other MNOs, this has not had the desired effect of leveling the market because it was done too late.

60 Ndemo, "Inside a Policymaker's Mind."

61 Ndung'u, "A Digital Financial Services Revolution in Kenya," 33.

62 Frankline Sunday, "State Now Declares M-Pesa, Bourse as Key Infrastructure," *The Standard,* January 8, 2022, available online: https://www.standardmedia.co.ke/business/news/article/2001436791/state-now-declares-m-pesa-bourse-as-key-infrastructure.

63 Notably, Safaricom shaped the market through collaboration with the government, as well as other actors in the political environment. Its first digital loan product, Mshwari, for example, was with Kenya's top bank, KCB. Its overdraft facility, known as Fuliza, is a collaboration with NCBA, a bank whose ownership is linked to the first family.

64 Safaricom, "Pochi La Biashara," 2022, available online: https://www.safaricom.co.ke/business/sme/m-pesa-payment-solutions/pochi-la-biashara.

65 Privacy International, "Fintech: Privacy and Identity in the New Data-Intensive Financial Sector" (Privacy International, 2017), available online: https://privacyinternational.org/sites/default/files/2017-12/Fintech%20report.pdf.

66 Keith Breckenridge, "The Failure of the 'Single Source of Truth' About Kenyans: The NDRS, Collateral Mysteries and the Safaricom Monopoly," *African Studies* 78, no. 1 (2019): 91–111, available online: https://doi.org/10.1080/00020184.2018.1540515.

67 Ayang Macdonald, "Kenyan Telco Requires Face Biometrics for SIM Card Re-Registration," Biometric Update, February 3, 2022, available online: https://www.biometricupdate.com/202202/kenyan-telco-requires-face-biometrics-for-sim-card-re-registration.

68 Safaricom, "Safaricom Introduces Measures to Curb Sim Fraud," 2018, available online: https://www.safaricom.co.ke/media-center-landing/press-releases/safaricom-introduces-measures-to-curb-sim-fraud; George Brian, "You Are Not Required to Submit Your Photo During SIM Card Registration," *People Daily*,

April 10, 2022, available online: https://www.pd.co.ke/news/you-are-not-required-to-submit-your-photo-during-sim-card-registration-chiloba-122677/.

69 DFS Lab, Caribou Digital, and Caribou Data, "Payment System Design and the Financial Inclusion Gender Gap- Will Implementing the Level One Project Principles Benefit Women?," Technical Report, Level One Project, 2021, available online: https://www.leveloneproject.org/wp-content/uploads/2021/01/Payment_System_Design_and_the_Financial_Inclusion_Gender_Gap.pdf.

70 Central Bank of Kenya, "Kenya National Payments System Vision and Strategy 2021–2025," National Policy, Nairobi, 2020, available online: https://www.centralbank.go.ke/wp-content/uploads/2020/12/CBK-NPS-Vision-and-Strategy.pdf.

71 Communications Authority, "Fourth Quarter Sector Statistics Report for the Financial Year 2024/25"; Central Bank of Kenya, "Mobile Payments," available online: https://www.centralbank.go.ke/national-payments-system/mobile-payments/; Victor Mukabi and Ian Okal, "Mobile Money Boom as Kenyans Move Sh8.7tr," *People Daily*, February 5, 2025, available online: https://peopledaily.digital/business/mobile-money-boom-as-kenyans-move-sh8-7tr.

72 Patrick Alushula, "Safaricom Contributes 6pc of GDP in One Year," *Business Daily*, October 15, 2020, available online: https://www.businessdailyafrica.com/bd/corporate/companies/safaricom-contributes6pc-of-gdp-in-one-year-2481500.

73 "Box 4.3 Leading Country Example: Kenya—Digital Tax Payments," in "Tax Administration 3.0: The Digital Transformation of Tax Administration," OECD, 2020, 51–2, available online: https://www.oecd.org/content/dam/oecd/en/publications/reports/2020/12/tax-administration-3-0-the-digital-transformation-of-tax-administration_886337a7/ca274cc5-en.pdf.

74 Central Bank of Kenya, "Expiry of Emergency Measures to Facilitate Mobile Money Transactions and the Introduction of Principles to Guide Pricing," December 17, 2020, available online: https://www.centralbank.go.ke/uploads/press_releases/546023682_Press%20Release%20-%20Expiry%20of%20Emergency%20Measures%20to%20Facilitate%20Mobile%20Money%20Transactions%20and%20the%20Introduction%20of%20Principles%20to%20Guide%20Pricing.pdf.

75 Grace Mutung'u, "Digital Rights in 2021: Perspectives from Kenya," *Digital Frontiers*, January 8, 2021, available online: https://www.orfonline.org/expert-speak/digital-rights-2021-perspectives-kenya/.

76 Tanzania's ex-ante approach to the mobile money market may be an interesting example to study in this case. Mazer and Rowan, "Competition in Mobile Financial Services."

77 Brian Ngugi, "Safaricom to Monetise Customer Location Data," *Business Daily*, September 20, 2020, available online: https://www.businessdailyafrica.com/bd/corporate/companies/safaricom-to-monetise-customer-location-data-2275336.

78 Safaricom, "Safaricom's PLC Submissions on the Draft Privacy and Data Protection Policy and Bill, 2018," 2018, available online: https://www.ca.go.ke/wp-content/uploads/2018/10/Safaricom-PLC.pdf.

79 Republic of Kenya, "Data Protection Act," 2019, sec. 44, available online: https://kenyalaw.org/kl/fileadmin/pdfdownloads/LegalNotices/2021/LN263_2021.pdf.

80 Otiato Guguyu, "Safaricom to Hide Identity of Lipa Na M-Pesa Users," *Business Daily*, July 26, 2021, available online: https://www.businessdailyafrica.com/bd/economy/safaricom-hide-identity-of-lipa-na-m-pesa-users-3486200.

81 Central Bank of Kenya, "Press Release—Emergency Measures to Facilitate Mobile Money Transactions," March 16, 2021, available online: https://www.centralbank.go.ke/uploads/press_releases/2125080701_Press%20Release%20-%20Emergency%20Measures%20to%20Facilitate%20Mobile%20Money%20Transactions.pdf.

82 Safaricom, "Innovation."

Bibliography

Adner, Ron. "Ecosystem as Structure: An Actionable Construct for Strategy." *Journal of Management* 43, no. 1 (2017): 39–58. https://doi.org/10.1177/0149206316678451.

Ahmed, Abiy. "The Council of Ministers Has Unanimously Made a Historic Decision Today Allowing Ethiopian Communications Authority to Grant a New Nationwide Telecom License to the Global Partnership for Ethiopia Which Offered the Highest Licensing Fee and a Very Solid Investment Case. 1/2 Https://T.Co/Ht6z95BHzZ." Tweet, @AbiyAhmedAli (blog), May 22, 2021. Available online: https://twitter.com/AbiyAhmedAli/status/1396060475184533505.

Alushula, Patrick. "New Skiza Tune 40pc Earnings Sweet Music to Artists' Ears." *Business Daily*, August 2, 2021. Available online: https://www.businessdailyafrica.com/bd/corporate/companies/new-skiza-40pc-earnings-sweet-music-to-artistes-ears-3496346.

Alushula, Patrick. "Safaricom Contributes 6pc of GDP in One Year." *Business Daily*, October 15, 2020. Available online: https://www.businessdailyafrica.com/bd/corporate/companies/safaricom-contributes6pc-of-gdp-in-one-year-2481500.

Bowmans. "Telecom Regulation: Kenya Introduces a Unified Licensing Framework." Bowmans, 2012. Available online: https://www.bowmanslaw.com/insights/technology-media-and-telecommunications/telecom-regulation-kenya-introduces-a-unified-licensing-framework/.

Breckenridge, Keith. "The Failure of the 'Single Source of Truth' about Kenyans: The NDRS, Collateral Mysteries and the Safaricom Monopoly." *African Studies* 78, no. 1 (2019): 91–111. https://doi.org/10.1080/00020184.2018.1540515.

Brian, George. "You Are Not Required to Submit Your Photo During SIM Card Registration." *People Daily*, April 10, 2022. Available online: https://www.pd.co.ke/news/you-are-not-required-to-submit-your-photo-during-sim-card-registration-chiloba-122677/.

Central Bank of Kenya. "Expiry of Emergency Measures to Facilitate Mobile Money Transactions and the Introduction of Principles to Guide Pricing." December 17, 2020. Available online: https://www.centralbank.go.ke/uploads/press_releases/546023682_Press%20Release%20-%20Expiry%20of%20Emergency%20Measures%20to%20Facilitate%20Mobile%20Money%20Transactions%20and%20the%20Introduction%20of%20Principles%20to%20Guide%20Pricing.pdf.

Central Bank of Kenya. "Kenya National Payments System Vision and Strategy 2021–2025." National Policy. Nairobi, 2020. Available online: https://www.centralbank.go.ke/wp-content/uploads/2020/12/CBK-NPS-Vision-and-Strategy.pdf.

Central Bank of Kenya. "Mobile Payments." Available online: https://www.centralbank.go.ke/national-payments-system/mobile-payments/.

Central Bank of Kenya. "Press Release—Emergency Measures to Facilitate Mobile Money Transactions." March 16, 2021. Available online: https://www

.centralbank.go.ke/uploads/press_releases/2125980791_Press%20Release%20-%20Emergency%20Measures%20to%20Facilitate%20Mobile%20Money%20Transactions.pdf.

Central Bank of Kenya and Fsd Kenya. "FinAccess Survey Report." 2021. Available online: https://www.fsdkenya.org/wp-content/uploads/2019/04/21-12-15-FinAccess-launch-FSD-Kenya-CEO-remarks.pdf.

Committee to Protect Journalists. "Ethiopian Law Criminalizes Independent Telecom Use." Committee to Protect Journalists, June 15, 2012. Available online: https://cpj.org/2012/06/ethiopian-law-criminalizes-independent-telecom-use/.

Communications Authority. "First Quarter Sector Statistics Report for the Financial Year 2021/22." 2021. Available online: https://www.ca.go.ke/consumers/industry-research-statistics/statistics/.

Communications Authority and National Cohesion and Integration Commission. "Guidelines on Prevention of Dissemination of Undesirable Bulk and Premium Rate Political Messages and Political Social Media Content Via Electronic Networks." Guidelines on Prevention of Dissemination of Undesirable Bulk and Premium Rate Political Messages and Political Social Media Content Via Electronic Networks § (2017). Available online: https://ca.go.ke/wp-content/uploads/2018/02/Guidelines-on-Prevention-of-Dissemination-of-Undesirable-Bulk-and-Premium-Rate-Political-Messages-and-Political-Social-Media-Content-Via-Electronic-Networks-1.pdf.

Computer Misuse and Cybercrimes Act. 2018. Available online: https://kenyalaw.org/kl/fileadmin/pdfdownloads/Acts/ComputerMisuseandCybercrimesActNo5of2018.pdf.

Copyright (Amendment) Act No. 14 of 2022. Available online: http://kenyalaw.org/kl/fileadmin/pdfdownloads/Acts/2022/TheCopyright_Amendment_Act_2022.pdf.

"Data Protection Act." Republic of Kenya. 2019, sec. 44. Available online: https://kenyalaw.org/kl/fileadmin/pdfdownloads/LegalNotices/2021/LN263_2021.pdf.

Departmental Committee on Communication, Information and Innovation. "Report on the Inquiry into Legislative and Regulatory Gaps Affecting Competition in the Telecommunications Sub-Sector." Departmental paper (National Assembly, Kenya, March 2019). Available online: http://www.parliament.go.ke/sites/default/files/2019-03/ICT%20Report%20on%20Inquiry%20on%20Competition%20in%20Telcom%20subsector.pdf.

DFS Lab, Caribou Digital, and Caribou Data. "Payment System Design and the Financial Inclusion Gender Gap-Will Implementing the Level One Project Principles Benefit Women?" Technical Report. Level One Project, 2021. Available online: https://www.leveloneproject.org/wp-content/uploads/2021/01/Payment_System_Design_and_the_Financial_Inclusion_Gender_Gap.pdf.

Fick, Maggie, and Duncan Miriri. "A Year of War in Ethiopia Batters Investors and Citizens." Reuters, December 16, 2021, sec. European Markets. Available online: https://www.reuters.com/markets/europe/year-war-ethiopia-batters-investors-citizens-2021-12-16/.

Flaig, Alexander, Daniel Kindström, and Mikael Ottosson. "Market-Shaping Strategies: A Conceptual Framework for Generating Market Outcomes." *Industrial Marketing Management* 96 (2021): 254–66. https://doi.org/10.1016/j.indmarman.2021.06.004.

Gillespie, Tarleton. "The Politics of 'Platforms.'" *New Media & Society* 12, no. 3 (2010): 347–64. https://doi.org/10.1177/1461444809342738.

Goldstein, Joshua, and Juliana Rotich. "Digitally Networked Technology in Kenya's 2007–2008 Post-Election Crisis." *Wajibu* 24, no. 2 (2009): 5–13. Available online: https://hdl.handle.net/10520/AJA10169717_364.

Gorwa, Robert. "What Is Platform Governance?" *Information, Communication & Society* 22, no. 6 (2019): 854–71. https://doi.org/10.1080/1369118X.2019.1573914.

Guguyu, Otiato. "Ethiopia Shields M-Pesa from Licence Freeze." *Business Daily*, February 7, 2022. Available online: https://www.businessdailyafrica.com/bd/corporate/industry/ethiopia-shield-m-pesa-from-licence-freeze-3707294.

Guguyu, Otiato. "Safaricom to Hide Identity of Lipa Na M-Pesa Users." *Business Daily*, July 26, 2021. Available online: https://www.businessdailyafrica.com/bd/economy/safaricom-hide-identity-of-lipa-na-m-pesa-users-3486200.

Hushyar, Kaveh, Harald Braun, and Hossein Eslambolchi. *Telecom Extreme Transformation: The Road to a Digital Service Provider*. CRC Press, 2021.

Independent Electoral and Boundaries Commission. "The Post Election Evaluation Report for the 8 August 2017 General Election and 26 October 2017 Fresh Presidential Election." IEBC, 2018. Available online: https://www.iebc.or.ke/uploads/resources/V9UUoGqVBK.pdf.

Institute for Human Rights and Business. "Digital Dangers: Corporate Responses to Hate Speech in the 2013 Kenya Presidential Elections." Case Study. London, 2014. Available online: https://www.ihrb.org/pdf/DD-Safaricom-Case-Study.pdf.

Juma, Victor. "Why Safaricom, Airtel Are Fighting over Call Rate Cuts." *Business Daily*, December 29, 2021. Available online: https://www.businessdailyafrica.com/bd/corporate/companies/why-safaricom-airtel-are-fighting-over-call-rate-cuts-3667010.

Kabengele, Christian, and Rüdiger Hahn. "Institutional and Firm-Level Factors for Mobile Money Adoption in Emerging Markets—A Configurational Analysis." *Technological Forecasting and Social Change* 171 (2021): 120934. Available online: https://doi.org/10.1016/j.techfore.2021.120934.

Kang'ara, Sylvia Wairimu. "When the Pendulum Swings Too Far: Structural Adjustment Programs in Kenya." *Third World Legal Studies* 15, no. 1 (2000): 109–51.

KEPSA. "ICT Sector Board Engages Senate Standing Committee on Legislative Issues in the Sector." KEPSA, March 15, 2021. Available online: https://kepsa.or.ke/ict-sector-board-engages-senate-standing-committee-on-legislative-issues-in-the-sector/.

Kerretts, Monica. "ICT Regulation and Policy at a Crossroads: A Case Study of the Licensing Process in Kenya." *South African Journal of Information and Communication* no. 5 (2004): 49–63. https://doi.org/10.23962/10539/19816.

KICTANet (Kenya ICT Action Network). "Talk to Safaricom Stakeholder Engagement 2017." July 19, 2019. Available online: https://www.kictanet.or.ke/mdocs-posts/talk-to-safaricom-stakeholder-engagement-2017/.

Kivuva, Mwendwa. "Memorandum on the ICT Practitioner's Bill 2020, Submitted to the National Assembly." KICTANet, February 26, 2021. Available online: https://www.kictanet.or.ke/mdocs-posts/memorandum-on-the-ict-practitioners-bill-2020-submitted-to-the-national-assembly.

Macdonald, Ayang. "Kenyan Telco Requires Face Biometrics for SIM Card Re-Registration." Biometric Update, February 3, 2022. Available online: https://www.biometricupdate.com/202202/kenyan-telco-requires-face-biometrics-for-sim-card-re-registration.

Mazer, Rafe, and Philip Rowan. "Competition in Mobile Financial Services: Lessons from Kenya and Tanzania." *African Journal of Information and Communication* no. 17 (2016): 39–59. https://doi.org/10.23962/10539/21629.

Minor, Dylan. "The Organization of Non-Market Strategy." In *Strategy Beyond Markets*, edited by John de Figueiredo, Michael Lenox, Felix Oberholzer-Gee, and Rick Van den Bergh. Emerald, 2016.

Msimang, Mandla. "Broadband in Kenya: Build It and They Will Come." Technical Report. InfoDev World Bank, 2011. Available online: https://policycommons.net/artifacts/1508875/kenya-broadband-in-kenya/2176217/.

Mukabi, Victor, and Ian Okal. "Mobile Money Boom as Kenyans Move Sh8.7tr." *People Daily*, February 5, 2025. Available online: https://peopledaily.digital/business/mobile-money-boom-as-kenyans-move-sh8-7tr.

Muthuri, Robert. "Internet Speed Throttling Surrounding Repeat Election?" Centre for Intellectual Property and Information Technology Law, October 29, 2017. Available online: https://cipit.strathmore.edu/internet-speed-throttling-surrounding-repeat-election/.

Mutung'u, Grace. "Digital Rights in 2021: Perspectives from Kenya." *Digital Frontiers*, January 8, 2021. Available online: https://www.orfonline.org/expert-speak/digital-rights-2021-perspectives-kenya/.

Mwaniki, Charles. "Who Will Take Over at Kenya's Most Profitable Firm?" *Business Daily*, September 24, 2020. Available online: https://www.businessdailyafrica.com/bd/news/who-will-take-over-at-kenya-s-most-profitable-firm--2255900.

Mwenda, Edeb. "Number of Mobile Money Accounts Rise to 80.8 Million." *Business Daily*, January 26, 2025. Available online: https://www.businessdailyafrica.com/bd/corporate/companies/number-of-mobile-money-accounts-rise-to-80-8-million-4902514#:~:text=M%2DPesa%20is%20the%20dominant%20mobile%20money%20platform,with%20T%2Dkash%20of%20Telkom%20Kenya%20and%20Equitel.&text=In%20the%20half%20year%20that%20ended%20in,Kenyan%20market%20grew%2016.6%20percent%20to%20Sh77.

N.A. "Safaricom Rejects KRA Bid for Free Access to Taxpayers M-Pesa Accounts." *Business Daily*, December 22, 2020. Available online: https://www.businessdailyafrica.com/bd/economy/safaricom-rejects-kra-bid-for-free-access-to-taxpayers-m-pesa-accounts-2118628.

Ndemo, Bitange. "Inside a Policymaker's Mind: An Entrepreneurial Approach to Policy Development and Implementation." In *Digital Kenya—An Entrepreneurial Revolution in the Making*, edited by Bitange Ndemo and Tim Weiss. Palgrave Macmillan, 2017. Available online: https://www.palgrave.com/gp/book/9781137578808.

Ndung'u, Njuguna S. "A Digital Financial Services Revolution in Kenya: The M-Pesa Case Study." African Economic Research Consortium, 2021. Available online: https://aercafrica.org/old-website/wp-content/uploads/2021/03/AERC-MPesa-Case-Study.pdf.

Ngugi, Brian. "Comesa Watchdog to Review Safaricom Ethiopia Entry Deal." *Business Daily*, September 30, 2021. Available online: https://www.businessdailyafrica.com/bd/markets/market-news/comesa-watchdog-safaricom-ethiopia-entry-deal-3568512.

Ngugi, Brian. "EU Watchdog Clears Vodafone, Safaricom Venture for Ethiopia Entry." *The East African*, September 8, 2021. Available online: https://www.theeastafrican.co.ke/tea/business/eu-watchdog-clears-vodafone-safaricom-ethiopia-entry-3542540.

Ngugi, Brian. "Safaricom to Monetise Customer Location Data." *Business Daily*, September 20, 2020. Available online: https://www.businessdailyafrica.com/bd/corporate/companies/safaricom-to-monetise-customer-location-data-2275336.

Nojiyeza, Simphiwe, and Jocelyn Muthoka. "Barriers to Entry of Kenya's Telecommunication Industry: Is There a Market Slice for New Entrants?" *Journal of Management & Administration* 11, no. 1 (2013): 136–96. Available online: https://hdl.handle.net/10520/EJC141733.

OECD. "Tax Administration 3.0: The Digital Transformation of Tax Administration." OECD, 2020. Available online: https://www.oecd.org/content/dam/oecd/en/publications/reports/2020/12/tax-administration-3-0-the-digital-transformation-of-tax-administration_886337a7/ca274cc5-en.pdf.

Park, Emma. "Intimacy and Estrangement: Safaricom, Divisibility, and the Making of the Corporate Nation-State." *Comparative Studies of South Asia, Africa and the Middle East* 41, no. 3 (2021): 423–40. https://doi.org/10.1215/1089201X-9407975.

Piot, Stéphane, Philip Bates, and Kerron Edmunson. "Telecommunication Competition Market Study in Kenya." Communications Authority, 2018. Available online: https://www.ca.go.ke/sites/default/files/2023-06/Presentation-on-Telecommunication-Competition-Study-to-Stakeholders-.pdf.

Privacy International. "Fintech: Privacy and Identity in the New Data-Intensive Financial Sector." Privacy International, 2017. Available online: https://privacyinternational.org/sites/default/files/2017-12/Fintech%20report.pdf.

Privacy International. "Track, Capture, Kill: Inside Communications Surveillance and Counterterrorism in Kenya." NGO Report, 2017. Available online: https://privacyinternational.org/sites/default/files/2017-10/track_capture_final.pdf.

Qingjun, Cheng. "Six IoT Models: Which Should Telcos Choose?" Huawei Publications, 2018. Available online: https://www.huawei.com/en/huaweitech/publication/84/iot-business-models-telcos.

Reuters. "Safaricom Signs Security Contract with Kenya's Government." Reuters, November 25, 2014, sec. Telecommunications Services. Available online: https://www.reuters.com/article/kenya-security-safaricom-idUSL6N0TF1A520141125.

Roberts, Simon. "Competition Law Prescriptions and Competitive Outcomes: Insight from Southern and East Africa." Centre for Competition, Regulation & Economic Development Working Paper No. 14/2017, 2017. https://dx.doi.org/10.2139/ssrn.2982387.

Safaricom. "Condensed Unaudited Results for the Six Months Ended 30 September 2020." 2021. Available online: https://www.safaricom.co.ke/images/Downloads/Resources_Downloads/H1_FY21_Press_Release.pdf.

Safaricom. "Innovation." 2021. Available online: https://www.safaricom.co.ke/sustainability report_2019/our-material-topics/innovation/.

Safaricom. "M-PESA Foundation." 2022. Available online: https://m-pesafoundation.org/.

Safaricom. "Pochi La Biashara." 2022. Available online: https://www.safaricom.co.ke/main-mpesa/for-your-business/pochi-la-biashara.

Safaricom. "Safaricom Board Charter." Safaricom PLC, 2022. Available online: https://www.safaricom.co.ke/images/directors/Safaricom-PLC-Board-Charter.pdf.

Safaricom. "Safaricom Foundation." 2022. Available online: https://www.safaricom foundation.org/.

Safaricom. "Safaricom Introduces Measures to Curb Sim Fraud." 2018. Available online: https://www.safaricom.co.ke/media-center-landing/press-releases/safaricom-introduces-measures-to-curb-sim-fraud.

Safaricom. "Safaricom Receives Award for the Top Taxpayer in the Country by the Kenya Revenue Authority." Safaricom Newsroom, March 17, 2021. Available online: https://www.safaricom.co.ke/about/media-center/publications/press-releases/release/1037.

Safaricom. "Safaricom Sustainability Report." 2020. Available online: https://www.safaricom.co.ke/sustainabilityreport_2020/stakeholder-engagement/employees/.

The Star. "IEBC Spent Sh939m for 2022 Polls Results Transmission." March 15, 2023. Available online: https://www.the-star.co.ke/news/2023-03-18-iebc-spent-sh939m-for-2022-polls-results-transmission.

Sunday, Frankline. "State Now Declares M-Pesa, Bourse as Key Infrastructure." *The Standard*, January 8, 2022. Available online: https://www.standardmedia.co.ke/business/news/article/2001436791/state-now-declares-m-pesa-bourse-as-key-infrastructure.

Tuwei, David, and Melissa Tully. "Producing Communities and Commodities: Safaricom and Commercial Nationalism in Kenya." *Global Media and Communication* 13, no. 1 (2017): 21–39. https://doi.org/10.1177/1742766517694471.

Waema, Timothy Mwololo. "A Brief History of the Development of an ICT Policy in Kenya." In *At the Crossroads: ICT Policy Making in East Africa*, edited by Florence E. Etta and Laurent Elder. East African Educational Publishers/International Development Research Centre, 2005.

11
CHINA'S CRACKDOWN ON BIG TECH

Angela Huyue Zhang

Introduction

Since late 2020, China's vast bureaucratic apparatus has been unleashing a wave of regulations targeted at the Chinese big tech sector. What started with Chinese businessman and philanthropist Jack Ma's infamous public criticism of China's financial system at the 2020 Bund Finance Summit culminated in a spate of harsh regulatory sanctions imposed across China's big tech sector.[1] First was the shocking cancellation of Ant Group's initial public offering (IPO) in November 2020, which was set to become the biggest in Chinese history.[2] Ant Group then faced pressure from Chinese financial regulators to revamp its business structure in a way that might have cut its valuation by one-third.[3] As financial regulation was ramping up, the State Administration for Market Regulation (SAMR), China's antitrust watchdog, issued a set of new guidelines on the platform economy and completed a high-profile investigation into Alibaba within four months, imposing an almost $2.8 billion fine on the e-commerce giant. Cybersecurity concerns also emerged as a major issue when the Cyberspace Administration of China (CAC) opened its investigation into Didi Chuxing just two days after the company listed on the New York Stock Exchange.[4] The investigation culminated in the crippling decision to remove Didi's ride-hailing app from Chinese app stores.[5] The CAC's drastic action has been regarded by some as retaliation against Didi for failing to heed the regulator's earlier advice to postpone the IPO.[6] Since then, Chinese tech firms have read the writing on the wall and have been hastily ceding to various regulatory demands. In April 2021, a meeting with Chinese market regulators saw thirty-four tech firms quickly make preemptive public vows to enhance legal compliance and improve consumer protection.[7]

The timing of the big tech crackdown, coming on the heels of Ma's fateful speech, has raised questions about the campaign's underlying motivations.

Prominent critics believed that the campaign was mainly driven by politics at the elite level of the Chinese Communist Party (CCP).[8] This chapter provides a more nuanced understanding of the driving forces behind China's crackdown. It starts by providing the context, particularly by outlining China's unruly tech environment. It then moves on to answer why the regulation of the tech sector went from being very lax to suddenly becoming very harsh between 2020 and 2021. And last but not least, it discusses the major impact this form of policy swing can have on Chinese technology, innovation, social welfare, and the growth of the regulatory state.

The Unruly Tech Sector

To a large extent, China's concerns about the unbridled growth of big tech are shared by antitrust regulators across the world. Take the United States, for example, where federal and state regulators have brought a number of high-profile lawsuits against Google, Facebook, and Amazon in the past couple of years.[9] The Federal Trade Commission recently filed a complaint against Facebook for its alleged exclusionary conduct, asking a judge to force a sell-off of Instagram and WhatsApp.[10] In addition to the lawsuits, legislators are introducing bills that could fundamentally alter big tech's business practices.[11] The European Commission has been even more aggressive, imposing ex ante regulations on tech platforms deemed digital gatekeepers.[12] The commission's proposed Digital Markets Act seeks to identify these so-called digital gatekeepers, empowering the commission to take specific action if necessary.

China is facing similar problems with its own domestic tech giants. The Chinese tech sector is highly concentrated, with Alibaba and Tencent dominating the landscape. In 2020, Amazon's share of the US e-commerce market was slightly less than 40 percent, whereas Alibaba's Tmall and Taobao held almost 56 percent of China's e-retail market.[13] Meituan and Ele.me dominated the food delivery business, together capturing almost 98 percent of the market, while Didi alone possessed 85 percent of the ride-hailing business.[14] Meanwhile, Alibaba and Tencent have carved up China's tech sector into two competing ecosystems, each side blocking users from sharing content to the other's. Because of the lack of interoperability between the two ecosystems, most new start-ups are forced to join either the Alibaba or Tencent camp to survive. Leading e-commerce firms, such as Alibaba and Meituan, have also imposed restrictive conditions to force merchants to stay on their platforms, further entrenching their dominant positions.

Moreover, as these tech firms have grown, risk factors that threaten financial stability and personal safety have also begun to emerge. Didi Chuxing's launch of its hitchhiking service "Shunfengche" was pulled just a few years into operations in response to public uproar at incidents involving "Shunfengche" drivers raping and murdering their passengers.[15] Shortly after this crisis erupted, regulators quickly tightened regulations and ordered Didi to overhaul its screening mechanism and safety protocols. Another scandal involving one of China's largest peer-to-peer (P2P) lenders, Ezubao, saw over 900,000 users defrauded of almost fifty billion RMB.[16] After Ezubao, authorities began to crack down on the industry and, by late 2020, had virtually eliminated it.[17]

Meanwhile, digital platforms have pervaded every facet of Chinese life, all the while bestowing upon their users both great benefits and harms. Consumers enjoy the myriad conveniences platforms provide but have had to hand over enormous amounts of their personal data in the process. On top of this, regulatory uncertainty has incentivized these platforms to operate in legal gray areas, where taking dangerous risks is often rewarded. As platforms act as intermediaries, disputes create massive problems as the law is often conveniently ambiguous about what liabilities lie in store for middlemen facilitating transactions between buyers and sellers. For example, delivery workers are often pushed to drive dangerously to appease the unreasonable demands of faceless algorithms. Food delivery platforms, Meituan and Ele.me, have both been criticized for this kind of behavior.[18] As competition between these two platforms intensified, their delivery time windows narrowed, which effectively encouraged drivers to run red lights or even drive the wrong way against traffic to meet their targets.[19] This explains why some drivers, after being involved in accidents, still try to complete their deliveries, often while having sustained serious injuries.[20] Yet when gig workers do get into accidents, the liability of the platform is often unclear due to their employment status, which classifies them as contractors rather than full employees. Companies are normally implicated when their employees come to harm over the course of their employment. However, as delivery drivers rarely enjoy full employee status, the situation for them is far murkier.

The Chinese fintech sector is also prone to moral hazard concerns as fintech intermediaries frequently encourage risky borrowing. For instance, Alibaba affiliate and microlending giant Ant Group achieved great success by providing user-friendly, easy-to-secure microloans, insurance plans, and wealth management products, all outside the confines of the regulatory framework. Throughout its success, Ant continued to insist that it was a technology company rather than a financial firm to evade regulatory scrutiny. This was despite the fact that Ant was built on providing financial products and the fact that Chinese financial regulators were already planning to regulate it as a financial institution.[21] Undoubtedly, Ant's attempted evasion has caused a number of problems. Its operations as a microlending company saw it get away with passing off default risk to partnering banks that had extended 98 percent of all loans, according to Ant's IPO filing.[22] This increased the prospect that Ant would engage in risky lending, and indeed the company has previously been accused of using deceptive tactics to lure young students into taking out loans with the company.[23] Indeed, its excessively high valuation as a tech firm, rather than a bank, during the IPO process stoked fears that a bubble might be emerging. Despite all these problems bubbling beneath the surface, Chinese regulators were nonetheless slow to take a tough stance.

From Lax to Strict Regulation

To be sure, new technologies present a challenge to regulators everywhere as the law cannot account for all possible eventualities. However, in China, regulatory lag in the digital economy has been further exacerbated by three elements unique to Chinese regulatory governance, namely, the top leadership's support for the tech sector, regulatory arbitrage sought by the tech firms, and the inertia of Chinese regulators.

As the Chinese economy began to slow down shortly after the 2008 financial crisis, the government decided to place innovation as a top priority to rebalance its mostly export and investment-led economy.[24] In 2015, the State Council announced the "Internet Plus" program to promote entrepreneurship in the internet sector.[25]

Astute tech companies recognize the opportunities available when the government lends its support to various sectors. Hence, they often take advantage of informal avenues to lobby for more favorable outcomes. For example, tech entrepreneurs secure CCP membership and have been known to actively participate in China's most significant political event, the annual Two Sessions, a move seen by some scholars as a way to garner preferential treatment and protection.[26]

Tech firms have also been observed to employ two kinds of intermediaries to exert influence on regulatory decision-making behind the scenes. The first type comprises former government officials and academics who understand the inner workings of the bureaucratic machine. These "information intermediaries" provide vital insights into an otherwise opaque regulatory system. Many scholars have pointed to the role these intermediaries have played in successfully watering down the harsher requirements of the E-commerce Law.[27] The expertise these intermediaries can bring to the table is vital for Chinese tech firms that would otherwise be stumbling blindly through the complex regulatory landscape. At the same time, the revolving door between government and business undoubtedly increases the risk of regulatory capture.

The second type comprises political elites who either have strong family connections with government officials (e.g., the princelings) or are highly ranked within the bureaucracy, such as powerful Chinese state-owned enterprises or state sovereign funds. These intermediaries are often given a chance to invest in a company at a very early stage. The presence of these intermediaries within a company's ownership structure gives it protection from regulators, who have to think twice about whose toes they might be stepping on.

Meanwhile, Chinese regulators face significant constraints operating within China's vast bureaucracy, tightly connected through the nomenklatura system that places bureaucratic agencies in a chain of accountability going all the way to the top leadership.[28] Officials thus pay very close attention to the party line, as straying away from it can entail severe consequences. China's tightly coupled administrative system is, therefore, in contrast to that of the United States, where regulatory authorities enjoy greater autonomy while being subject to close scrutiny by the judiciary, press, and public.

Indeed, although Chinese agencies are rarely challenged in court, their success depends on their understanding of the formal and unspoken rules woven into the fabric of the bureaucratic machine. Thus, before any decision is made, authorities need to carefully evaluate whether pursuing a case is worth the trouble. These bureaucratic considerations determine the kinds of cases that are brought and how they are pursued. Regulatory agencies, therefore, had to refrain from taking an aggressive stance in regulating Chinese big tech given the central government's generous support of the sector.

As such, Chinese antitrust regulators adopted a rather "cautious and tolerant" approach in their regulation of the tech sector.[29] Instead of applying antitrust law, they preferred to rely on weak regulatory tools, such as the Anti-Unfair Competition Law and the E-Commerce Law, which both greatly limit the maximum fine an authority can ask for. Authorities also shied away from reviewing merger transactions involving a "variable interest entity (VIE)," a structure used to circumvent government restrictions on foreign investment in the internet sector. The fact that Tencent and Alibaba made hundreds of acquisitions free of any antitrust scrutiny up until 2020 shows just how lax regulation had been.

However, one random event completely distorted these regulatory dynamics. On October 24, 2020, Jack Ma publicly criticized China's financial regulatory system, chiding state banks for operating with a "pawn shop mentality."[30] Regulators quickly retaliated with their own criticisms of Jack Ma and Ant Group, their displeasure culminating in the stunning cancellation of Ant's IPO, dashing Ma's hopes of listing the biggest IPO in Chinese history.

So how did Jack Ma's speech and Ant's mega IPO, which would have brought China tremendous pride, become the tipping point in regulating the Chinese platform economy? I propose four reasons for this change, namely, a heightened sensitivity for financial risk among top leaders, deep concerns from financial players with vested interests, unbridled regulatory arbitrage, and the existence of a persistent regulator.

First, the Chinese government has oriented itself toward reducing the risk of financial instability in the wake of rampant fraud in the P2P sector and high-profile financial scandals brought about by the likes of HNA Group and Anbang

Group. As such, the balance was already tilting toward more regulation since 2018, well before the collapse of Ant's IPO.

The second reason came from the strong opposition of vested interests in the financial sector, which was largely dominated by state-owned banks. Though Ant initially tried to partner with these banks, they often had to shoulder most of the risk, leading many to feel they had struck a bad deal.[31]

Third, as a result of aggressively seeking regulatory arbitrage, Ant was able to win massive concessions from regulators. Amid several Chinese companies getting delisted in the United States, China launched the Technology and Innovation Board (the STAR market),[32] a new Chinese technology stock market similar to NASDAQ. As Ant's IPO debut could give a significant boost to the STAR market, the China Securities Regulatory Commission fast-tracked the company's listing process. Ant's IPO was highly oversubscribed, gaining the firm a high valuation as a technology company rather than as a bank. Indeed, Jack Ma's controversial speech in Shanghai appears to have been the entrepreneur's last attempt to lobby for favorable regulatory treatment in anticipation of tightening regulations over his business.

Last, the presence of a persistent regulator was crucial in tipping the balance. As the People's Bank of China (PBOC) is the lender of last resort, it saw curbing the moral hazards presented by Ant as vital to protecting the whole system.[33] The PBOC had long been calling to regulate Ant as a financial holding company and, in 2018, was already drafting regulations that proposed increased regulation of fintech companies via stricter capital-reserve requirements and risk management rules. Moreover, during Ant's IPO process, the PBOC and other financial regulators grew even more alarmed as Ant's high valuation as a tech company stoked fears that a bubble was emerging.[34]

The debacle of Ant Group's IPO saw an end to the regulator's leniency. When antitrust regulators received a clear signal from China's central government to rein in tech firms, they responded with targeted legislation and enforcement. This type of regulatory campaign is reminiscent of the campaign-style law enforcement efforts common in the revolutionary period of the CCP.[35] In the absence of formal state institutions at that time, the CCP relied heavily on these mass movements to implement policy. Although mass campaigns have largely vanished after Mao, the Chinese government continued to employ campaign techniques by mobilizing grassroots party networks along with propaganda blitzes intended to enlist mass support.[36]

In the current law enforcement campaign against the tech firms, the PBOC was the first to express its criticisms of Ant. A few days after Jack Ma's controversial speech in Shanghai, *Financial News,* a newspaper affiliated with the PBOC, published three days of commentaries that rebutted Ma's Shanghai speech argument by argument.[37] These commentaries elaborated on the financial risks involved with Ant's business model and called for greater regulation. Such a bold rebuke of Ant and Jack Ma demonstrates how committed the PBOC was to reining in the sector and strongly indicates that tensions between Ant and financial regulators were the spark that blew the powder keg. On October 31, 2020, the Financial Stability and Development Committee, headed by Liu He, decided that all kinds of financial activities and similar businesses should be regulated in the same way, clearing the way for regulators to tighten their scrutiny over Ant.[38] This message was further reiterated by the Politburo on December 11, 2020, when it declared "strengthening antitrust regulation and preventing the excessive expansion of capital" to be a work priority.[39]

This was followed by a flurry of legislative and enforcement actions aimed at reducing risk in the financial sector. For instance, SAMR conducted a number of high-profile investigations into firm misconduct, past mergers, and the use of VIE structures, which culminated in several fines.[40] On Christmas Eve of 2020, SAMR announced an investigation into Alibaba for conducting its anticompetitive "choose one from two" business practice. The regulator concluded its investigation in four months and imposed a record fine of almost $2.8 billion on Alibaba.[41] In October 2021, SAMR imposed a fine of almost $500 million on Meituan for conducting exclusionary practices similar to Alibaba.[42] The lightning speed of the Alibaba and Meituan investigation stands in sharp contrast with other investigations of a similar nature, which can take years to conclude.

These campaigns seek to coalesce the public around a common cause, making the media an invaluable tool in the hands of antitrust authorities seeking to accelerate their enforcement efforts. As I elaborate in my book *Chinese Antitrust Exceptionalism: How the Rise of China Challenges Global Regulation*, Chinese antitrust authorities mostly stay under the radar when investigating cases, especially those involving state-owned firms, to avoid damaging the stock price of a targeted company.[43] However, in certain cases, the agency chooses to take the opposite approach by announcing its investigation through the media.[44] This approach has the effect of causing a significant drop in a firm's stock price. At this stage, businesses tend to accept the antitrust agency's demands in order to limit the damage caused by the initial media exposure. This saves the agency time and effort as they no longer need to pursue their enforcement once a firm is left with no choice but to give in.

The investigation into Alibaba was one such example of the agency using the media to bolster its enforcement. Minutes after the antitrust authority announced its case online, the *People's Daily* published a commentary endorsing the agency's investigation.[45] Likely having been prepared ahead of time, the commentary may be viewed as an attempt to control the narrative from the outset. Like clockwork, the announcement saw $100 billion in Alibaba's market capitalization disappear overnight.[46] Indeed, the final official sanction of $2.8 billion was minuscule compared to the damage caused by the unwanted public attention.

The distinctive approach of Chinese antitrust enforcement enabled the Chinese government to move forward very quickly in reining in its tech sector—a task that has presented unprecedented challenges for regulators in the West. Meanwhile, it carries significant implications for Chinese innovation and social welfare, as elaborated below.

Impact of the Crackdown

One important consequence of the law enforcement campaign is the way in which it further aligned the private sector's incentives with the Chinese government's agenda to stay competitive with the United States. Since the intensification of the US–China tech rivalry in recent years, moving China up the technological ladder has become the Chinese leadership's top priority.[47] In March 2021, Premier Li Keqiang outlined key areas where major breakthroughs in core technologies are needed, including semiconductors, operating systems, computer processors, and cloud computing.[48] However, despite their success at home, China's largest tech firms such as Alibaba and Tencent have yet to become internationally competitive and have been criticized by officials for not investing more in foundational technologies capable of closing the gap in the Sino-US tech war.[49] Because China is the only country apart from the United States to have internet giants, these tech firms have both deep pockets and the talent needed to develop cutting-edge technologies for the country. As tech firms increasingly become a target of regulation, their incentives to adhere to the government's policy directives grow stronger. The Chinese big tech sector's recent investment spree in innovation may be a sign of this phenomenon in action.[50] Alibaba has pledged $1 billion to nurture 100,000 developers and tech start-ups over the next three years, and another $28 billion dollars to boost its cloud computing division to invest in technologies related to operating systems, servers, chips, and networks.[51] Meituan raised a record $10 billion to develop autonomous delivery vehicles and robotics.[52]

Chinese authorities also used this round of the law enforcement campaign to tackle lingering concerns over welfare redistribution. At the moment, Chinese administrative authorities are using a variety of soft legal tools to curb high prices and improve conditions for contractors, employees, and suppliers. For example, after SAMR released its penalty decision against Alibaba, it issued nonbinding administrative guidance for the firm to take heed of.[53] This guidance included requests that Alibaba staff undergo compliance training, produce public compliance reports, and create an external review system, among other suggestions. However, absent clear institutional authority to do so, it remains to be seen whether these attempts will bear any fruit. Though at least in the short term, Alibaba has promised to invest billions of dollars to reduce access fees for merchants and to enhance merchant experience, despite not being legally required to do so.[54] These promises seem to align with the goals set out in

SAMR's administrative guidance. Apart from softer regulatory tools, propaganda has also been employed by the government to address wealth distribution. A recent commentary from an affiliated newspaper of China's top political advisory body invoked Marxist language in its criticism of the 9:00 a.m. to 9:00 p.m., six days a week, or "996," work culture.[55] Many tech companies quickly took heed, announcing changes to their work cultures while adding new work opportunities for college graduates.[56] In line with this trend, several tech CEOs have publicly declared their desire to "give back to society," with many collectively donating billions of dollars to charity.[57] Such economic redistribution helps the government accrue popular support, aligning the interests of the masses with the government, harkening back to similar policies typical of the Mao era.

This law enforcement also strengthens China's regulatory state, as administrative agencies saw their prestige and policy control expand significantly as the campaign progressed. Indeed, this round of the law enforcement campaign has also brought with it long-lasting institutional changes, such as increased personnel and budget. This is particularly the case for the PBOC, China's central bank, SAMR, the market and antitrust regulator, as well as the CAC, China's internet watchdog. In January 2021, the PBOC announced new draft guidelines aimed at regulating the online payment industry.[58] Under the guidelines, the PBOC can make a request to SAMR to break up any "nonbank payment company" that controls more than 50 percent of the relevant market. These guidelines appear to have expanded the PBOC's regulatory control to include antitrust enforcement, going well beyond the central bank's original ambit.

Similarly, SAMR's administrative guidance leveled at Alibaba encompassed the agency's broader mandate, touching on many areas of platform governance beyond antitrust. In mid-November 2021, China upgraded its Anti-Monopoly Bureau within SAMR to vice ministerial status, adding more budget and personnel to this small agency that has long suffered from severe capacity constraints.

Meanwhile, the CAC has emerged as a prominent regulator in charge of data security by issuing a spate of related draft measures. For instance, the CAC's draft guidelines, published in November 2021, place hefty restrictions on the use of recommendation algorithms, deeply concerning firms that rely on them. Since its investigation into Didi Chuxing, the CAC has created rules that require data-rich firms to undergo cybersecurity reviews before listing overseas. By expanding its regulatory control, the CAC has gone from a once relatively obscure bureau to becoming the key gatekeeper in overseeing cross-border data transfer issues.[59]

Conclusion

Beijing's unprecedented regulatory campaign to rein in the Chinese tech sector represented a great reversal from its previous lax regulatory policy. Although

Jack Ma's speech and Ant's IPO were the direct trigger for this massive law enforcement campaign, the regulatory tensions between Chinese online platforms and their platform participants have been present for a long time. As such, China is hardly unique in its demand to regulate tech giants. What is unique about China, however, is its heavy-handed campaign-style approach to implementing regulations. Whether China will succeed in achieving its goals is far from certain. What is certain, however, is that these newly added laws and legal institutions will have far-reaching implications on Chinese society and beyond.

Notes

1 Jing Yang and Lingling Wei, "China's President Xi Jinping Personally Scuttled Jack Ma's Ant IPO," *The Wall Street Journal*, November 12, 2020, available online: https://www.wsj.com/articles/china-president-xi-jinping-halted-jack-ma-ant-ipo-11605203556.

2 Ibid.

3 Julie Zhu, Kane Wu, and Nikhil Nainan, "Exclusive Investor Warburg Cuts Ant Valuation by 15% to Below $200 Bln—Source," Reuters, November 24, 2021, available online: https://www.reuters.com/business/exclusive-warburg-cuts-ant-valuation-by-15-below-200-bln-source-2021-11-24/.

4 Angela Huyue Zhang, "Didi's Failure to Listen Forces Rewrite of Chinese Tech Listing Rules," *Nikkei Asia*, July 8, 2021, available online: https://asia.nikkei.com/Opinion/Didi-s-failure-to-listen-forces-rewrite-of-Chinese-tech-listing-rules.

5 Raymond Zhong, "China Orders Didi off App Stores in an Escalating Crackdown," *The New York Times*, July 4, 2021, available online: https://www.nytimes.com/2021/07/04/technology/china-didi-app-removed.html.

6 Lingling Wei and Keith Zhai, "Chinese Regulators Suggested Didi Delay Its U.S. IPO," *The Wall Street Journal*, July 5, 2021, available online: https://www.wsj.com/articles/chinese-regulators-suggested-didi-delay-its-u-s-ipo-11625510600.

7 Stephanie Yang, "China's Tech Giants Vow, in Unison, to Play by Regulator's Rules," *The Wall Street Journal*, April 14, 2021, available online: https://www.wsj.com/articles/chinas-tech-giants-vow-in-unison-to-play-by-regulators-rules-11618402448.

8 Barry Naughton and Jude Blanchette, "The Party Politics Driving Xi Jinping," *The Wire China*, October 3, 2021, available online: https://www.thewirechina.com/2021/10/03/the-party-politics-driving-xi-jinping/.

9 John D. McKinnon, "These Are the U.S. Antitrust Cases Facing Google, Facebook and Others," *The Wall Street Journal*, December 17, 2020, available online: https://www.wsj.com/articles/these-are-the-u-s-antitrust-cases-facing-google-facebook-and-others-11608150564.

10 Federal Trade Commission, "FTC Sues Facebook for Illegal Monopolization," Federal Trade Commission, March 18, 2021, available online: https://www.ftc.gov/news-events/press-releases/2020/12/ftc-sues-facebook-illegal-monopolization.

11 Dana Mattioli and Ryan Tracy, "House Bills Seek to Break up Amazon and Other Big Tech Companies," *The Wall Street Journal*, June 11, 2021, available online:

https://www.wsj.com/articles/amazon-other-tech-giants-could-be-forced-to-shed-assets-under-house-bill-11623423248.

12 Damien Geradin, "What Is a Digital Gatekeeper? Which Platforms Should Be Captured by the EC Proposal for a Digital Market Act?," SSRN, April 2, 2021, available online: https://papers.ssrn.com/sol3/papers.cfm?abstract_id=3788152.

13 N.A., "China Internet Report 2021?," China Internet Report, *South China Morning Post* (scmp.com).

14 Ibid.

15 Sui-lee Wee, "Didi Suspends Carpooling Service in China after 2nd Passenger Is Killed," *The New York Times*, August 26, 2018, available online: https://www.nytimes.com/2018/08/26/business/didi-chuxing-murder-rape-women.html.

16 Chuanman You, "Recent Developments of FinTech Regulation in China: A Focus on the New Regulatory Regime for the P2P Lending (Loan-based Crowdfunding) Market," *Capital Market Law Review* 13, no. 1 (2018): 85, 96.

17 Frank Tang, "How China's P2P Purge Has Left Millions of Investors in Debt and Desperate," *South China Morning Post*, December 28, 2020, available online: https://www.scmp.com/economy/china-economy/article/3115580/chinas-p2p-purge-leaves-millions-victims-out-cold-losses.

18 Carol Huang, "Driven to Death? China Food-Delivery Services Criticized for Pressuring Drivers: News," *Campaign Asia*, September 10, 2020, available online: https://www.campaignasia.com/article/driven-to-death-china-food-delivery-services-criticised-for-pressuring-drivers/463537.

19 Ibid.

20 Ibid.

21 Nan Li and John Darwin Van Fleet, "Ant's Road to Redemption: How the Fintech Giant Can Save Itself," SupChina, May 19, 2021, available online: https://supchina.com/2021/05/18/ants-road-to-redemption-how-the-fintech-giant-can-save-itself/.

22 Ibid.

23 "Jueshou Zhou, "Daxing Hulianwang Qiye Jinru Jinrong Lingyu de Qianzai Fengxian yu Jianguan," *Financial News*, October 31, 2020, available online: https://www.financialnews.com.cn/gc/gz/202011/t20201102_204376.html.

24 Elizabeth Economy, "Xi Sets Targets for China's Innovation," China.org.cn, available online: http://www.china.org.cn/china/2016-05/31/content_38568066.htm.

25 N.A., "China Unveils 'Internet Plus' Action Plan to Fuel Growth," Chinadaily.com.cn, July 4, 2015, available online: https://www.chinadaily.com.cn/bizchina/tech/2015-07/04/content_21181256.htm.

26 Bruce J. Dickson, *Red Capitalists in China* (Cambridge University Press, 2009).

27 Jingting Deng and Pinxin Liu, "Consultative Authoritarianism: The Drafting of China's Internet Security Law and E-Commerce Law," *Journal of Contemporary China* 26, no. 107 (2017): 679, 686.

28 Sebastian Heilmann, "Regulatory Innovation by Leninist Means: Communist Party Supervision in China's Financial Industry," *China Quarterly* 181 (2005): 4.

29 Angela Zhang, "Agility over Stability: China's Great Reversal in Regulating the Platform Economy," *Harvard International Law Journal* 63, no. 2 (2022): 457–514.

30 Jing Yang and Lingling Wei, "China's President Xi Jinping Personally Scuttled Jack Ma's Ant IPO," *The Wall Street Journal*, November 12, 2020, available online: https://www.wsj.com/articles/china-president-xi-jinping-halted-jack-ma-ant-ipo-11605203556.

31 Jane Zhang and Iris Deng, "China Issues Final Antitrust Rules as Beijing Moves to Rein in Big Tech," *South China Morning Post*, February 9, 2021, available online: https://www.scmp.com/tech/policy/article/3120977/china-issues-final-version-anti-monopoly-guidelines-beijing-moves-rein.

32 Shi Jing, "Star Market Listings to Drive China's Technology Innovation Efforts," Chinadaily.com.cn, December 25, 2020, available online: https://global.chinadaily.com.cn/a/202012/25/WS5fe53dc7a31024ad0ba9e725.html.

33 Logan Wright and Daniel Rosen, "Credit and Credibility: Risks to China's Economic Resilience," Center for Strategic and International Studies, October 5, 2021, available online: https://www.csis.org/analysis/credit-and-credibility-risks-chinas-economic-resilience.

34 Angela Huyue Zhang, "China's Regulatory War on Ant," Project Syndicate, March 12, 2021, available online: https://www.project-syndicate.org/commentary/china-bureaucracy-regulatory-war-on-ant-group-by-angela-huyue-zhang-2021-03#:~:text=The%20Shanghai%20Stock%20Exchange%20suspended,crackdown%20on%20Chinese%20Big%20Tech.

35 Xin Frank He, "Sporadic Law Enforcement Campaigns as a Means of Social Control: A Case Study from a Rural-Urban Migrant Enclave in Beijing," *Columbia Journal of Asian Law* 17 (2003): 121, 134; Angela Huyue Zhang, "In China, Behave or Face a Campaign," Bloomberg, January 7, 2021, available online: https://www.bloomberg.com/opinion/articles/2021-01-06/china-s-regulators-turn-to-communist-style-campaigns-to-keep-things-in-line.

36 Elizabeth J. Perry, "Mass Campaigns to Managed Campaigns: 'Constructing a New Socialist Countryside,'" in *Mao's Invisible Hand: The Political Foundations of Adaptive Governance in China*, ed. Sebastian Heilmann and Elizabeth J. Perry (Harvard University Press, 2011), 30–61.

37 Feiyu Zhang, "Guanyu Jinrong Chuangxin Yu Jianguan De Ji Dian Renshi," *Financial News*, October 31, 2020, available online: https://www.financialnews.com.cn/hg/202010/t20201031204309.html; Shi Yu, "Zai Jinrong Keji Fazhan Zhong Xuyao Sikao He Liqing De Jige Wenti," Caixin, November 2, 2020, available online: https://opinion.caixin.com/2020-11-02/101622131.html; Jueshou Zhou, "Daxing Hulianwang Qiye Jinru Jinrong Lingyu De Qianzai Fengxian Yu Jianguan," *Financial News*, November 2, 2020, available online: https://www.financialnews.com.cn/gc/gz/202011/t20201102_204376.html.

38 Jing Yang and Lingling Wei, "China's President Xi Jinping Personally Scuttled Jack Ma's Ant IPO," *The Wall Street Journal*, November 12, 2020, available online: https://www.wsj.com/articles/china-president-xi-jinping-halted-jack-ma-ant-ipo-11605203556.

39 N.A., "Zhongyang Yizhou Liang Ti Qianghua Fan Longduan He Fangzhi Ziben Wuxu Kuozhang Dui Ziben Shichang," *Sina News*, December 18, 2020, available online: https://finance.sina.com.cn/stock/stockptd/2020-12-18/doc-iiznctke7264478.shtml.

40 Hazel Yin, "The Coming Wave of Stringent Enforcement Actions in China," Freshfields, March 19, 2021, available online: https://www.freshfields.com/en-gb/our-thinking

/knowledge/briefing/2021/03/the-coming-wave-of-stringent-enforcement-actions-in-china-4425/.

41 Coco Liu, "China Fines Alibaba Record $2.8 Billion After Monopoly Probe," Bloomberg, April 10, 2021, available online: https://www.bloomberg.com/news/articles/2021-04-10/china-fines-alibaba-group-2-8-billion-in-monopoly-probe.

42 Minghe Hu, "Meituan Becomes the Focus of China's Antitrust Investigation as Government's Scrutiny of Business Practice Shifts," *South China Morning Post*, April 26, 2021, available online: https://www.scmp.com/tech/policy/article/3131121/china-antitrust-fury-drops-upon-meituan-after-record-fine-alibaba [https://perma.cc/H62U-3EWJ].

43 Angela Huyue Zhang, *Chinese Antitrust Exceptionalism: How the Rise of China Challenges Global Regulation* (Oxford University Press, 2021), 93.

44 Ibid., 93–105.

45 Angela Huyue Zhang, "In China, Behave or Face a Campaign."

46 Angela Huyue Zhang, "Why Is China Cracking down on Alibaba," Project Syndicate, February 2, 2021, available online: https://www.project-syndicate.org/commentary/chinese-government-alibaba-antitrust-investor-confidence-by-angela-huyue-zhang-2021-02.

47 Li Yuan, "ZTE's Near-Collapse May Be China's Sputnik Moment," *The New York Times*, June 10, 2018, available online: https://www.nytimes.com/2018/06/10/technology/china-technology-zte-sputnik-moment.html.

48 Colum Murphy, "China to Pour More Money into Chips, AI and 5G to Catch U.S.," Bloomberg, March 5, 2021, available online: https://www.bloomberg.com/news/articles/2021-03-05/chinese-premier-calls-for-major-breakthroughs-in-core-tech.

49 N.A., "Renmin Ribao Ping Shequ Tuangou: Bie Zhi Dianji Zhe Ji Kun Baicai, Keji Chuangxin De Xingchen Dahai Geng Lingren Xinchaopengpai," *People's Daily*, December 11, 2020, available online: https://wallstreetcn.com/articles/3613229.

50 Coco Liu, "Alibaba Kicks Off Spending Spree With $1 Billion for Cloud," Bloomberg, June 8, 2021, available online: https://www.bloomberg.com/news/articles/2021-06-08/alibaba-kicks-off-spending-spree-with-1-billion-for-cloud.

51 Arjun Kharpal, "China's Alibaba to Invest $28.2 Billion in Cloud Infrastructure as It Battles Amazon, Microsoft, CNBC," April 20, 2020, available online: https://www.cnbc.com/2020/04/20/alibaba-to-invest-28-billion-in-cloud-as-it-battles-amazon-microsoft.html#:~:text=Alibaba%20said%20Monday%20it%20would,%2C%20servers%2C%20chips%20and%20networks.

52 "China Tech Giants Spend Billions to Fuel Growth After Crackdown," Bloomberg, May 27, 2021, available online: https://www.bloomberg.com/news/articles/2021-05-26/china-tech-giants-spend-billions-to-fuel-growth-after-crackdown.

53 N.A., "Chinese Regulator Fines Alibaba, Sends Policy Signal to Ensure Development and Fairness of Online Economy," *Global Times*, April 10, 2021, available online: https://www.globaltimes.cn/page/202104/1220682.shtml. Coco Feng, "China's Big Tech Urged to Follow Karl Marx's Lead, Get Rid of 996 Culture," *South China Morning Post*, July 15, 2021, available online: https://www.scmp.com/tech/big-tech/article/3141129/chinas-big-tech-sector-urged-abide-karl-marxs-ideals-do-away-996-work.

54 Raymond Zhong, "Alibaba Will Lower Merchant Fees After Antitrust Fine," *The New York Times*, April 12, 2021, available online: https://www.nytimes.com/2021/04/11/business/alibaba-fees-antitrust-case.html.

55 Feng, "China's Big Tech Urged to Follow Karl Marx's Lead, Get Rid of 996 Culture."

56 Josh Ye, "China's Tech Giants Go on Hiring Spree Despite Historic Crackdown," *South China Morning Post*, July 26, 2021, available online: https://www.scmp.com/tech/big-tech/article/3142572/chinas-tech-giants-go-hiring-spree-fresh-graduates-despite-beijings.

57 Yuan Yang, "How China Is Targeting Big Tech," *Financial Times*, June 18, 2021, available online: https://www.ft.com/content/baad4a14-efac-4601-8ce4-406d5fd8f2a7.

58 Zhang, "China's Regulatory War on Ant."

59 Minghe Hu and Coco Feng, "How an Obscure Government Office Has Struck Fear into China's Big Tech," *South China Morning Post*, July 9, 2021, available online: https://www.scmp.com/tech/big-tech/article/3140432/chinas-big-tech-crackdown-how-obscure-office-beijings-cybersecurity.

Bibliography

Deng, Jingting, and Pinxin Liu. "Consultative Authoritarianism: The Drafting of China's Internet Security Law and E-Commerce Law." *Journal of Contemporary China* 26, no. 107 (2017): 679–95.

Dickson, Bruce J. *Red Capitalists in China*. Cambridge University Press, 2009.

Economy, Elizabeth. "Xi Sets Targets for China's Innovation." China.org.cn. Available online: http://www.china.org.cn/china/2016-05/31/content_38568066.htm.

Federal Trade Commission. "FTC Sues Facebook for Illegal Monopolization." Federal Trade Commission, March 18, 2021. Available online: https://www.ftc.gov/news-events/press-releases/2020/12/ftc-sues-facebook-illegal-monopolization.

Feng, Coco. "China's Big Tech Urged to Follow Karl Marx's Lead, Get Rid of 996 Culture." *South China Morning Post*, July 15, 2021. Available online: https://www.scmp.com/tech/big-tech/article/3141129/chinas-big-tech-sector-urged-abide-karl-marxs-ideals-do-away-996-work.

Geradin, Damien. "What Is a Digital Gatekeeper? Which Platforms Should Be Captured by the EC Proposal for a Digital Market Act?" SSRN, April 2, 2021. Available online: https://papers.ssrn.com/sol3/papers.cfm?abstract_id=3788152.

He, Xin Frank. "Sporadic Law Enforcement Campaigns as a Means of Social Control: A Case Study from a Rural-Urban Migrant Enclave in Beijing." *Columbia Journal of Asian Law* 17 (2003): 121–45.

Heilmann, Sebastian. "Regulatory Innovation by Leninist Means: Communist Party Supervision in China's Financial Industry." *The China Quarterly* 181 (2005): 1–21.

Heilmann, Sebastian, and Elizabeth J. Perry, eds. *Mao's Invisible Hand: The Political Foundations of Adaptive Governance in China*. Harvard University Press, 2011.

Hu, Minghe. "Meituan Becomes the Focus of China's Antitrust Investigation as Government's Scrutiny of Business Practice Shifts." *South China Morning Post*, April 26, 2021. Available online: https://www.scmp.com/tech/policy/article/3131121/china-antitrust-fury-drops-upon-meituan-after-record-fine-alibaba.

Hu, Minghe, and Coco Feng. "How an Obscure Government Office Has Struck Fear into China's Big Tech." *South China Morning Post*, July 9, 2021. Available online: https://www.scmp.com/tech/big-tech/article/3140432/chinas-big-tech-crackdown-how-obscure-office-beijings-cybersecurity.

Huang, Carol. "Driven to Death? China Food-Delivery Services Criticized for Pressuring Drivers: News." *Campaign Asia*, September 10, 2020. Available online: https://www.campaignasia.com/article/driven-to-death-china-food-delivery-services-criticised-for-pressuring-drivers/463537.

Jing, Shi. "Star Market Listings to Drive China's Technology Innovation Efforts." Chinadaily.com.cn, December 25, 2020. Available online: https://global.chinadaily.com.cn/a/202012/25/WS5fe53dc7a31024ad0ba9e725.html.

Kharpal, Arjun. "China's Alibaba to Invest $28.2 Billion in Cloud Infrastructure as It Battles Amazon, Microsoft, CNBC." April 20, 2020. Available online: https://www.cnbc.com/2020/04/20/alibaba-to-invest-28-billion-in-cloud-as-it-battles-amazon-microsoft.html#:~:text=Alibaba%20said%20Monday%20it%20would,%2C%20servers%2C%20chips%20and%20networks.

Li, Nan, and John Darwin Van Fleet. "Ant's Road to Redemption: How the Fintech Giant Can Save Itself." SupChina, May 19, 2021.

Liu, Coco. "Alibaba Kicks Off Spending Spree with $1 Billion for Cloud." Bloomberg, June 8, 2021. Available online: https://www.bloomberg.com/news/articles/2021-06-08/alibaba-kicks-off-spending-spree-with-1-billion-for-cloud.

Liu, Coco. "China Fines Alibaba Record $2.8 Billion After Monopoly Probe." Bloomberg, April 10, 2021. Available online: https://www.bloomberg.com/news/articles/2021-04-10/china-fines-alibaba-group-2-8-billion-in-monopoly-probe.

Mattioli, Dana, and Ryan Tracy. "House Bills Seek to Break up Amazon and Other Big Tech Companies." *The Wall Street Journal*, June 11, 2021. Available online: https://www.wsj.com/articles/amazon-other-tech-giants-could-be-forced-to-shed-assets-under-house-bill-11623423248.

McKinnon, John D. "These Are the U.S. Antitrust Cases Facing Google, Facebook and Others." *The Wall Street Journal*, December 17, 2020. Available online: https://www.wsj.com/articles/these-are-the-u-s-antitrust-cases-facing-google-facebook-and-others-11608150564.

Murphy, Colum. "China to Pour More Money into Chips, AI and 5G to Catch U.S." Bloomberg, March 5, 2021. Available online: https://www.bloomberg.com/news/articles/2021-03-05/chinese-premier-calls-for-major-breakthroughs-in-core-tech.

N.A. "China Internet Report 2021?" China Internet Report | *South China Morning Post*.

N.A. "China Tech Giants Spend Billions to Fuel Growth After Crackdown." Bloomberg, May 27, 2021. Available online: https://www.bloomberg.com/news/articles/2021-05-26/china-tech-giants-spend-billions-to-fuel-growth-after-crackdown.

N.A. "China Unveils 'Internet Plus' Action Plan to Fuel Growth." Chinadaily.com.cn, July 4, 2015. Available online: https://www.chinadaily.com.cn/bizchina/tech/2015-07/04/content_21181256.htm.

N.A. "Chinese Regulator Fines Alibaba, Sends Policy Signal to Ensure Development and Fairness of Online Economy." *Global Times*, April 10, 2021. Available online: https://www.globaltimes.cn/page/202104/1220682.shtml.

N.A. "Renmin Ribao Ping Shequ Tuangou: Bie Zhi Dianji Zhe Ji Kun Baicai, Keji Chuangxin De Xingchen Dahai Geng Lingren Xinchaopengpai." Huaerjie jianwen, December 11, 2020. Available online: https://wallstreetcn.com/articles/3613229.

Naughton, Barry, and Jude Blanchette. "The Party Politics Driving Xi Jinping." *The Wire China*, October 3, 2021. Available online: https://www.thewirechina.com/2021/10/03/the-party-politics-driving-xi-jinping/.

Sina News. "Zhongyang Yizhou Liang Ti Qianghua Fan Longduan He Fangzhi Ziben Wuxu Kuozhang Dui Ziben Shichang." *Sina News*, December 18, 2020. Available online: https://finance.sina.com.cn/stock/stockptd/2020-12-18/doc-iiznctke7264478.shtml.

Tang, Frank. "How China's P2P Purge Has Left Millions of Investors in Debt and Desperate." *South China Morning Post*, December 28, 2020. Available online: https://www.scmp.com/economy/china-economy/article/3115580/chinas-p2p-purge-leaves-millions-victims-out-cold-losses.

Wee, Sui-lee. "Didi Suspends Carpooling Service in China After 2nd Passenger Is Killed." *The New York Times*, August 26, 2018. Available online: https://www.nytimes.com/2018/08/26/business/didi-chuxing-murder-rape-women.html.

Wei, Lingling, and Keith Zhai. "WSJ News Exclusive | Chinese Regulators Suggested Didi Delay Its U.S. IPO." *The Wall Street Journal*, July 5, 2021. Available online: https://www.wsj.com/articles/chinese-regulators-suggested-didi-delay-its-u-s-ipo-11625510600.

Wright, Logan, and Daniel Rosen. "Credit and Credibility: Risks to China's Economic Resilience." Center for Strategic and International Studies, October 5, 2021. Available online: https://www.csis.org/analysis/credit-and-credibility-risks-chinas-economic-resilience.

Yang, Jing, and Lingling Wei. "China's President Xi Jinping Personally Scuttled Jack Ma's Ant IPO." *The Wall Street Journal*, November 12, 2020. Available online: https://www.wsj.com/articles/china-president-xi-jinping-halted-jack-ma-ant-ipo-11605203556.

Yang, Stephanie. "China's Tech Giants Vow, in Unison, to Play by Regulator's Rules." *The Wall Street Journal*, April 14, 2021. Available online: https://www.wsj.com/articles/chinas-tech-giants-vow-in-unison-to-play-by-regulators-rules-11618402448.

Yang, Yuan. "How China Is Targeting Big Tech." *Financial Times*, June 18, 2021. Available online: https://www.ft.com/content/baad4a14-efac-4601-8ce4-406d5fd8f2a7.

Ye, Josh. "China's Tech Giants Go on Hiring Spree despite Historic Crackdown." *South China Morning Post*, July 26, 2021. Available online: https://www.scmp.com/tech/big-tech/article/3142572/chinas-tech-giants-go-hiring-spree-fresh-graduates-despite-beijings.

Yin, Hazel. "The Coming Wave of Stringent Enforcement Actions in China." English (United Kingdom), March 19, 2021. Available online: https://www.freshfields.com/en-gb/our-thinking/knowledge/briefing/2021/03/the-coming-wave-of-stringent-enforcement-actions-in-china-4425/.

You, Chuanman. "Recent Developments of FinTech Regulation in China: A Focus on the New Regulatory Regime for the P2P Lending (Loan-Based Crowdfunding) Market." *Capital Market Law Review* 13, no. 1 (2018): 85–115.

Yu, Shi. "Zai Jinrong Keji Fazhan Zhong Xuyao Sikao He Liqing De Jige Wenti." Caixin, November 2, 2020. Available online: https://opinion.caixin.com/2020-11-02/101622131.html.

Yuan, Li. "ZTE's Near-Collapse May Be China's Sputnik Moment." *The New York Times*, June 10, 2018. Available online: https://www.nytimes.com/2018/06/10/technology/china-technology-zte-sputnik-moment.html.

Zhang, Angela Huyue. "Agility over Stability: China's Great Reversal in Regulating the Platform Economy." *Harvard International Law Journal* 63, no. 2 (2022): 457–514.

Zhang, Angela Huyue. "China's Regulatory War on Ant." Project Syndicate, March 12, 2021. Available online: https://www.project-syndicate.org/commentary/china

-bureaucracy-regulatory-war-on-ant-group-by-angela-huyue-zhang-2021-03#:~:text=The%20Shanghai%20Stock%20Exchange%20suspended,crackdown%20on%20Chinese%20Big%20Tech.

Zhang, Angela Huyue. *Chinese Antitrust Exceptionalism: How the Rise of China Challenges Global Regulation*. Oxford University Press, 2021.

Zhang, Angela Huyue. "Didi's Failure to Listen Forces Rewrite of Chinese Tech Listing Rules." *Nikkei Asia*, July 8, 2021. Available online: https://asia.nikkei.com/Opinion/Didi-s-failure-to-listen-forces-rewrite-of-Chinese-tech-listing-rules.

Zhang, Angela Huyue. "In China, Behave or Face a Campaign." Bloomberg, January 7, 2021. Available online: https://www.bloomberg.com/opinion/articles/2021-01-06/china-s-regulators-turn-to-communist-style-campaigns-to-keep-things-in-line.

Zhang, Angela Huyue. "Why Is China Cracking Down on Alibaba?" Project Syndicate, February 2, 2021. Available online: https://www.project-syndicate.org/commentary/chinese-government-alibaba-antitrust-investor-confidence-by-angela-huyue-zhang-2021-02.

Zhang, Feiyu. "Guanyu Jinrong Chuangxin Yu Jianguan De Ji Dian Renshi." *Financial News*, October 31, 2020. Available online: https://www.financialnews.com.cn/hg/202010/t20201031204309.html.

Zhang, Jane, and Iris Deng. "China Issues Final Antitrust Rules as Beijing Moves to Rein in Big Tech." *South China Morning Post*, February 9, 2021. Available online: https://www.scmp.com/tech/policy/article/3120977/china-issues-final-version-anti-monopoly-guidelines-beijing-moves-rein.

Zhong, Raymond. "Alibaba Will Lower Merchant Fees after Antitrust Fine." *The New York Times*, April 12, 2021. Available online: https://www.nytimes.com/2021/04/11/business/alibaba-fees-antitrust-case.html.

Zhong, Raymond. "China Orders Didi off App Stores in an Escalating Crackdown." *The New York Times*, July 4, 2021. Available online: https://www.nytimes.com/2021/07/04/technology/china-didi-app-removed.html.

Zhou, Jueshou. "Daxing Hulianwang Qiye Jinru Jinrong Lingyu De Qianzai Fengxian Yu Jianguan." *Financial News*, November 2, 2020. Available online: https://www.financialnews.com.cn/gc/gz/202011/t20201102_204376.html.

Zhu, Julie, Kane Wu, and Nikhil Nainan. "Exclusive Investor Warburg Cuts Ant Valuation by 15% to Below $200 Bln—Source." Reuters, November 24, 2021. Available online: https://www.reuters.com/business/exclusive-warburg-cuts-ant-valuation-by-15-below-200-bln-source-2021-11-24/.

PART FOUR

INFRASTRUCTURE

12
A POLITICAL ECONOMY OF CHINA'S GLOBAL DIGITAL INFRASTRUCTURE

Hong Shen

China's ambition of building a China-centered global digital infrastructure is a hotly debated topic in both academic and policy circles. On one hand, China has been actively engaging in global infrastructural expansion and provision for a long time, including the construction of the Freedom Railway, one of Africa's most vital transportation corridors.[1] Only this time, its tech giants have become the forerunners. On the other hand, the expansion of China's global digital infrastructure was also deeply intertwined with the state's geopolitical ambitions, strategies, and challenges and, therefore, by no means evenly distributed. For example, although Huawei, the powerful Chinese network supplier, has developed a significant presence in Europe and Africa, it has been consistently blocked out of the US market.[2]

Starting in the early 2000s and accelerating under the recent policy slogan of building a "digital silk road,"[3] China-based internet entities have projected enormous capital into global cyberspace. For example, following a record $25 billion IPO in 2014, China's e-commerce giant Alibaba spent $1 billion for a controlling stake of Lazada, the biggest e-commerce firm in Southeast Asia.[4] Search engine Baidu, similarly, confirmed its 2014 investment in Uber, the US-based taxi sharing company, with some estimating the figure to be around $600 million.[5] In mid-2016, social media giant Tencent led an investment group to purchase 84 percent of Finnish mobile games maker Supercell for $8.6 billion.[6] With market values of $89 billion (Baidu), $484 billion (Alibaba), and $447 billion (Tencent) by mid-2018, the Baidu, Alibaba, and Tencent (BAT) have entered the club of the world's most valuable tech companies, sharing the stage with American tech giants such as Apple, Amazon, Alphabet, and Meta.[7] It is worth noting that starting from late 2020, the Chinese state has initiated a series of regulatory moves to regain control over its burgeoning tech sector, including the cancellation of the much-anticipated IPO by Ant Group—Alibaba's financial arm. These recent tech crackdowns have, to a certain extent, negatively impacted some of the most powerful Chinese tech giants; however, by early 2022, Tencent and Alibaba were still listed as top 10 tech companies worldwide, with market values of $561 billion (Tencent) and $303 billion (Alibaba).[8]

Those significant waves of growth and outward expansion, as well as many contradictions, have puzzled some analysts and policymakers. For example, existing frameworks have often portrayed the Chinese internet as a state-dominated walled garden, but this falls short in understanding this new phenomenon.[9] Should equipment manufacturer ZTE, a partly state-owned enterprise, be considered as having closer ties to the Chinese government than Huawei, a private telecom vendor? Or should Alibaba, a company largely owned by foreign capital, be considered as autonomous from the state? This chapter challenges these ownership-based policy frameworks and calls for more nuanced research on state–capital interactions in different layers of China's globalizing digital infrastructure.

I argue that China's digital infrastructure needs to be disaggregated to better understand the country's multifaceted expansion into the global internet. My approach builds on previous scholarly work on China's telecommunications industry. In particular, China scholar Eric Harwit points out that in order to fully grasp China's highly dynamic telecommunication revolution, the definition of telecommunications needs to include both the service and the equipment manufacturing sector.[10] Political scientist Roselyn Hsueh adds to the picture by arguing that an analysis of China's telecommunications policy should pay attention to both equipment (network and consumer) and services (basic and value-added) and should clarify significant differences among these industrial subsectors as they hold different strategic value to the state.[11] Drawing on these previous insights into China's telecommunications sector—within which the internet is contained—I disaggregate China's digital infrastructure into three different layers: (1) hardware layer that is represented by network and consumer equipment manufacturers such as Huawei and Xiaomi; (2) networking layer that is dominated by telecom operators such as China Mobile, Telecom, and Unicom; and (3) web applications layer that includes service providers such as Alibaba and Tencent. This enables me to observe the complicated forms of state–capital interactions at each of these layers in a historically evolving process.

By foregrounding complex forms of state-business interactions in these industrial layers, I argue that neither the label of "China Inc." nor the characterization of "state capitalism" accurately captures China's rising global digital infrastructure. Instead, China's growing efforts in building this vital infrastructure are not only constrained by internal fragmentation and contradiction but are further weakened by the conflicts between state objectives and business incentives in different industrial subsectors. Instead of viewing China's global digital infrastructure as a monolithic endeavor, policymakers need to pay attention to the changing state–capital dynamics across different industrial subsectors, which will be detailed below.

The Hardware Layer

The first layer of China's global digital infrastructure is the hardware layer, led by information and communications technology (ICT) equipment manufacturers such as Huawei, ZTE, Lenovo, and Xiaomi, the pioneers in constructing China's global digital infrastructure. For example, Huawei and ZTE started to build their telecom networks in Africa in the early 2000s. Over the years, these companies have enjoyed generous financial and diplomatic support from the state to expand their reach to many of the countries in the Global South. However, in certain cases, they may also need to distance themselves from the Chinese government's agenda due to the growing tension in the geopolitics of the global internet, as well as their increasingly internationalized business scope and profit strategies.

Chinese equipment makers such as Huawei and ZTE spearheaded the outward expansion of the Chinese internet. Their initial global expansion, however, was largely propelled by the intensive competition in China's domestic market, rather than state strategies. As communication scholar Hong Yu has shown, many Chinese network gear suppliers turned to overseas markets for development after the inward foreign direct investment (FDI)-driven developmental model of the 1980s and 1990s created domestic market saturation and allowed for foreign domination in China's domestic telecommunications space. For example, a number of powerful transnational corporations, such as Cisco and IBM, essentially controlled China's then-emerging domestic ICT market.[12] Indeed, in the 1990s, long before the state officially implemented its "going out" initiatives in the 2000s, Huawei had already received its first overseas contract from a Hong Kong company and extended its international business to Russia.[13]

However, state support has also played an important role in those companies' globalization strategies, mainly through financial support and diplomatic assistance. On the one hand, Chinese network gear providers have received significant financial support from China's policy banks. In 2004 and 2009, Huawei was granted a $10 billion and $30 billion line of credit by China's Development Bank, respectively. ZTE, in 2009 alone, received a $10 billion credit line from China Exim Bank and $15 billion from China's Development Bank; the latter increased ZTE's credit line to $20 billion in 2012.[14] Apart from these strategic credits from policy banks, the Chinese state also utilized foreign aid programs to support its "national champions." For example, in 2010, China and Nigeria reached a $900 million concessional loan agreement for basic infrastructure building. Nigeria's government, in turn, awarded ZTE a $400 million contract to build its Public Safety Communication System.[15]

On the other hand, the Chinese state has also offered considerable diplomatic assistance in the internationalization of its equipment makers. As scholar Wen Yun has demonstrated, Huawei's entry into Russia and later into Africa has significantly benefited from the state's diplomatic efforts, such as the establishment of the Forum on China-Africa Cooperation in 2000. Such entries, therefore, largely mirrored the state's diplomatic trajectories.[16] The Chinese state has also hoped that the international operations of these Chinese vendors would reciprocally reinforce its diplomatic relationships with host countries and enhance its international status. Sometimes, these vendors' overseas projects have even been elevated as a manifestation of Chinese foreign policy. For example, in 2011, during his visit to Ethiopia, China's then propaganda officer, Liu Yunshan, visited ZTE's local branch and openly praised the company's Ethiopian network infrastructure project as "a model of Sino-Africa cooperation."[17]

Even so, this close and highly complex relationship between the state and Chinese network gear suppliers in their outward expansion should not be oversimplified. First, although government credit has certainly helped China's companies to gain a foothold in the international market, the real impact of these credit lines still requires careful evaluation. In 2011, Fred Hockber, the then chair of US Exim Bank, criticized Huawei for unfair competition and government support; Huawei pointed out that government credit had actually played a limited role in its business operation.[18] For example, although China Exim Bank had granted a total $40 billion credit line (mainly in the form of exporter's credit) to Huawei, only a small portion of that credit—$2.99 billion—was actually used, while during the same time period, the company had made a far more substantial $110 billion in its revenue.[19]

Second, it is unclear how far the Chinese state still exercises control over its "national champions," because foreign markets have become crucial for some leading firms in this sector. In 2008, Huawei's overseas revenues accounted for a historical high of 75 percent of its total revenue.[20] In certain cases, Chinese vendors, under the logic of capital accumulation, may need to distance themselves from the state's agenda. For example, when the state decided to promote China's own third-generation (3G) networking standard, TD-SCDMA, in the late 2000s, leading Chinese vendors such as Huawei and ZTE only offered limited support. Instead, they prioritized the application of European-backed WCDMA and the US-backed CDMA 2000 standards in their global development, since those non-Chinese 3G standards enjoyed wider global market penetration.[21]

Moreover, when facing obstacles in entering the lucrative markets in the Global North, sometimes, Chinese firms had to align themselves with the structures of global digital capitalism, a pattern that has been consistently observed by scholars working in other domains.[22] Huawei's arduous journey in the United States is illustrative of this conflict zone. For example, the US government has repeatedly forced the company to drop its investments in several US equipment manufacturers and network operators, including its investment in 3Com in 2008 and in 2Wire, Motorola, and Sprint in 2010. The Committee on Foreign Investment in the United States (CFIUS) rejected those deals based on national security grounds. Entrenched players in the US market, notably Cisco, have also lobbied aggressively to protect their domestic markets. To counter these accusations, Huawei has adopted Western rules of game playing: It hired a group of high-level executives from transnational corporations (e.g., Cisco and Ericsson), involved in extensive lobbying activities in Washington and, eventually, opened all its source code to the US government.[23] Those practices, however, seemed to have little effect.

Finally, the fierce global competition among major players in this sector has further undercut the idea of a monolithic "China, Inc." Huawei and ZTE are sworn rivals in African telecom markets, as costly price wars have become common practice between the two firms. When Huawei first entered the African market, its bidding price was 5 percent—15 percent lower than that of Ericsson and Nokia Siemens—which helped the company win significant market share from well-entrenched Western players; however, when ZTE came in, it offered an even more aggressive price that was 30 percent—40 percent lower—and snatched part of the market share from Huawei.[24] The increasingly overlapping markets and similar low-price strategies of the two firms reached a high conflicting point in 2011. In March 2011, Huawei filed lawsuits in Germany, France, and Hungary, accusing ZTE of patent infringements; ZTE, in response, filed similar cases against Huawei in China. The battle was so intense that China's Ministry of Industry and Information Technology (MIIT), as the industry regulator, eventually stepped in and arranged talks with executives from both firms, but achieved limited results.[25]

With the growing global impact of China's digital footprints, these complicated state–capital dynamics in the hardware layer have only intensified recently. On the one hand, Chinese equipment makers are facing an increasingly hostile geopolitical environment, especially in the Global North. In 2018, Meng Wanzhou, one of Huawei's top executives, was arrested in Vancouver by Canadian authorities in response to an extradition request from the United States. In 2019, the Trump administration added Huawei and ZTE to a trade blacklist, blocking their access to US suppliers in critical areas such as semiconductors.[26] In 2021, the Biden administration signed the Secure Equipment Act, officially banning Huawei and ZTE from receiving new equipment licenses from US regulators.[27] Such challenging geopolitical environments, on the other hand, have also pushed these powerful companies to form a closer relationship with the Chinese state. For instance, with a big decline in overseas markets, Huawei's revenues from the domestic market increased from 59 percent in 2019 to 66 percent in 2020, benefiting significantly from China's New Infrastructure Initiative.[28] Not without conflicts, the profit maximization interests of China's hardware suppliers seem to have increasingly aligned and associated with the strategic consideration of the state.

The Networking Layer

The second layer of China's global digital infrastructure is networking, including major telecommunication network operators such as China Mobile, Telecom, and Unicom. Starting in the early 2000s but significantly accelerating under the recent "Belt and Road Initiative," China has been aggressively pushing the construction of a China-centered network system that ties neighboring countries more closely to it through submarine, terrestrial, and satellite links. Its own network operators, namely, China Telecom, China Unicom, and China Mobile, however, have been largely unsuccessful in their global adventures. Because of their strategic position in digital infrastructure, these companies have received the strictest regulations from the Chinese state. Over the years, they have been controlled by the state through both ownership and personnel management but still need to strike a balance between often-contradictory economic incentives and political objectives.

The global journey of Chinese network carriers started in the early 2000s. In anticipation of fierce competition after China joined the World Trade Organization (WTO) in 2001, the Chinese state restructured its basic telecom sector to cultivate a group of globally competitive corporations. In particular, to absorb foreign capital, it allowed all state-owned operators to adopt corporate structure reform and list part of their assets on foreign stock exchanges. The "plugging" of those network operators into transnational financial markets has resulted in an extremely high degree of involvement of transnational financial institutions in the process, including investment banks such as Goldman Sachs and law and accounting firms such as Linklaters LLP.[29]

Despite this high degree of involvement, foreign equity investment has been tightly regulated in this strategic area. By 2015, foreign investment remained under 10 percent in all three Chinese carriers, although the country's WTO commitment promised that it would open its operating sector up to 49 percent.[30] Furthermore, all three Chinese telecom carriers remain state owned. Specifically, the Chinese state has retained its power of executive regulation and ownership control over this strategic layer, as demonstrated in the 2004 reshuffle of the chief executives among the three networking companies. China's network operators, therefore, have been transformed into state-owned enterprises with corporate structures.

This transformation has two major implications. On the one hand, the companies superficially exhibit the logic of capital accumulation, performing as corporate entities with a prominent goal of profit maximization and capitalist expansion. On the other hand, the state tightly controls them through both the industry regulator (the MIIT) and the ownership agency (the State-owned Assets Supervision and Administration Commission of the State Council [SASAC]). Therefore, they are also obliged to undertake special political missions, such as adopting China's own 3G mobile standard, TD-SCDMA. This dual identity creates significant contradictions and has become prominent in their overseas expansion.

China Mobile's global route illustrates this dual identity. On the one hand, state support and geopolitical considerations have certainly infused its global projects. For example, in 2007, China Mobile spent a total of $560 million in acquiring Paktel, the fifth largest mobile operator in Pakistan, and has since operated local networks under the "Zong" brand. As the first successful overseas project completed by China Mobile, Pakistan was not a random choice. Wang Jianzhou, the company's former chair, was quoted as saying, "If we can't do well in Pakistan, we wouldn't be able to do well in other places."[31] As one of China's closest allies since the 1950s, China Mobile's expansion into Pakistan has certainly built upon the diplomatic assistance of the Chinese state; the establishment of a Chinese telecom brand in Pakistan, in turn, might also serve to boost the close connections between the two countries.

Apart from geopolitical considerations, another prominent role played by Chinese operators in their journey abroad is to promote China-owned network standards. In the 2008 restructuring, the MIIT assigned China Mobile, as the strongest among the three, to be the single major carrier of China's Indigenous 3G networking standard, TD-SCDMA, and, subsequently, as one of the major carriers of the China-developed fourth generation (4G) TD-LTE standard. As I have discussed elsewhere, technological standards are important arenas for global power competition as they not only constitute the foundation of the global network system but also play a major role in shaping related equipment industries.[32] The outward expansion of China Mobile, therefore, also shoulders the political responsibility of promoting China's homegrown standards. The company is well aware of this situation. Xi Guohua, China Mobile's chair, in his proposal to the National People's Congress in 2014, reportedly stated that China Mobile would actively promote the internationalization of TD-LTE; meanwhile, it would also use this opportunity to expand its own overseas territory.[33] In November 2021, China Mobile had reportedly built the largest number of fifth generation (5G) base stations worldwide, with over 560,000 units, leading with 134 international 5G benchmark programs and 3,300 5G patents.[34]

It is worth noting that intragovernment conflicts have also played a role in potentially weakening the state's agenda in promoting China-centered tech standards. A prominent example was the development of the wireless local area network (WLAN) standard and WLAN Authentication and Privacy Infrastructure

(WAPI) in the early 2000s. As Zhao argued, since the promotion of WAPI was more in line with the interests of China's national security division, it received greater endorsement from agencies such as the People's Liberation Army (PLA), while China's trade and commerce division, which has closer ties with transnational political and economic forces, showed very limited support.[35]

For all this, however, it might be misleading to consider political aims as the *only* logic that has driven China's network operators' global expansion. Profit maximization, sometimes, plays a more decisive role. For example, the state strongly encourages Chinese internet companies to work together in conquering foreign markets—a practice called "go global in groups" (*Jituan Chuhai*). Operators' overseas expansion, in particular, carries the aim of promoting the export of Chinese network products. To some extent, China Mobile has built part of its overseas network based on equipment provided by Chinese makers such as Huawei and ZTE. It has also, however, collaborated with foreign vendors. For example, in 2007, Alcatel-Lucent, Ericsson, ZTE, and Huawei jointly shared a $500 million network expansion contract from China Mobile's Pakistan subsidiary.[36] Sometimes, instead of granting a contract to the members in its home team, China Mobile has chosen to let the vendors compete and has benefited from the price wars.[37] Such practices, driven by the corporate rationale of profit maximization, have certainly decreased the company's procurement expenditure; however, they have also weakened the state's agenda of promoting a unified "Chinese team" in the global arena.

Thanks to China's growing domestic market and its state's protectionist policy, by the end of 2015, all three network operators had grown into the top-tier telecom companies in the world. For example, the 2018 Fortune Global 500 ranks China Mobile as 53, China Telecom as 141, and China Unicom as 273 on its list.[38] Their international presence, however, has so far been rather limited. China Telecom has not yet had any large overseas acquisitions. This pattern persisted for China Unicom, as two of its three large overseas projects in the past ten plus years were minority equity investments into Spain's Telefonica—1 percent in 2009 and 1 percent in 2011. In contrast, Telefonica once held a 9.57 percent stake in China Unicom and recently decreased this number to 5.01 percent due to financial constraints.[39] For China Mobile, the most powerful among the three, not only has Pakistan remained the only overseas market, but by the middle of 2021, the company only possessed a market share of 20 percent in Pakistan.[40]

But this trend might start to change as the internet sector has been assigned an unprecedented role in the current leadership's "Belt and Road Initiatives." The internet's growing importance in both China's domestic market and its foreign diplomacy might reinforce the territorial power of the state in these network operators' global strategies. Indeed, Chinese network carriers have been busy in constructing a China-centered transnational network infrastructure alongside the Belt and Road countries. It is reported that from 2012 to 2015, Chinese firms participated in 7 percent of transnational undersea cable projects; this number rose to 20 percent from 2016 to 2019.[41] In 2015, China Unicom invested $490 million in Cameroon's Camtel to build a transatlantic submarine cable connecting Africa to Latin America. Supported by Telefonica's international facilities and constructed by Huawei Marine, this project is expected not only to improve local internet service but also to serve "Chinese enterprises which have entered into the African and Latin American markets."[42]

The Web Application Layer

Finally, the most visible layer of China's global digital infrastructure is probably its web services and applications companies. Led by Baidu, Alibaba, and Tencent—and more recently, the TMDs (news and information content provider Toutiao, online food delivery-to-ticketing services giant Meituan [formerly Meituan-Dianping], and ride-hailing platform Didi)—they are at the forefront of China's global ambition. Having secured a dominant position in their respective areas in the Chinese market, Chinese application providers have also started to increasingly set their sights on the international market. Despite their status as private companies largely funded by foreign capital, these companies are still, to a certain extent, subject to state influence in their outward expansion, given the dominant role of the Chinese market in their profit strategies. Indeed, state influence seems to have become even stronger recently, with the People's Republic of China's continuing rollout of antitrust and data security regulations to further exercise power over its internet application companies.

As discussed elsewhere, the internet services and applications sector in China has largely been funded by transnational capital from the beginning.[43] Although the state has controlled China's domestic internet through various regulatory measures, it has exhibited a high degree of tolerance toward foreign capital *as a portfolio investor* in this sector. One possible reason behind this strategy is the relatively less sensitive nature of value-added telecom services in terms of national security threats.[44] In addition, because the state in the late 1990s only perceived web applications as "an extension of telecom services," companies in this sector had a low priority in terms of state funding.[45] The rise of the dot.com bubble in the United States also prompted many transnational financial firms to look into emerging digital markets for investment opportunities, especially in China. As a result, a large amount of transnational capital poured into the Chinese online market in the late 1990s and early 2000s, often through an extremely complex variable interest entity (VIE) structure. This literally jump-started China's internet applications sector. Due to the highly speculative and short-term nature of venture capital investments,[46] these firms—many of them were registered in offshore tax havens such as the Cayman Islands—have also rushed to list shares on foreign stock markets to raise capital and, to some extent, to further "internationalize" their assets. The Chinese state, therefore, does not hold significant influence over these companies in terms of ownership and financing structure, especially compared with its close relationship to hardware manufacturers and network operators.

For China's web applications companies, this relatively detached relationship with the state has significantly influenced their global adventures. Indeed, their deep ties with global financial networks mean that global banks, instead of the Chinese state, have often stood behind their global investment projects. For example, in 2015–16, with help from foreign investment banks such as Citigroup, Deutsche Bank, Goldman Sachs, JP Morgan, and Morgan Stanley, all the three internet giants in China have secured some types of syndicated loans to fund their overseas buying spree: Alibaba $4 billion, Tencent $4.4 billion, and Baidu $2 billion.[47] Furthermore, China's internet firms have used these loans to invade each other's turf. For example, Alibaba, the e-commerce behemoth, has elbowed into Tencent's core businesses—the social media and online gaming market—through aggressive transborder capital projections. In 2014–15, Alibaba invested over $400 million in mobile messaging apps such as TangoMe and Snapchat and another $120 million in Kabam, an online gaming company. In other words, China-based internet firms have competed ruthlessly with each other on a global scale based on the support of transnational financial networks. There is indeed no unified "Chinese team" to speak of.

Moreover, for these China-based internet services and applications companies, to keep some form of distance from the Chinese state might be beneficial for their expansion into the center of neoliberal capitalism, notably, the United States. Only after 2016 did the United States start to seek more scrutiny of Chinese web investments. This contrasts sharply with the equipment-manufacturing sector, where the US state has repeatedly forced several Chinese vendors, including ZTE and Huawei, to drop their investment deals in the US market. Then what is the territorial logic behind the United States having intervened only modestly—and very recently—into the merger and acquisition activities of Chinese internet application companies? Some scholars have argued that one possible reason is that value-added services present fewer security concerns for states.[48] Another possible reason, however, might lie in the transnational nature of these companies. As Alibaba's IPO prospectus reveals, in 2014, SoftBank of Japan held a 34.4 percent stake of the company, Yahoo owned 22.6 percent, and the founder, Jack Ma, only 8.9 percent.[49] To what extent are Alibaba—and many other companies in this sector—Chinese? Furthermore, under certain circumstances, these companies might choose to delink themselves from the state and realign with neoliberal transnational capitalism. Indeed, when the *New York Times* raised questions over Alibaba's potential political ties with some high-level Chinese politicians, the company firmly responded through its Weibo account that "our only background is the market."[50] This response, of course, has concealed the fact that Alibaba, and other Chinese internet companies, are dependent on state-controlled operators for access to the Chinese market.

This does not mean, however, that the state has lost its control over its homegrown internet companies. First, it is worth noting that in some cases, the state still offered critical financial support to those internet firms through its now highly capable and complex financial arms. Alibaba's 2012 deal with Yahoo to buy back half of its stock is illustrative in this regard. It is reported that this $7.6 billion project was funded by a group of mixed investors, including not only foreign banks but also Chinese investors. For example, China Development Bank made a $2 billion loan to Alibaba. Alibaba also raised part of the funds by selling its stocks to China-based investors, including China's sovereign wealth fund (the China Investment Corporation (CIC)), CITIC Capital Holdings Limited, an investment management firm under the state-owned CITIC, and CDB Capital, the private investment arm of the China Development Bank.[51] Apart from providing loans, the Chinese state has also teamed up with China-based internet firms in their overseas buying activities. For example, in October 2015, China's sovereign wealth fund collaborated with Didi, China's dominant ride-hailing company, to inject $100 million into GrabTaxi, Uber's rival in Southeast Asia, with a possible aim to distract Uber from its fierce competition with Didi in the Chinese market. Such financial muscle, under certain circumstances, might be able to translate into some maneuvering power over these internet firms.

Second, although in some cases, China-based internet companies may want to distance themselves from the state, in other cases, they also need to rely on the state's diplomatic relations to further their global journey. Indeed, it has now become a common practice that high-level executives of China's internet companies often accompany Chinese leaders in their diplomatic visits. For example, in July 2014, Baidu's CEO, Robin Li, accompanied Chinese President Xi Jinping on a visit to Brazil. During the visit, Baidu launched its Portuguese search engine, with an opening ceremony attended by both Xi Jinping and Brazilian President Dilma Rousseff.[52] The same year, Baidu acquired Peixe Urbano, a Brazilian online-discount company, to gain a foothold in a country whose e-commerce market is expected to maintain a strong annual growth of 18 percent in 2016.[53] Apart from significant market potential, Brazil was chosen by Baidu probably also for geopolitical reasons. South Asian historian Vijay Prashad illustrates the deepening connections between China and Brazil in the era of neoliberal globalization. He documents how the Non-Aligned Movement in the 1970s, which was originally constructed as an alternative South–South movement to Western capitalism, was demolished and how the BRICS countries (Brazil, Russia, India, China, and South Africa) noteworthily reemerged as the "locomotives of the South" pulling the "wagons of the North."[54] Deep divisions and conflicts notwithstanding, sociologist Zhao Yuezhi reminds us in her case study of the BRICS cable that in a post-Snowden cyberspace where the US hegemonic power has been—at least to some extent—destabilized, there might exist possibilities that the BRICS would start to form a potential power bloc to rebalance the US-dominated global communication order.[55] Unfortunately, Baidu's engagement with Brazil ended unsuccessfully in 2018, five years after it set up shop in the country.[56]

Finally, and probably most importantly, the Chinese state has so far still retained a strong command over its domestic online market. This is especially relevant for China's web services and applications companies because the majority, if not all, of them are still heavily, if not exclusively, reliant on the domestic market for profit and growth. In 2017, the overseas revenues of the three strongest internet applications companies in China—Alibaba, Tencent, and Baidu—only accounted for 11 percent, 5 percent, and 1 percent of their annual revenues, respectively.[57] In other words, despite their extensive and deep ties with transnational financial capital, in terms of revenue distribution, China's internet applications companies are still dominantly "Chinese." Indeed, domestic markets have become even more important, given the challenging geopolitical environments the firms are facing. For example, even with large amounts of capital investment, Alibaba's overseas revenue has only accounted for a small amount of its total revenue, and this has been declining—from 11 percent in 2017 down to 7 percent in 2019 and 2020.[58] The state's tight control over the domestic digital market, in turn, can be converted into leverage over these companies to keep them in line with the state's developmental and international agenda. A series of regulatory initiatives has reinforced this trend, including the recently passed antitrust and data security regulations.[59]

Policy Implications

How can we better understand China's efforts in building a global digital infrastructure? By breaking this vital sector into three layers and by observing how the complicated forms of state–capital interactions have played out at each of these layers over the years, the chapter offers three policy lessons.

First, China's presence in global cyberspace is by no means a recent phenomenon. In other words, to claim that China has only recently started to "move beyond the 'Great Firewall'" is misleading. For example, Chinese telecom equipment vendor Huawei started its global journey in the late 1990s, way before the Chinese state even officially announced its "going out" initiative in the mid-2000s. In 2008, Huawei's overseas revenue already accounted for over 75 percent of its total revenue, making it officially an international tech giant by revenue distribution. Only by fully accounting for this longer history can we understand the current and future behavior of these China-based tech giants.

For example, even being blacklisted by the United States and other Western nations, Huawei has remained a key pillar in Africa, partly because of its long engagement with Africa's basic telecommunication infrastructure from the early 2000s. In 2021, Huawei worked on twenty-five projects across Africa, and many African nations have announced that they would move their government data and digital platforms to Huawei's data center.[60]

Second, Chinese political and economic entities are not the only architects in building a China-centered international internet. The outward expansion of China's internet industry is often perceived as a one-dimensional power projection from China to the rest of the world, although transnational capital has played a far more important role in this process. China's e-commerce giant Alibaba offers an illustrative example in this regard. As I have discussed elsewhere,[61] instead of being a "Chinese" company, Alibaba's corporate nationality has been an extremely complicated issue for a long time. For instance, it was once owned primarily by foreign capital, including Japan's SoftBank and Yahoo. Furthermore, many transnational investment banks have been the major forces supporting Alibaba's global shopping spree. For example, in 2015–16, with help from foreign investment banks such as Citigroup, Deutsche Bank, Goldman Sachs, JP Morgan, and Morgan Stanley, Alibaba secured $3 billion in syndicated loans to fund its overseas projects.[62] Even in the wake of a recent crackdown led by the government, Alibaba continues to receive strong support from transnational capital. It is reported that in 2021, JP Morgan announced that it supported credit card payments processing for Alibaba.com, the B2B business unit of Alibaba Group in the United States.[63]

Finally, China's efforts to build a global digital infrastructure do not represent a single-minded state-oriented action. Often, we assume that the Chinese internet is dominated by a monolithic authoritarian state that exercises its power over every aspect of the Chinese digital economy. However, this chapter has demonstrated that there are actually complicated forms of power struggles among different government entities and units of internet capital across hardware, network, and application layers in China's global digital infrastructure. For example, led by equipment vendors such as Huawei, ZTE, Lenovo, and Xiaomi, companies in the hardware layer are the pioneers in constructing China's global digital infrastructure. They have, in general, enjoyed generous support from the state over the years to reach many of the countries in the Global South. The growing geopolitics of the global internet, however, may sometimes require them to distance themselves from Chinese interests. For instance, in 2015, a Huawei executive had expressed concern about the trade implications of China's then newly formulated information security laws. He worried that the policies would have adverse effects on global trade openness and Huawei's own internationalization plans.[64] Such power struggles, however, have not precluded many China-based tech companies from prioritizing their global expansion based on the state's geopolitical interests, as shown in the recent development of the "Belt and Road Initiative."

Conclusion

A global digital China is rising. This process, however, is complicated and multifaceted, demanding a longer historical perspective and a structural understanding of the transformation of the global internet. Instead of viewing China's efforts as simply dominated by state strategies, we need to remind ourselves that the priorities and interests of many China-based digital entities are not always in line with the Chinese state. It is important, therefore, to move beyond the abstract notion of "great power competition" to more closely monitor what is actually happening on the ground in the construction of China's global digital infrastructure.[65] For policymakers, this means moving beyond the binary framing of "state- versus private-owned companies" and engaging instead with concrete analysis of how those companies, operating in different layers of China's global digital infrastructure, have interacted differently with the state. Will the future structure of the global internet be significantly shaped by China-based business actors across hardware, network, and applications layers? If so, for whom and to what ends?

Notes

1 Jamie Monson, *Africa's Freedom Railway: How a Chinese Development Project Changed Lives and Livelihoods in Tanzania* (Indiana University Press, 2009).

2 Yun Wen, *The Huawei Model: The Rise of China's Technology Giant* (University of Illinois Press, 2020).

3 Hong Shen, "Building a Digital Silk Road? Situating the Internet in China's Belt and Road Initiative," *International Journal of Communication* 12 (2018): 2683–701.

4 Newley Purnell and Alyssa Abkowitz, "Alibaba Thinks Outside the China Box," *The Wall Street Journal*, August 12, 2016.

5 Lulu Yilun Chen, "Baidu Said to Buy Stake in Uber, Boosting App in China," Bloomberg, December 11, 2014, available online: http://www.bloomberg.com/news/articles/2014-12-12/baidu-said-to-buy-stake-in-uber-boosting-app-in-china.

6 Lulu Yilun Chen, Pavel Alpeyev, and Eric Nakamura, "Tencent Leads $8.6 Billion Deal for Clash of Clans Studio," Bloomberg, June 21, 2016.

7 Jeff Desjardins, "Tech's 20 Largest Companies Are Based in Two Countries," Business Insider, July 9, 2018, available online: https://www.businessinsider.com/techs-20-largest-companies-are-based-in-2-countries-2018-7.

8 Olga Protska, "Top 10 World's Most Valuable Tech Companies in 2022," FXSSI, February 3, 2022, available online: https://fxssi.com/most-valuable-tech-companies.

9 See Gady Epstein, "China's Internet: A Giant Cage," *The Economist*, April 6, 2013, available online: https://www.economist.com/special-report/2013/04/06/a-giant-cage.

10 Eric Harwit, *China's Telecommunications Revolution* (Oxford University Press, 2008).

11 Roselyn Hsueh, *China's Regulatory State: A New Strategy for Globalization* (Cornell University Press, 2011).

12 Yu Hong, *Networking China: The Digital Transformation of the Chinese Economy* (University of Illinois Press, 2017).

13 Wen, *Huawei Model*.

14 Zhao Hejuan and Zhang Yuzhe, "The Chinese Telecommunications War in Africa," *Caixin New Century*, January 16, 2012, available online: http://magazine.caixin.com/2012-01-13/100348416.html.

15 Zhang Weiwei, "ZTE Received 400 Million Contract from Nigeria to Build its Public Safety Communication System," Caixin, December 28, 2010.

16 Wen, *Huawei Model*.

17 Zhao and Zhang, "The Chinese Telecommunications War in Africa."

18 Although many countries, including the United States, have their own Exim Banks, the Chinese ones are usually much bigger. It is reported in early 2017 that the China Development Bank had $1.8 trillion in assets, bigger than the US Exim Bank "by a multiple of 64." See Scott Cendrowski, "Is the World Big Enough for Huawei?," *Fortune*, February 1, 2017, available online: http://fortune.com/huawei-china-smartphone.

19 Stephen Lawson, "Huawei Calls Charge of Government Help 'Hogwash,'" *IDG News Service*, March 9, 2011, available online: http://www.pcworld.com/article/230671/Huawei_Calls_Charge_of_Government_Help_hogwash.html.

20 Zhao and Zhang, "The Chinese Telecommunications War in Africa."

21 Yuezhi Zhao, "China's Pursuits of Indigenous Innovations in Information Technology Developments: Hopes, Follies and Uncertainties," *Chinese Journal of Communication* 3, no. 3 (2010): 266–89.

22 See Jan Zofka, "Chairman Cotton: Socialist Bulgaria's Cotton Trade with African Countries During the Early Cold War (1946–70)," *Journal of Global History* (2021): 1–19.

23 Sheridan Prasso, "What Makes China Telecom Huawei So Scary?," *Fortune*, July 28, 2011, available online: http://fortune.com/2011/07/28/what-makes-china-telecom-huawei-so-scary.

24 Zhao and Zhang, "The Chinese Telecommunications War in Africa."

25 Guo Haifei and Yan Yu, "The Battle Between Huawei and ZTE," *People's Daily*, May 18, 2011.

26 David Shepardson and Karen Freifeld, "China's Huawei, 70 Affiliates Placed on US Trade Blacklist," Reuters, May 15, 2019.

27 David Shepardson, "Biden Signs Legislation to Tighten U.S. Restrictions on Huawei, ZTE," Reuters, November 11, 2021.

28 Cheng Ting-fang and Lauly Li, "Huawei's Grip on China Market Softens Blow of US Crackdown," *Nikkei Asia*, March 31, 2021, available online: https://asia.nikkei.com/Spotlight/Huawei-crackdown/Huawei-s-grip-on-China-market-softens-blow-of-US-crackdown.

29 Dariusz Wójcik and James Camilleri, "'Capitalist Tools in Socialist Hands'? China Mobile in Global Financial Networks," *Transactions of the Institute of British Geographers* 40, no. 4 (2015): 464–78.

30 Roselyn Hsueh, "Nations or Sectors in the Age of Globalization: China's Policy Toward Foreign Direct Investment in Telecommunications," *Review of Policy Research* 32, no. 6 (2015): 627–48.

31 Ma Xiaofang, "Wang Jianzhou: If We Can't Do Well in Pakistan, We Wouldn't Be Able to Do Well in Other Places," *China Business News*, June 23, 2010.

32 Hong Shen, "China and Global Internet Governance: Toward an Alternative Analytical Framework," *Chinese Journal of Communication* 9, no. 3 (2016): 304–24.

33 Nan Shan, "Xi Guohua: China Mobile Restarted Its Globalization Through Developing TD-LTE," March 5, 2014.

34 Juan Pedro Tomás, "China Mobile Already Deployed More Than 560,000 5G Base Stations Nationwide," RCR Wireless, November 4, 2021.

35 Zhao, "China's Pursuits of Indigenous Innovations in Information Technology Developments."

36 Syed Fazl-E-Haider, "China Mobile Expanding Its Network in Pakistan," *Pakistan Economist*, September 17–23, 2007, available online: http://www.pakistaneconomist.com/pagesearch/Search-Engine2007/S.E600.php.

37 Zhao Hejuan, "China Mobile's Pakistani Subsidiary Ranked the Lowest Again This Year," Caixin, May 23, 2011.

38 Fortune Global 500, available online: http://fortune.com/global500/.

39 Zhang Huanping, "A Review of Spain's Telefonica's Equity Investment in China Unicom," Caixin, June 13, 2012, available online: http://economy.caixin.com/2012-06-13/100400074.html.

40 CGTN, "Going Global Series: How China Mobile Pakistan Expanded in the Country," April 5, 2021, available online: https://news.cgtn.com/news/2021-04-05/VHJhbnNjcmlwdDUzNDcw/index.html.

41 Stacia Lee, "The Cybersecurity Implications of Chinese Undersea Cable Investment," Henry M. Jackson School of International Studies, January 25, 2017, available online: https://jsis.washington.edu/news/cybersecurity-implications-chinese-undersea-cable-investment.

42 Winston Qiu, "Camtel and China Unicom Signed C&MA for South Atlantic Inter Link (SAIL) Cable System," August 13, 2016, available online: https://www.submarinenetworks.com/en/systems/brazil-africa/sail/camtel-and-china-unicom-signed-c-ma-for-south-atlantic-inter-link-sail-cable-system.

43 Hong Shen, *Across the Great (Fire) Wall: China and the Global Internet* (PhD diss., University of Illinois at Urbana-Champaign, 2017).

44 Roselyn, "Nations or Sectors in the Age of Globalization," 637; Harwit, *China's Telecommunications Revolution*, 105.

45 Yu Hong, "Pivot to Internet Plus: Molding China's Digital Economy for Economic Restructuring," *International Journal of Communication* 11 (2017): 1486–506.

46 Matthew Crain, "Financial Markets and Online Advertising: Reevaluating the Dotcom Investment Bubble," *Information, Communication & Society* 17, no. 3 (2014): 371–84.

47 Sandra Tsui, "Tencent Said to Increase Size of Syndicated Loan to $4.4 Billion," Bloomberg, June 6, 2016, available online: http://www.bloomberg.com/news/articles/2016-06-06/tencent-said-to-increase-size-of-syndicated-loan-to-4-4-billion.

48 Hsueh, "Nations or Sectors in the Age of Globalization," 637; Harwit, *China's Telecommunications Revolution*, 105.

49 Alibaba, "Form F1 Submitted to the United States Securities and Exchange Commission," May 6, 2014, available online: https://www.sec.gov/Archives/edgar/data/1577552/000119312514184994/d709111df1.htm.

50 Alibaba, "The market is our background," *International Business Times*, July 23, 2014, available online: http://www.ibtimes.com.cn/articles/38199/20140723/a-li-ba-ba-wo-men-de-bei-jing-shi-shi-chang.htm.

51 Michael Forsythe, "Alibaba's I.P.O. Could Be a Bonanza for the Scions of Chinese Leaders," *The New York Times*, July 21, 2014.

52 Ministry of Foreign Affairs, "Xi Jinping Holds Talks with President Dilma Rousseff of Brazil, Inheriting the Past and Ushering in the Future to Forge More Splendid Future for China-Brazil Relations," July 18, 2014.

53 Guillermo Parra-Bernal, "China's Baidu Buys Control of Brazil's Peixe Urbano in Expansion Push," Reuters, October 9, 2014.

54 Vijay Prashad, *The Poorer Nations: A Possible History of the Global South* (Verso, 2013), 10–12.

55 Yuezhi Zhao, "The BRICS Formation in Reshaping Global Communication: Possibilities and Challenges," in *Mapping BRICS Media*, ed. Kaarle Nordenstreng and Daya Kishan Thussu (Routledge, 2015), 66–86.

56 Angelica Mari, "Baidu Ends Brazil Operations," ZDNet, July 17, 2018, available online: https://www.zdnet.com/article/baidu-ends-brazil-operations.

57 Rebecca Fannin, "China's BAT Won't Battle the FANGS in the US Anytime Soon," *Forbes*, May 21, 2018, available online: https://www.forbes.com/sites/rebeccafannin/2018/05/21/dont-count-on-chinas-baidu-alibaba-tencent-to-go-mainstream-in-the-u-s/#191319745f28.

58 "Alibaba Group Announces March Quarter and Full Fiscal Year 2020 Results," Business Wire, May 22, 2020, available online: https://www.businesswire.com/news/home/20200522005178/en/Alibaba-Group-Announces-March-Quarter-and-Full-Fiscal-Year-2020-Results.

59 Josh Bramble, "Beijing's Tech Sector Crackdown Sends a Clear Warning to Companies Going Global," Center for Strategic & International Studies, October 4, 2021, available online: https://www.csis.org/blogs/new-perspectives-asia/beijings-tech-sector-crackdown-sends-clear-warning-companies-going.

60 Jevans Nyabiage, "African Nations Continue to Put Trust in Huawei for Data Management," *South China Morning Post*, June 28, 2021, available online: https://www.scmp.com/news/china/diplomacy/article/3138917/african-nations-continue-put-trust-huawei-data-management.

61 Hong Shen, *Alibaba: Infrastructuring Global China* (Routledge, 2021).

62 Adam Jourdan, "China's Alibaba Says Agrees $3 Billion Five-Year Loan," Reuters, March 9, 2016, available online: http://www.reuters.com/article/us-alibaba-loan-idUSKCN0WC00D.

63 J.P. Morgan, "J.P. Morgan Supports Alipay to Provide Card Payment Services for Alibaba.com in the US," September 16, 2021, available online: https://www.jpmorgan.com/news/jpmorgan-provides-alibaba-card-payment-services.

64 Gerry Shih, "Huawei CEO Says Chinese Cybersecurity Rules Could Backfire," Reuters, April 21, 2015, available online: https://www.reuters.com/article/us-huawei-cybersecurity/exclusive-huawei-ceo-says-chinese-cybersecurity-rules-could-backfire-idUSKBN0NC1G920150421.

65 Yujia He and Hong Shen, "Beyond the Great Power Competition Narrative: Exploring Labor Politics and Resistance behind AI Innovation in China," *Georgetown Journal of Asian Affairs* 7 (2021): 5–15.

Bibliography

Alibaba. "Form F1 Submitted to the United States Securities and Exchange Commission." May 6, 2014. Available online: https://www.sec.gov/Archives/edgar/data/1577552/000119312514184994/d709111df1.htm.

Alibaba. "Women De Beijing Shi Shichang." 我们的背景是市场 [The Market Is Our Background]. *International Business Times*, July 23, 2014. Available online: http://www.ibtimes.com.cn/articles/38199/20140723/a-li-ba-ba-wo-men-de-bei-jing-shi-shi-chang.htm.

Bramble, Josh. "Beijing's Tech Sector Crackdown Sends a Clear Warning to Companies Going Global." Center for Strategic & International Studies, October 4, 2021. Available online: https://www.csis.org/blogs/new-perspectives-asia/beijings-tech-sector-crackdown-sends-clear-warning-companies-going.

Business Wire. "Alibaba Group Announces March Quarter and Full Fiscal Year 2020 Results." May 22, 2020. Available online: https://www.businesswire.com/news/home/20200522005178/en/Alibaba-Group-Announces-March-Quarter-and-Full-Fiscal-Year-2020-Results.

Cendrowski, Scott. "Is the World Big Enough for Huawei?" *Fortune*, February 1, 2017. Available online: http://*fortune*.com/huawei-china-smartphone.

CGTN. "Going Global Series: How China Mobile Pakistan Expanded in the Country." April 5, 2021. Available online: https://news.cgtn.com/news/2021-04-05/VHJhbnNjcmlwdDUzNDcw/index.html.

Chen, Lulu Yilun. "Baidu Said to Buy Stake in Uber, Boosting App in China." Bloomberg, December 11, 2014. Available online: http://www.bloomberg.com/news/articles/2014-12-12/baidu-said-to-buy-stake-in-uber-boosting-app-in-china.

Cheng, Ting-fang, and Lauly Li. "Huawei's Grip on China Market Softens Blow of US Crackdown." *Nikkei Asia*, March 31, 2021. Available online: https://asia.nikkei.com/Spotlight/Huawei-crackdown/Huawei-s-grip-on-China-market-softens-blow-of-US-crackdown.

Crain, Matthew. "Financial Markets and Online Advertising: Reevaluating the Dotcom Investment Bubble." *Information, Communication & Society* 17, no. 3 (2014): 371–84.

Desjardins, Jeff. "Tech's 20 Largest Companies Are Based in Two Countries." Business Insider, July 9, 2018. Available online: https://www.businessinsider.com/techs-20-largest-companies-are-based-in-2-countries-2018-7.

Epstein, Gady. "China's Internet: A Giant Cage." *The Economist*, April 6, 2013. Available online: https://www.economist.com/special-report/2013/04/06/a giant cage.

Fannin, Rebecca. "China's BAT Won't Battle the FANGS in the US Anytime Soon." *Forbes*, May 21, 2018. Available online: https://www.*forbes*.com/sites/rebeccafannin/2018/05/21/dont-count-on-chinas-baidu-alibaba-tencent-to-go-mainstream-in-the-u-s/#191319745f28.

Fazl-E-Haider, Syed. "China Mobile Expanding Its Network in Pakistan." *Pakistan Economist*, September 17–23, 2007.

Forsythe, Michael. "Alibaba's I.P.O. Could Be a Bonanza for the Scions of Chinese Leaders." *The New York Times*, July 21, 2014. Available online: http://dealbook.nytimes.com/2014/07/20/alibabas-i-p-o-could-be-a-bonanza-for-the-scions-of-chinese-leaders/?_r=0.

Fortune Global 500. Available online: http://*fortune*.com/global500/.

Gewirtz, Julian. *Unlikely Partners: Chinese Reformers, Western Economists, and the Making of Global China*. Harvard University Press. 2017.

Guo Haifei, and Yan Yu. "Huawei Zhongxin roubozhan." 华为中兴肉搏战 [The Battle Between Huawei and ZTE]. *People's Daily*, May 18, 2011. Available online: http://paper.people.com.cn/jhzk/html/2011-05/18/content_959339.htm?div=-1.

Harwit, Eric. *China's Telecommunications Revolution*. Oxford University Press, 2008.

He, Yujia, and Hong Shen. "Beyond the Great Power Competition Narrative: Exploring Labor Politics and Resistance Behind AI Innovation in China." *Georgetown Journal of Asian Affairs* 7 (2021): 5–15.

Hong, Yu. *Networking China: The Digital Transformation of the Chinese Economy*. University of Illinois Press, 2017.

Hong, Yu. "Pivot to Internet Plus: Molding China's Digital Economy for Economic Restructuring." *International Journal of Communication* 11 (2017): 1486–506.

Hsueh, Roselyn. "Nations or Sectors in the Age of Globalization: China's Policy Toward Foreign Direct Investment in Telecommunications." *Review of Policy Research* 32, no. 6 (2015): 627–48, 637.

Jourdan, Adam. "China's Alibaba Says Agrees $3 Billion Five-Year Loan." Reuters, March 9, 2016. Available online: http://www.reuters.com/article/us-alibaba-loan-idUSKCN0WC00D.

"J.P. Morgan Supports Alipay to Provide Card Payment Services for Alibaba.com in the U.S." J.P. Morgan, September 16, 2021. Available online: https://www.jpmorgan.com/news/jpmorgan-provides-alibaba-card-payment-services.

Lawson, Stephen. "Huawei Calls Charge of Government Help 'Hogwash'." IDG News Service. Available online: http://www.pcworld.com/article/230671/Huawei_Calls_Charge_of_Government_Help_hogwash.html.

Lee, Stacia. "The Cybersecurity Implications of Chinese Undersea Cable Investment." The Henry M. Jackson School of International Studies, January 25, 2017. Available online: https://jsis.washington.edu/news/cybersecurity-implications-chinese-undersea-cable-investment.

Mari, Angelica Mari. "Baidu Ends Brazil Operations." ZDNet, July 17, 2018. Available online: https://www.zdnet.com/article/baidu-ends-brazil-operations.

Ma Xiaofang. "Wang Jianzhou: Bajisitan zuobuhao buqu qitadifang." 王建宙: 巴基斯坦做不好去其他地方 [Wang Jianzhou: If We Can't Do Well in Pakistan, We Wouldn't Be Able to Do Well in Other Places]. *China Business News*第一财经日报, June 23, 2010. Available online: http://tech.qq.com/a/20100623/000234.htm.

Ministry of Foreign Affairs. "Xi Jinping Holds Talks with President Dilma Rousseff of Brazil, Inheriting the Past and Ushering in the Future to Forge More Splendid Future for China-Brazil Relations." July 18, 2014. Available online: http://www.fmprc.gov.cn/mfa_eng/topics_665678/xjpzxcxjzgjldrdlchwdbxagtwnrlgbjxgsfwbcxzlldrhw/t1176222.shtml.

Monson, Jamie. *Africa's Freedom Railway: How a Chinese Development Project Changed Lives and Livelihoods in Tanzania*. Indiana University Press, 2009.

Nan Shan. "Xi Guohua: Zhongyidong zaiqi guojihua, jie TD-LTE yangfan chuhai." 奚国华: 中移动再启国际化 借TD-LTE扬帆出海 [Xi Guohua: China Mobile Restarted Its Globalization Through Developing TD-LTE]. March 5, 2014. Available online: http://www.c114.net/news/22/c16710.html.

Nyabiage, Jevans. "African Nations Continue to Put Trust in Huawei for Data Management." *South China Morning Post*, June 28, 2021. Available online: https://www.scmp.com/news/china/diplomacy/article/3138917/african-nations-continue-put-trust-huawei-data-management.

Parra-Bernal, Guillermo. "China's Baidu Buys Control of Brazil's Peixe Urbano in Expansion Push." Reuters, October 9, 2014. Available online: http://www.reuters.com/article/us-peixe-urbano-m-a-baidu-idUSKCN0HY1EN20141009.

Prashad, Vijay. *The Poorer Nations: A Possible History of the Global South*. Verso, 2013.

Prasso, Sheridan. "What Makes China Telecom Huawei So Scary?" *Fortune*, July 28, 2011. Available online: http://*fortune*.com/2011/07/28/what-makes-china-telecom-huawei-so-scary.

Protska, Olga. "Top 10 World's Most Valuable Tech Companies in 2022." February 3, 2022. Available online: https://fxssi.com/most-valuable-tech-companies.

Purnell, Newley, and Alyssa Abkowitz. "Alibaba Thinks Outside the China Box." *The Wall Street Journal*, August 12, 2016. Available online: https://www.wsj.com/articles/alibaba-thinks-outside-the-china-box-1470995037.

Qiu, Winston. "Camtel and China Unicom Signed C&MA for South Atlantic Inter Link (SAIL) Cable System." August 13, 2016. Available online: https://www.submarinenetworks.com/en/systems/brazil-africa/sail/camtel-and-china-unicom-signed-c-ma-for-south-atlantic-inter-link-sail-cable-system.

Sanchez-Sibony, Oscar. *Red Globalization: The Political Economy of the Soviet Cold War from Stalin to Khrushchev*. Cambridge University Press, 2014.

Shen, Hong. "Across the Great (Fire) Wall: China and the Global Internet." PhD diss., University of Illinois at Urbana-Champaign, 2017.

Shen, Hong. "Building a Digital Silk Road? Situating the Internet in China's Belt and Road Initiative." *International Journal of Communication* 12 (2018): 2683–701.

Shen, Hong. "China and Global Internet Governance: Toward an Alternative Analytical Framework." *Chinese Journal of Communication* 9, no. 3 (2016): 304–24.

Shepardson, David. "Biden Signs Legislation to Tighten U.S. Restrictions on Huawei, ZTE." Reuters, November 11, 2021. Available online: https://www.reuters.com/technology/biden-signs-legislation-tighten-us-restrictions-huawei-zte-2021-11-11/.

Shepardson, David, and Karen Freifeld. "China's Huawei, 70 Affiliates Placed on US Trade Blacklist." Reuters, May 15, 2019. Available online: https://www.reuters.com/article/uk-usa-china-huaweitech-idUKKCN1SL2VW.

Shih, Gerry. "Huawei CEO Says Chinese Cybersecurity Rules Could Backfire." Reuters, April 21, 2015. Available online: https://www.reuters.com/article/us-huawei-cybersecurity/exclusive-huawei-ceo-says-chinese-cybersecurity-rules-could-backfire-idUSKBN0NC1G920150421.

Tomás, Juan Pedro. "China Mobile Already Deployed More Than 560,000 5G Base Stations Nationwide." November 4, 2021. Available online: https://www.rcrwireless.com/20211104/5g/china-mobile-already-deployed-over-560000-5g-base-stations-nationwide.

Tsui, Sandra. "Tencent Said to Increase Size of Syndicated Loan to $4.4 Billion." Bloomberg, June 6, 2016. Available online: http://www.bloomberg.com/news/articles/2016-06-06/tencent-said-to-increase-size-of-syndicated-loan-to-4-4-billion.

Wen, Yun. *The Huawei Model: The Rise of China's Technology Giant*. University of Illinois Press, 2020.

Wójcik, Dariusz, and James Camilleri. "'Capitalist Tools in Socialist Hands'? China Mobile in Global Financial Networks." *Transactions of the Institute of British Geographers* 40, no. 4 (2015): 464–78.

Zhang, Huanping. "Xibanya dianxin rugu, zengchi yu jianchi liantong guiji huigu." 西班牙电信入股、增持与减持联通轨迹回顾 [A Review of Spain's Telefonica's Equity Investment in China Unicom]. *Caixin*财新, June 13, 2012. Available online: http://economy.*caixin*.com/2012-06-13/100400074.html.

Zhang, Weiwei. "Zhongxing huo niriliya guojia gonggong anquan tongxun xitong xiangmu 4yi meiyuan dingdan." 中兴获尼日利亚国家公共安全通讯系统项目4亿美元订单 [ZTE Received 400 Million Contract from Nigeria to Build Its Public Safety Communication System]. December 28, 2010. Available online: http://www.c114.net/news/127/a572092.html.

Zhao, Hejuan. "Zhongyidong bajisitan zigongsi paimindiandi nianfuyinian." 中移动巴基斯坦子公司排名垫底年复一年 [China Mobile's Pakistani Subsidiary Ranked the Lowest Again This Year]. *CaiXin* 财新, May 23, 2011. Available online: http://www.c114.net/news/118/a603483.html.

Zhao, Hejuan, and Zhang Yuzhe. "Dianxin zhan feizhou." 电信战非洲 [The Chinese Telecommunications War in Africa]. *Caixin New Century*财新《新世纪》, January 16, 2012. Available online: http://magazine.*caixin*.com/2012-01-13/100348416.html.

Zhao, Yuezhi. "The BRICS Formation in Reshaping Global Communication: Possibilities and Challenges." In *Mapping BRICS Media*, edited by Kaarle Nordenstreng and Daya Kishan Thussu. Routledge, 2015.

Zhao, Yuezhi. "China's Pursuits of Indigenous Innovations in Information Technology Developments: Hopes, Follies and Uncertainties." *Chinese Journal of Communication* 3, no. 3 (2010): 266–89.

Zofka, Jan. "Chairman Cotton: Socialist Bulgaria's Cotton Trade with African Countries During the Early Cold War (1946–70)." *Journal of Global History* 17 (2021): 1–19.

13

CHINA'S DIGITAL INFRASTRUCTURES IN AFRICA

Moral Panics and Critical Engagements

Iginio Gagliardone

Western policymaking often approaches the rise of Chinese tech firms in Africa with fear and anxiety, powered by the concern that China may seek to export its model of the information society, favor authoritarian tendencies in the shaping of digital spaces, or covertly promote its interests.[1] The repeated—and often self-inflicted—blows to the ideals of hope, freedom, and opportunity that had accompanied the initial expansion of the internet from its epicenter in the United States have fueled this sentiment further. The romantic conception of digital technologies as "liberation technologies"[2] has dramatically faded. Authoritarian rulers have demonstrated their ability to retain or claw back control—as testified by the endurance of leaders in Russia, Cameroon, or China, or by the aftermath of the Arab Spring. Scandals and leaks—from Cambridge Analytica to Edward Snowden and Frances Haugen—and the heightened attention and reporting of hate speech and mis/disinformation have undermined the once convincing tale of social media as forces for good.

Compared to the early stages of China's expansion into Africa's digital space at the turn of the millennium, empirical evidence distinguishing real from imagined risks posed by Chinese technology has become increasingly abundant.[3] And yet analysts and policymakers seem to have selectively engaged with it, privileging accounts heightening over those diffusing the perception of impending threats. The "digital authoritarianism" hypothesis, based on the assumption that an authoritarian regime—China—would seek to export its model abroad, has found no empirical evidence[4] but continues to inform public statements and actions.[5]

Both the Trump and the Biden administrations have relied on it to present their own projects, developed to counter China's Belt and Road Initiative as the responses of the democratic world to the spread of authoritarianism. Trump's Blue Network and Biden's Build Back Better World (B3W), and their digital versions, Clean Network and the Alliance for the Future of the Internet, were designed to generate products "with our [the US] democratic values front and center"[6] or to "reassess [. . .] the aspirational vision of the internet that prevailed from the 90s through the 00s."[7] At the same time, news of the signing of new contracts with China in sensitive areas such as urban surveillance or facial recognition has been given ample attention and framed with alarmist tones. Deployments of Huawei's Safe City and ZTE's Smart City or CloudWalk's ambitions to step up facial recognition in Zimbabwe have been associated with the rise of a global panopticon[8] or used as evidence of China's rise as a new digital colonizer.[9]

Reflecting on the heightening of sentiments of fear and anxiety, this chapter proposes a shift in perspective. I argue that many of the reactions and responses described above emerge from an ultimately insular process of soul-searching and exaggerated characterization of China as "the other," which disregards the technological imageries and materialities that have progressively emerged in Africa, acquiring momentum and defying simplistic narratives. In most African countries, digital infrastructures have evolved—and continue to evolve—by combining material artifacts, solutions, and ideas from the West and from the East, in stark contrast with the expectation that nations should choose one or the other camp. The noncompliance of African states with the ban on Huawei issued by Donald Trump in 2019, for example, is not the result of supposed new allegiances to China and its "model" of the internet. Rather, it reflects Africa's greater confidence in developing specific strategies for digital innovation, where foreign partners may be recognized as more resourceful but are brought in to implement those strategies rather than impose their own.

The chapter builds on extensive research conducted in Ethiopia, Rwanda, Kenya, Ghana, and South Africa in the past decade, as well as on critical accounts that have emerged from African academic institutions and/or from scholars, mostly anthropologists, who have examined China–Africa relations from the bottom up. These works are combined to illustrate how, away from sweeping narratives and Cold War tropes, greater awareness of overlooked forms of resistance and of some of the failures of Chinese tech on the ground may ultimately tame fears and panics.

The chapter is organized in three sections, each reflecting on a distinctive aspect of Chinese-built and/or financed digital infrastructures in Africa: (1) how they compare to other types of Chinese infrastructures (e.g., roads, dams, and railways); (2) how they interact with preexisting infrastructures, both technical (e.g., legacy equipment, projects deployed by non-Chinese companies) and sociopolitical (e.g., acceptance/resistance vis-à-vis surveillance tech, law enforcement agencies' ability to act on information acquired through surveillance tech); and (3) whether and how far deployments of Chinese digital infrastructure reinforce a state-centered and sovereign internet advocated by China on the international stage.

The Unique Trajectories of Chinese Digital Infrastructures in Africa

Digital infrastructures have distinctive features compared to other large-scale Chinese projects in Africa, which have made them an easier target of criticism from China's adversaries.

When China scaled up its involvement in Africa in the early 2000s, it focused on constructing roads, railways, dams, and power plants for at least three reasons. First, exporting capital and labor abroad responded to China's crisis of overaccumulation after waves of stimulus packages in real estate and infrastructure had created "ripple bubbles" at home.[10] Moving overcapacity to new markets offered an opportunity to expand the Chinese accumulation system and replicate strategies that had been tried and tested at the domestic level.[11]

Second, financing infrastructure projects represented a "safer" conduit to strengthen diplomatic relations with African partners. Betting on increasing global consensus on "infrastructure-led development"[12] to boost African states' capacity to move goods across and from the continent and generate power was likely to attract less criticism than venturing into contentious spaces of international cooperation, such as governance or education, where China's authoritarian tendencies could generate stronger resistance.

Third, large infrastructural projects were able to communicate China's new presence and "friendship" to large audiences, signaling the beginning of a new phase after limited exposure on the continent. As writer and professor Brian Larkin has pointed out, for many infrastructures, their aesthetic or "poetic" value, their ability to communicate a message—of progress, power, or prowess—is as relevant as their function. As he explained, in the poetic mode, "infrastructures [become] the means by which a state [but this can be extended to external agents] proffers representations to its citizens and asks them to take those representations as social facts."[13] During one of my visits to Addis Ababa in 2015, an Ethiopian colleague offered a vivid illustration of this principle, signaling how China's attempt to "communicate via infrastructure" had produced significant results: "If you go out in the streets of Addis and ask people if they know of any project funded by the United States, they will have no idea. Ask them about China, and they won't stop pointing their fingers at all that's around them."[14] In two decades, China shifted from a marginal player to Africa's "infrastructure giant," with funding for infrastructure coming second only to Africa's own governments.[15]

Of these three drivers, digital infrastructures share only the first. They are highly intensive in terms of capital expenditure—and even more intensive in terms of skill set—required for their implementation. The expansion of Chinese tech firms laying fiber-optic backbones and 5G antennae not only in Africa but also in Europe and North and South America is also a testimony to China's leap from replicating to leading innovation and building the foundations for new generations of communication systems.

Regarding the second aspect of Chinese infrastructural expansion, digital infrastructures broke into riskier territory, as illustrated by the ban issued by US President Donald Trump on Huawei in 2019. On the surface, the ban did not produce significant repercussions for digital infrastructures in Africa. Contrary to many US allies that issued similar bans, most African governments and service providers continued renewing or signing new contracts with Huawei to expand national backbone infrastructures, implement solutions in urban surveillance, and launch 5G networks. At a deeper level, however, the discrepancies in how different blocs responded to the ban have created the preconditions for a scenario that has heightened, rather than diffused, concerns that China may be exporting technologies with potential vulnerabilities. China is now deploying its advanced technologies mostly in countries with fewer checks and balances, experimenting in spaces that offer opportunities to test solutions that are likely to find stronger scrutiny elsewhere.

These concerns are strengthened even further by how digital infrastructures function in apparent contradiction to the third feature of Chinese large-scale projects highlighted above. Unlike roads, railways, and ports, they are largely invisible to the end users. They are either underground or in disguise. This invisibility has stripped digital infrastructure of its ability to act as a symbol of China's supposed benevolence to the continent. More critically, it has created ample room for speculation. Fiber-optic backbones, 5G repeaters, data centers, and transmission protocols, mostly invisible to end users, have been turned into hyper-visible objects in geopolitical contentions, allowing claims about vulnerabilities or backdoors in Chinese equipment to spread widely.

Western powers, the United States above all, have exploited this fragility to warn African partners, and the world at large, of the ambiguities of China's projects, seeking to present Chinese and Western visions as diametrically different and incompatible, not only at a discursive but also at a material level. The Blue Network initiative and B3W became the responses of the "democratic world" to China's Belt and Road Initiative, designed to develop "values-driven, high-standard and transparent infrastructure partnerships"[16] as opposed to "aggressive intrusions by malign actors, such as the Chinese Communist Party" or "the rise [of] an alternative vision of the Internet as a tool of State control promoted by authoritarian powers."[17]

The effort spent to spin these macro-narratives not only seems surprisingly unaware of their lack of credibility, considering the incessant stream of leaks and scandals highlighting the hypocrisy of US tech giants,[18] but it also prevents policymakers and analysts from noticing other critiques and forms of resistance to Chinese infrastructure that are emerging from the ground up. These critiques may be understandably harder to process and accept, as they are directed not only at China but also at all foreign actors exploiting power imbalances with the African continent. If taken seriously, however, they can disclose opportunities to chart processes of innovation that do not, once again, impose grand but unrealistic visions onto Africa but appreciate the unique trajectories of change and transformation in specific socio-technical spaces on the continent. Below, I highlight two examples, one locating new infrastructural projects in the long history of capital accumulation and exploitation on the continent and the other focusing on how infrastructure development is perceived at the margins.

The first example emerges from a critical analysis of one of Africa's largest and most debated Chinese-funded infrastructural projects: Kenya's Standard Gauge Railway (SGR), built by the China Road and Bridge Corporation (CRBC). When Kenya's President, Uhuru Kenyatta, launched the project on May 31, 2017, he referred to the new train designed to ride on it, the "Madaraka Express" ("Freedom Express") as a "new dawn for Kenya," which would "begin to reshape the story of Kenya for the next 100 years."[19] Anthropologist Wangui Kimari and geographer and political ecologist Henrik Ernston[20] articulate a critique that defies widespread tropes—neither challenging nor replicating recent narratives on China's debt traps—and originally locate the project in the "longer histories of imperial racial pathologizing of Africa, despite rhetorical claims to the opposite."[21] They reconnect the new train to the "Lunatic Express" built by British colonizers at the end of the nineteenth century, which created a racialized infrastructural regime in Kenya and in neighboring countries. While residues of colonialism continue to exist in the form of "imperial remains," new infrastructures can be interpreted as the result of "imperial invitations," rearticulating distinctions in a new form. As they continue:

> Though infrastructures emerging from imperial invitations are said to represent a "new dawn" from "new" partners, they do not help shift the centres of knowledge, or in fact provide the space for other epistemes about what else (or who else) can count as appropriate infrastructure. These projects uphold that there are limited centres from where infrastructural knowledge is constructed. And this centre is never Africa.[22]

In their reading, China ceases to be framed as the opposite, or the alternative, to colonial powers, which extended their domination after the end of colonial rule in the form of aid or technical assistance and became the largest financers of infrastructure in Africa, which amounted to 60 percent of aid in 1973, to be discontinued a few years later when many large projects failed to yield the expected spillover effects.[23] The Chinese government and Chinese companies are presented as uninterested and unable to *displace* the actors who had generated racialized infrastructural regimes, promoting new and supposedly fairer economic and social relations, as claimed in formal declarations. Rather, they are described as simply *replacing* those actors, appropriating, rather than challenging, their logic.

The second example emerges from interrogating how populations affected by, but not immediately benefiting from, new infrastructures interpret China's development projects and compare them with those implemented by other actors. Anthropologist Miriam Driessen has offered a fascinating account of perceptions and self-perceptions of Chinese aid—of the gap between how its recipients think of it and how Chinese actors expect it will be received—when examining infrastructural projects in rural Ethiopia. As she reported, Ethiopians living alongside construction sites seemed not to appreciate the difference between "new" Chinese actors and previous agents of development. They often stole material owned by Chinese companies "to level their front or back yards" or to build "chapels and churches."[24] This appeared to infuriate Chinese managers and workers and brought to light substantial contradictions between different conceptions of development. Like their Western counterparts, Chinese development actors adopted a high-modernist[25] view of development as progressive and unilinear; they tended to ignore alternative, local ideas about development and were prone to universalizing human motivation. As Driessen reported:

> Chinese managers attempt to fashion young Ethiopian men into diligent workers who submit themselves to management and to the higher cause of wealth accumulation. According to the Chinese viewpoint, these workers care more about religion (or what the Chinese migrants referred to as "Jesus") than about money. The Ethiopians steal rather than struggle to make a living for themselves, as one Chinese accountant put it, and as a result are labelled as lazy. Once again, the colonial trope of the indolent native is repeated. What the Chinese see as a novel and fairer form of development assistance in Africa actually shares many characteristics with the old, and arguably superseded, Western approach to delivering "aid."[26]

These studies offer a concrete illustration of how resisting simple dichotomies and Cold War tropes does not amount to making concessions to China. On the contrary, bracketing out China–US competition and focusing on understanding contemporary large-scale projects from the ground up, as encased in the long-term histories of infrastructure building in Africa, enables other, possibly more complex, but also more realistic narratives and forms of contestation to emerge.

The Technopolitics of Chinese Successes and Failures in Africa

Another trigger of the fears and anxieties following deployments of Chinese tech in Africa is the framing, in reports and analyses emerging from the West, of the implementation of large-scale projects as uncomplicated and able to swiftly produce the expected outcomes. The *Atlantic*, for example, in 2020 sensationally titled its article "The Panopticon Is Already Here"[27] to report the expansion of Huawei's Safe City and ZTE's Smart City projects across the continent. A closer analysis of these projects on the ground, however, offers a significantly different picture.

Huawei and ZTE have aggressively marketed their Safe City and Smart City solutions, as they respectively branded their technology-aided urban law enforcement packages. Using language that seems to contradict the subdued tones usually employed by Chinese authorities when providing support in the communication sector (but that is quite ordinary for corporate actors seeking to sell their products), the two companies have boasted about how their solutions could uniquely match the needs of overcrowded and chaotic African cities. Their presentations and promotional materials sought to create an image of unparalleled efficiency, stressing their ability to offer tangible results over short time frames.[28] Huawei and ZTE have also capitalized on perceptions of Chinese technology and surveillance strategies as particularly effective, drawing on examples from Chinese cities as proof of the benefits of a comprehensive deployment of Smart City and Safe City solutions.[29]

As a result, Huawei soon became the leader in this emerging segment of the industry, providing advanced tools, either as part of its Safe City solution or in support of interventions aimed at stepping up local surveillance capabilities in numerous African countries. According to data released by Huawei and ZTE, as well as collected by the Carnegie Endowment for International Peace[30] and the Center for Strategic and International Studies,[31] by 2019, fifteen African countries had signed contracts with Huawei in this area: Algeria, Botswana, Côte d'Ivoire, Egypt, Ethiopia, Ghana, Kenya, Mauritius, Morocco, Nigeria, Rwanda, South Africa, Uganda, Zambia, and Zimbabwe. ZTE had a smaller presence, with projects launched only in five countries: Egypt, Ethiopia, Nigeria, Sudan, and Zambia.

Both companies have developed diverse and layered packages. Relying on a system connecting an operation center able to analyze vast amounts of data in real time with a multiplicity of sensors and cameras deployed across the city, they have offered services ranging from mundane smart metering to more worrying emergency assessments aimed at keeping "social peace" and predictive policing.[32] Public authorities have strongly supported the deployment of these systems on African soil, invoking increasingly pervasive discourses of securitization and the need to protect citizens.

Western journalists and policymakers have interpreted the implementation of these and similar projects with a sense of doom, stressing how Huawei and ZTE's solutions represent a threat to freedom and civil liberties. They certainly have the ingredients for being so. Data emerging from Asia and Africa, however, has begun to reveal how Huawei's own promises of curbing crime and improving centralized city management clash with the (quite predictable) complexity of the sociopolitical and technological realities of different locales.[33] Reports from Pakistan, one of the main beneficiaries of China's Belt and Road Initiative, indicate that, after a slight reduction in the year following the installation of Huawei's Safe City in the country's major urban centers, violent crime has continued to rise.[34] Kenya, an early African adopter of Huawei's Safe City, experienced a similar trajectory, with crime rates apparently unaffected by the installation of new surveillance technologies in Nairobi and Mombasa.[35]

These failures should not be surprising. The hype surrounding surveillance technologies (as happens for most innovations framed as "disruptive") and the fear provoked by these technologies' Chinese origins have led to some overlooking the fact that every artifact is part of wider networks that profoundly influence its functioning.[36] As much as prior promises of "liberation technologies" did not free the world from abuse and dictators, so new surveillance technologies risk faltering and failing when inserted into very different contexts from their origins. The "successes" recorded by Safe City and Smart City when deployed in China only partly occurred due to Huawei and ZTE's technological solutions. They also depend on larger networks shaped by norms, bureaucracies, and policies that significantly affect the outcomes these technologies produce.

Also, in this case, the excessive focus on the perceived threat posed by China's expansion into new markets and sectors, and the little interest in understanding the distinctive technopolitical trajectories characterizing different African states, has led to overestimating the ability of new technological solutions to produce transformative effects, for better or for worse. More than loud cries about digital panopticons descending onto African citizens, empirical and extensive investigations of actual deployments of surveillance systems should guide both expert and popular responses to these increasingly pervasive technologies, providing tools to distinguish between impending risks and hyped phobias.

The Mirage of a Sovereign and Bordered Internet

One of the most recent fears around China's global expansion in the digital space is its intention to fragment the internet. Unlike the "digital authoritarianism" hypothesis, based on the assumption that an authoritarian regime—China—would seek to export its model abroad, of which there is little empirical evidence[37] or trace in public statements by Chinese authorities, the "digital sovereignty" hypothesis is corroborated by the Chinese government's very assertive moves to theorize and promote the concept of a bordered and sovereign internet as more fitting for countries in the Global South.

The first of these moves was the publication, in 2010, of the "White Paper on the Internet in China," as the first comprehensive manifesto detailing China's own vision of the internet. As researcher Johan Lagerkvist noted, until then, "there was no single cardinal document that specified an official ideology of what exactly the Chinese Internet should be about—apart from scattered, amorphous and hazy ideas of its being harmonious and protecting the psychology of the Chinese youth from overseas hostile values and forces."[38] The White Paper not only aimed to stress the Chinese government's right to build its own version of the internet but was also informed by the ambition of initiating a broader process to legitimize a new internet doctrine to make the Chinese case less exceptional. As the document stressed, broadening the focus beyond China: "Though connected, the Internet of various countries belongs to different sovereignties." The importance of respecting distinctions among countries and their political and cultural institutions was made even clearer when addressing particularly sensitive issues, including internet security.

> National situations and cultural traditions differ among countries, and so concern about Internet security also differs. Concerns about Internet security of different countries should be fully respected. We should seek common ground and reserve differences, promote development through exchanges, and jointly protect international Internet security.

The White Paper on the internet in China created the foundations to build a broader and more ambitious strategy and progressively transform China from a "norm taker" to a "norm shaper" and, possibly, a "norm maker" in the long term.[39] This strategy has significantly strengthened since Xi Jinping became president in 2012 and has evolved along two distinct, but related, trajectories.

A first component of this strategy has consisted in the Chinese government's increasingly decisive participation in debates and fora on internet governance and standard-setting. Representation at the Internet Engineering Task Force

(IETF)—the institution mandated to produce technical documents and standards related to the design, use, and management of the internet—has been dramatically stepped up. Similarly, Chinese representation has increased dramatically in formal standard-setting organizations, including the International Telecommunication Unit (ITU) and International Telecommunication Union Telecommunication Standardization Sector (ITU-T), where China has been gaining secretarial positions in an increasing number of technical committees and subcommittees.[40] This new phase of international exposure in charting the future of the global internet has also been characterized by a push to shift from the multistakeholder approach favored by the United States to a multilateral approach to internet governance.

The second component of the strategy to assert a Chinese vision of a sovereign internet has consisted in consolidating parallel venues of like-minded states, all seeking to reduce external interference in the shaping of their national information societies. The most notable initiatives originated in the context of the Shanghai Cooperation Organization (SCO), a forum established in 2001 to explore normative and legal consensus around security threats like terrorism, separatism, and extremism, and counting Kazakhstan, Kyrgyzstan, Russia, Tajikistan, Uzbekistan, India, and Pakistan as its members. In 2011, China, Russia, Tajikistan, and Uzbekistan elaborated a document—the "International Code of Conduct for Information Security"—detailing their vision for a set of global standards to regulate the protection of national information spaces and persecute those seeking to penetrate into national information and network infrastructure. Another key venue to collectively advance the ideal of a sovereign internet was created by the Cyberspace Administration of China in 2014 in Wuzhen, near Hangzhou, under the name of "World Internet Conference" (WIC). In 2015, the WIC was opened by President Xi Jinping, who used assertive tones to elaborate on the Chinese government's internet doctrine. He made it clear that "no country should pursue cyber hegemony, interfere in other countries' internal affairs or engage in, connive at or support cyber activities that undermine other countries' national security" and that all should "respect the right of individual countries to independently choose their own path of cyber development, model of cyber regulation and Internet public policies, and participate in international cyberspace governance on an equal footing."[41]

The promises of internet sovereignty may indeed appeal to authoritarian regimes that have struggled to translate their capacity to control the press, radio, and television into the digital sphere. In Africa, only a few countries have sought to incorporate some of their premises into formal legislation or have taken proactive measures to design tools that could translate them into a concrete form. Ethiopia is one of these countries. In 2020, it passed a new law introducing harsh measures against hate speech and disinformation that could threaten "social harmony, political stability, national unity, human dignity, diversity and equality."[42]

A year later, after Facebook deactivated some pro-government accounts, Ethiopia's Information Network Security Agency (INSA) declared it would begin developing its own social media platform to rival Facebook, Twitter (now X), and WhatsApp.[43]

In most cases, African governments—especially if led by authoritarian rulers who have served many terms in office, such as Paul Biya in Cameroon or Yoweri Museveni in Uganda[44]—have asserted their sovereign rights over digital communication in a cruder fashion through internet shutdowns. China has never been mentioned as an inspiration, and authorities have tended to invoke the need to guarantee security and peace to justify network disruptions. However, the defiance that has characterized these actions indicates how China's doctrine that "concerns about Internet security of different countries should be fully respected," no matter what these concerns are, seems to have gained traction. Measures once considered extreme and disproportionate have progressively become the new normal. While at the beginning of the global internet, countries censoring online communication tended to deny doing so, or sought to present disruptions as technical failures for fear of becoming the target of international condemnation,[45] the same countries are now implementing far more abusive and disruptive measures and getting away with it.

Do these developments indicate that the threats of a bifurcated, fractured internet are becoming real? Is China winning the battle to assert a conception of sovereign, state-dominated digital spaces? As in the case of infrastructures discussed above, it depends on the perspective adopted to examine these processes, on the attention paid to understand how ideas of internet sovereignty resonate with different components of African societies, and on the choice to locate recent developments within shorter or longer historical trajectories.

The idea of digital sovereignty is indeed attractive for many governments. As David Fischer suggested, "the fact that digital sovereignty is simultaneously vague and elusive and at the same time charged with idealist imaginaries of political autonomy repurposes the theoretical term into a vessel that governments and other actors attempt to fill with meaning according to their needs."[46]

Enforcing internet sovereignty, however, is a more complex endeavor when it comes to translating the abstract concept into concrete measures and tools. Scholar and author Milton Mueller has offered detailed explanations of how the fragmented internet is more akin to a hyped threat used in rhetorical battles than a project that can find actualization on a large scale.[47] A full control of the national digital space, in a Westphalian sense, would require establishing "technical incompatibilities between their part of the Internet and the other part(s); and the incompatibilities must be both sustainable over a significant period of time and able to obstruct communications among parties that are willing to communicate."[48] This is a route very few states would embark on as it would annihilate the network effects and benefits the internet has brought to most economies worldwide. Below this extreme level of separation, however, different degrees of alignment between digital and national boundaries are possible and have been enacted by democracies and autocracies alike. It is beyond the scope of this chapter to delve into different taxonomies of political and technical alignments, and there is now ample literature detailing the complex interactions between political wills, technical standards, and governance structures.[49] I want to focus instead on another aspect or, rather, a paradox of internet sovereignty that is seldom discussed but is particularly relevant when examined from an African perspective. What does internet sovereignty mean for postcolonies? What is its place in the long history of liberation from colonial rule and other forms of external interference in the politics and economics of the African continent?

China has pitched the idea of internet sovereignty as particularly appealing for countries in the Global South, presenting it as a response to US hegemony and interference and to power imbalances in institutions mandated to shape and regulate the internet. In developing the concept of internet sovereignty, China has, paradoxically, appropriated and accepted a Westphalian definition of the state—one forged in the history of wars between European powers—even when this move was presented as a form of resistance to Western influence. For China, this move can be interpreted, in realistic terms, as opportunistic and self-interested, a way to exploit widely accepted principles on the international stage—territoriality and noninterference—to affirm its own right to shape a distinctive model of the internet within its borders.

The same move takes on different connotations on African soil. The history of how the model of the modern state as the "Westphalian state" took roots in Africa contains significantly more violent connotations.[50] Africa's borders were drawn by colonial powers violating demographic, ethnographic, and topographic factors, mostly to prevent the conflicts that could have erupted between European countries scrambling for new territories.[51] If colonial borders were kept, rather than redrawn, by liberation movements in the 1960s, it was to avoid plunging the continent into war immediately after independence. As Nigerian Prime Minister Abubakar Tafawa Balewa remarked during one of the first conferences convening the leaders of African independent states in 1963:

> On the problem of boundaries, our view is that although in the past some of these were created artificially by the European powers, which even went so far as to split some communities into three parts, each administered by a different colonial power, nevertheless those boundaries should be respected and, in the interest of peace, must remain the recognised boundaries. [. . .] Any attempt, on the part of any African country to disregard this fact might bring trouble to this continent.[52]

Since Balewa's speech, two different conceptions of sovereignty have coexisted and competed on the continent. One, Pan-Africanism, sought not only to capitalize on the peaceful coexistence among newly created independent states but also to extend the spirit that informed liberation struggles to chart new avenues for a more united Africa. In this view, accepting to replicate the sovereign conception of the nation-state enforced by colonial powers would amount to a form of regression, and only attempts to create a multinational polity could have been interpreted as real progress.[53] The other conception, which prevailed in the end, strengthening borders, rather than making them more fluid, is critically described by historian Achille Mbembe. As he stressed, what replaced the initial commitment to avoid conflict among liberated states, and thus maintain colonial boundaries, was a "fetishization" of the concept of nation-state. To justify controls and restrains on the mobility of people and information, African governments "borrowed concepts from the Western lexicon such as 'national interest,' 'risks,' 'threats,' or 'national security' [which] refer to a philosophy of movement and a philosophy of space entirely predicated on the existence of an enemy in a world of hostility" disregarding "our own long held traditions of flexible, networked sovereignty."[54]

Digital media, praised—especially in the initial phases of their global diffusion—for its ability to disregard physical and political boundaries, was interpreted by a few African innovators and intellectuals as an opportunity to bring some of the communities split by colonial borders closer together, even to recreate and reinterpret modes of being and communicating that had characterized precolonial Africa. As Achille Mbembe[55] wrote, describing the types of mobility that had prevailed in the continent before colonization in a language that deeply resonates with the one commonly used to refer to digital media and their modes of connection:

> Precolonial Africa might not have been a borderless world. But where they existed borders were always porous and permeable. [. . .] Networks, flows and crossroads were more important than borders. What mattered the most was the extent to which flows intersected with other flows.

At a concrete level, in September 2006, Celtel, the telecommunication company funded by Sudanese engineer Mo Ibrahim, launched an initiative, under the brand of "One Network," which sought to harness the power of some of these flows to intersect, once again, across borders. Establishing the world's first borderless mobile network, Celtel's scheme allowed users in Kenya, Uganda, and Tanzania to make transboundary calls at local rates, free of roaming charges.[56] Defying stereotypes of Africa as condemned to catch up with or adopt technical and normative innovations, African citizens were the first to experience the power of mobile technology to draw new boundaries to encompass preexisting or imagined communities (for comparison, it took another ten years for the European Union to end roaming charges among Member States).[57] And yet, despite its symbolic potential, One Network failed to inspire a critical mass of African leaders and entrepreneurs to more assertively experiment with similar forms of borderless communication.

Imageries of networked sovereignty, to date, appear more aspirational than able to inspire concrete avenues to unite African communities across borders. This does not mean, however, that critical reflections and contestations of the idea of sovereignty, as rooted in the history of colonialism and liberation in Africa, should be excluded from debates on the future of the internet. The deeper appreciation of the contradictions of the concept of internet sovereignty, when examined from Africa, could, at least, offer a new type of critique to claims that a bordered internet would benefit the Global South, whether they come from African or Chinese leaders.

Conclusion

This chapter has sketched possible avenues to repackage the global competition for the future of the internet, as perceived in and from Africa. Accusations traded between the United States and China on self-asserted and real intents in expanding their spheres of influence on the continent have clogged avenues for more constructive conversations on the emergence of alternative conceptions of the information society. Alongside the exhortation for greater attention to other forms of critique emerging from the South, the chapter has also sought to illustrate how more empirically grounded and inclusive research may ultimately reduce the anxieties that have emerged from a principled, rather than factual, interpretation of China's inroads into African digital spaces.

Notes

1 Khwezi Nkwanyana, "China's AI Deployment in Africa Poses Risks to Security and Sovereignty," *The Strategist*, May 5, 2021, available online: https://www.aspistrategist.org.au/chinas-ai-deployment-in-africa-poses-risks-to-security-and-sovereignty/; Yomi Kazeem, "Amid Mixed Messages and Inconsistency China Is the Only Constant of Trump's US-Africa Policy," Quartz (blog), February 19, 2020, available online: https://qz.com/africa/1804762/pompeos-africa-visit-is-about-trumps-china-obsession/.

2 Larry Diamond, "Liberation Technology," *Journal of Democracy* 21, no. 3 (2010): 69–83.

3 Matthew S. Erie and Thomas Streinz, "The Beijing Effect: China's Digital Silk Road as Transnational Data Governance," *NYU Journal of International Law and Politics* 54 (2021): 1; Iginio Gagliardone, *China, Africa, and the Future of the Internet* (Zed Books, 2019); Steven Feldstein, "The Global Expansion of AI Surveillance," Carnegie Endowment, 2019, available online: https://carnegieendowment.org/2019/09/17/global-expansion-of-ai-surveillance-pub-79847; Arhan S. Ertan and H. Akın Ünver, "Politics of Artificial Intelligence Adoption: Unpacking the Regime Type Debate," Available at SSRN 4024365, 2022.

4 Gagliardone, *China, Africa, and the Future of the Internet*; Erie and Streinz, "The Beijing Effect"; Feldstein, "The Global Expansion of AI Surveillance"; Alvaro Artigas, "Surveillance, Smart Technologies and the Development of Safe City Solutions: The Case of Chinese ICT Forms and Their International Expansion to Emerging Markets" (Institut Barcelona d'Estudis Internacionals, 2017); Samuel Woodhams, "China, Africa, and the Private Surveillance Industry," *Georgetown Journal of International Affairs* 21 (2020): 158–65.

5 Issie Lapowsky, "The Scramble to Fix Biden's Plan for the Future of the Internet," Protocol, December 4, 2021, available online: https://www.protocol.com/policy/white-house-alliance-future-internet.

6 Anita Powell, "'Build Back Better World' to Launch 50 Projects, White House Says," VOA, 2021, available online: https://www.voanews.com/a/build-back-better-world-to-launch-50-projects-white-house-says/6307433.html.

7 Lapowsky, "The Scramble to Fix Biden's Plan for the Future of the Internet."

8 Ross Andersen, "China's Artificial Intelligence Surveillance State Goes Global," 2020, available online: https://www.theatlantic.com/magazine/archive/2020/09/china-ai-surveillance/614197/.

9 Willem H. Gravett, "Digital Coloniser? China and Artificial Intelligence in Africa," *Survival* 62, no. 6 (2020): 153–78.

10 Ngai-Ling Sum, "The Intertwined Geopolitics and Geoeconomics of Hopes/Fears: China's Triple Economic Bubbles and the 'One Belt One Road' Imaginary," *Territory, Politics, Governance* 7, no. 4 (2019): 528–52.

11 Xin Zhang, "Chinese Capitalism and the Maritime Silk Road: A World-Systems Perspective," *Geopolitics* 22, no. 2 (2017): 310–31.

12 Seth Schindler and J. Miguel Kanai, "Getting the Territory Right: Infrastructure-Led Development and the Re-Emergence of Spatial Planning Strategies," *Regional Studies* 55, no. 1 (2021): 40–51.

13 Brian Larkin, "The Politics and Poetics of Infrastructure," *Annual Review of Anthropology* 42 (2013): 335.

14 Fellow of the Forum for Social Studies, Addis Ababa, Ethiopia, May 15, 2015.

15 Tim Zajontz and Ian Taylor, "Capitalism and Africa's (Infra) Structural Dependency: A Story of Spatial Fixes and Accumulation by Dispossession," in *Africa and the Global System of Capital Accumulation*, ed. Emmanuel Oritsejafor and Allan Cooper (Routledge, 2021), 190–213.

16 Powell, "'Build Back Better World' to Launch 50 Projects, White House Says."

17 Lapowsky, "The Scramble to Fix Biden's Plan for the Future of the Internet."

18 Kari Paul and Dan Milmo, "Facebook Putting Profit Before Public Good, Says Whistleblower Frances Haugen," *The Guardian*, 2021; Henry Farrell and Martha Finnemore, "The End of Hypocrisy: American Foreign Policy in the Age of Leaks," *Foreign Affairs* 92, no. 6 (2013): 22–6; Mercedes Bunz, "As You Like It: Critique in the Era of an Affirmative Discourse," in *Unlike Us Reader: Social Monopolies and Their Alternatives*, ed. Geert Lovink (Institute of Network Cultures, 2013), 137–45; Harry Davies et al., "Uber Broke Laws, Duped Police and Secretly Lobbied Governments, Leak Reveals," *The Guardian*, July 11, 2022, sec. News, available online: https://www.theguardian.com/news/2022/jul/10/uber-files-leak-reveals-global-lobbying-campaign.

19 Wangui Kimari and Henrik Ernstson, "Imperial Remains and Imperial Invitations: Centering Race within the Contemporary Large-Scale Infrastructures of East Africa," *Antipode* 52, no. 3 (2020): 829.

20 Ibid.

21 Ibid., 837.

22 Ibid.

23 Zajontz and Taylor, "Capitalism and Africa's (Infra) Structural Dependency."

24 Miriam Driessen, "The African Bill: Chinese Struggles with Development Assistance," *Anthropology Today* 31, no. 1 (2015): 3.

25 See, for example, James C. Scott, *Seeing Like a State: How Certain Schemes to Improve the Human Condition Have Failed* (Yale University Press, 1998).

26 Driessen, "The African Bill," 4.

27 Andersen, "China's Artificial Intelligence Surveillance State Goes Global."

28 Iginio Gagliardone, "The Impact of Chinese Tech Provision on Civil Liberties in Africa" (South African Institute for International Affairs, 2020).

29 Artigas, "Surveillance, Smart Technologies and the Development of Safe City Solutions: The Case of Chinese ICT Forms and Their International Expansion to Emerging Markets"; Feldstein, "The Global Expansion of AI Surveillance."

30 Feldstein, "The Global Expansion of AI Surveillance."

31 Jonathan Hillman and Maesea McCalpin, "Watching Huawei's 'Safe Cities'" (Center for Strategic and International Studies, 2019).

32 Artigas, "Surveillance, Smart Technologies and the Development of Safe City Solutions: The Case of Chinese ICT Forms and Their International Expansion to Emerging Markets."

33 Nicole Hao, "Huawei 'Safe City' Systems Are Ineffective, Crime Figures Show," *The Epoch Times*, December 29, 2019, available online: https://www.theepochtimes.com/huawei-safe-cities-are-ineffective-according-to-crime-figures_3187283.html; Sheridan Prasso, "Huawei's Claims That It Makes Cities Safer Mostly Look Like Hype," Bloomberg, November 12, 2019, available online: https://www.bloomberg.com/news/articles/2019-11-12/huawei-s-surveillance-network-claims-face-scrutiny.

34 Hao, "Huawei 'Safe City' Systems Are Ineffective, Crime Figures Show."

35 Prasso, "Huawei's Claims That It Makes Cities Safer Mostly Look Like Hype."

36 Iginio Gagliardone, *The Politics of Technology in Africa* (Cambridge University Press, 2016).

37 Gagliardone, *China, Africa, and the Future of the Internet*; Ertan and Ünver, "Politics of Artificial Intelligence Adoption."

38 Johan Lagerkvist, *After the Internet, Before Democracy: Competing Norms in Chinese Media and Society* (Peter Lang, 2010), 61, 62.

39 Jinghan Zeng, Tim Stevens, and Yaru Chen, "China's Solution to Global Cyber Governance: Unpacking the Domestic Discourse of 'Internet Sovereignty,'" *Politics & Policy* 45, no. 3 (2017): 432–64; Jinghan Zeng and Shaun Breslin, "China's 'New Type of Great Power Relations': A G2 with Chinese Characteristics?," *International Affairs* 92, no. 4 (2016): 773–94.

40 Sorina Teleanu, "The Geopolitics of Digital Standards: China's Role in Standard-Setting Organisations" (DiPLO, 2021), available online: https://www.diplomacy.edu/wp-content/uploads/2021/12/Geopolitics-of-digital-standards-Dec-2021.pdf.

41 Xi Jinping, "Remarks by H.E. Xi Jinping President of the People's Republic of China at the Opening Ceremony of the Second World Internet Conference," 2015, available online: http://www.fmprc.gov.cn/mfa_eng/wjdt_665385/zyjh_665391/t1327570.shtml.

42 Federal Democratic Republic of Ethiopia, "Hate Speech and Disinformation Prevention and Suppression Proclamation" (Federal Democratic Republic of Ethiopia, 2020).

43 Reuters, "Ethiopia to Build Local Rival to Facebook, Other Platforms," Reuters, August 23, 2021, sec. Media & Telecom, available online: https://www.reuters.com/business/media-telecom/ethiopia-build-local-rival-facebook-other-platforms-2021-08-23/.

44 CIPESA, "Despots and Disruptions: Five Dimensions of Internet Shutdowns in Africa" (Kampala, 2019).

45 Ronald Deibert et al., *Access Denied: The Practice and Policy of Global Internet Filtering* (MIT Press, 2008).

46 David Fischer, "The Digital Sovereignty Trick: Why the Sovereignty Discourse Fails to Address the Structural Dependencies of Digital Capitalism in the Global South," *Zeitschrift für Politikwissenschaft* 32 (2022): 3.

47 Milton Mueller, *Will the Internet Fragment?: Sovereignty, Globalization and Cyberspace* (John Wiley, 2017).

48 Ibid., 42.

49 Laura DeNardis, "Hidden Levers of Internet Control: An Infrastructure-Based Theory of Internet Governance," *Information, Communication & Society* 15, no. 5 (2012): 720–38; Laura DeNardis and Francesca Musiani, "Governance by Infrastructure," in *The Turn to Infrastructure in Internet Governance,* ed. Francesca Musiani, Derrick L. Cogburn, Laura DeNardis, and Nanette S. Levinson (Springer, 2016), 3–21; Mueller, *Will the Internet Fragment?*

50 Navnita Chadha Behera, "State and Sovereignty," in *International Relations from the Global South: Worlds of Difference*, ed. Arlene Tickner, David Blaney, and Inanna Hamati-Ataya (Routledge, 2020), 139–60.

51 Jeffrey Herbst, "The Creation and Maintenance of National Boundaries in Africa," *International Organization* 43, no. 4 (1989): 673–92.

52 Abubakar Tafawa Balewa, as cited in Ajala Adekunle, "The Nature of African Boundaries," *Africa Spectrum* 18, no. 2 (1983): 177–89.

53 Amy Niang, "The International," in *International Relations from the Global South: Worlds of Difference*, ed. Arlene Tickner, David Blaney, and Inanna Hamati-Ataya (Routledge, 2020), 97–114.

54 Achille Mbembe, "Scrap the Borders That Divide Africans," *Mail & Guardian* 17 (2017), available online: https://mg.co.za/article/2017-03-17-00-scrap-the-borders-that-divide-africans/.

55 Ibid., 3.

56 Robert Horvitz and Simon Forge, "A Case Study of ONA—East Africa One Network Area Roaming Initiative" (International Telecommunication Union, 2016), available online: https://www.researchgate.net/publication/336319415_A_Case_Study_of_ONA_-_East_Africa's_One_Network_Area_Roaming_Initiative.

57 Elizabeth Goldberg, "'Better Regulation': European Union Style" (Harvard Kennedy School, 2018).

Bibliography

Ajala, Adekunle. "The Nature of African Boundaries." *Africa Spectrum* 18, no. 2 (1983): 177–89.

Andersen, Ross. "China's Artificial Intelligence Surveillance State Goes Global." *The Atlantic*, 2020. Available online: https://www.theatlantic.com/magazine/archive/2020/09/china-ai-surveillance/614197/.

Artigas, Alvaro. "Surveillance, Smart Technologies and the Development of Safe City Solutions: The Case of Chinese ICT Forms and Their International Expansion to Emerging Markets." Institut Barcelona d'Estudis Internacionals, 2017.

Behera, Navnita Chadha. "State and Sovereignty." In *International Relations from the Global South: Worlds of Difference*, edited by Arlene Tickner, David Blaney, and Inanna Hamati-Ataya. Routledge, 2020.

Bunz, Mercedes. "As You Like It: Critique in the Era of an Affirmative Discourse." In *Unlike Us Reader: Social Monopolies and Their Alternatives*, edited by Geert Lovink. Institute of Network Cultures, 2013.

CIPESA. "Despots and Disruptions. Five Dimensions Shutdowns in Africa." Kampala, 2019.

Davies, Harry, Simon Goodley, Felicity Lawrence, Paul Lewis, Lisa O'Carroll, and Sam Cutler. "Uber Broke Laws, Duped Police and Secretly Lobbied Governments, Leak Reveals." *The Guardian*, July 11, 2022, sec. News. Available online: https://www.theguardian.com/news/2022/jul/10/uber-files-leak-reveals-global-lobbying-campaign.

Deibert, Ronald, John Palfrey, Rafal Rohozinski, Jonathan Zittrain, and Janice Gross Stein. *Access Denied: The Practice and Policy of Global Internet Filtering*. MIT Press, 2008.

DeNardis, Laura. "Hidden Levers of Internet Control: An Infrastructure-Based Theory of Internet Governance." *Information, Communication & Society* 15, no. 5 (2012): 720–38.

DeNardis, Laura, and Francesca Musiani. "Governance by Infrastructure." In *The Turn to Infrastructure in Internet Governance*, edited by Francesca Musiani, Derrick L. Cogburn, Laura DeNardis, and Nanette S. Levinson. Springer, 2016.

Diamond, Larry. "Liberation Technology." *Journal of Democracy* 21, no. 3 (2010): 69–83.

Driessen, Miriam. "The African Bill: Chinese Struggles with Development Assistance." *Anthropology Today* 31, no. 1 (2015): 3–7.

Erie, Matthew S., and Thomas Streinz. "The Beijing Effect: China's Digital Silk Road as Transnational Data Governance." *NYU Journal of International Law and Politics* 54 (2021): 1.

Ertan, Arhan S., and H. Akın Ünver. "Politics of Artificial Intelligence Adoption: Unpacking the Regime Type Debate." Available at SSRN 4024365, 2022. Available online: https://papers.ssrn.com/sol3/papers.cfm?abstract_id=4024365.

Farrell, Henry, and Martha Finnemore. "The End of Hypocrisy: American Foreign Policy in the Age of Leaks." *Foreign Affairs* 92, no. 6 (2013): 22–6.

Federal Democratic Republic of Ethiopia. "Hate Speech and Disinformation Prevention and Suppression Proclamation." Federal Democratic Republic of Ethiopia, 2020. Available online: https://justice.gov.et/en/law/hate-speech-and-disinformation-prevention-and-suppression-proclamation/.

Feldstein, Steven. "The Global Expansion of AI Surveillance." Carnegie Endowment, 2019. Available online: https://carnegieendowment.org/research/2019/09/the-global-expansion-of-ai-surveillance.

Fellow of the Forum for Social Studies. Addis Ababa, Ethiopia, May 15, 2015. Available online: https://fss-ethiopia.org.

Fischer, David. "The Digital Sovereignty Trick: Why the Sovereignty Discourse Fails to Address the Structural Dependencies of Digital Capitalism in the Global South." *Zeitschrift für Politikwissenschaft* 32 (2022): 1–20.

Gagliardone, Iginio. *China, Africa, and the Future of the Internet*. Zed Books, 2019.

Gagliardone, Iginio. "The Impact of Chinese Tech Provision on Civil Liberties in Africa." South African Institute for *International Affairs*, 2020.

Gagliardone, Iginio. *The Politics of Technology in Africa*. Cambridge University Press, 2016.

Goldberg, Elizabeth. "'Better Regulation': European Union Style." Harvard Kennedy School, 2018.

Gravett, Willem H. "Digital Coloniser? China and Artificial Intelligence in Africa." *Survival* 62, no. 6 (2020): 153–78.

Hao, Nicole. "Huawei 'Safe City' Systems Are Ineffective, Crime Figures Show." *The Epoch Times*, December 29, 2019. Available online: https://www.theepochtimes.com/huawei-safe-cities-are-ineffective-according-to-crime-figures_3187283.html.

Herbst, Jeffrey. "The Creation and Maintenance of National Boundaries in Africa." *International Organization* 43, no. 4 (1989): 673–92.

Hillman, Jonathan, and Maesea McCalpin. "Watching Huawei's 'Safe Cities.'" Center for Strategic and International Studies, 2019.

Horvitz, Robert, and Simon Forge. "A Case Study of ONA—East Africa One Network Area Roaming Initiative." International Telecommunication Union, 2016. Available online: https://www.researchgate.net/publication/336319415_A_Case_Study_of_ONA_-_East_Africa's_One_Network_Area_Roaming_Initiative.

Jinping, Xi. "Remarks by H.E. Xi Jinping President of the People's Republic of China at the Opening Ceremony of the Second World Internet Conference." 2015. Available online: http://www.fmprc.gov.cn/mfa_eng/wjdt_665385/zyjh_665391/t1327570.shtml.

Kazeem, Yomi. "Amid Mixed Messages and Inconsistency China Is the Only Constant of Trump's US-Africa Policy." Quartz (blog), February 19, 2020. Available online: https://qz.com/africa/1804762/pompeos-africa-visit-is-about-trumps-china-obsession/.

Kimari, Wangui, and Henrik Ernstson. "Imperial Remains and Imperial Invitations: Centering Race within the Contemporary Large-Scale Infrastructures of East Africa." *Antipode* 52, no. 3 (2020): 825–46.

Lagerkvist, Johan. *After the Internet, before Democracy: Competing Norms in Chinese Media and Society*. Peter Lang, 2010.

Lapowsky, Issie. "The Scramble to Fix Biden's Plan for the Future of the Internet." *Protocol*, December 4, 2021. Available online: https://www.protocol.com/policy/white-house-alliance-future-internet.

Larkin, Brian. "The Politics and Poetics of Infrastructure." *Annual Review of Anthropology* 42 (2013): 327–43.

Mbembe, Achille. "Scrap the Borders That Divide Africans." *Mail & Guardian* 17 (2017). Available online: https://mg.co.za/article/2017-03-17-00-scrap-the-borders-that-divide-africans/.

Mueller, Milton. *Will the Internet Fragment?: Sovereignty, Globalization and Cyberspace*. John Wiley, 2017.

Niang, Amy. "The International." In *International Relations from the Global South: Worlds of Difference*, edited by Arlene Tickner, David Blaney, and Inanna Hamati-Ataya. Routledge, 2020.

Nkwanyana, Khwezi. "China's AI Deployment in Africa Poses Risks to Security and Sovereignty." *The Strategist*, May 5, 2021. Available online: https://www.aspistrategist.org.au/chinas-ai-deployment-in-africa-poses-risks-to-security-and-sovereignty/.

Paul, Kari, and Dan Milmo. "Facebook Putting Profit Before Public Good, Says Whistleblower Frances Haugen." *The Guardian*, 2021.

Powell, Anita. "'Build Back Better World' to Launch 50 Projects, White House Says." VOA, 2021. Available online: https://www.voanews.com/a/build-back-better-world-to-launch-50-projects-white-house-says/6307433.html.

Prasso, Sheridan. "Huawei's Claims That It Makes Cities Safer Mostly Look Like Hype." Bloomberg, November 12, 2019. Available online: https://www.bloomberg.com/news/articles/2019-11-12/huawei-s-surveillance-network-claims-face-scrutiny.

Reuters. "Ethiopia to Build Local Rival to Facebook, Other Platforms." Reuters, August 23, 2021, sec. Media & Telecom. Available online: https://www.reuters.com/business/media-telecom/ethiopia-build-local-rival-facebook-other-platforms-2021-08-23/.

Schindler, Seth, and J. Miguel Kanai. "Getting the Territory Right: Infrastructure-Led Development and the Re-Emergence of Spatial Planning Strategies." *Regional Studies* 55, no. 1 (2021): 40–51.

Scott, James C. *Seeing Like a State: How Certain Schemes to Improve the Human Condition Have Failed*. Yale University Press, 1998.

Sum, Ngai-Ling. "The Intertwined *Geopolitics* and Geoeconomics of Hopes/Fears: China's Triple Economic Bubbles and the 'One Belt One Road' Imaginary." *Territory, Politics, Governance* 7, no. 4 (2019): 528–52.

Teleanu, Sorina. "The *Geopolitics* of Digital Standards: China's Role in Standard-Setting Organisations." DiPLO, 2021. Available online: https://www.diplomacy.edu/wp-content/uploads/2021/12/*Geopolitics*-of-digital-standards-Dec-2021.pdf.

Woodhams, Samuel. "China, Africa, and the Private Surveillance Industry." *Georgetown Journal of International Affairs* 21 (2020): 158–65.

Zajontz, Tim, and Ian Taylor. "Capitalism and Africa's (Infra) Structural Dependency: A Story of Spatial Fixes and Accumulation by Dispossession." In *Africa and the Global System of Capital Accumulation*, edited by Emmanuel Oritsejafor and Allan Cooper. Routledge, 2021.

Zeng, Jinghan, and Shaun Breslin. "China's 'New Type of Great Power Relations': A G2 with Chinese Characteristics?" *International Affairs* 92, no. 4 (2016): 773–94.

Zeng, Jinghan, Tim Stevens, and Yaru Chen. "China's Solution to Global Cyber Governance: Unpacking the Domestic Discourse of 'Internet Sovereignty.'" *Politics & Policy* 45, no. 3 (2017): 432–64.

Zhang, Xin. "Chinese Capitalism and the Maritime Silk Road: A World-Systems Perspective." *Geopolitics* 22, no. 2 (2017): 310–31.

14
WHEN ROBOT BOSSES ARE ALGORITHMS OF SUSPICION

Lilly Irani

Introduction

Platform workers, for whom jobs might be a lifeline, could wake up one day to find themselves cut off from work without notice. The reasons might be a software glitch, a change of address, or myriad others, as this chapter's analysis will reveal. For those workers brave or stubborn enough to contest it, they may be met by silence from platform technical support. They may be told that there is nothing the platform can do. Or, if they are lucky, the platform may investigate their case and determine their account was suspended in error. In those cases of repair, companies have not redressed their error by restoring earnings that workers lost when they were shut out of their accounts. Turkopticon, a platform worker advocacy project, assists many workers across the globe in this situation. The consequences are lost access to livelihood, already earned wages trapped in platform accounts, and a deep sense of frustration and unfairness. Workers report experiences of automated firing, wage theft, and platform silence on myriad global gig work platforms, including Uber, Lyft, DoorDash, Zomato, Ola, and, the focus of this chapter, Amazon Mechanical Turk (AMT).

This chapter builds on scholarship on automated shop floor management, a problem that includes but is also broader than platforms. Legal scholar Jeremias Adams-Prassl has examined how the introduction of algorithms into employer functions of hiring, monitoring, and firing concentrates managerial control over work while also making responsibility and accountability difficult to track.[1] Labor scholar Nantina Vgontzas explains how algorithms in Amazon's warehouse operations are central to controlling workers. They do this through surveillance and control of rates that produce gendered and racialized hierarchies in the workplace. The algorithms, engineered by Amazon's own tech workers, also direct packing and shipping to work around sites of work slowdowns or strikes, making it more difficult for workers to engage in effective, concerted collective action.[2] More broadly, wide-ranging scholarship on gig work has debated platforms' forms of control through reputation systems, gamification, and debt, as well as platforms' strategies of legal and, especially, employment (mis) classification.[3]

This chapter contributes to these debates by drawing attention to a form of algorithmic control and wage theft through account suspensions on one such platform, AMT. Common digital rights policy frameworks give platforms a wide berth to suspend worker and consumer rights under laws that exempt "fraud detection" activities from oversight and transparency requirements. In many jurisdictions, workers are also (mis)classified as independent contractors, lacking rights of recourse in cases of firing. Finally, Amazon's algorithms—marketed to other companies as Amazon Fraud Detector—have wider implications, not only for its platform workers but also to small businesses and consumers on its wider website and to internet users at large.[4] As goes Amazon, so goes the world.

This chapter draws on the experiences and insights of AMT workers faced with the problem of account suspensions, analyses of how AMT's interfaces and policies structure and automate employer–worker interactions, and analyses of patents that give clues as to Amazon's black-box fraud-detection algorithms, unleashed on workers at scale. I show legitimate reasons why workers might get caught up by Amazon's algorithms, a computational data process with no social or political knowledge of workers' lives. The chapter concludes by arguing that existing digital rights frameworks must be revised to give workers rights and protections against platforms' algorithmic forms of suspicion. I offer preliminary suggestions to this end.

This is a work of engaged scholarship, accountable to workers on the frontlines experiencing these workplace issues at the intersection of policies, practices, and algorithms. The research is particularly indebted to the work of AMT workers organizing as Turkopticon, a project that advocates better working conditions for workers. An important part of their work is assisting AMT workers who are contesting account suspensions. Workers' problems and insights motivate and inform this chapter's inquiry. Workers' comments on this chapter and conversations have informed its development. This work is informed by methods such as Community-Based Participatory Research and Design Justice.[5] From these methods, I adopt accountability to communities and a respect for communities' expertise in many circumstances that affect their lives.

Policy, practices, and design are mutually constitutive in complex systems design.[6] Workers encountering these problems propose solutions that might require shifts in one or more of these three aspects. Solutions to the problem of account suspensions likely require changes in intermediary (e.g., platform, company, and employer) practices, including algorithm design processes, how employers (e.g., platforms) employ algorithmic judgments, and how they prevent or repair unwarranted harm to workers from those judgments. Solutions may also require changes to the algorithms themselves, the datasets on which the algorithms are trained, or the ways in which outputs are applied. Finally, policy environments set the conditions in which companies configure these algorithmic processes, create risks for workers, and distribute the costs of those risks. This chapter analyzes AMT's fraud practices as coconstituted by organizational practices, algorithms, and a permissive legal environment that allows algorithmic managers a wide berth to opaquely regulate workers without worker redress.

AMT: Classifying Cultural Data for Artificial Intelligence

AMT is a data work marketplace that powers machine learning (ML) and artificial intelligence (AI) pipelines across the tech industry.[7] Amazon launched AMT in 2006 to allow programmers to issue data processing calls directly from their computer code. Rather than other code answering the calls, thousands of workers wait at their computers, ready to perform cognitive piecework on demand. The system, and systems like it, are critical to the production of ML and AI.

AMT workers choose from tasks such as transcription, content moderation, and image classification, getting paid per piece of data processed. They categorize and classify data so that ML algorithms can learn to approximate Turkers' judgments (evaluations made by crowd workers). Sometimes, the workers help train AI. Other times, they make up for AI's shortcomings. A company that scans customer receipts into budget software, for example, would send the faded or irregular receipts that confused its algorithms to AMT workers to transcribe and enter into the software. AMT workers may also participate in social science experiments and data gathering as paid participants. AMT workers, in short, perform those tasks of cultural judgment they learn to perform through a lifetime of cognitive and cultural development.

Amazon first patented the system in 2007 to help organize products from different sellers on Amazon's marketplace.[8] Engineers faced a problem: They had data, including pictures and text, about products from different merchants to display on their websites. A stream of products uploaded by merchants of, say, pens may not have a standardized identification number. For example, are products titled Lamy Safari, Lamy Safari Pen, Lamy Safari Fountain Pen, and Lamy Fountain Pen Cartridge the same product? Computers cannot tell without human interaction. A person familiar with fountain pens might easily say that the first three are names for the same thing, but the last is a different kind of object, even though each phrase differs from the next by only one word. So, Amazon's engineers had a problem. How could they automate the process of creating just one page for a product and linking to different merchants that offer the product but describe it in varying ways?

This kind of problem is one of organizing cultural data—data that contains cultural categories produced and changed by people as they interact through language and symbols.[9] AI, ML, and platform content moderation are all examples of attempts to automate at least part of the process of organizing, filtering, and responding to cultural data. The engineer's goal is to extract correct categorizations from workers to train ML or substitute for it when it fails. Just as a lot of work goes into quantifying and scaling the messy world so it can be represented statistically, a lot of work also goes into both producing correctly classified datasets to produce these models and correcting the answers of models when they fail. Correct here is employers who enforce dominant culture definitions and conventions through their task design and criteria.[10]

On AMT, this work is completed by over 120,000 registered workers, though only 30,000 were active in a given month, according to a 2020 study.[11] A 2016 International Labour Organization (ILO) study found that 45.2 percent of US and 90.7 percent of Indian AMT workers had college or postgraduate degrees, belying assumptions that workers on the platform lacked sufficient education to gain higher-paying work. The ILO study found that almost 85 percent of workers were based in the United States, 15 percent were from India, and a small percentage were from other countries. Workers, the ILO found, came to the platform for many reasons, including complementing pay from other jobs, combining work with child- or eldercare, and earning a living with a disability.[12]

Imagining Workers as "Bad Actors"

Employers outsourcing data processing work to the AMT platform create batches of tasks, called "human intelligence tasks," or "HITs," in Amazon parlance. HITs are web-based forms, hosted on Amazon's platform, which specify an information task and allow workers to input a response. Tasks include structuring unstructured data (e.g., entering a given web page into an employer's structured form fields), transcribing snippets of audio, and labeling an image (e.g., as pornography or violating the given Terms of Service). Employers define the structure of the data that workers must input, create instructions, specify the pool of information that must be processed, and set a price.

The employer then defines criteria that candidate workers must meet to work on the task. These criteria include the worker's "approval rating" (the percentage of tasks the worker has performed that employers have approved and, by consequence, paid for), the worker's self-reported country, and whether the worker has completed certain skill-specific qualification exams offered on the platform. This filter approach to choosing workers, as compared to more individualized evaluation and selection, allows employers to request work from thousands of temporary workers in a matter of hours.

One consequence of seeing people at scale has been that engineers imagine a world of "customers" and "bad actors." In their public writings to one another, engineers worry about two kinds of bad actors: workers using scripts to generate random answers and hoping to get away with it and workers not competent in the cultural categories specified by requesters.[13] Workers might also produce "errors" because of interface design, exhaustion, undesirable interpretations, or simply by accident. AMT's restrictive interface prevents employers from knowing the difference between good faith errors, good faith cultural mistranslation, and bad faith "spam" work in many cases.

The language of bad actors reflects a wider culture of security beyond AMT. It is common for large computer system operators, from corporations to the military, to operate in an imaginative geography of "good" and "bad actors." In such a world, engineers often see themselves in warfare with bad actors trying to "game the system." The more bad actors know about how the system operates, the more they can game it, or so the "security by obscurity" story goes. Conversely, engineers charged with protecting systems use the data available to them to identify and block bad actors from accessing the system. In a world of platforms made into a cybersecurity battleground, collateral damage is common.

In 2018, the "bot scare" erupted in the world of AMT workers and employers, illustrating how employers imagine mundane workplace challenges through this "bad actor" lens. The scare began when a graduate student posted to a Facebook group of other AMT employers, observing that he was seeing more surveys with nonsense answers and respondents with identical locations. By the end of the week, researchers all over the internet were reporting similar concerns, fearing that their published research papers had analyzed spurious data produced by automated scripts and the workers inappropriately using them. Crowdsourcing research firm CloudResearch produced a study involving a range of tasks meant to discern whether answers were produced through automation or human input.[14] They reported that odd results were not bots at all but rather workers who performed well on certain questions and poorly on others. These workers, often in South Asia, performed worse on certain kinds of tasks not designed with their capabilities in mind but actually performed better than US workers on tasks geared toward their cultural knowledge. The "bot scare" unfolded based on racialized stereotypes of Asian workers as "lower quality." Requesters' racist panic about fraudulent workers, in fact, masked their lack of awareness of who their workers were, what their skills were, and what tasks they might be suited to. Instead of seeking an understanding with workers, engineers design algorithms to automate trust.

They do this both at the scale of assessing work products, or HIT results, and also at the scale of assessing workers.

How Engineers Assess Work Products

Engineer–employers need to authenticate answers from untrusted workers to common data classification tasks that provide fuel (training sets, algorithmic evaluations) for ML. The engineer can extract answers from workers, but how can they know which answers are correct by their standards? Remember, they are working with large volumes of data work output, so they can't review answers individually. And they are dealing with socially negotiated categories and meanings. *Is this porn or not porn* is only the most extreme example. I have not yet seen an engineer grapple with anthropological questions of whether multiple answers can be "correct" in different contexts.

Engineers have several ways of dealing with this uncertainty. Sometimes, employers will have a trusted "gold standard" dataset of "ground truth" answers—correctly classified cultural symbols. These datasets might be produced and validated by AMT (or similar) workers or acquired from trusted projects, labs, or other public datasets.[15] They can use this gold standard to test workers, slipping in tasks with known correct answers into a stream of tasks with unknown correct answers. Another strategy, not only detailed in a patent but also commonly discussed by engineers, can be summarized as "the most plural judgements."[16] This can mean simply assigning several workers the same task and using a majority vote to decide on the "true" answer.

With both the "gold standard" test and the "plurality agreement" test, engineers face a trade-off: the more gold standard test tasks or duplicated tasks, the greater the certainty that the workers giving the correct answers are actually trustworthy, rather than lucky. But the more test tasks employers pay for, the greater the "human capital investment."[17] In patents and trade show presentations alike, engineers treat the confidence level needed in a worker as a kind of knob that can be dialed up or down, adding more or less information about workers.[18] This additional information can come from testing workers or gathering other information about them, such as through surveillance. I will return to the latter.

How Engineers Assess Workers

Assessing human *judgments* can be a lot of extra work for engineers, who have to put out multiple instances of a task, compare the answers, and figure out which workers to distrust or even blacklist. To reduce this work, Amazon has developed a program it calls "Masters." Amazon promotes Masters workers as trusted producers of high-quality work and charges a premium for them. Masters workers do not earn a higher wage per task, but they get exclusive access to a large stream of work. Amazon makes Masters workers a default for employers setting up tasks on the platform.

Workers find the Masters designation puzzling and frustrating. There is no application process or clarity about the criteria to achieve this. You wake up one day and find out you've been chosen as a Master. On forums, workers will talk to each other to compare their statistics and try to decode why some get the designation and some do not. Excellent performance by the simple statistics workers get on the platform—the percentage of approved work tasks and the number of tasks they've done—does not seem to predict getting the designation. What is interesting here, though, is that Amazon has developed a meritocracy among workers, and its mechanisms are intentionally opaque, likely to prevent gaming by those imagined bad actors. (This is a world in which studying for the test is considered cheating.)

A 2011 Amazon patent holds some clues. The patent suggests that Amazon may calculate a "judge error rate" or confidence rating it assigns to workers behind the scenes.[19] Amazon has an advantage over engineer–employers in that it can maintain a record of the workers' error rates across their whole work history on the platform, across all employers. The patent suggests that Amazon, like the engineers I described, might use the kinds of gold standard and plurality techniques I described to evaluate "judges." The patent suggests a wide range of qualities by which a worker may be evaluated, including accuracy, error rate, and speed of task performance.[20]

While these may seem straightforward attributes of competence, the algorithm is agnostic to conditions that explain the differences, such as disabilities or multitasked care work in the home. Turk workers work in varied conditions—in their homes, at the library, and while at school. As independent contractors, this kind of flexibility is touted as precisely part of the appeal of gig work. But as Amazon judges the "judges," these variations in bodies, environments, and work processes manifest to the algorithm as differences in speed or even interpretive variations that manifest as "error rate." Together, these can mean the difference between being algorithmically judged a Master and being judged a fraudster.

An Exception: Finding a Trusted Pool

Once they have identified workers they trust, some engineers will develop custom lists of worker IDs they will clear for their tasks and treat this group as a trusted pool (Gray & Suri 2019). Some might create a Slack channel to communicate with these workers or participate in worker-run forums to engage these workers through informal channels. These communication forums allow workers and employers to engage in more dialogue about the labor process and how to adjust it. These more stable relationships might seem to indicate a tendency, as described by economist Ronald Coase, for firms to form as a way of decreasing transaction costs of operating on the open market (1937). These trusted pool formations reveal a tension, as argued by anthropologists Ilana Gershon and Melissa Cefkin, between neoliberal autonomy and transactional efficiencies.[21] The emergent organizational forms reveal one way that workers and employers cobble together platforms and software, usually leaving platform operators, such as Amazon, untouched, to negotiate these tensions in organizing a less wasteful and fairer labor process.

Such employers, from a worker's perspective, are the exception. I show this exceptional form of collaboration to underscore how work organization could be otherwise from the approach to filtering and testing workers en masse and through automated surveillance and managerial action. Why is it exceptional? Elsewhere, I've argued that part of the appeal of AMT for engineers is that their managerial relationships and responsibilities are displaced into the technological platform. Engineers describe feeling like the platform is "magic" because it allows them to focus on the coding work they are attached to, rather than the enactment of managerial authority that violates their image of Silicon Valley work cultures.[22] Most employers want to keep their workers across the programming interface out of sight to be filtered, transacted, and extracted.

Enforcing One Login, One Body

These techniques of assessing workers all depend on a one-to-one relationship between an Amazon worker's login and the working body behind the screen. A login identifies the data object that holds the work history. When Amazon algorithms detect a possible violation of their assumption, they label accounts as at risk of being fraudulent. Workers only discover this when their accounts are suspended.

One practice that Amazon penalizes is the sharing of a single worker's login among several workers. This is a problem especially for Indian workers, who often face barriers to getting an AMT login. AMT does not accept all people who apply to be workers and, true to form for black-boxed fraud governance, does not explain why they reject applications. It may be because Indian workers are less likely to be Amazon customers and thus lack a digital history, or it may be because Indian workers were more likely to be rejected by requesters for giving undesirable task responses, and, thus, ML algorithms have learned to discriminate against workers from India in general. Some Indian workers, unable to get their own account, respond by sharing logins with others, working around the clock and dividing up the wages that accrue to the account. Amazon seeks to shut down this behavior that violates the integrity of one login, one body. Workers may suddenly find their accounts suspended, unable to access the previous earnings already held in their Amazon account.

Algorithms policing violations to one login, one body sometimes shut down practices that Amazon later determines, under pressure from workers, to be legitimate. In one case, a mother and son found their logins suspended because they were logged in from the same house, and thus the same Wi-Fi router and, thus, had the same IP address. The accounts were only restored after Turkopticon worker organizers intervened to bring the case to an Amazon manager. Amazon explained its policy as a way of protecting the authenticity of social science research results. Amazon had interpreted the second login on the same IP address as a worker trying to get paid to do the same social science study twice, corrupting research results. While Amazon did admit its mistake when it reinstated the mother whose son turked from her home, for two weeks of lost earnings, they gifted her a $10 Amazon gift card—far less than what she would have earned.[23]

Enforcing one login, one body means platform operators scan data flows with suspicion that one login hosts many bodies, as well as suspicion that multiple logins can host one body. Both are problems for the political economies of knowledge extraction. As Amazon's algorithms automate fraud judgments, they may learn to simply exclude workers from Indian IP addresses or IP addresses from Starbucks or IP addresses from libraries in low-income neighborhoods without, as researchers Jenna Burrell and Anne Jonas argue, "understanding the systematic social and political conditions that produce differential behaviors online."[24]

Platformizing Amazon's Vision of Fraud

The techniques described above are of consequence not only to AMT employers and workers but also to internet users at large. While Amazon's approaches to fraud remain opaque to outsiders (and likely even many insiders), the company has made its cloud-based Fraud Detector available as a platform service it sells to other organizations. This is significant for several reasons. First, it means Amazon disseminates its techniques to the internet at large. Second, Amazon becomes a central broker of data signals on users and can leverage data and risk assessments made for one client to inform assessments for another client. Amazon Fraud Prevention team lead Ryan Schmiedl described this bleed of risk data across sites as a "lift" clients get from Amazon: "We're taking patterns from repeated bad actors . . . so you're benefiting not just from what you know, but from what we know."[25]

Amazon's Fraud Detector might label as higher risk those whose self-declared country and customer address are different or whose IP address country and phone numbers are different. A user facing precarity and moving across state and country borders, as is common between San Diego and Tijuana, here becomes suspect. Similarly, someone couch surfing in a different location than their listed address might be flagged. The ML algorithm, according to Schmiedl, also flags practices that are simply outliers, "unlike anything it has seen from legitimate customers."[26] To be risky, then, is not to demonstrate threatening behaviors. It might simply be that one seems dissimilar to others represented in the dataset.

Fraud reduction can justify creative and expansive forms of surveillance. One patent describes a data-thirsty technique that tracks user behavior habits, such as sequences of applications opened in the morning, combined with contextual markers, such as location, microphone data, and relationship to surrounding objects. That's the "behavioral data collector" indicated in the patent. The system authenticates users when they are acting habitually, as discerned by the algorithm. When use patterns change, the system forces reauthentication.[27] The patent claims an expansive range of surveillance modalities to protect the sanctity of digitized finance systems and firm financial flows. This patent also appears perfectly aligned with Amazon's fight against people consensually sharing a single internet login.

Penalties for those informally labeled as "fraudsters" include loss of work, loss of accrued wages, and even login-restricted services across the web. As a login infrastructure provider, Amazon controls access not only to its sites but also to all kinds of other sites across the internet.

Fraud risk techniques do not always present users with clear consequences. It can, according to Amazon presentations, result in "friction." Friction can take many forms. It can be those CAPTCHAs that ask you to mark all the trucks, bridges, or stop signs in a set of images. It can come as requests for additional authenticating data (address, phone number, social security number). It can come as a temporary delay pending a customer service call. Friction allows Amazon to titrate caution against fraudsters against the desire to allow customers to pay them. When dealing with customers who purchase products, Amazon needs to balance potential costs of fraudulent activity against the costs of slowing or blocking revenue-generating customers. But when dealing with workers in AMT, Amazon faces a surplus of interested workers and even turns applicants away.[28] Thus, it can aggressively suspend longtime workers or even block newer, untried workers with little consequence to the company.[30]

Governing Algorithmic Judgment

Scholarship on algorithmic judgment has identified several distinct kinds of problems, each of which implies distinct resolutions or mitigation strategies. AMT workers facing reputational harm and account suspensions can face problematic data, problematic engineering assumptions, problematic algorithmic inferences, or the criminalization of practices that are inconvenient for company business models. While the first two kinds of problems have been discussed widely in scholarship, the latter two have attracted less attention among those concerned with workers' or consumers' rights.

Rights to See and Repair Data about Platform Users

The simplest kind of problem faced by workers confronting account suspensions is the correction or updating of data. Workers, such as financial service users, might be flagged when they log in from a location distinct from the address registered to their account. Unlike financial service users, however, workers rarely have the opportunity to set an updated location status on the platform to avoid getting flagged.

Legal scholar Frank Pasquale has called for policies that guarantee the right to review data records about oneself. The fraud algorithms that are the central concern of this chapter are a key element, I argue, of what Pasquale calls "the black box society"—a society in which opaque and automated surveillance and reputational judgments restrict one's access to resources and activities.[29] The right to review and correct data ensures one mechanism for contesting unfair judgments. Companies can be expected to resist such transparency, arguing that it would allow bad actors crucial tactical knowledge about the cybersecurity battlefield. However, cybersecurity researchers argue that a truly secure system is one that is robust against an adversary who understands how it is constructed.[30] Transparency, conversely, improves security by expanding the community of people who can point out problems in the system and suggest mechanisms for repair.

Evidence from this chapter shows how the term "bad actors" occludes the unjust consequences of platform operator design, algorithms, and policies. For workers and users confronting algorithmic judgments, account suspensions exemplify an emergency—a moment when technical and social conditions create an unusual event. These events do not happen every day or even to most users. For this reason, data transparency ought not to place the responsibility for maintaining correct data on workers, adding an extra burden to the time they spend producing. Rather, it ought to be one means of mitigating harm in a larger process of repair when algorithms, such as people, inevitably misjudge the social world and fail.[31]

Beyond Ethics Education: Oversight and Accountability to Those Impacted

In some cases, patents reveal engineering assumptions that explicitly encode a model of knowledge or ability that reproduces hierarchies among differences.

Recall, for example, the patent that assumed speed as one indicator of worker quality, ignoring differences in competing obligations, pacing preferences, or body mobilities. Such an assumption seems especially unjustifiable on a platform on which workers are paid piece wages, rather than per hour.[32] Such an assumption is also especially problematic given the propensity of computer work to produce repetitive stress injuries that might slow workers down.

Simply educating engineers in ethics or social science methods cannot address such gaps, though such education may make engineers more aware of the gaps and the need to address them. Social justice approaches have focused on such assumptions and argued that those who design must do so in ways accountable to those directly affected by the design.[33] Drawing on a wide range of scholarship in feminist studies, disability studies, and the knowledge of social movement actors, such an approach draws on the knowledge of differently situated actors about the emergent effects designs may have on their lives. Technology transparency and oversight policy approaches require companies to reveal details of algorithms and data practices that affect users; they also create mechanisms of public regulatory oversight over platform operators, giving users one lever for understanding, redress, and advocacy.

These transparency and oversight approaches must not exempt fraud algorithms from rights and oversight claims, but some currently do. For example, California Assembly Bill AB 1790 sets out requirements for how online marketplaces such as eBay or Amazon resolve user disputes with what the law calls "minimum fairness," including specifying in writing grounds for suspensions.[34] Yet the law exempts the disclosure of "*information that would hinder any investigation or prevention of deceptive, fraudulent, or illegal activity*." This exemption gives a broad berth for platform operators to deny transparency and oversight to users. Another example of a policy that exempts fraud algorithms was the California Privacy Rights Act (CPRA) of 2018, passed by the legislature, which required businesses to respond to consumer requests to delete their personal information. This law also offered exemptions for consumer datakept to detect "fraudulent . . . activity."

Shield Platform Users from Systemic Risks

The problem of algorithms, geographer and scholar Louise Amoore argues, is not only "the power to perceive, to see, to collect, or to survey a vast data landscape, but the power to perceive and distill something for action."[35] When algorithms of suspicion target a user for outlier behavior or behavior that pattern matches to prior examples of bad actors fed to the system, that person might find themselves snatched out of an ocean of users for reasons of correlation rather than observed malfeasance.

This algorithmic power to focus and make actionable based on correlation introduces a kind of systemic risk—an expansion of vulnerabilities as systems become more interconnected and complex.[36] Algorithms draw on divorse sources of data through diverse modeling techniques being deployed and tested on people in their real lives, rather than in the lab. I argue that this generates an accumulation of risks in the platform management system, but the consequences of accumulated risk, then, are concentrated on those workers who find themselves suspended by mistake.

We need policies, norms, and practices that account for this risk and protect people from the harms such risks can generate. A simple example for AMT workers might be estimating the lost wages from a mistaken account suspension based on past earnings and adding compensation duress for time spent working toward a resolution. Actual solutions should be developed in collaboration with those most directly impacted by these risks.

Refuse Simple and Criminalizing Claims of Fraud

Algorithms of suspicion are not only harmful because their inferences or data are problematic. They can also be harmful by scanning for and targeting behaviors that might not be morally wrong but are inconvenient, undesirable, or costly for those who profit through algorithms.

To illustrate how socially acceptable practices might be inconvenient for and thus targeted by companies, I offer an example from the history of Google. When I worked for Google in the early 2000s, it was common for ad agencies to have a single login shared among staff to bid on Google AdWords keywords and craft ads. When Google transitioned the AdWords system (now called Google Ads) onto the master Google Accounts system, we forced each agency worker to create their own login. Google wanted to impose an identity between login and person in order to collect individualized data and create profiles for "personalized search" and personally targeted advertisements. (Prior to this, Google ads were contextual, based on what you searched for at that specific moment.)

Like Google, Amazon imposes an authenticated vision of an individual subject, penalized for interdependence with others and sharing of resources. The "wisdom of crowds" relies on the people as sensors of their environments, and requires—in fact, enforces—their independence.[37] It recasts collaboration—between mother and son, or workers in a coworking space—as collusion.

Part of the work of this chapter has been to denaturalize fraud and its associated discourse of "bad actors." The meaning of fraud has shifted historically, from concerns about forged documents leading to improper property claims[38] to concerns about compromising investors when uncertain statements about the future cross over into lies.[39] The language and techniques of fraud I have traced here are less concerned with whether a person has documentary authority or is truthful, but rather whether they can be trusted as a cultural worker and, in turn, as an authority on legitimate cultural meanings. A worker who offers a less "popular" answer or an answer the employer does not consider sensible can be labeled fraudulent, rather than simply culturally different. On platforms, as in domains of public services in the United States, accusations of fraud can serve the goals of accusing organizations of evading responsibilities as part of a broader social contract.[40]

Conclusion

What does it mean that fraud regimes are now being imposed on everyday communicational and work transactions, suppressing or even criminalizing other systems of ethics and truth, such as care, cooperation, or infrastructure sharing? Further, Amazon is generating a market for fraud detection as a service, spreading practices drawn from finance, internet security, and international relations, with their anxieties about bad actors who must be kept in the dark. In generating a market, Amazon generates desire and extends its infrastructure into new arenas of social life. In describing fraud detection systems, engineers easily slip into deploying quasi-criminalizing language that renarrates unusual digital traces as individuals who are malicious and untrustworthy. Such an orientation forecloses avenues for recognizing harm to workers and other users, recognizing badly designed platform workflows, or repairing problematic data and algorithmic inferences. Finally, algorithms of suspicion generate systemic risk unaddressed by ethics approaches that focus on transparency and accountability. Such approaches do not account for how algorithmic management generates new kinds of uncertainty and risk and then concentrates impacts on the shoulders of just a few. We need policies, norms, and practices that account for such risks and protect people from the harms such risks can generate and offer redress and compensation when an algorithm shuts them out.

Acknowledgments

I am indebted to helpful readings and discussions with scholars at AI Now, UCSD's Critical Data Studies group, participants in an SSRC workshop on authenticity organized by Wendy Chun, linguistic anthropologists at the Michicagoan Conference, graduate students at Cornell University, and the Platform Governance volume editors. I also thank Stuart Geiger, Ilana Gershon, Nick Seaver, and the editors of this volume for reading and discussing drafts of this work. I am indebted to Turkopticon workers the wider labor community for developing language and knowledge at the frontlines of harmful digital management practices.

Notes

1 Jeremias Adams-Prassl, "What If Your Boss Was an Algorithm? Economic Incentives, Legal Challenges, and the Rise of Artificial Intelligence at Work Automation, Artificial Intelligence, & Labor Law," *Comparative Labor Law & Policy Journal* 41, no. 1 (2019): 123–46.

2 Nantina Vgontzas, "Toward Degrowth: Worker Power, Surveillance Abolition, and Climate Justice at Amazon," *New Global Studies* 16, no. 1 (2022): 49–67, https://doi.org/10.1515/ngs-2022-0008.

3 Alex Rosenblat and Luke Stark, "Algorithmic Labor and Information Asymmetries: A Case Study of Uber's Drivers," *International Journal of Communication* 10 (2016): 27; Veena B. Dubal, "Wage Slave or Entrepreneur? Contesting the Dualism of Legal Worker Identities," *California Law Review* 105 (2017): 65–123; Jeremias Prassl, *Humans as a Service* (Oxford University Press, 2017); Niels van Doorn and Julie Yujie Chen, "Odds Stacked against Workers: Datafied Gamification on Chinese and American Food Delivery Platforms," *Socio-Economic Review* 19, no. 4 (2021): 1345–67, https://doi.org/10.1093/ser/mwab028.

4 José Van Dijck, Thomas Poell, and Martijn De Waal, *The Platform Society: Public Values in a Connective World* (Oxford University Press, 2018), 13–15.

5 Nina Wallerstein, Bonnie Duran, John G. Oetzel, and Meredith Minkler, *Community-Based Participatory Research for Health: Advancing Social and Health Equity* (John Wiley, 2017); Sasha Costanza-Chock, *Design Justice* (MIT Press, 2020).

6 Steven J. Jackson, Tarleton Gillespie, and Sandy Payette, "The Policy Knot: Re-Integrating Policy, Practice and Design in CSCW Studies of Social Computing," in *Proceedings of the 17th ACM Conference on Computer Supported Cooperative Work & Social Computing*. CSCW '14 (ACM, 2014), 588–602, https://doi.org/10.1145/2531602.2531674.

7 Lilly Irani, "The Cultural Work of Microwork," *New Media & Society* 17, no. 5 (2015): 720–39, https://doi.org/10.1177/1461444813511926; Lilly Irani, "Justice for Data Janitors," in *Think in Public*, ed. Sharon Marcus and Caitlin Zaloom (Columbia University Press, 2019), 23–40, https://doi.org/10.7312/marc19008-003; Mary L. Gray and Siddharth Suri, *Ghost Work: How to Stop Silicon Valley from Building a New Global Underclass* (Houghton Mifflin Harcourt, 2019).

8 Venky Harinarayan, Anand Rajaraman, and Anand Ranganathan, "Hybrid Machine/Human Computing Arrangement," Patent No. 7,197,459. USA (2007).

9 Terry Winograd and Fernando Flores, *Understanding Computers and Cognition: A New Foundation for Design* (Addison-Wesley Professional, reissue 1987).

10 Milagros Miceli and Julian Posada, "The Data-Production Dispositif," arXiv, May 24, 2022, https://doi.org/10.48550/arXiv.2205.11963.

11 Aaron Moss, "Five Years of Mechanical Turk Data in Five Figures," available online: https://www.cloudresearch.com/resources/blog/mechanical-turk-data-five-years-in-five-figures/.

12 Janine Berg, "Income Security in the On-Demand Economy: Findings and Policy Lessons from a Survey of Crowdworkers," *Comparative Labor Law & Policy Journal* 37, no. 3 (2016): 543.

13 Aaron Moss and Leib Litman, "After the Bot Scare: Understanding What's Been Happening with Data Collection on MTurk and How to Stop It," CloudResearch, September 18, 2018, available online: https://www.cloudresearch.com/resources/blog/after-the-bot-scare-understanding-whats-been-happening-with-data-collection-on-mturk-and-how-to-stop-it/.

14 CloudResearch, "How Many Amazon Mechanical Turk Workers Are There in 2019?," June 25, 2019, available online: https://www.cloudresearch.com/resources/blog/how-many-amazon-mturk-workers-are-there/.

15 Stacy Stanford, Roberto Iriondo, and Pratik Shukla, "Best Public Datasets for Machine Learning and Data Science," Medium (blog), August 28, 2020, available online: https://medium.com/towards-artificial-intelligence/best-datasets-for-machine-learning-data-science-computer-vision-nlp-ai-c9541058cf4f.

16 Irani, "The Cultural Work of Microwork."

17 Ryan Schmiedl, Nick Tostenrude, and Kara Suro. "AWS Re:Invent 2019: [REPEAT 1] Fraud: How to Detect and Prevent It Using ML (AIM322-R1)," August 31, 2020, available online: https://www.youtube.com/watch?v=ZkPQtjETrBw.

18 Ibid.; Gregory N. Hullender, Evaluation of Task Judging Results. United States US8868471B1, filed September 21, 2011, and issued October 21, 2014.

19 Hullender, Evaluation of Task Judging Results.

20 Ibid.

21 Ilana Gershon and Melissa Cefkin, "Click for Work: Rethinking Work Through Online Work Distribution Platforms," *Ephemera: Theory & Politics in Organization* 20, no. 4 (2020): 103–29.

22 Irani, "The Cultural Work of Microwork."

23 K. Kauffman, Personal Conversation, October 17, 2020.

24 Anne Jonas and Jenna Burrell, "Friction, Snake Oil, and Weird Countries: Cybersecurity Systems Could Deepen Global Inequality Through Regional Blocking," *Big Data & Society* 6, no. 1 (2019): 2053951719835238, https://doi.org/10.1177/2053951719835238.

25 Schmiedl, Tostenrude, and Suro, "AWS Re:invent."

26 Ibid.

27 Michael Frederick Masterman, Authentication and Fraud Detection Based on User Behavior. United States US10108791B1, filed March 19, 2015, and issued October 23, 2018.

28 Panos Ipeirotis, "Why Was My Amazon Mechanical Turk Registration Denied?," January 17, 2017, available online: https://www.behind-the-enemy-lines.com/2017/01/why-was-my-amazon-mechanical-turk.html.

29 Frank Pasquale, *The Black Box Society: The Secret Algorithms That Control Money and Information* (Harvard University Press, 2015). For policy calls to allow such redress for workers, see Emlyn Bottomley, "Data and Algorithms in the Workplace: An Overview of Current Public Policy Strategies," Working Paper, Technology and

Work Program, UC Berkeley Labor Center, November 17, 2020; see also "Top 10 Principles for Workers' Data Privacy and Protection," UNI Global Union, November 2, 2017, available online: https://uniglobalunion.org/report/principles-for-workers-data-rights/.

30 Julia Slupska, Jeanette Lowrie, Lilly Irani, and Deian Stefan, "How Secrecy Leads to Bad Public Technology," 2021, available online: https://escholarship.org/content/qt89d7826n/qt89d7826n.pdf.

31 Louise Amoore, *Cloud Ethics: Algorithms and the Attributes of Ourselves and Others* (Duke University Press, 2020), 18–19.

32 Veena Dubal, "The Time Politics of Home-Based Digital Piecework," Center for Ethics Journal: Perspectives on Ethics, July 4, 2020, available online: https://doi.org/10.2139/ssrn.3649270.

33 Costanza-Chock, *Design Justice*; Aimi Hamraie, "Designing Collective Access: A Feminist Disability Theory of Universal Design," *Disability Studies Quarterly* 33, no. 4 (2013), https://doi.org/10.18061/dsq.v33i4.3871.

34 "Today's Law as Amended—AB-1790," available online: https://leginfo.legislature.ca.gov/faces/billCompareClient.xhtml?bill_id=201920200AB1790.

35 Amoore, *Cloud Ethics*, 16.

36 Stephen J. Collier and Andrew Lakoff, "Introduction: Systemic Risk," *Limn* 1, no. 1 (2011), available online: https://escholarship.org/uc/item/0j88z94p.

37 Alek Felstiner, "The Weakness of Crowds," *Limn* 2 (2012), available online: https://limn.press/article/the-weakness-of-crowds/.

38 Levi Roach, *Forgery and Memory at the End of the First Millennium* (Princeton University Press, 2021).

39 Kaushik Sunder Rajan, *Biocapital: The Constitution of Post-Genomic Life* (Duke University Press, 2006), 115.

40 Virginia Eubanks, *Automating Inequality: How High-Tech Tools Profile, Police, and Punish the Poor* (St. Martin's Press, 2018).

Bibliography

"Today's Law as Amended—AB-1790." Available online: https://leginfo.legislature.ca.gov/faces/billCompareClient.xhtml?bill_id=201920200AB1790.

Amoore, Louise. *Cloud Ethics: Algorithms and the Attributes of Ourselves and Others*. Duke University Press, 2020.

Binns, Reuben, and Elettra Bietti. "Dissolving Privacy, One Merger at a time: Competition, Data and Third Party Tracking." *Computer Law & Security Review* 36 (2020): 1–19.

Bottomley, Emlyn. "Data and Algorithms in the Workplace: An Overview of Current Public Policy Strategies." Working Paper, Technology and Work Program. UC Berkeley Labor Center, November 17, 2020.

Collier, Stephen J., and Andrew Lakoff. "Introduction: Systemic Risk." *Limn* 1, no. 1 (2011). Available online: https://escholarship.org/uc/item/0j88z94p.

Costanza-Chock, Sasha. *Design Justice*. MIT Press, 2020. https://doi.org/10.7551/mitpress/12255.001.0001.

Dubal, Veena. "The Time Politics of Home-Based Digital Piecework." *Center for Ethics Journal: Perspectives on Ethics*, July 4, 2020. https://doi.org/10.2139/ssrn.3649270.

Dubal, Veena. "Wage Slave or Entrepreneur? Contesting the Dualism of Legal Worker Identities." *California Law Review* 105 (2017): 65–123.

Eubanks, Virginia. *Automating Inequality: How High-Tech Tools Profile, Police, and Punish the Poor*. St. Martin's Press, 2018.

Felstiner, Alek. "The Weakness of Crowds." *Limn* 2 (2012). Available online: https://limn.press/article/the-weakness-of-crowds/.

Gray, Mary L., and Siddharth Suri. *Ghost Work: How to Stop Silicon Valley from Building a New Global Underclass*. Houghton Mifflin Harcourt, 2019.

Hamraie, Aimi. "Designing Collective Access: A Feminist Disability Theory of Universal Design." *Disability Studies Quarterly* 33, no. 4 (2013). https://doi.org/10.18061/dsq.v33i4.3871.

Hullender, Gregory N. "Evaluation of Task Judging Results." United States US8868471B1, filed September 21, 2011, and issued October 21, 2014. Available online: https://patents.google.com/patent/US8868471B1.

Ipeirotis, Panos. "Why Was My Amazon Mechanical Turk Registration Denied?" January 17, 2017. Available online: https://www.behind-the-enemy-lines.com/2017/01/why-was-my-amazon-mechanical-turk.html.

Irani, Lilly. *Chasing Innovation: Making Entrepreneurial Citizens in Modern India*. Princeton University Press, 2019.

Irani, Lilly. "The Cultural Work of Microwork." *New Media & Society* 17, no. 5 (2019): 720–39.

Jackson, Steven J., Tarleton Gillespie, and Sandy Payette. "The Policy Knot: Re-Integrating Policy, Practice and Design in CSCW Studies of Social Computing." In *Proceedings of the 17th ACM Conference on Computer Supported Cooperative Work & Social Computing*. CSCW '14. ACM, 2014. https://doi.org/10.1145/2531602.2531674.

Marcus, Sharon, and Caitlin Zaloom, eds. *Think in Public: A Public Books Reader*. Columbia University Press, 2019.

Masterman, Michael Frederick. "Authentication and Fraud Detection Based on User Behavior." United States US10108791B1, filed March 19, 2015, and issued October 23, 2018. Available online: https://patents.google.com/patent/US10108791B1.

Moss, Aaron, and Leib Litman. "After the Bot Scare: Understanding What's Been Happening with Data Collection on MTurk and How to Stop It." CloudResearch, September 18, 2018. Available online: https://www.cloudresearch.com/resources/blog/after-the-bot-scare-understanding-whats-been-happening-with-data-collection-on-mturk-and-how-to-stop-it/.

Pasquale, Frank. *The Black Box Society: The Secret Algorithms That Control Money and Information*. Harvard University Press, 2015.

Prop 24. Available online: https://vig.cdn.sos.ca.gov/2020/general/pdf/topl-prop24.pdf.

Roach, Levi. *Forgery and Memory at the End of the First Millennium*. Princeton University Press, 2021.

Schmiedl, Ryan, Nick Tostenrude, and Kara Suro. "AWS Re:Invent 2019: [REPEAT 1] Fraud: How to Detect and Prevent It Using ML (AIM322-R1)." August 31. Available online: https://www.youtube.com/watch?v=ZkPQtjETrBw.

Slupska, Julia, Jeanette Lowrie, Lilly Irani, and Deian Stefan. “How Secrecy Leads to Bad Public Technology.” 2021. Available online: https://escholarship.org/content/qt89d7826n/qt89d7826n.pdf.

Stanford, Stacy, Roberto Iriondo, and Pratik Shukla. 2020. “Best Public Datasets for Machine Learning and Data Science.” Medium (blog), August 28, 2020. Available online: https://medium.com/towards-artificial-intelligence/best-datasets-for-machine-learning-data-science-computer-vision-nlp-ai-c9541058cf4f.

Sunder Rajan, Kaushik. *Biocapital: The Constitution of Post-Genomic Life*. Duke University Press, 2006.

“Top 10 Principles for Workers’ Data Privacy and Protection.” UNI Global Union, November 2, 2017. Available online: https://uniglobalunion.org/report/principles-for-workers-data-rights/.

Van Dijck, José, Thomas Poell, and Martijn De Waal. *The Platform Society: Public Values in a Connective World*. Oxford University Press, 2018.

Vgontzas, Nantina. “Toward Degrowth: Worker Power, Surveillance Abolition, and Climate Justice at Amazon.” *New Global Studies* 16, no. 1 (2022): 49–67. https://doi.org/10.1515/ngs-2022-0008.

Wallerstein, Nina, Bonnie Duran, John G. Oetzel, and Meredith Minkler. *Community-Based Participatory Research for Health: Advancing Social and Health Equity*. John Wiley, 2017. Available online: http://ebookcentral.proquest.com/lib/ucsd/detail.action?docID=5097167.

Walsh, Nicholas, and Robert Zhu. 2020. “AWS What’s Next Ft.” Amazon Fraud Detector. Available online: https://www.youtube.com/watch?v=FnFckqGa7XE.

INDEX